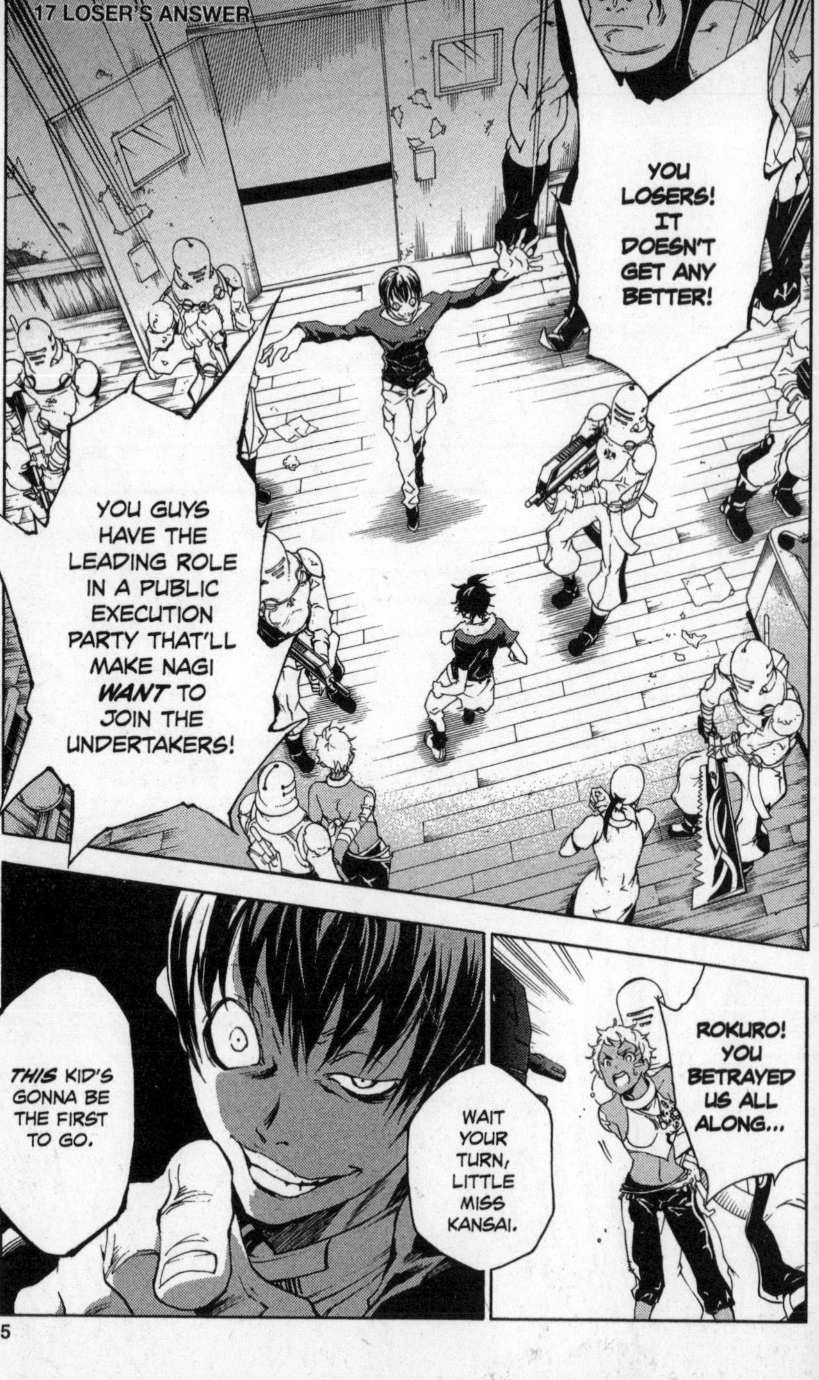
YOU LOSERS! IT DOESN'T GET ANY BETTER!
YOU GUYS HAVE THE LEADING ROLE IN A PUBLIC EXECUTION PARTY THAT'LL MAKE NAGI *WANT* TO JOIN THE UNDERTAKERS!
ROKURO! YOU BETRAYED US ALL ALONG...
WAIT YOUR TURN, LITTLE MISS KANSAI.
THIS KID'S GONNA BE THE FIRST TO GO.

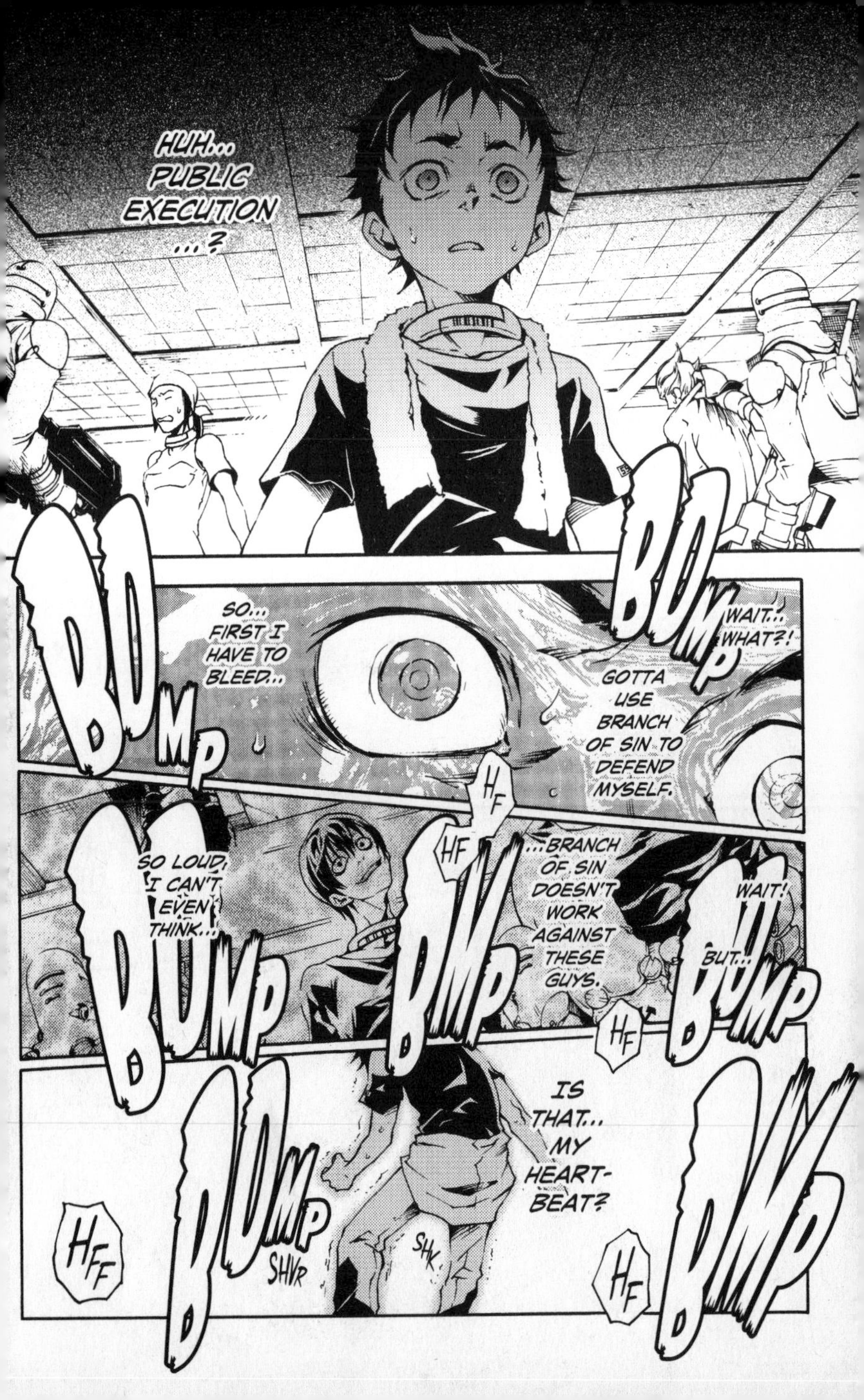
HUH... PUBLIC EXECUTION ...?
BOMP
WAIT... WHAT?!
GOTTA USE BRANCH OF SIN TO DEFEND MYSELF.
SO... FIRST I HAVE TO BLEED...
BOMP
HF
BUMP
WAIT!
BUT...
HF
...BRANCH OF SIN DOESN'T WORK AGAINST THESE GUYS.
HF
BMP
SO LOUD, I CAN'T EVEN THINK...
BUMP
BMP
HF
IS THAT... MY HEART-BEAT?
SHK
BUMP
SHVR
HFF

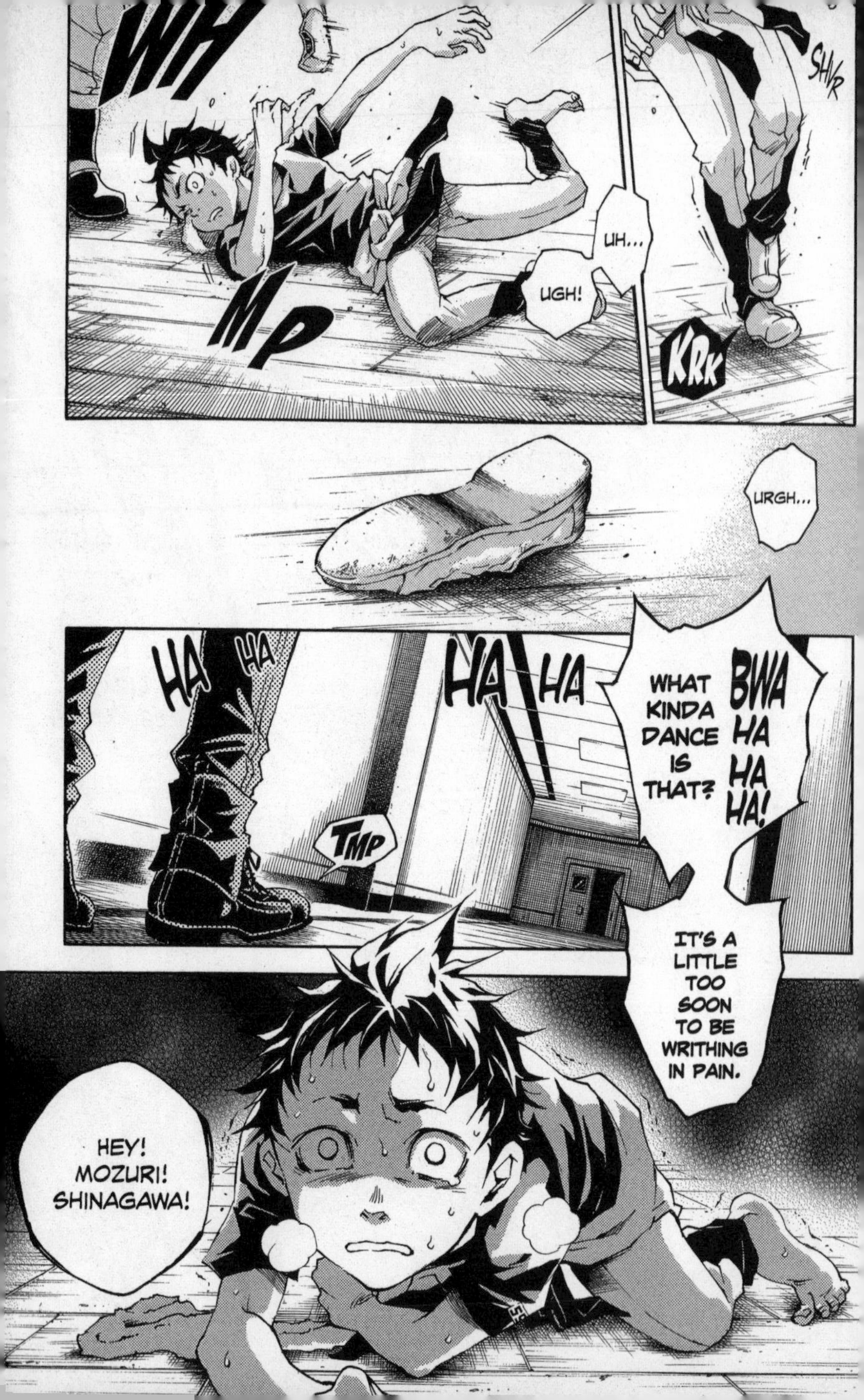
SHVR
KRK
UH...
UGH!
WH
MP
URGH...
BWA HA HA HA!
WHAT KINDA DANCE IS THAT?
HA HA
HA HA
TMP
IT'S A LITTLE TOO SOON TO BE WRITHING IN PAIN.
HEY! MOZURI! SHINAGAWA!

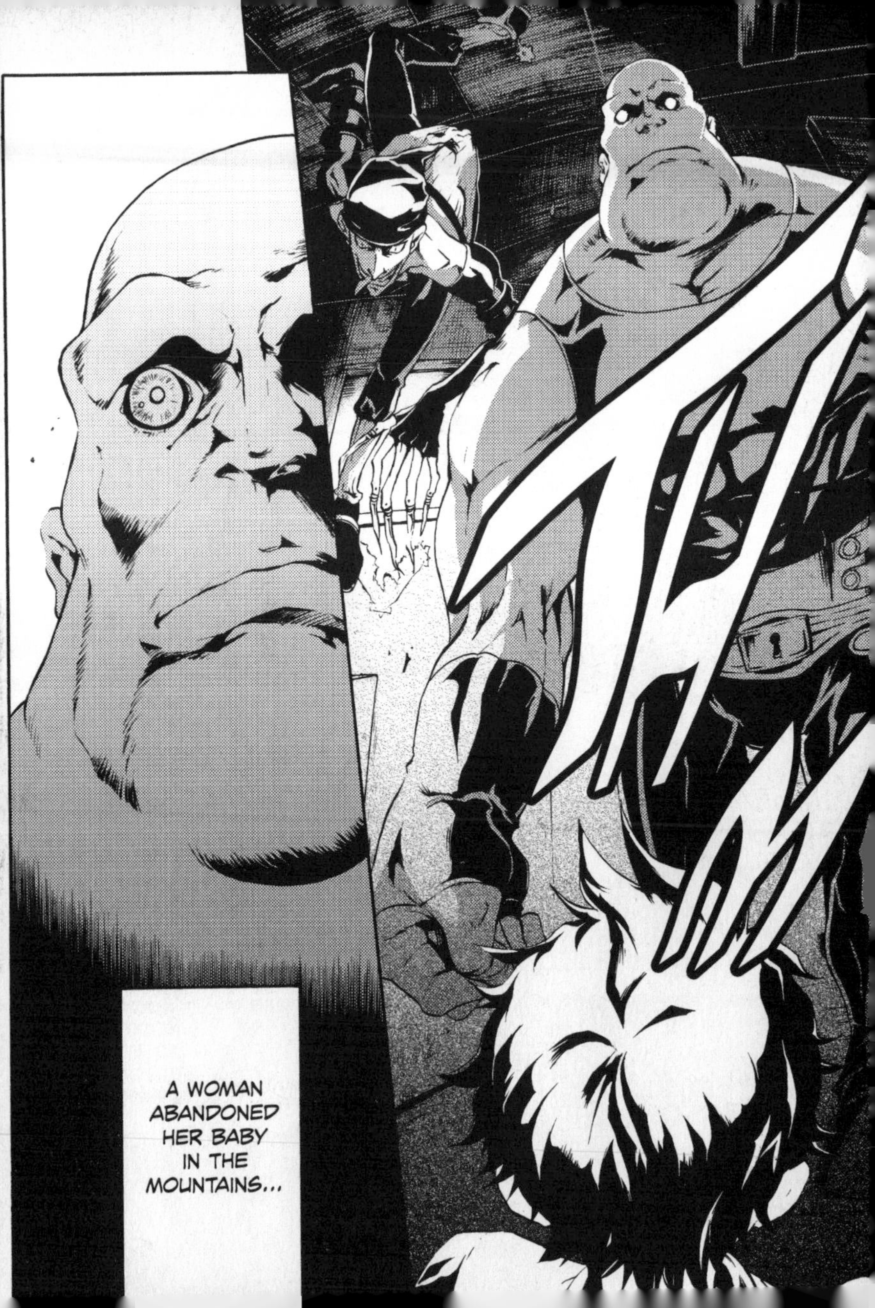
A WOMAN ABANDONED HER BABY IN THE MOUNTAINS...

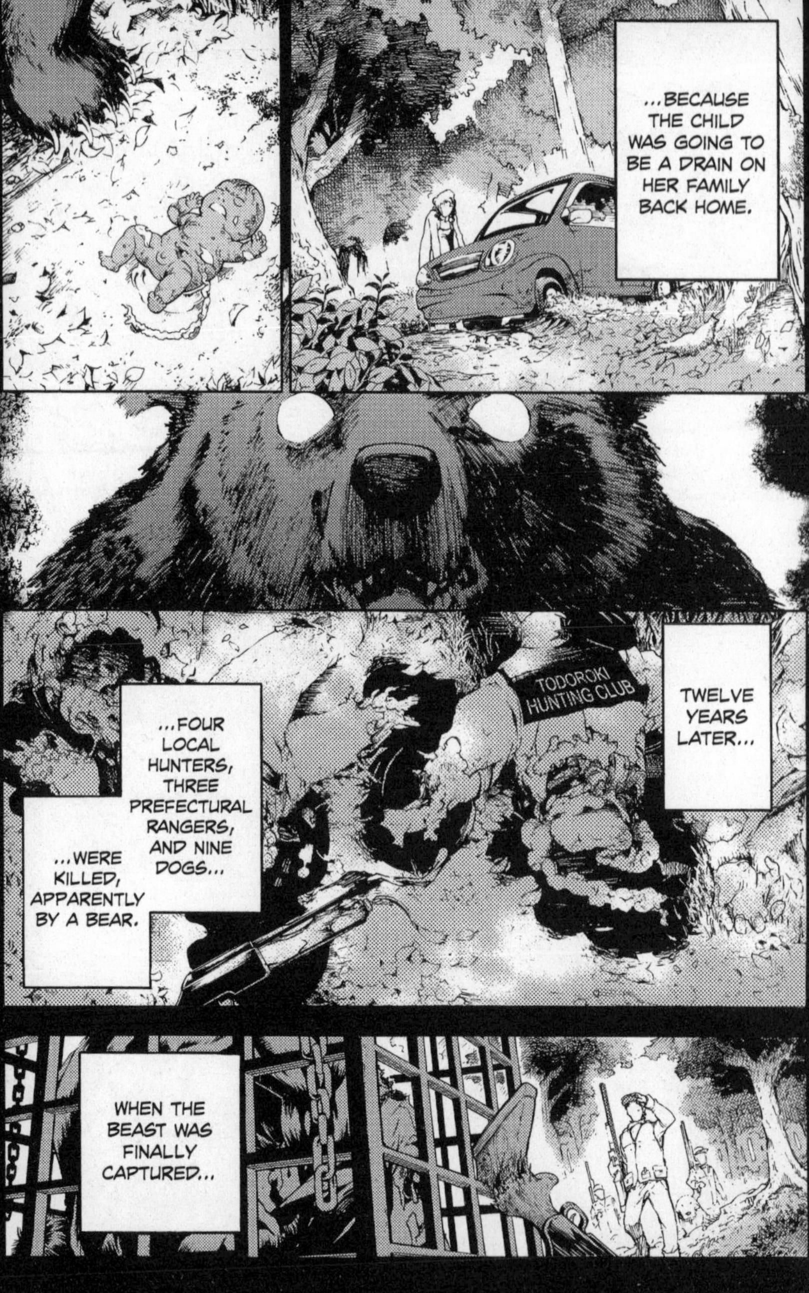
...BECAUSE THE CHILD WAS GOING TO BE A DRAIN ON HER FAMILY BACK HOME.
TWELVE YEARS LATER...
TODOROKI HUNTING CLUB
...FOUR LOCAL HUNTERS, THREE PREFECTURAL RANGERS, AND NINE DOGS...
...WERE KILLED, APPARENTLY BY A BEAR.
WHEN THE BEAST WAS FINALLY CAPTURED...

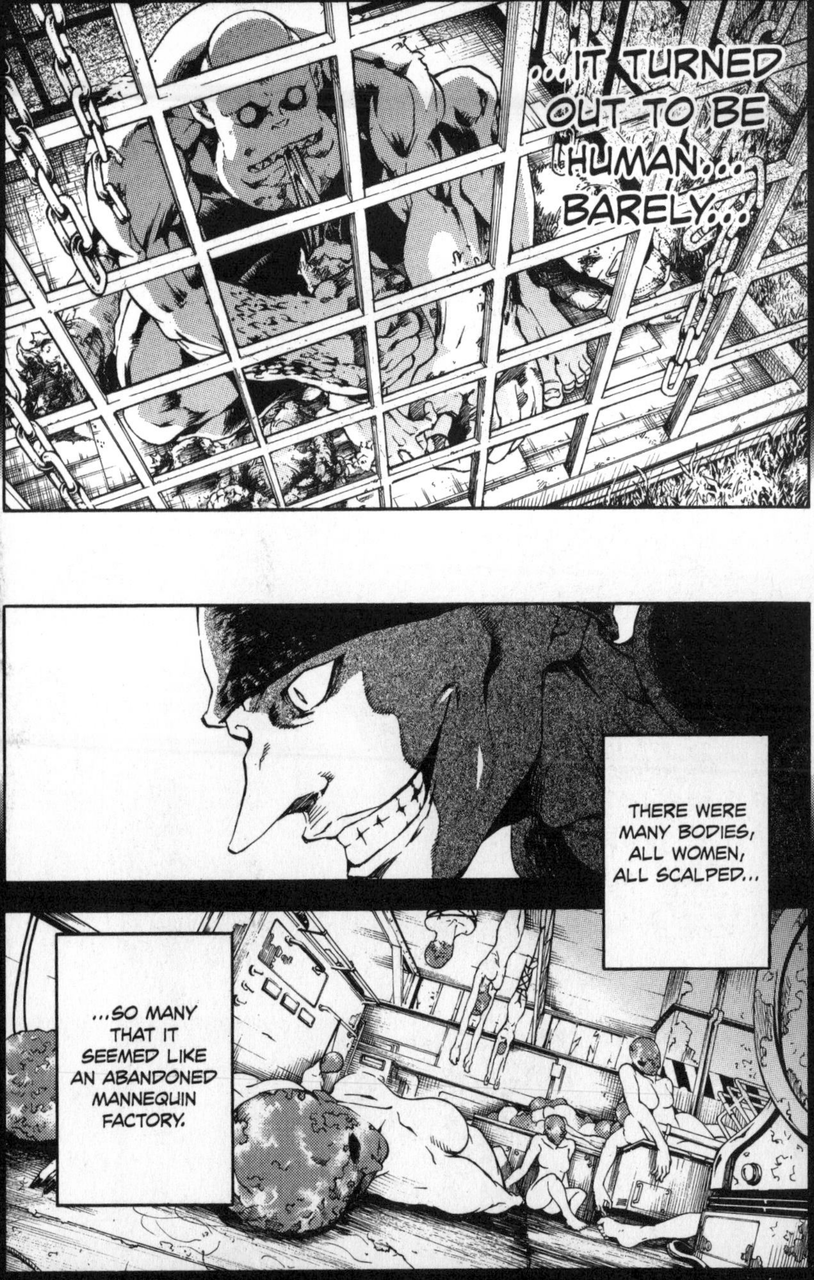
...IT TURNED OUT TO BE HUMAN... BARELY...
THERE WERE MANY BODIES, ALL WOMEN, ALL SCALPED...
...SO MANY THAT IT SEEMED LIKE AN ABANDONED MANNEQUIN FACTORY.

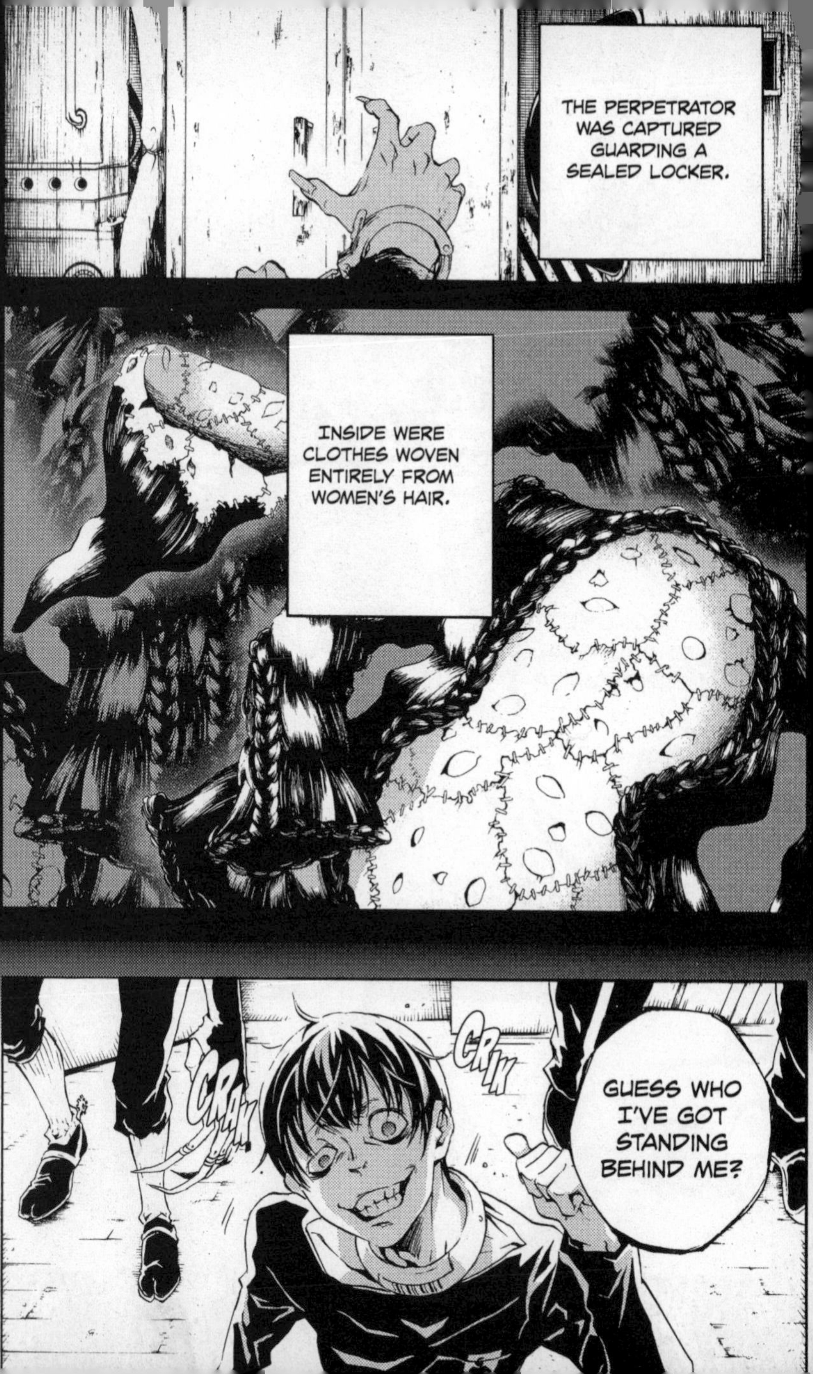
THE PERPETRATOR WAS CAPTURED GUARDING A SEALED LOCKER.
INSIDE WERE CLOTHES WOVEN ENTIRELY FROM WOMEN'S HAIR.
GUESS WHO I'VE GOT STANDING BEHIND ME?
CRIK
CRAK

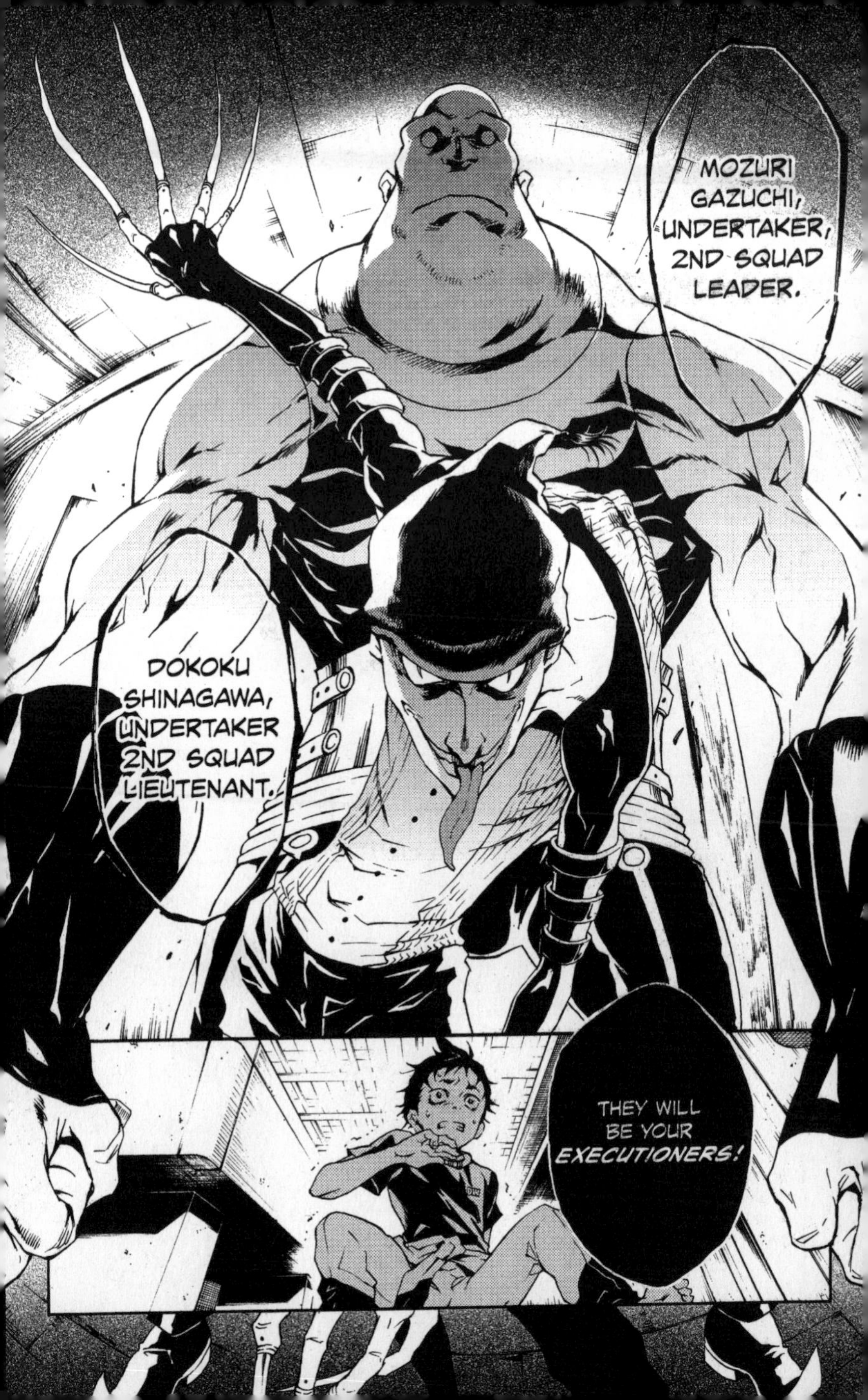
MOZURI GAZUCHI, UNDERTAKER, 2ND SQUAD LEADER.
DOKOKU SHINAGAWA, UNDERTAKER 2ND SQUAD LIEUTENANT.
THEY WILL BE YOUR *EXECUTIONERS!*

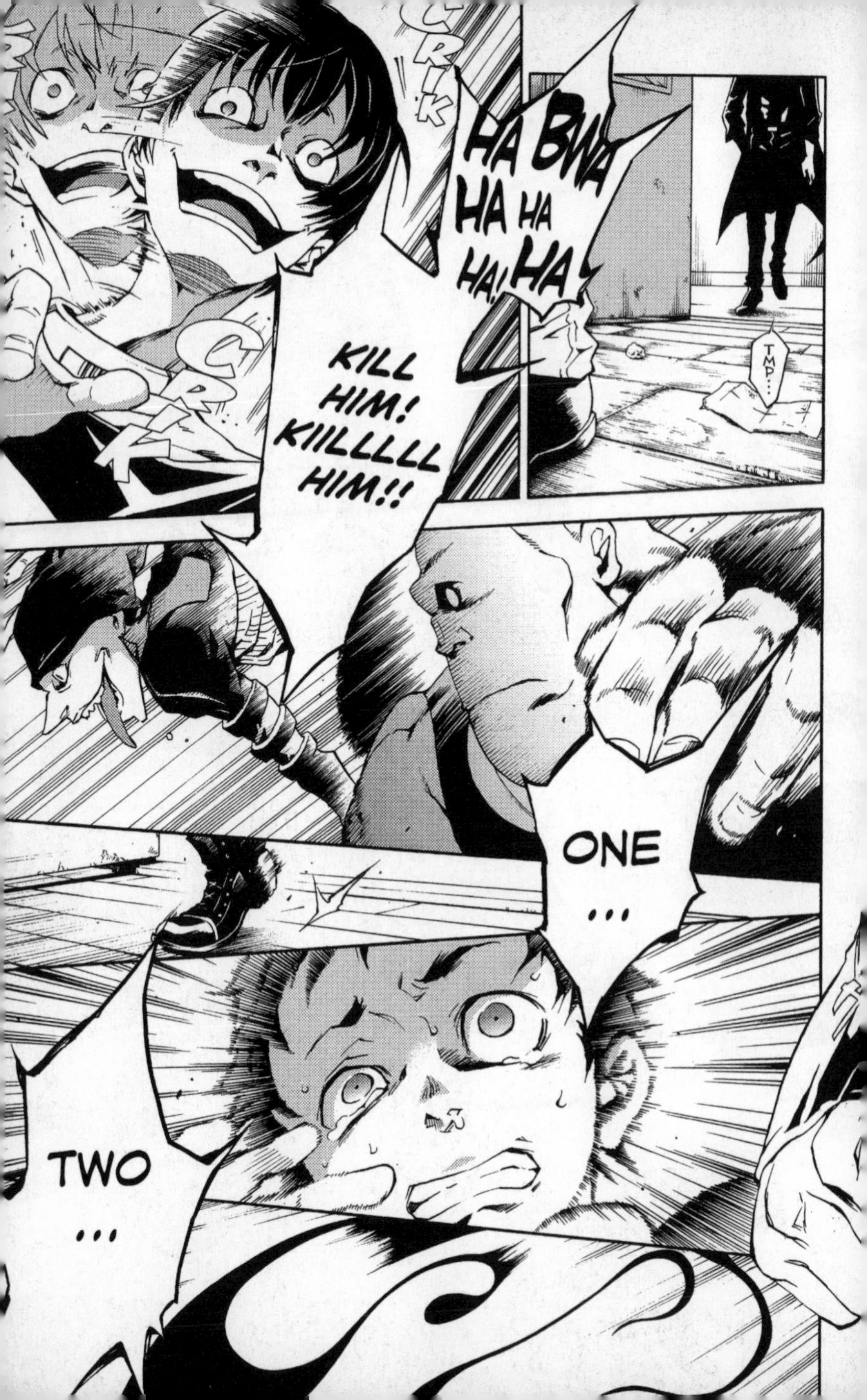
TMP...
HA BWA HA HA HA HA!
CRIK
KILL HIM! KIILLLLLL HIM!!
CRIK
ONE ...
TWO ...

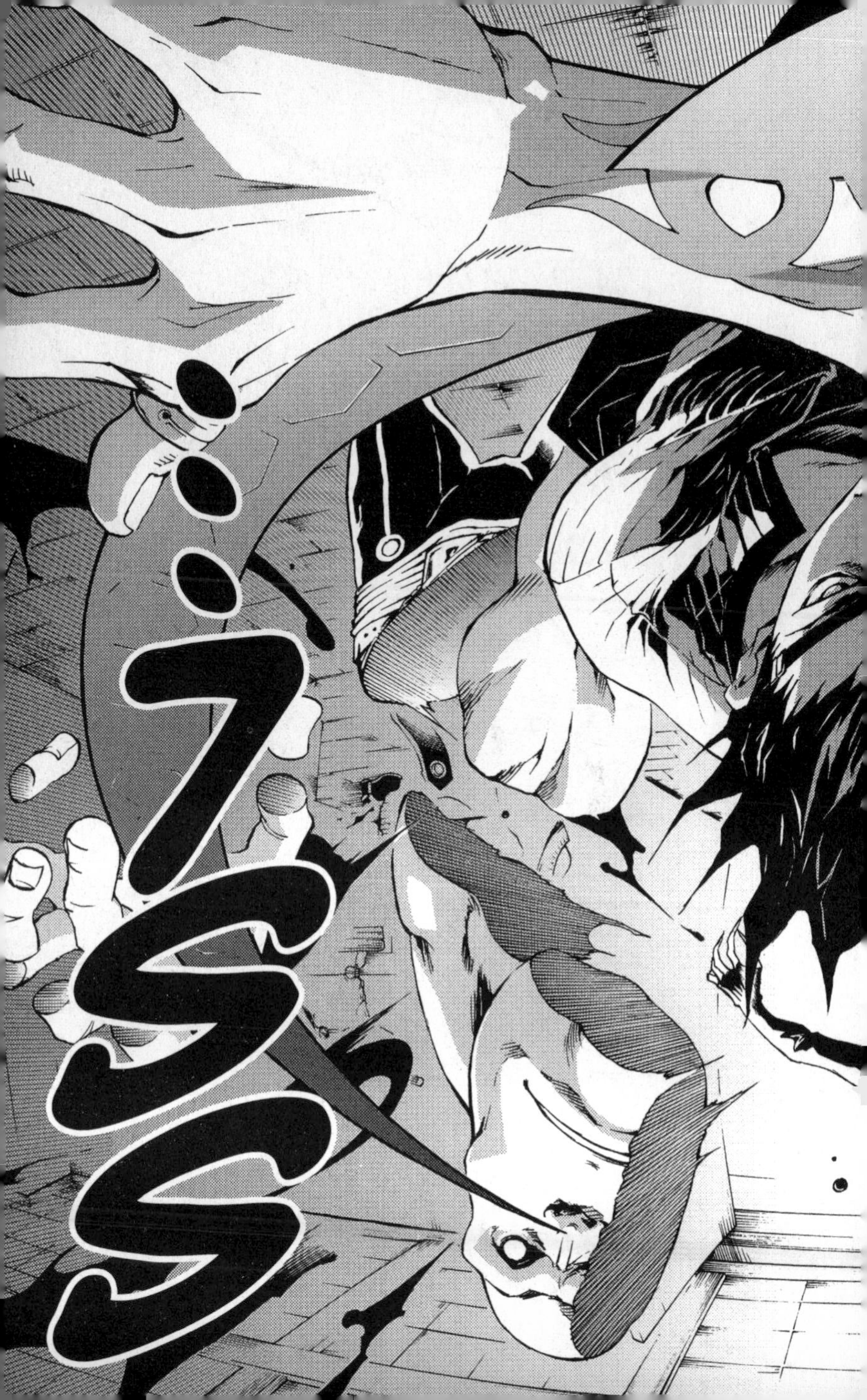

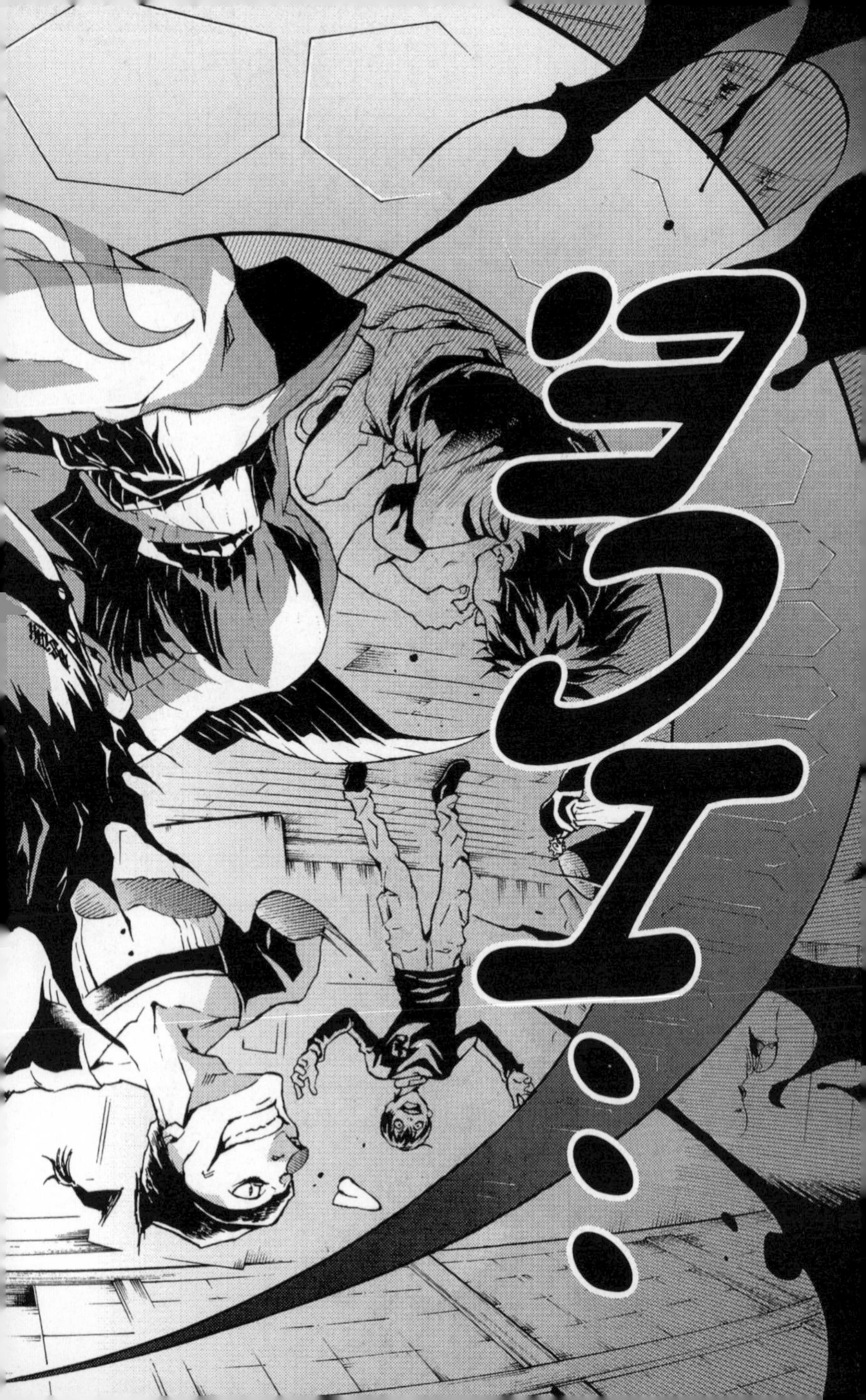

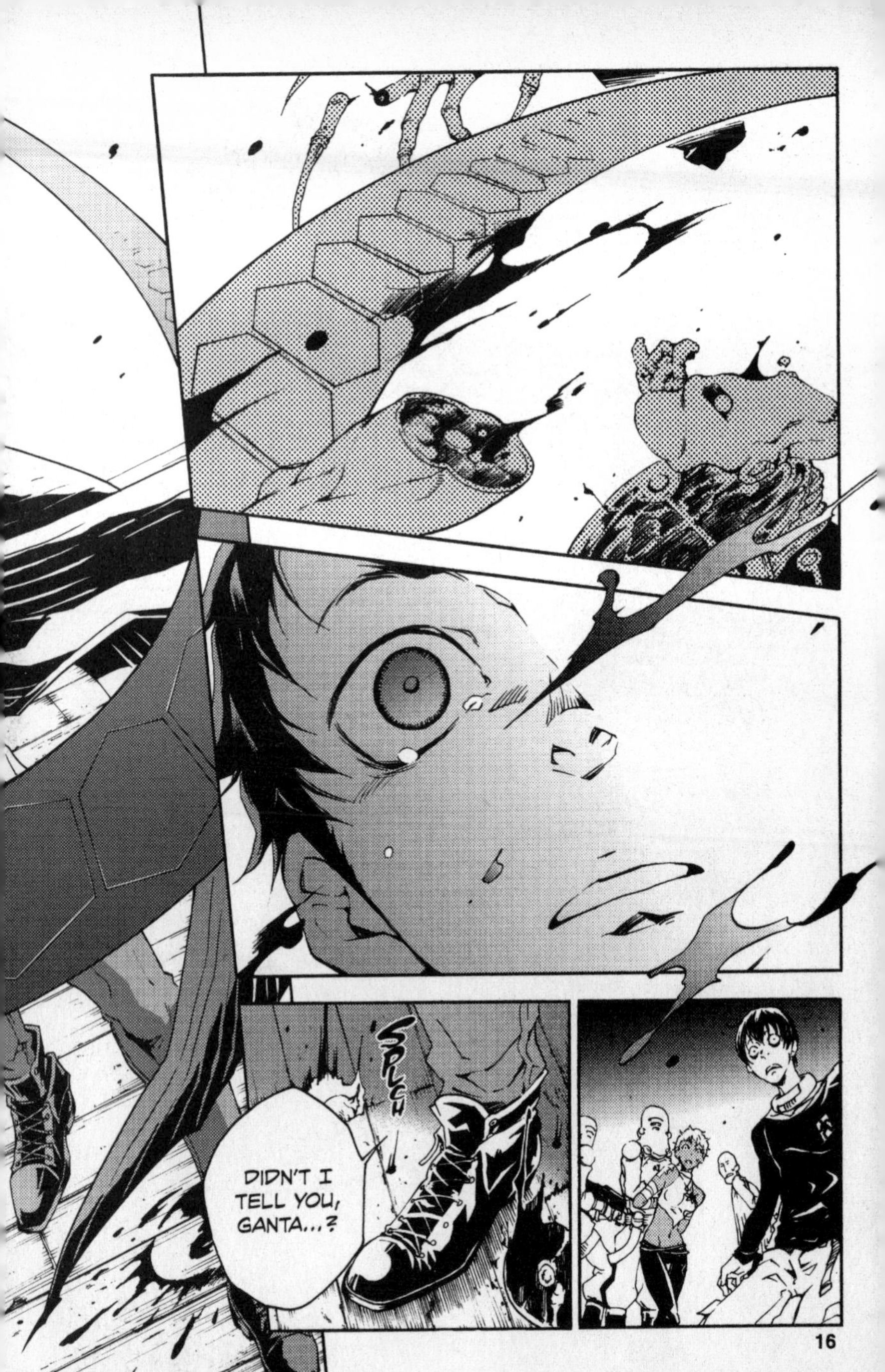
SPLCH
DIDN'T I TELL YOU, GANTA...?

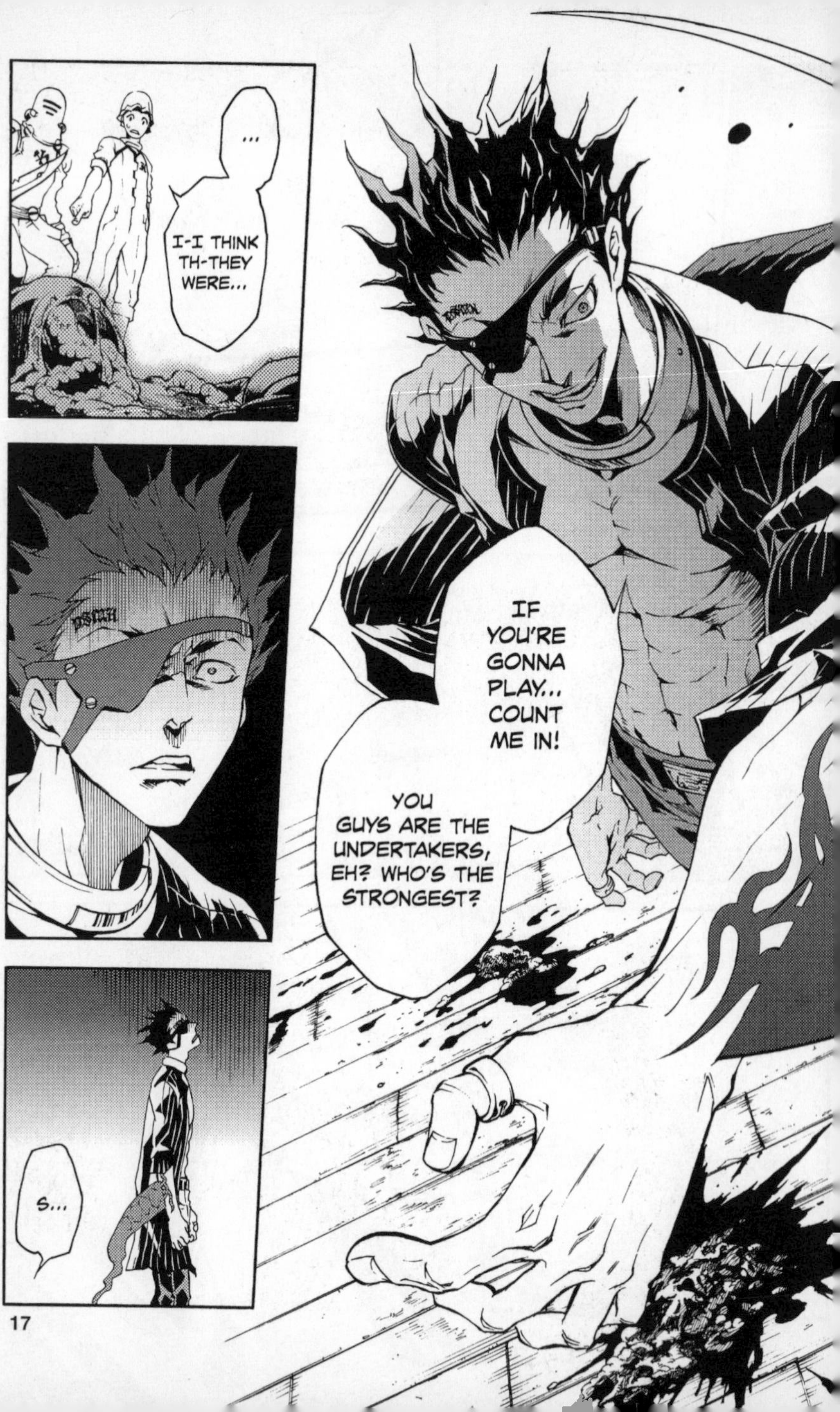
IF YOU'RE GONNA PLAY... COUNT ME IN!
YOU GUYS ARE THE UNDERTAKERS, EH? WHO'S THE STRONGEST?
...
I-I THINK TH-THEY WERE...
S...

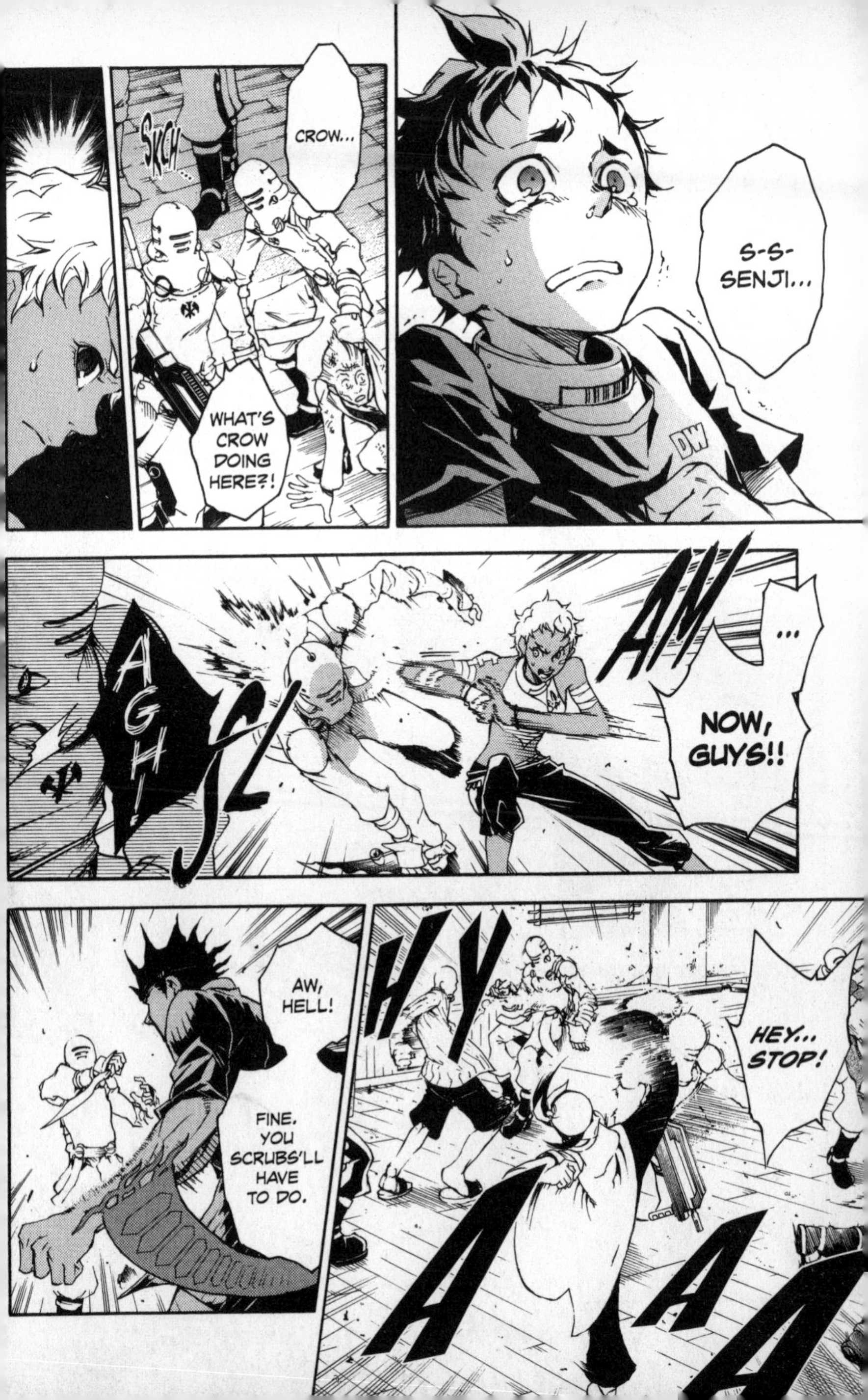
S-S-SENJI...
CROW...
SKCH...
WHAT'S CROW DOING HERE?!
AM
...NOW, GUYS!!
AGH!
HEY... STOP!
HYAAA
AW, HELL!
FINE. YOU SCRUBS'LL HAVE TO DO.

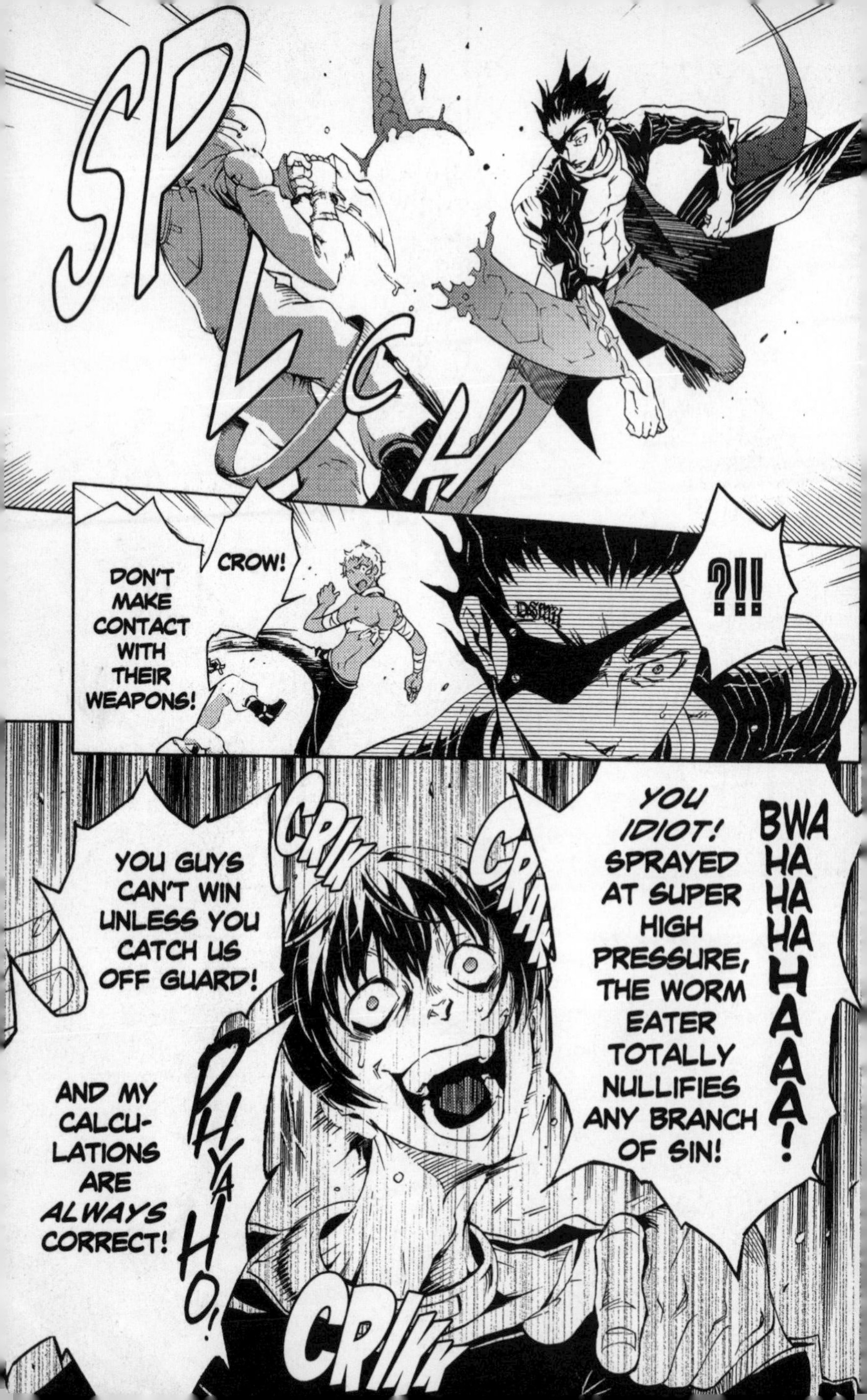
SPLCH
?!!
CROW!
DON'T MAKE CONTACT WITH THEIR WEAPONS!
BWA HA HA HA HA HAAAA!
YOU IDIOT! SPRAYED AT SUPER HIGH PRESSURE, THE WORM EATER TOTALLY NULLIFIES ANY BRANCH OF SIN!
CRAK
CRIK
YOU GUYS CAN'T WIN UNLESS YOU CATCH US OFF GUARD!
PHYAHO!
AND MY CALCULATIONS ARE ALWAYS CORRECT!
CRIKK

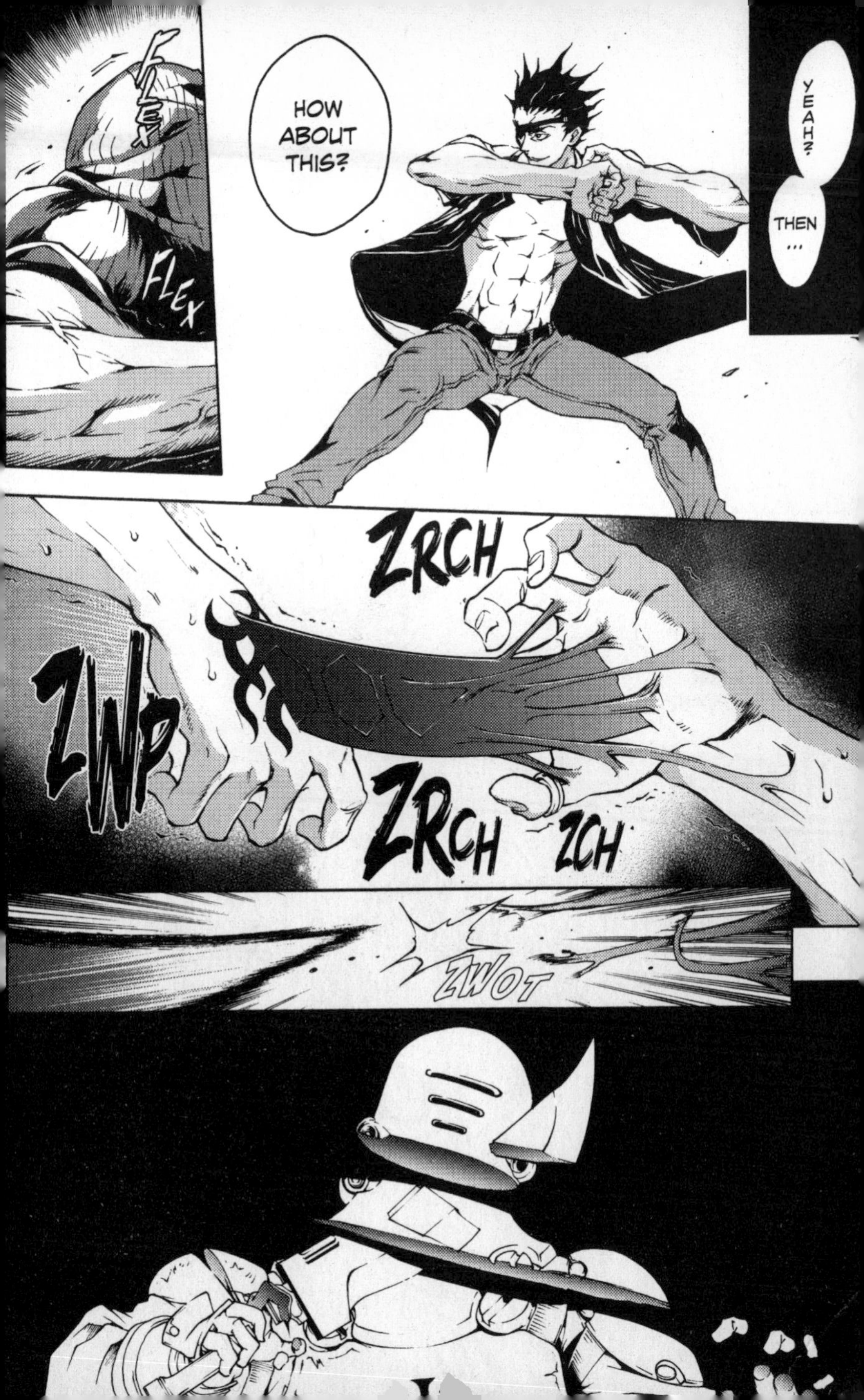
YEAH?
THEN...
HOW ABOUT THIS?
FLEX
FLEX
ZRCH
ZWP
ZRCH
ZCH
ZWOT

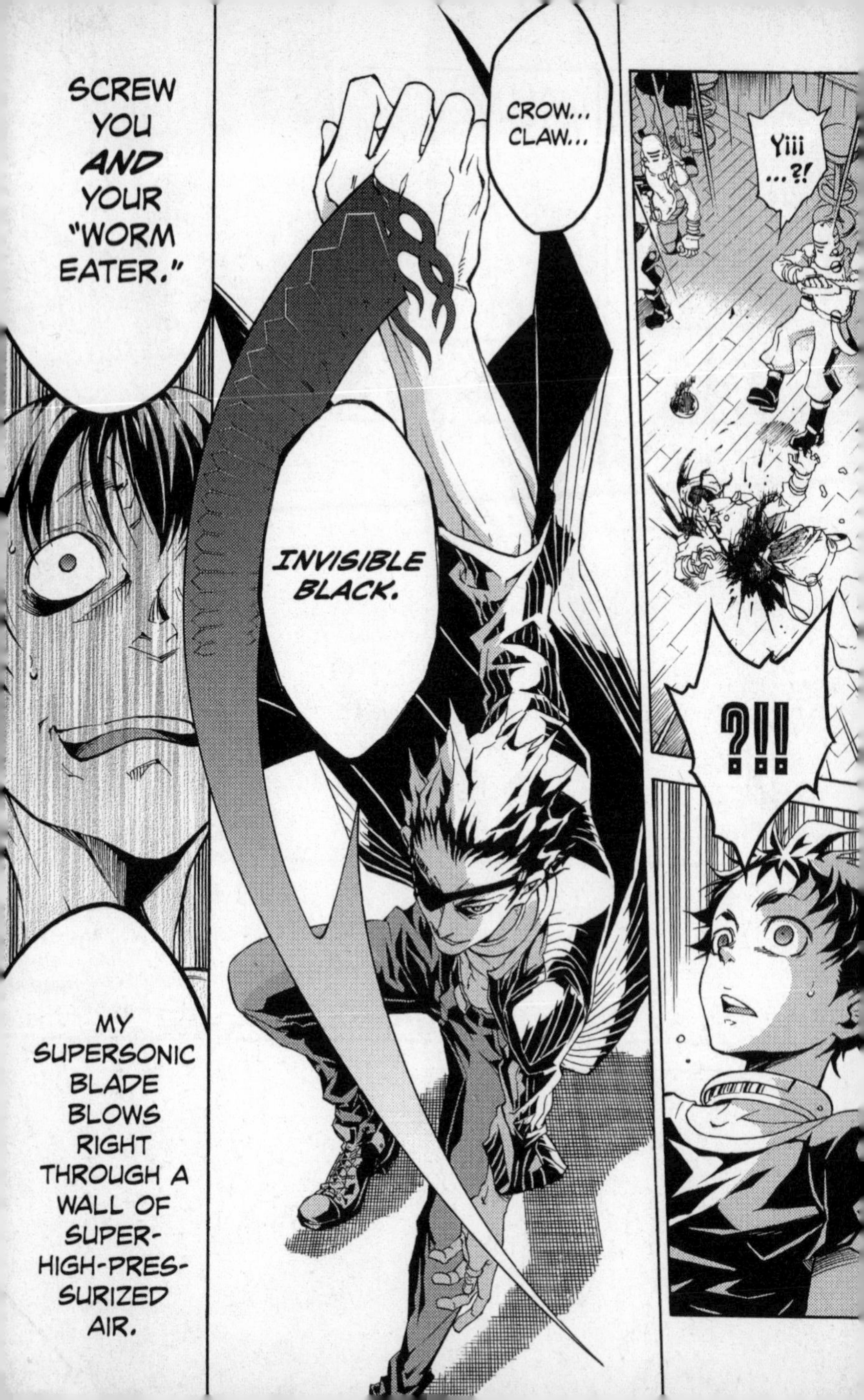
Yiii ...?!
?!!
CROW... CLAW...
INVISIBLE BLACK.
SCREW YOU AND YOUR "WORM EATER."
MY SUPERSONIC BLADE BLOWS RIGHT THROUGH A WALL OF SUPER-HIGH-PRES-SURIZED AIR.

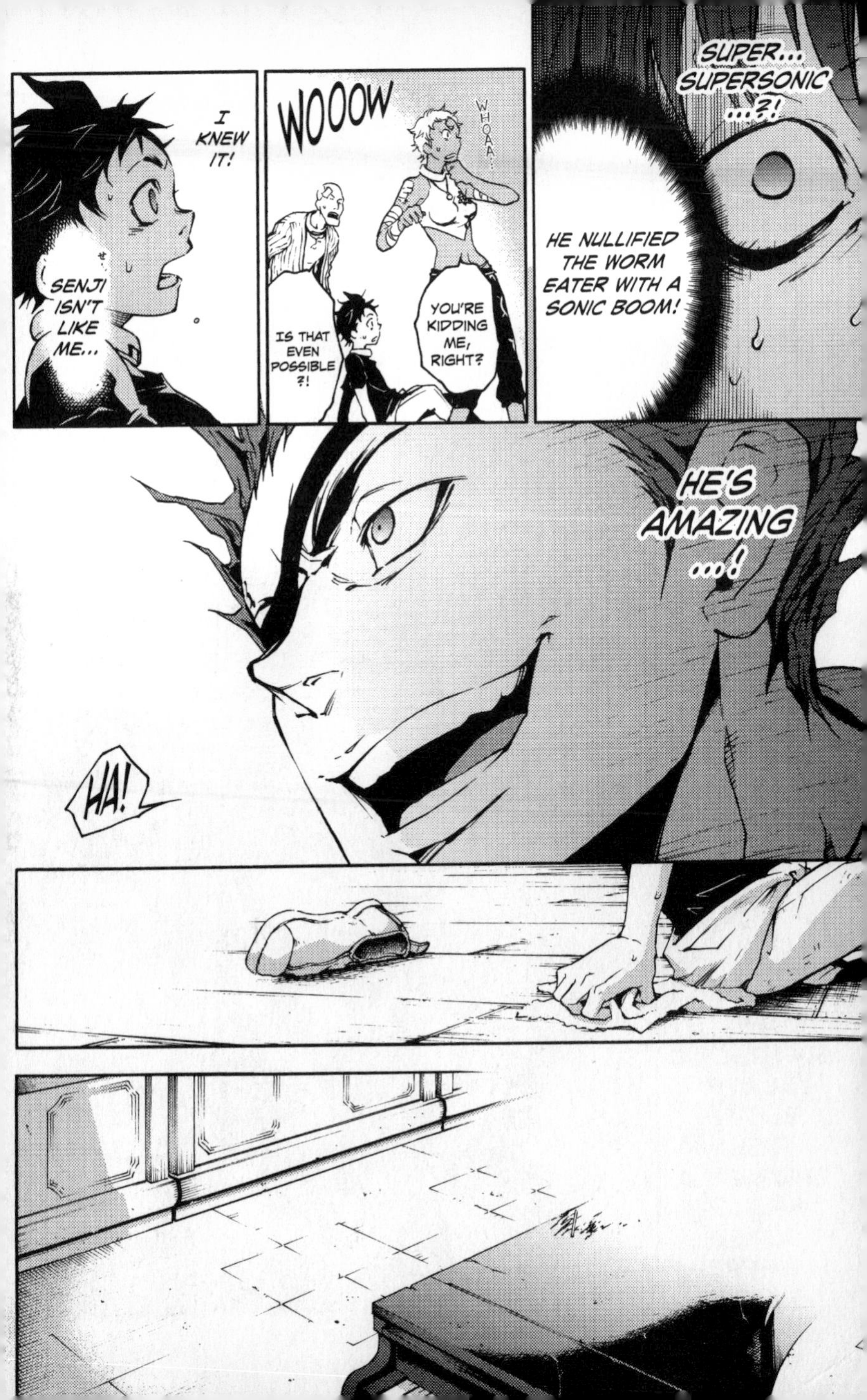
SUPER... SUPERSONIC ...?!
HE NULLIFIED THE WORM EATER WITH A SONIC BOOM!
WOOOW
WHOAA...
YOU'RE KIDDING ME, RIGHT?
IS THAT EVEN POSSIBLE ?!
I KNEW IT!
SENJI ISN'T LIKE ME...
HE'S AMAZING ...!
HA!

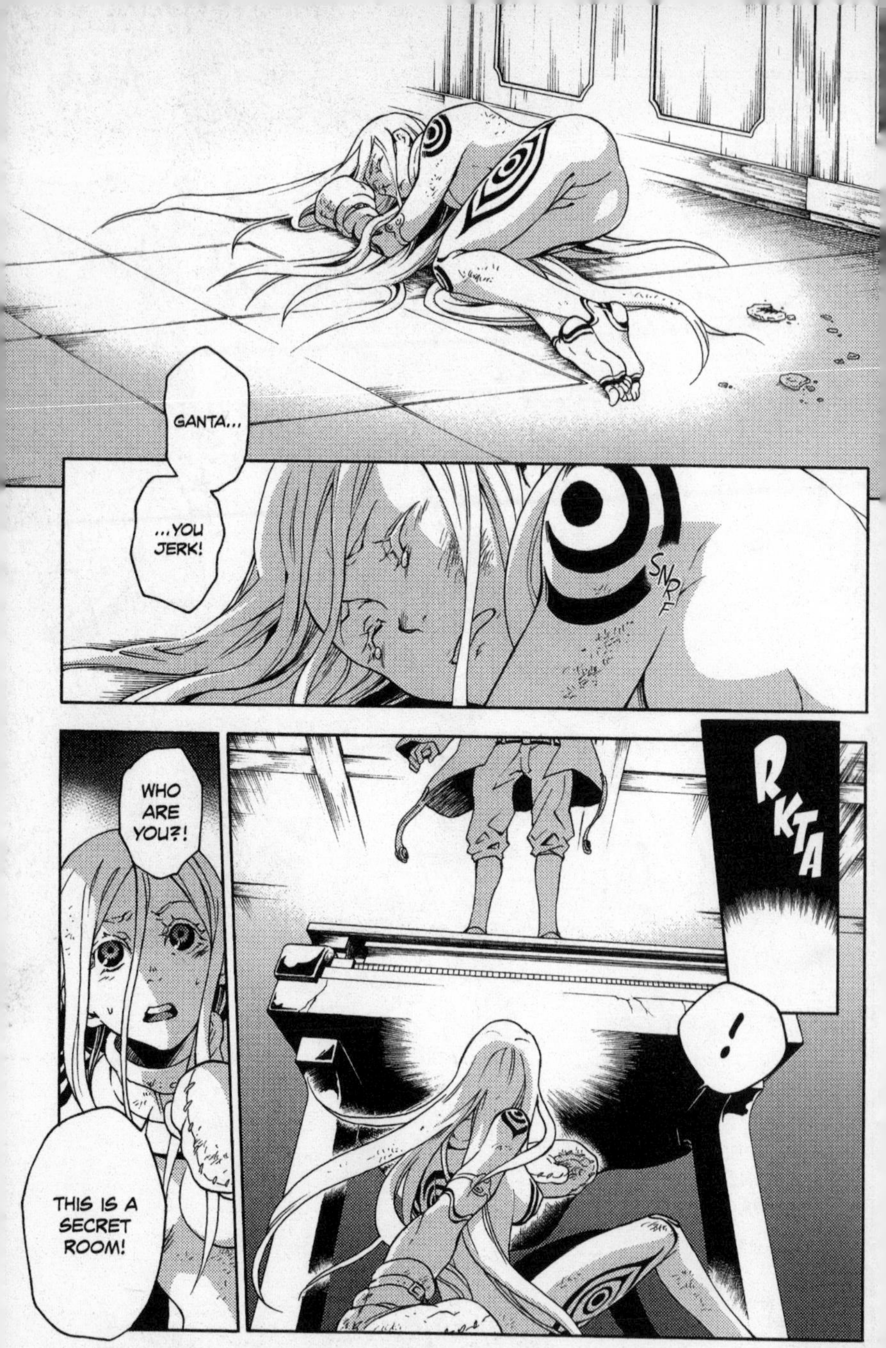
GANTA...
...YOU JERK!
SNRF
RKTA
!
WHO ARE YOU?!
THIS IS A SECRET ROOM!

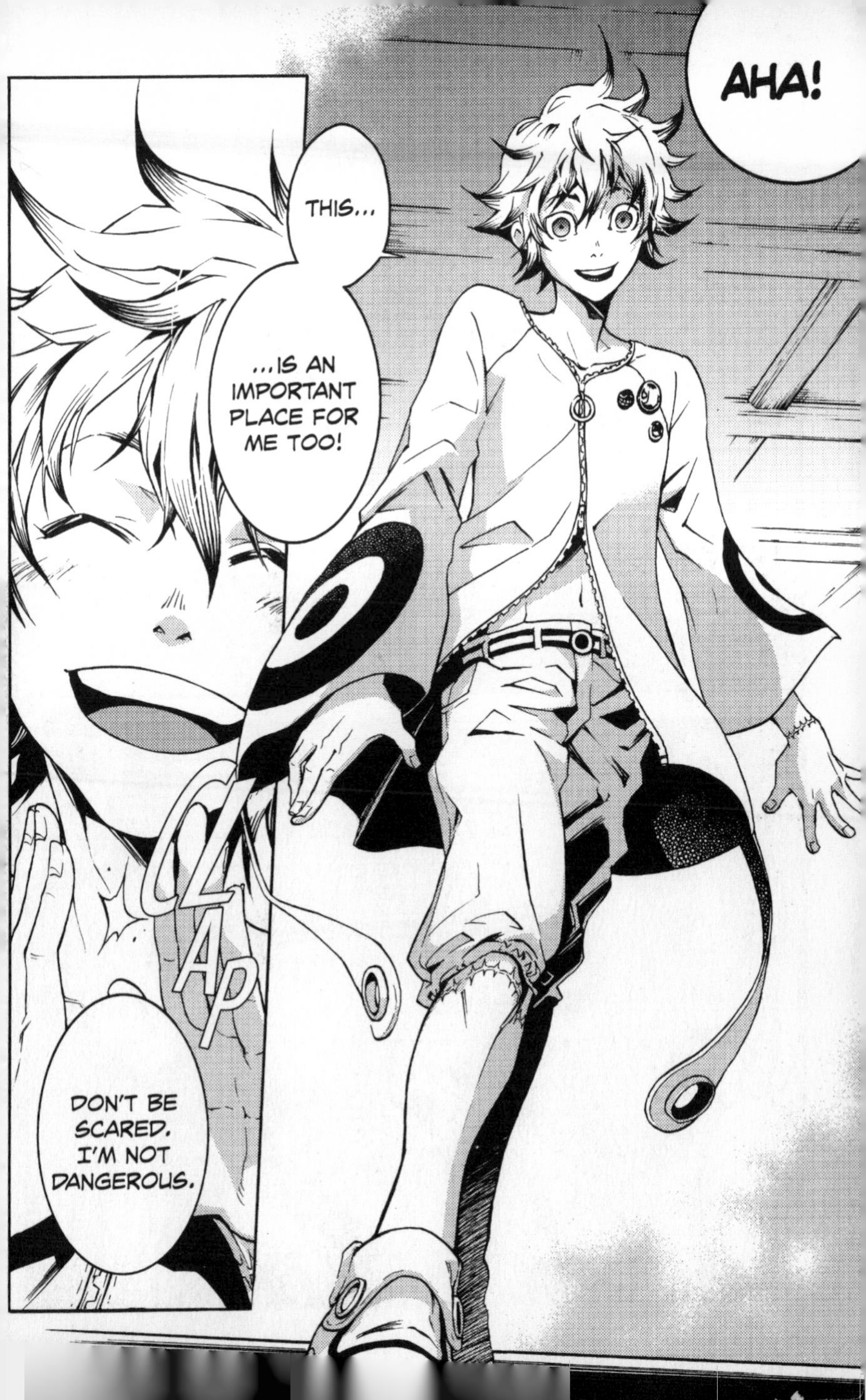
AHA!
THIS...
...IS AN IMPORTANT PLACE FOR ME TOO!
CLAP
DON'T BE SCARED. I'M NOT DANGEROUS.

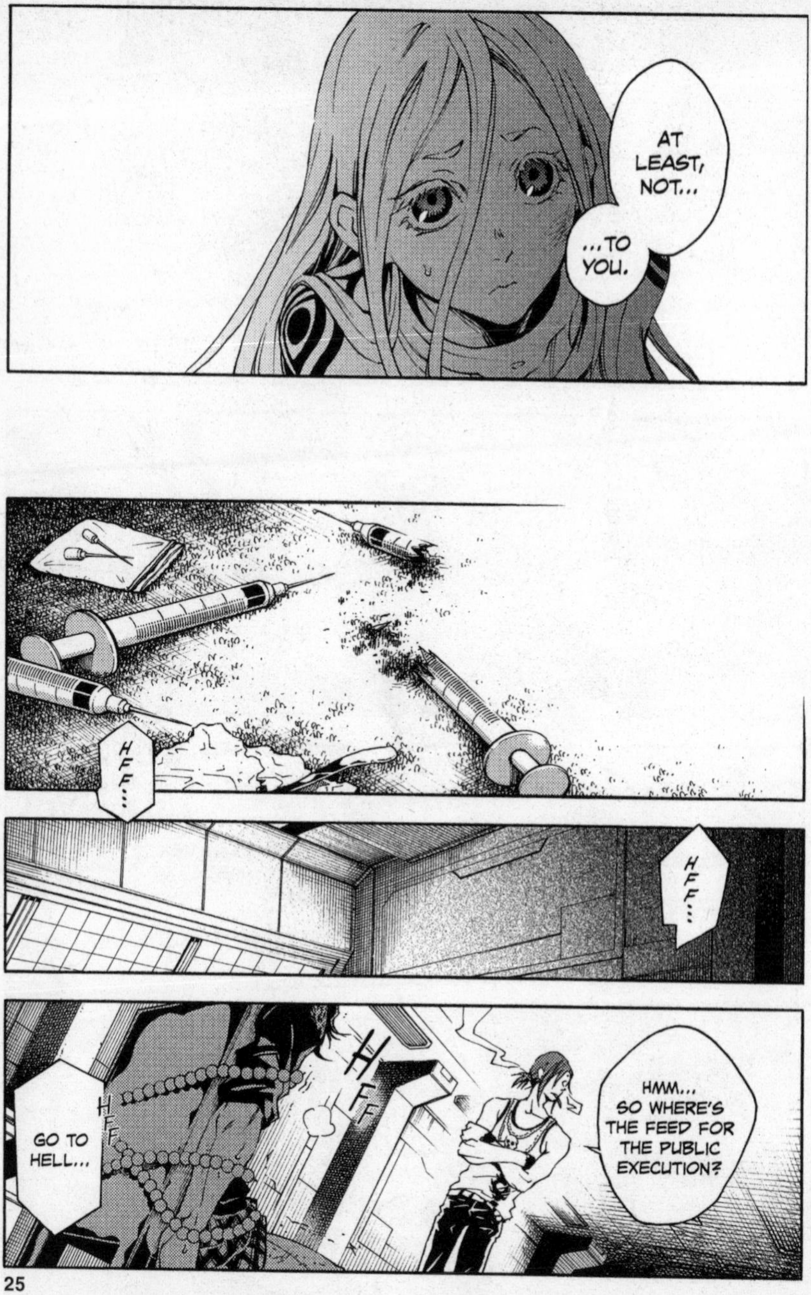
AT LEAST, NOT...
...TO YOU.
HFF...
HFF...
HMM... SO WHERE'S THE FEED FOR THE PUBLIC EXECUTION?
HFF
HFF
GO TO HELL...

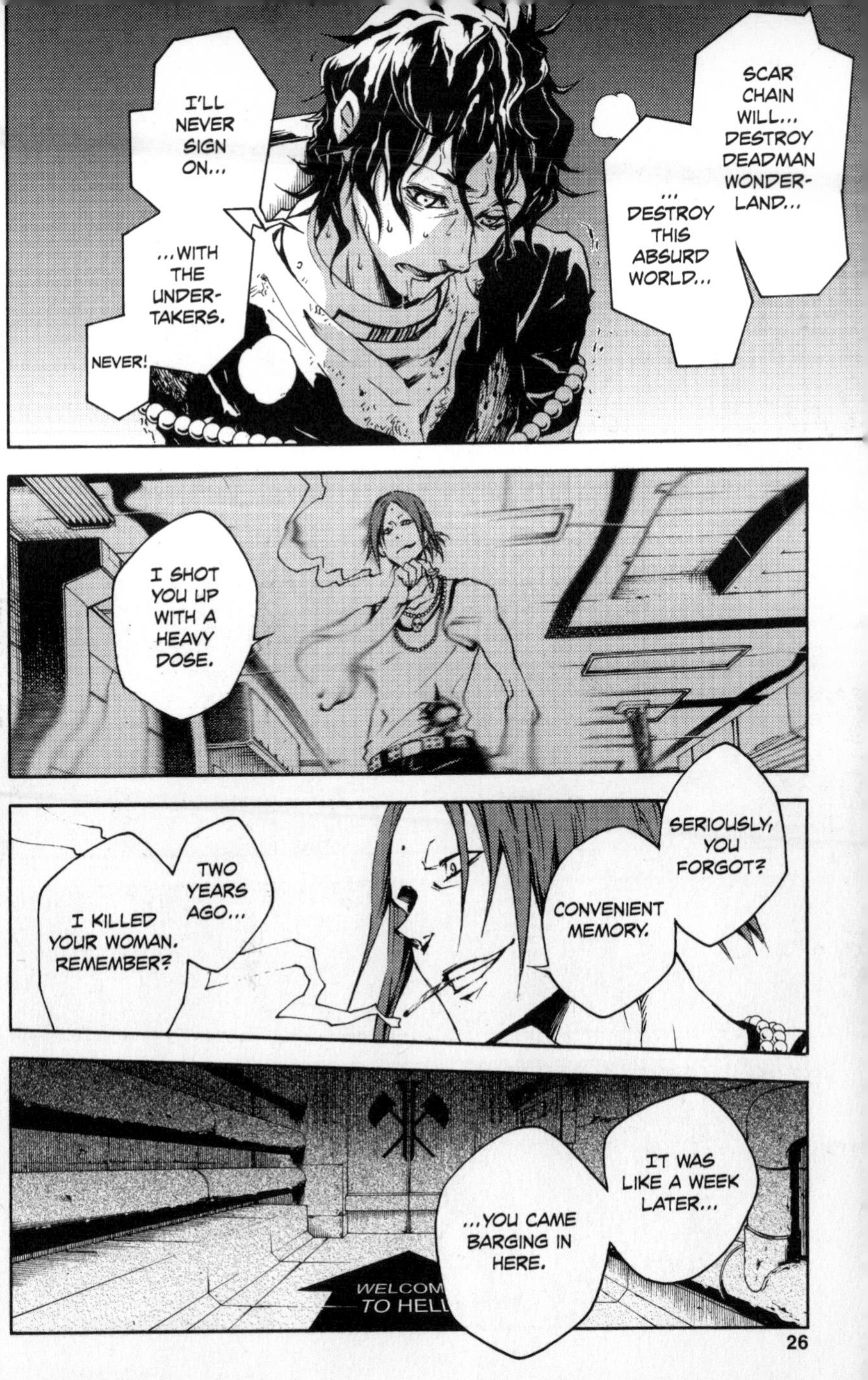
SCAR CHAIN WILL... DESTROY DEADMAN WONDER-LAND...
... DESTROY THIS ABSURD WORLD...
I'LL NEVER SIGN ON...
...WITH THE UNDER-TAKERS.
NEVER!
I SHOT YOU UP WITH A HEAVY DOSE.
SERIOUSLY, YOU FORGOT?
CONVENIENT MEMORY.
TWO YEARS AGO...
I KILLED YOUR WOMAN. REMEMBER?
IT WAS LIKE A WEEK LATER...
...YOU CAME BARGING IN HERE.
WELCOM
TO HELL

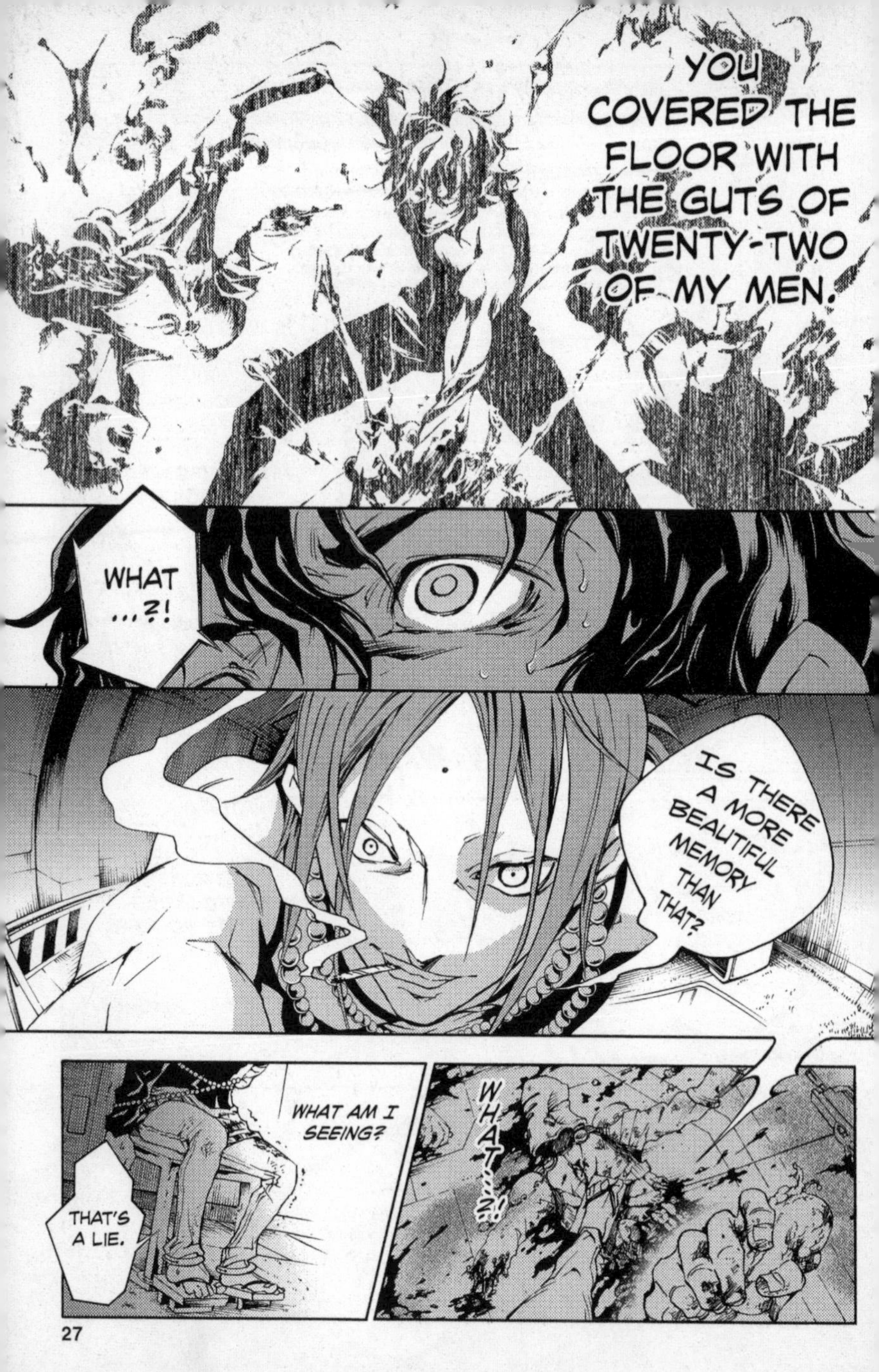
YOU COVERED THE FLOOR WITH THE GUTS OF TWENTY-TWO OF MY MEN.
WHAT ...?!
IS THERE A MORE BEAUTIFUL MEMORY THAN THAT?
WHAT...?!
WHAT AM I SEEING?
THAT'S A LIE.

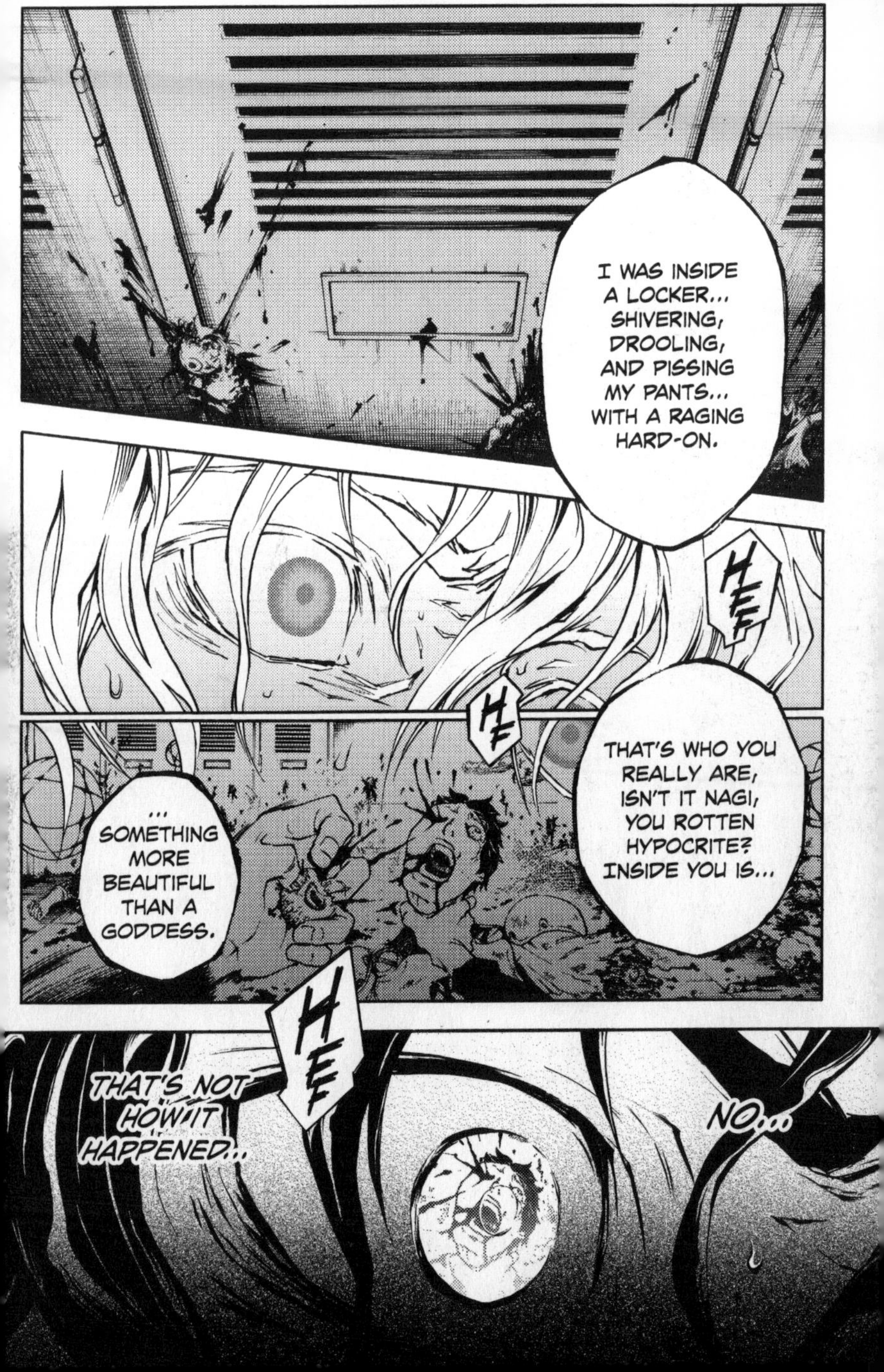
I WAS INSIDE A LOCKER... SHIVERING, DROOLING, AND PISSING MY PANTS... WITH A RAGING HARD-ON.
HEF
HEF
THAT'S WHO YOU REALLY ARE, ISN'T IT NAGI, YOU ROTTEN HYPOCRITE? INSIDE YOU IS...
... SOMETHING MORE BEAUTIFUL THAN A GODDESS.
HEF
NO...
THAT'S NOT HOW IT HAPPENED...

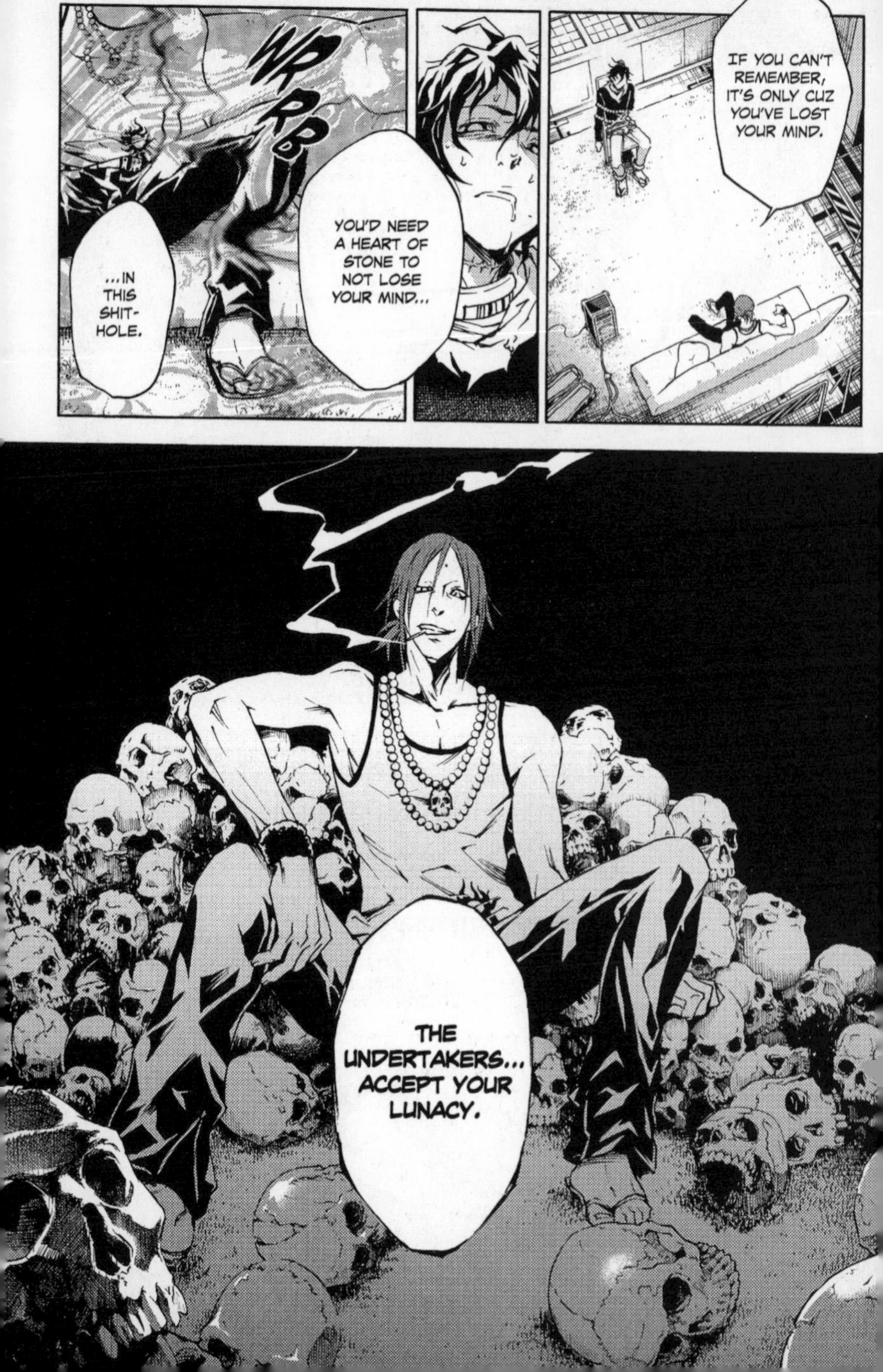
IF YOU CAN'T REMEMBER, IT'S ONLY CUZ YOU'VE LOST YOUR MIND.
YOU'D NEED A HEART OF STONE TO NOT LOSE YOUR MIND...
WRRB
...IN THIS SHIT-HOLE.
THE UNDERTAKERS... ACCEPT YOUR LUNACY.

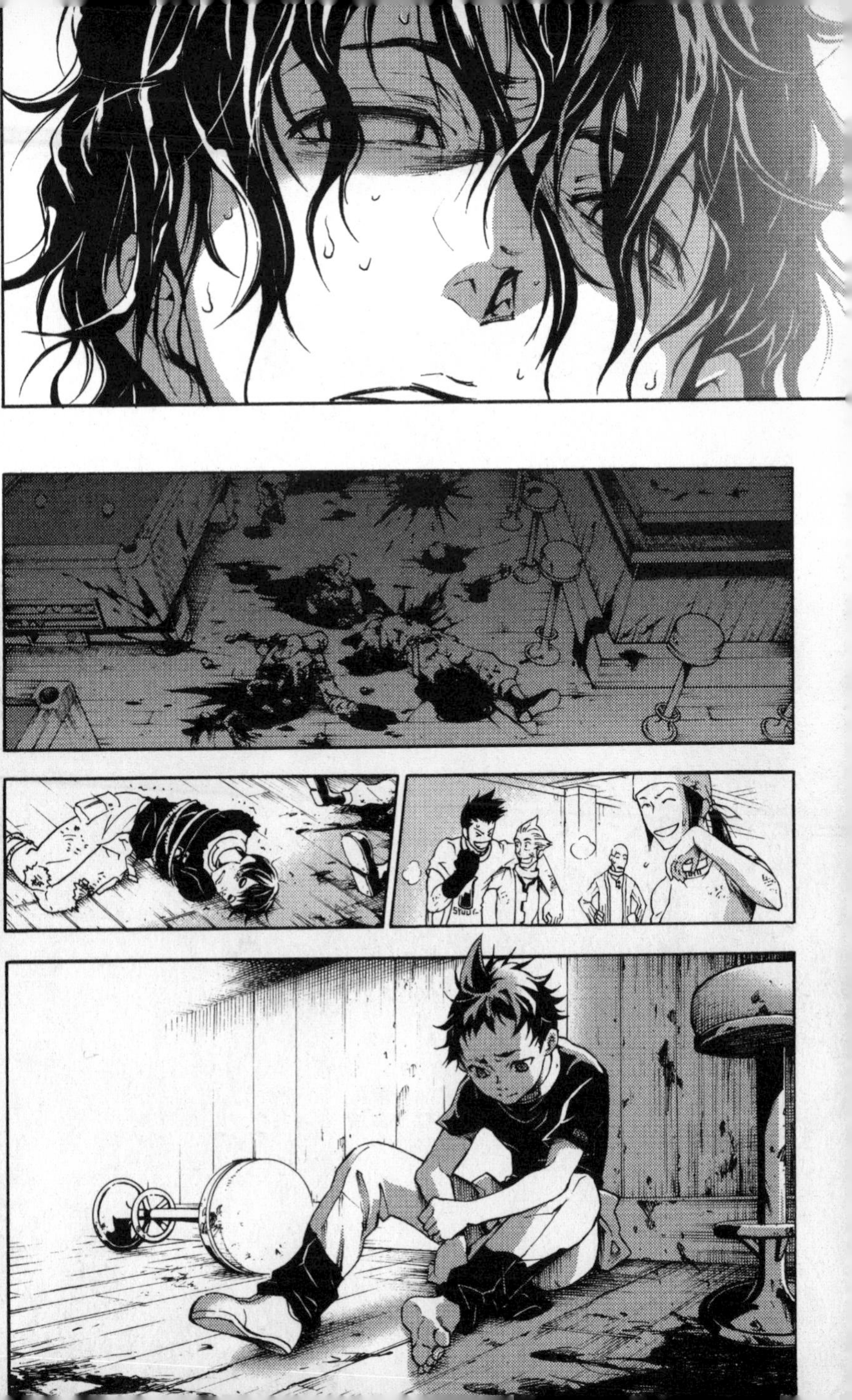

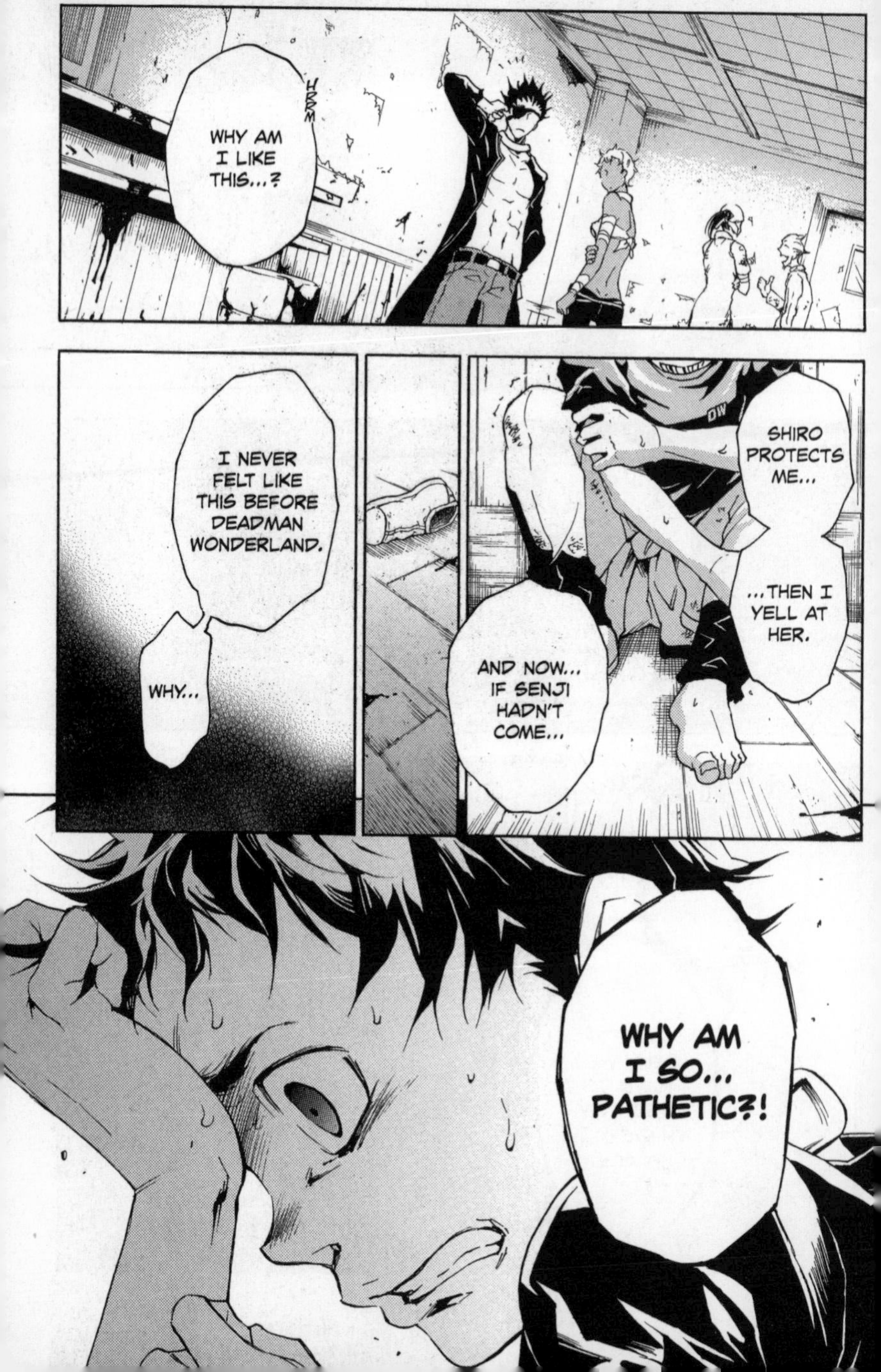
HRRM
WHY AM I LIKE THIS...?
SHIRO PROTECTS ME...
...THEN I YELL AT HER.
AND NOW... IF SENJI HADN'T COME...
I NEVER FELT LIKE THIS BEFORE DEADMAN WONDERLAND.
WHY...
WHY AM I SO... PATHETIC?!

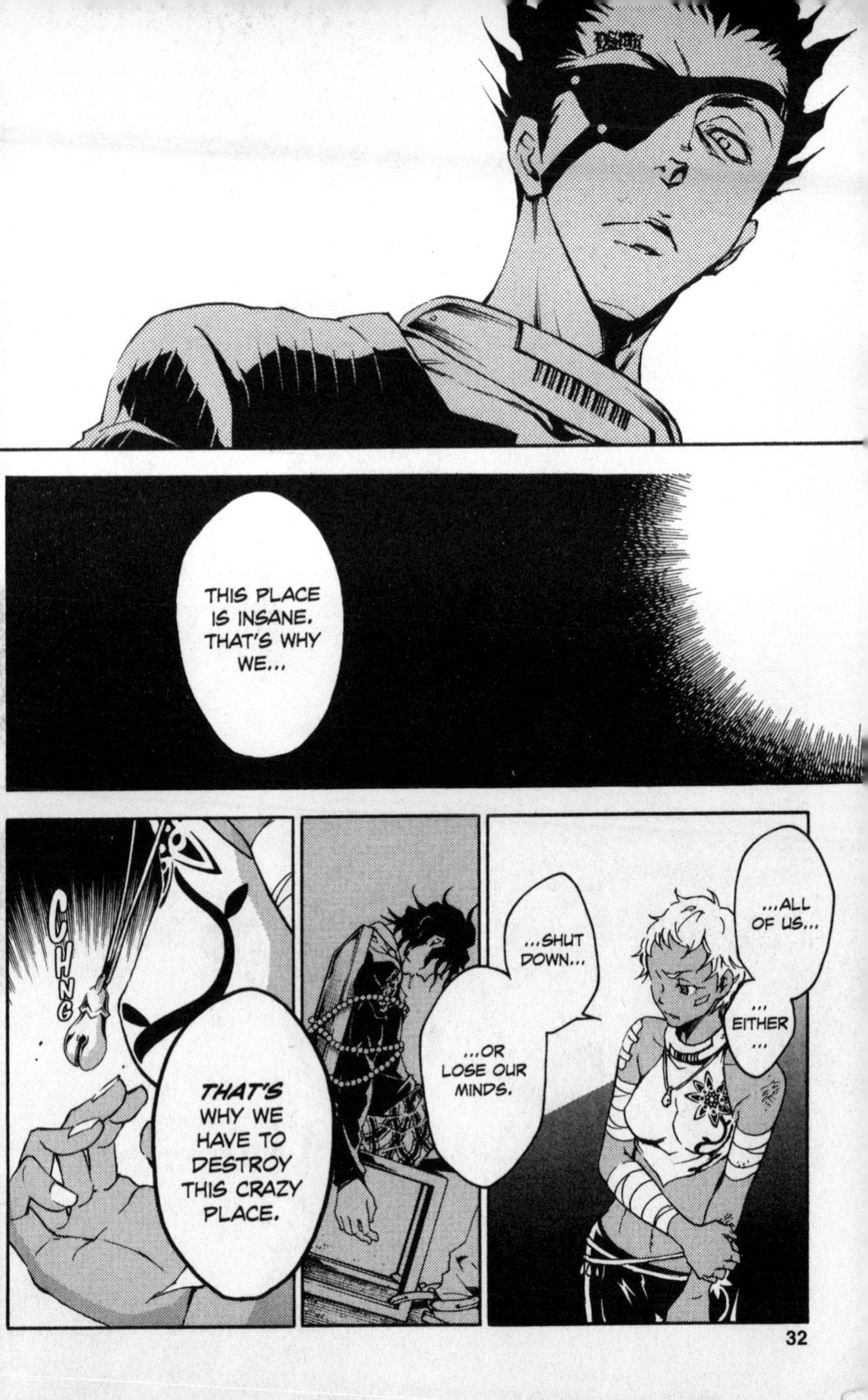
THIS PLACE IS INSANE. THAT'S WHY WE...
...ALL OF US...
... EITHER ...
...SHUT DOWN...
...OR LOSE OUR MINDS.
CHNG
THAT'S WHY WE HAVE TO DESTROY THIS CRAZY PLACE.

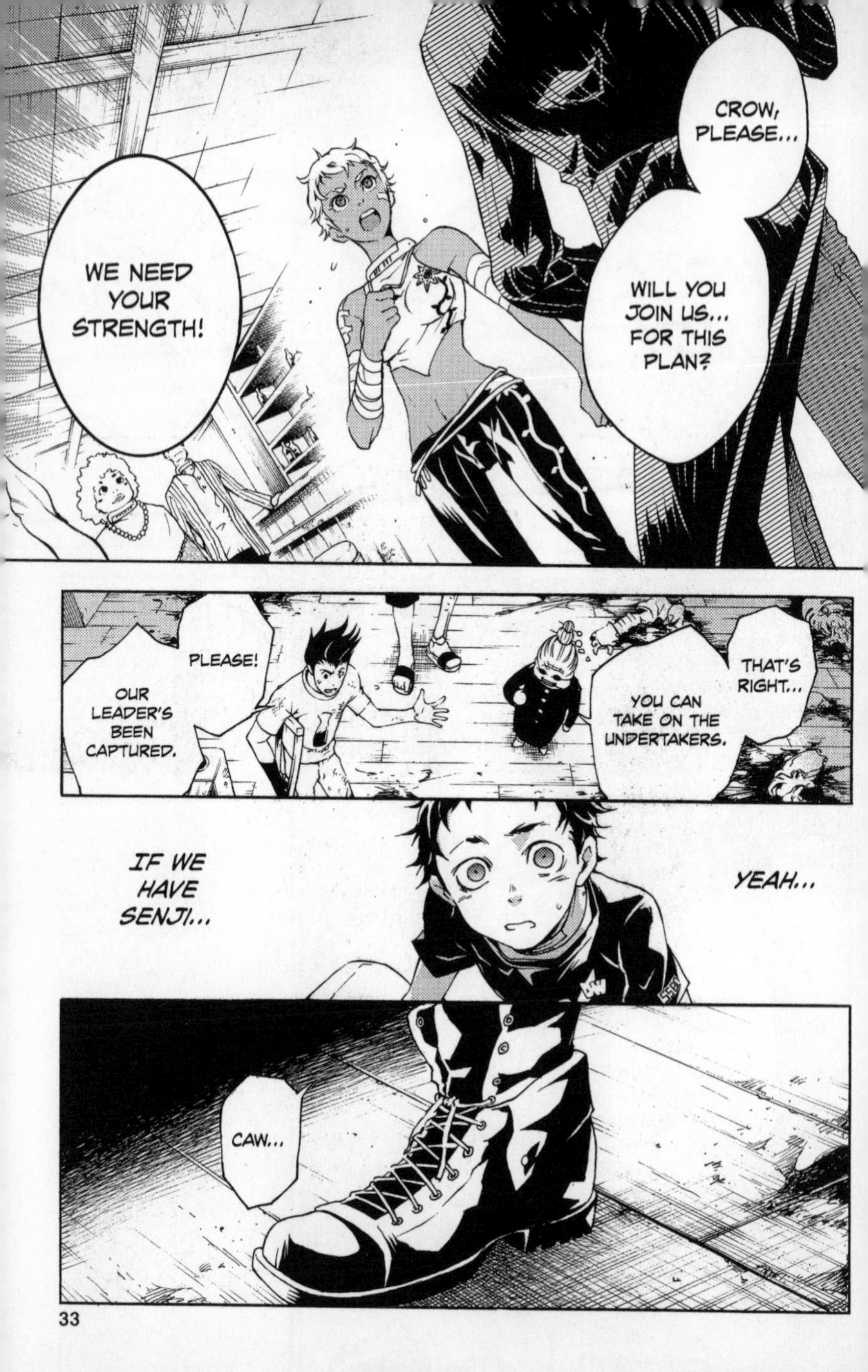
CROW, PLEASE...
WILL YOU JOIN US... FOR THIS PLAN?
WE NEED YOUR STRENGTH!
THAT'S RIGHT...
YOU CAN TAKE ON THE UNDERTAKERS.
PLEASE!
OUR LEADER'S BEEN CAPTURED.
YEAH...
IF WE HAVE SENJI...
CAW...

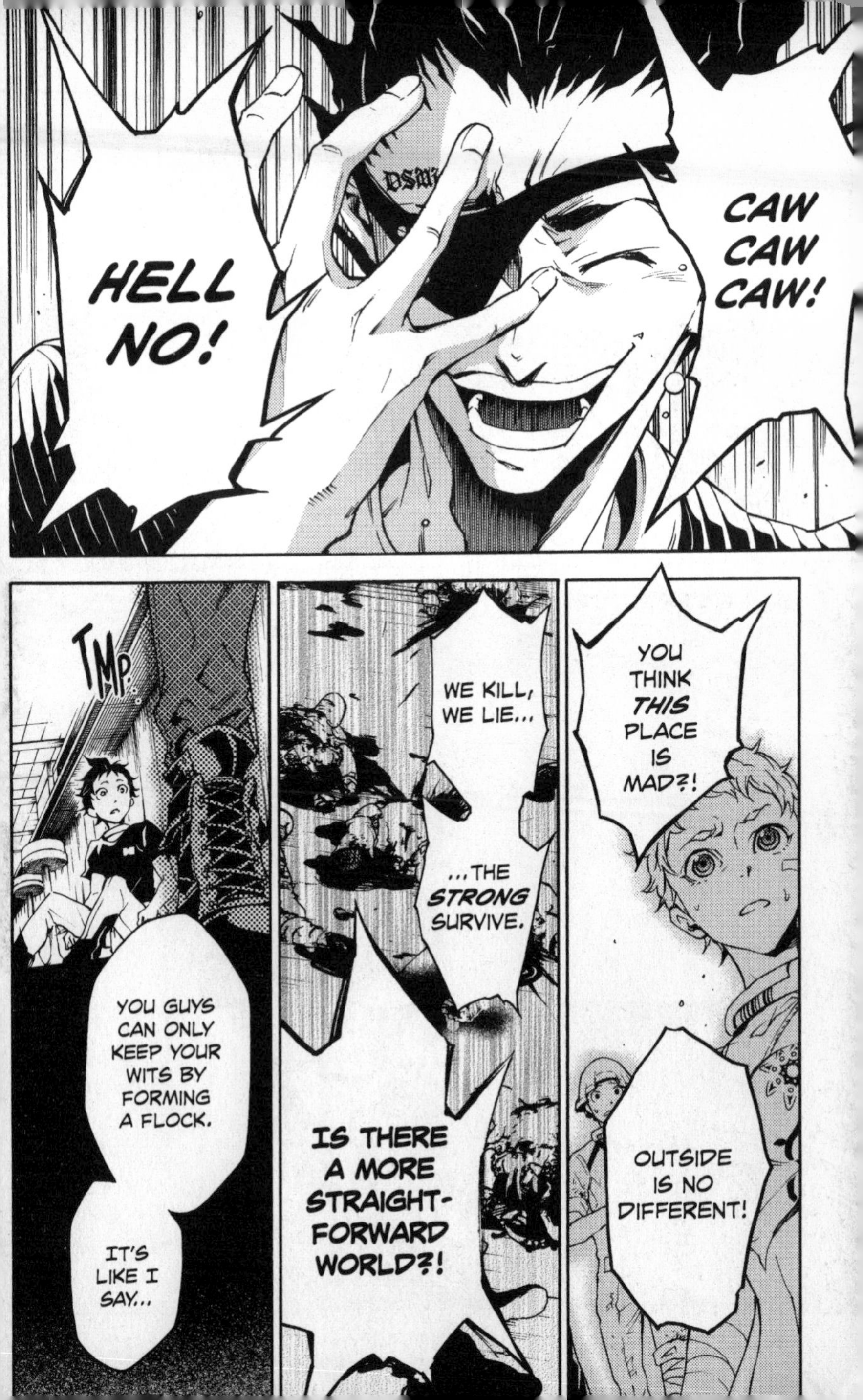
CAW CAW CAW!
HELL NO!
YOU THINK *THIS* PLACE IS MAD?!
OUTSIDE IS NO DIFFERENT!
WE KILL, WE LIE...
...THE *STRONG* SURVIVE.
IS THERE A MORE STRAIGHT-FORWARD WORLD?!
TMP
YOU GUYS CAN ONLY KEEP YOUR WITS BY FORMING A FLOCK.
IT'S LIKE I SAY...

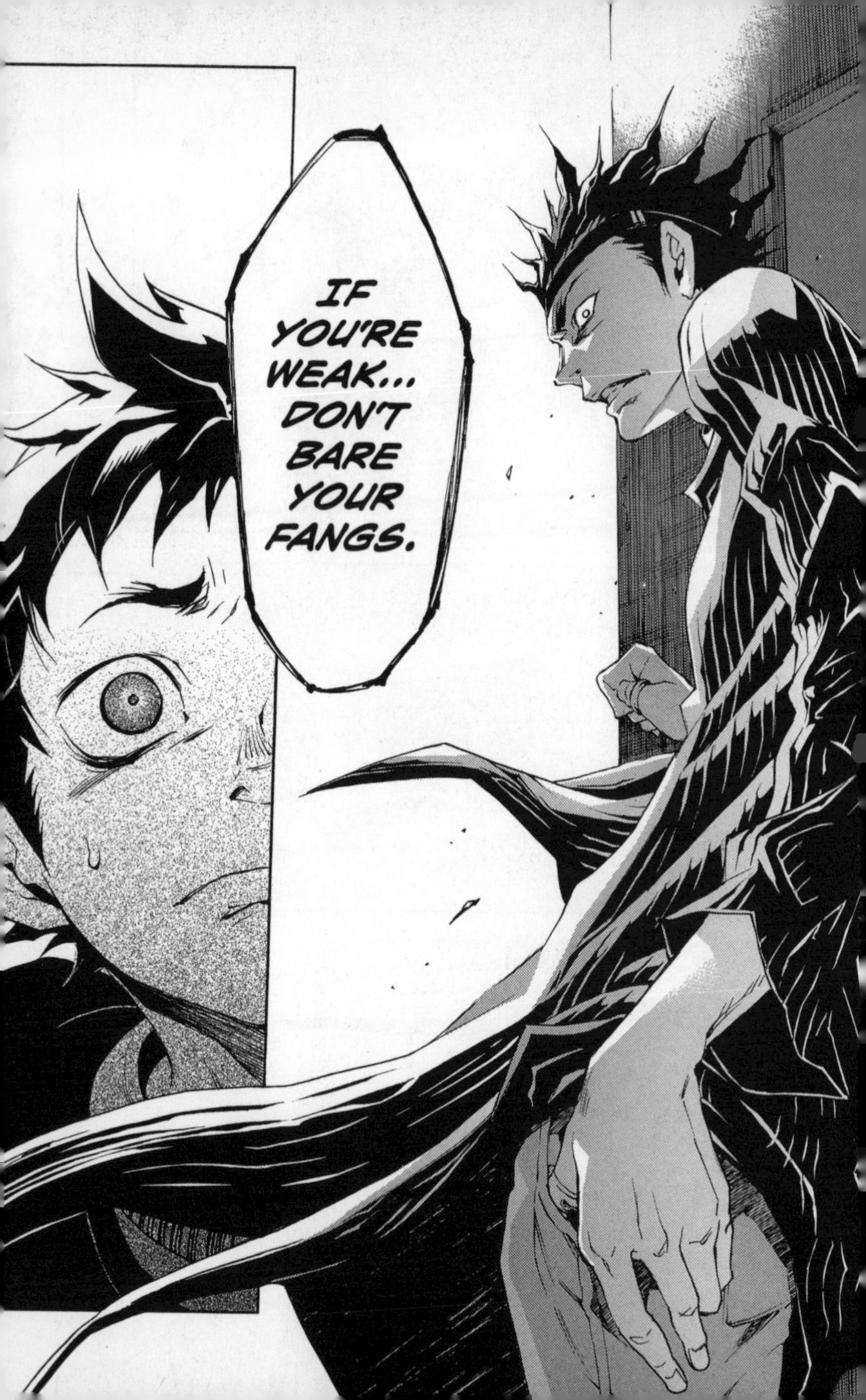
IF YOU'RE WEAK... DON'T BARE YOUR FANGS.

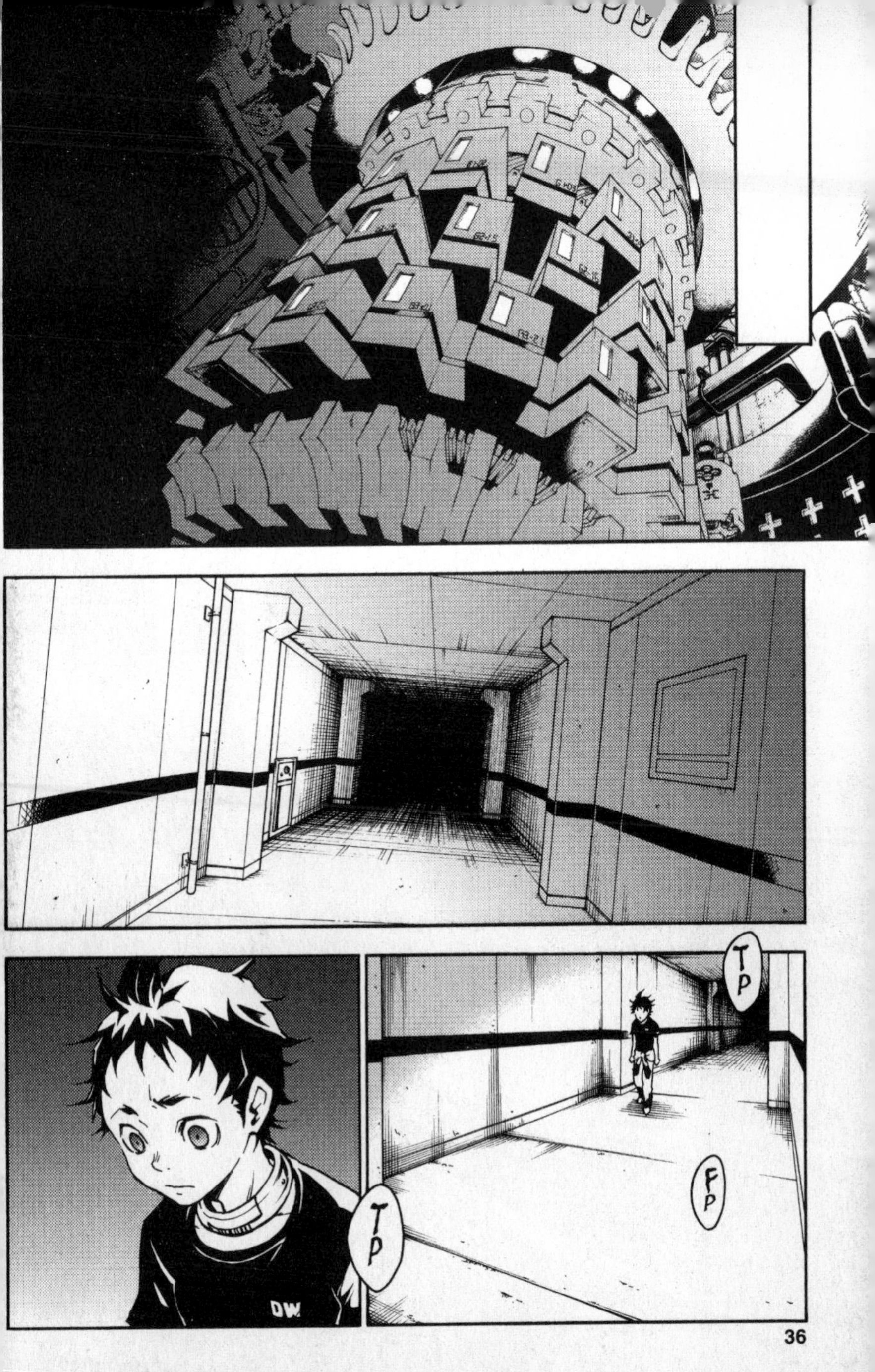
TP
FP
TP
DW

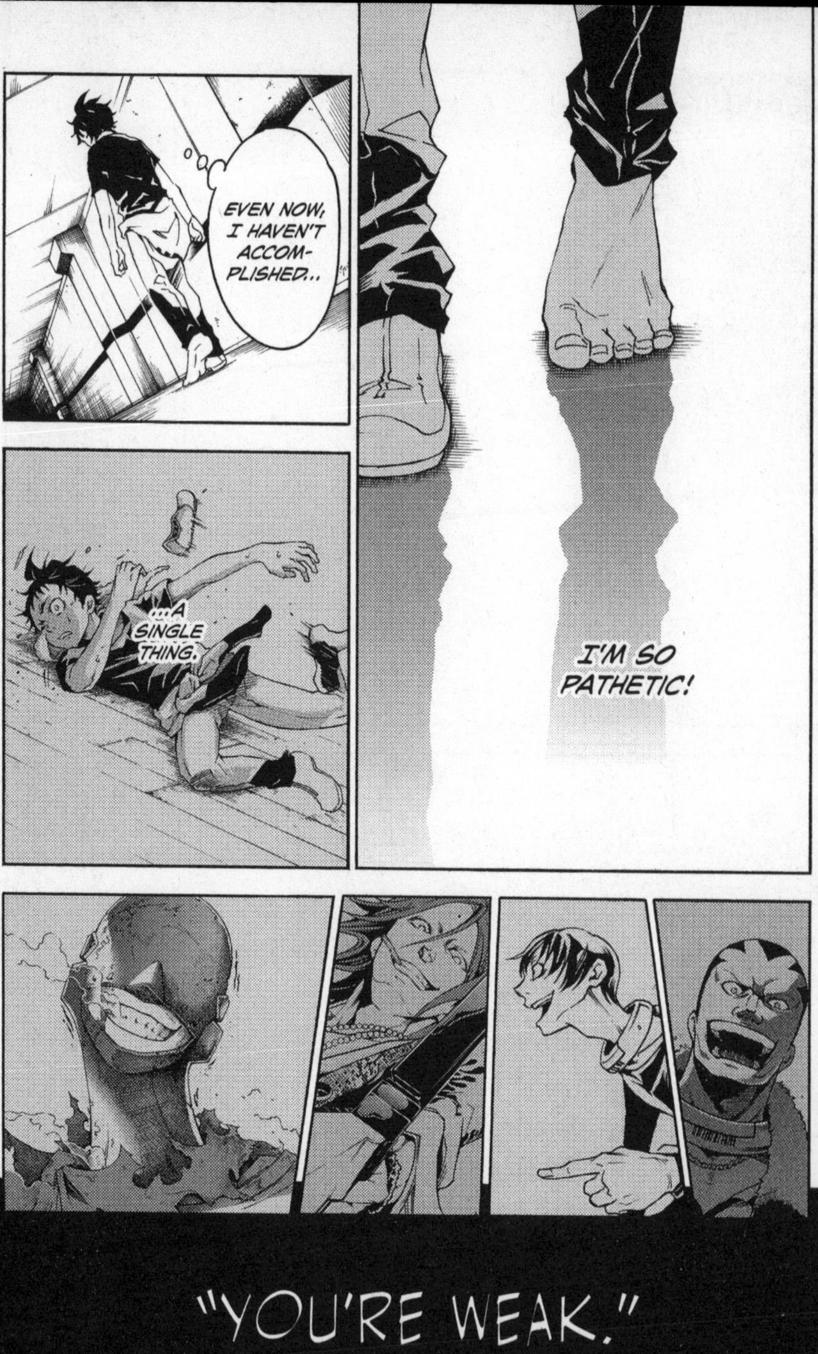
I'M SO PATHETIC!
EVEN NOW, I HAVEN'T ACCOMPLISHED...
...A SINGLE THING.
"YOU'RE WEAK."

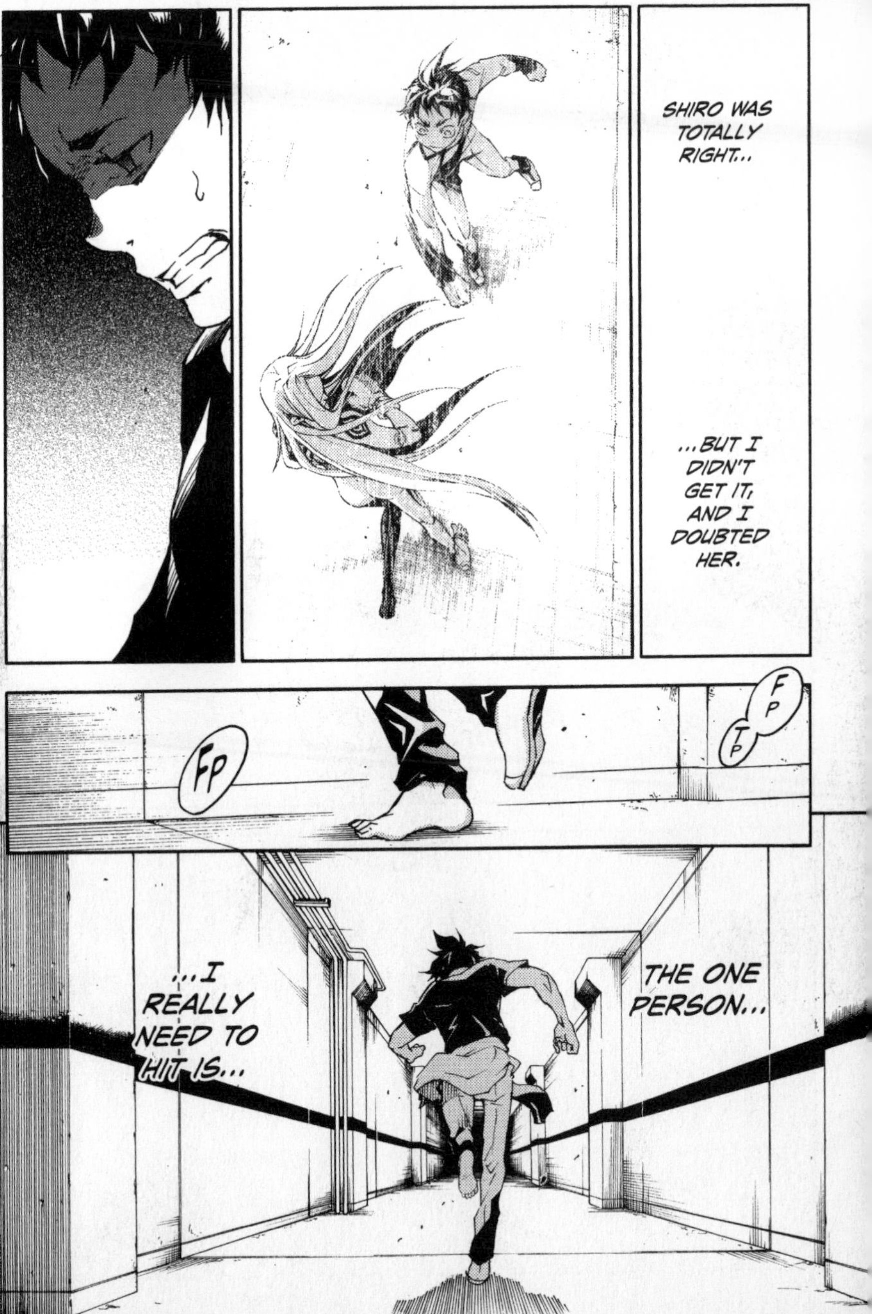
SHIRO WAS TOTALLY RIGHT...
...BUT I DIDN'T GET IT, AND I DOUBTED HER.
FP TP
FP
THE ONE PERSON...
...I REALLY NEED TO HIT IS...

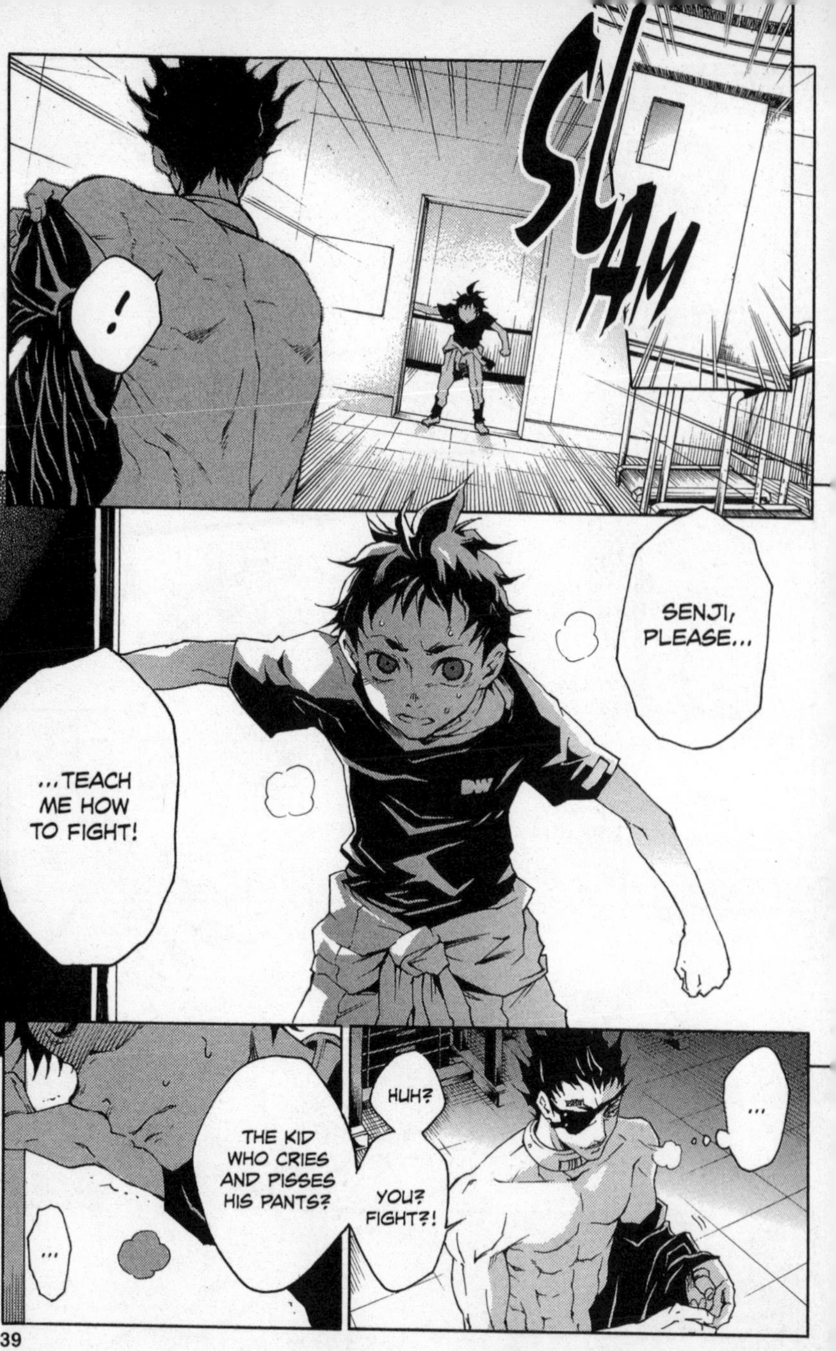
SLAM
!
SENJI, PLEASE...
...TEACH ME HOW TO FIGHT!
...
HUH?
YOU? FIGHT?!
THE KID WHO CRIES AND PISSES HIS PANTS?
...

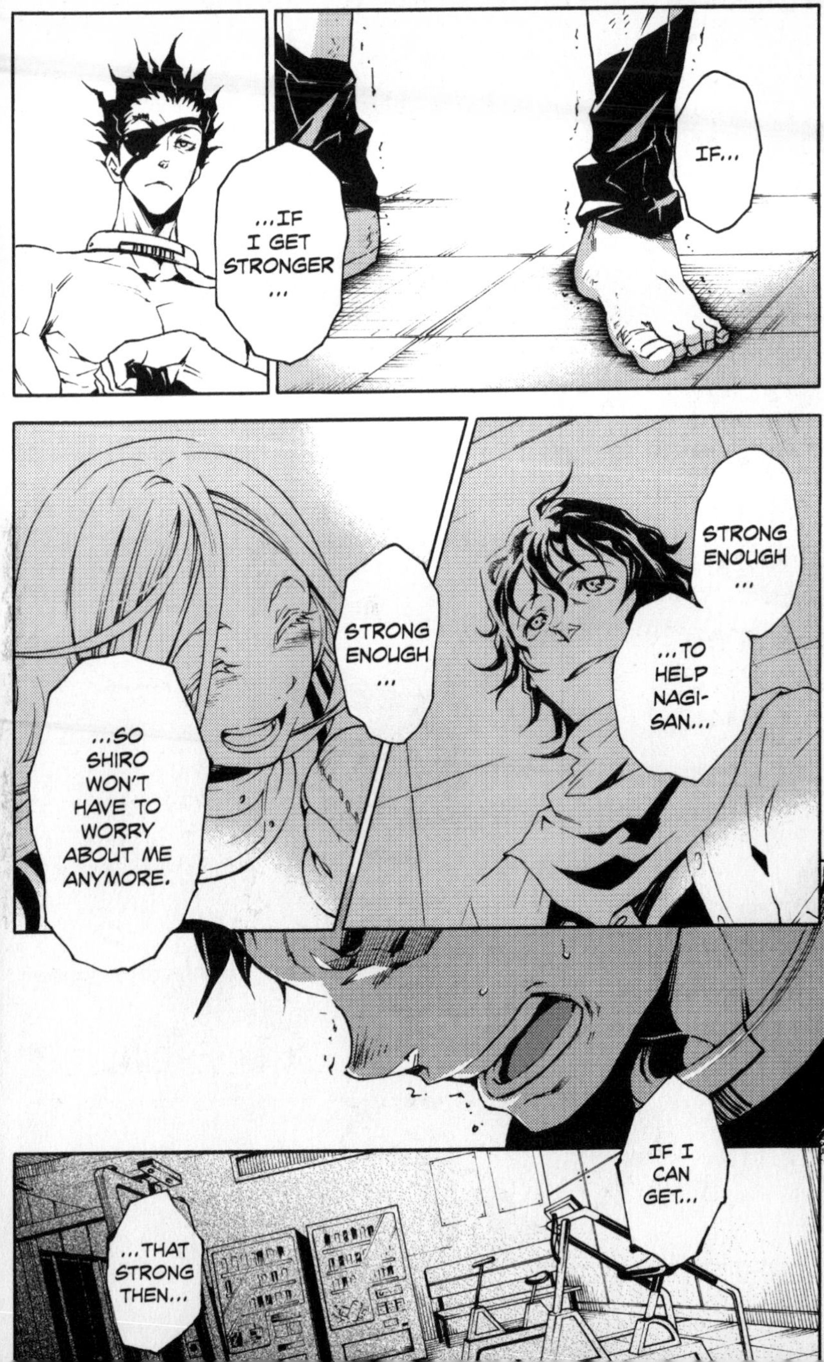
IF...
...IF I GET STRONGER ...
STRONG ENOUGH ...
...TO HELP NAGI-SAN...
STRONG ENOUGH ...
...SO SHIRO WON'T HAVE TO WORRY ABOUT ME ANYMORE.
IF I CAN GET...
...THAT STRONG THEN...

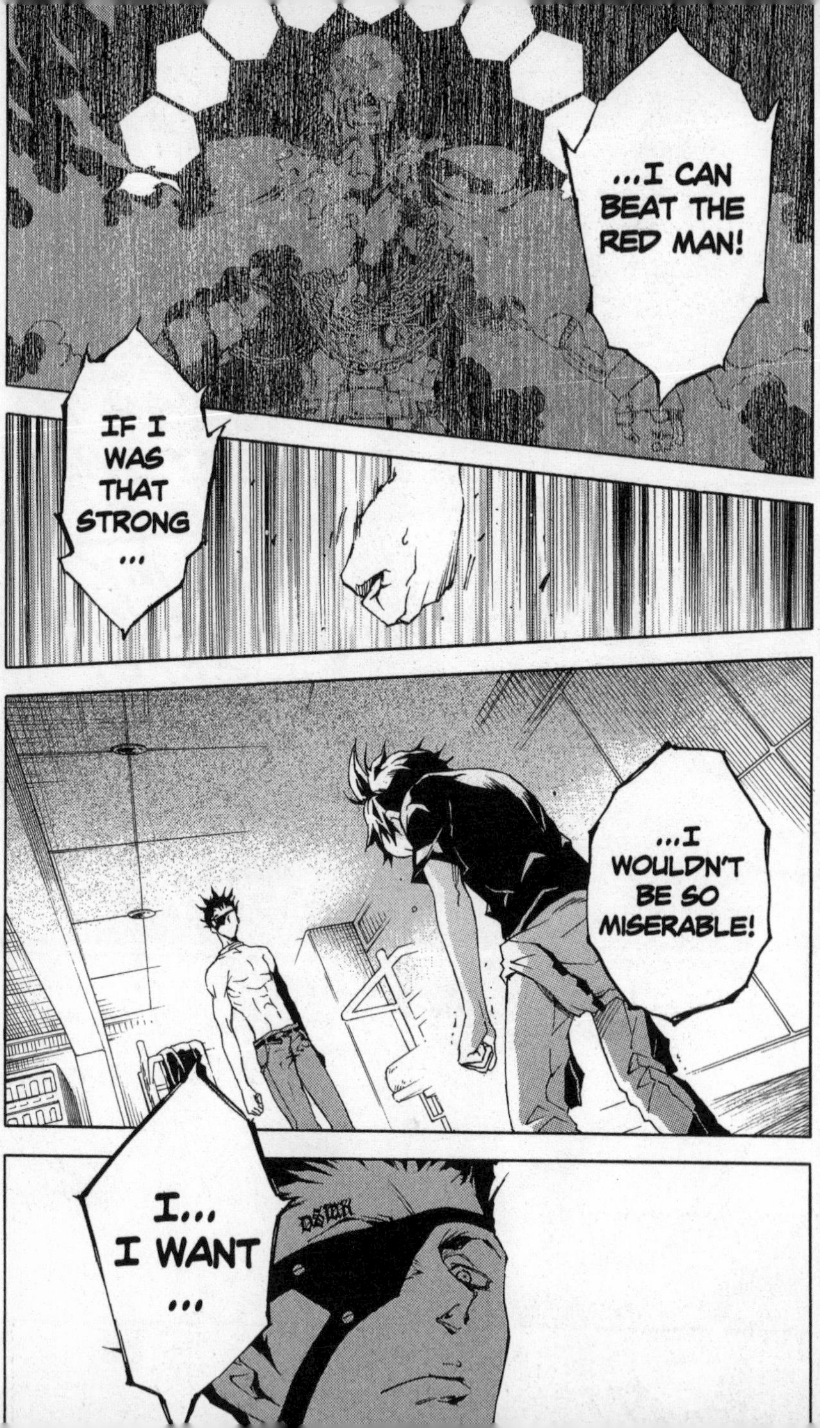
...I CAN BEAT THE RED MAN!
IF I WAS THAT STRONG...
...I WOULDN'T BE SO MISERABLE!
I... I WANT...

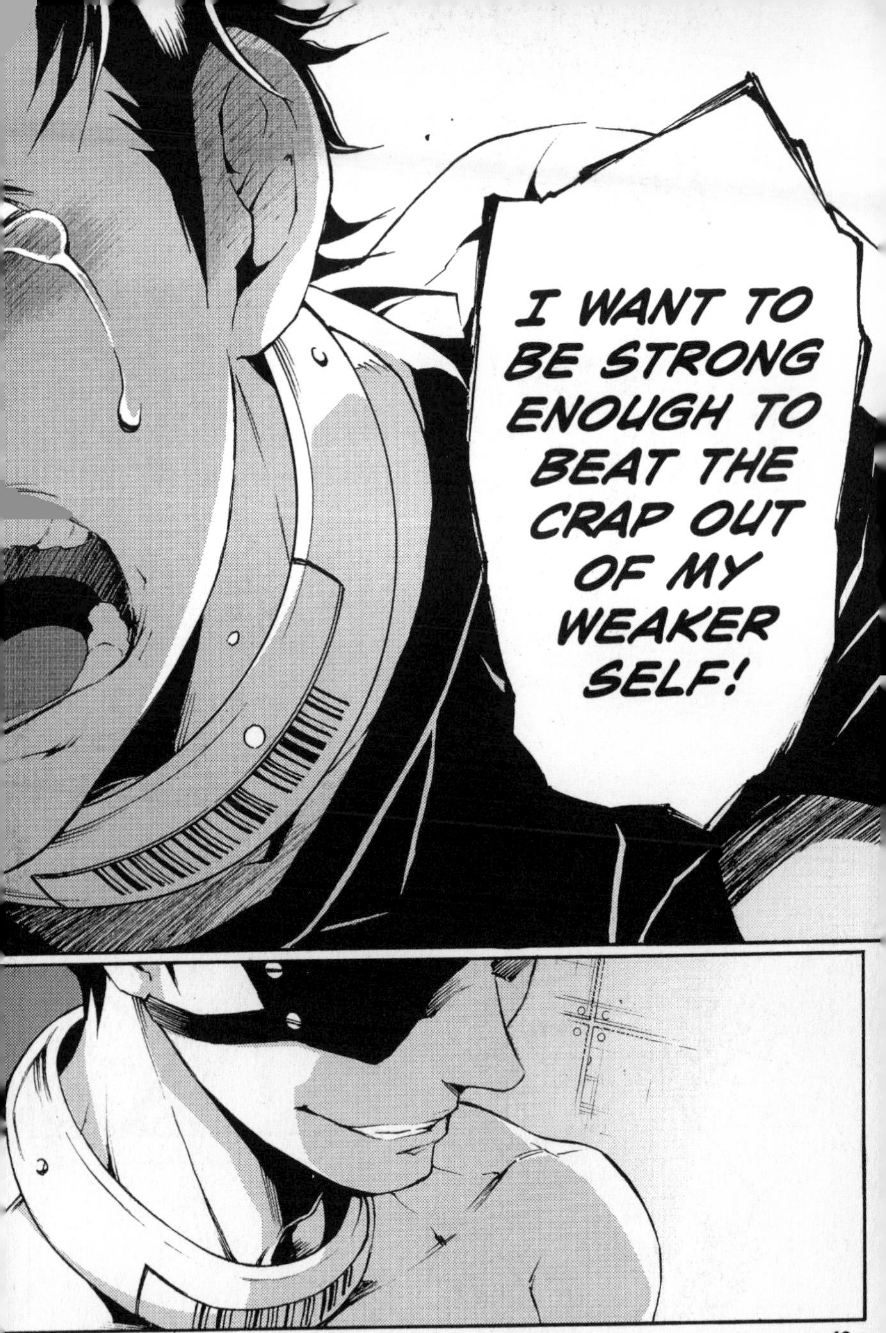
I WANT TO BE STRONG ENOUGH TO BEAT THE CRAP OUT OF MY WEAKER SELF!

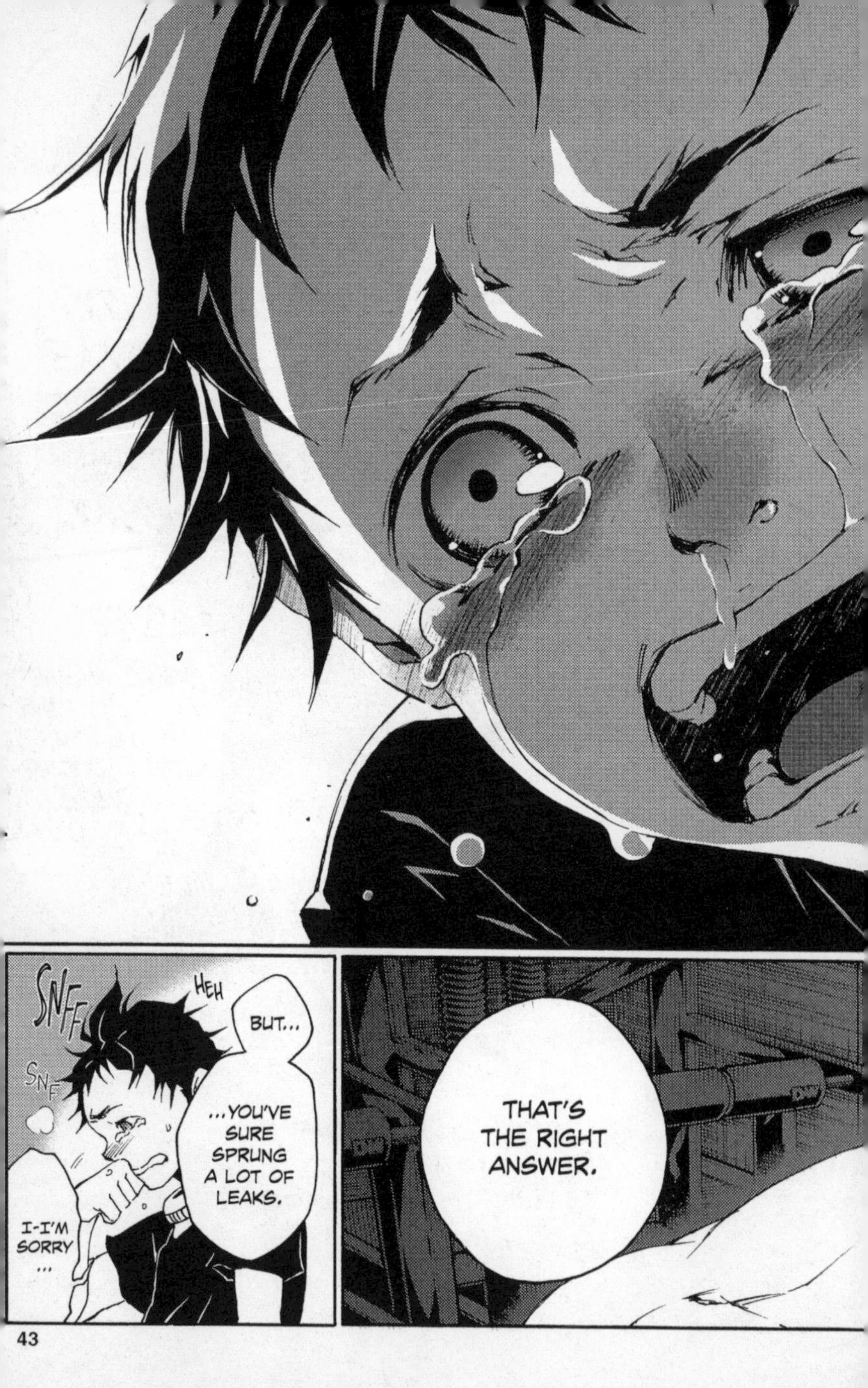
THAT'S THE RIGHT ANSWER.
HEH
BUT...
...YOU'VE SURE SPRUNG A LOT OF LEAKS.
SNFF
SNF
I-I'M SORRY ...

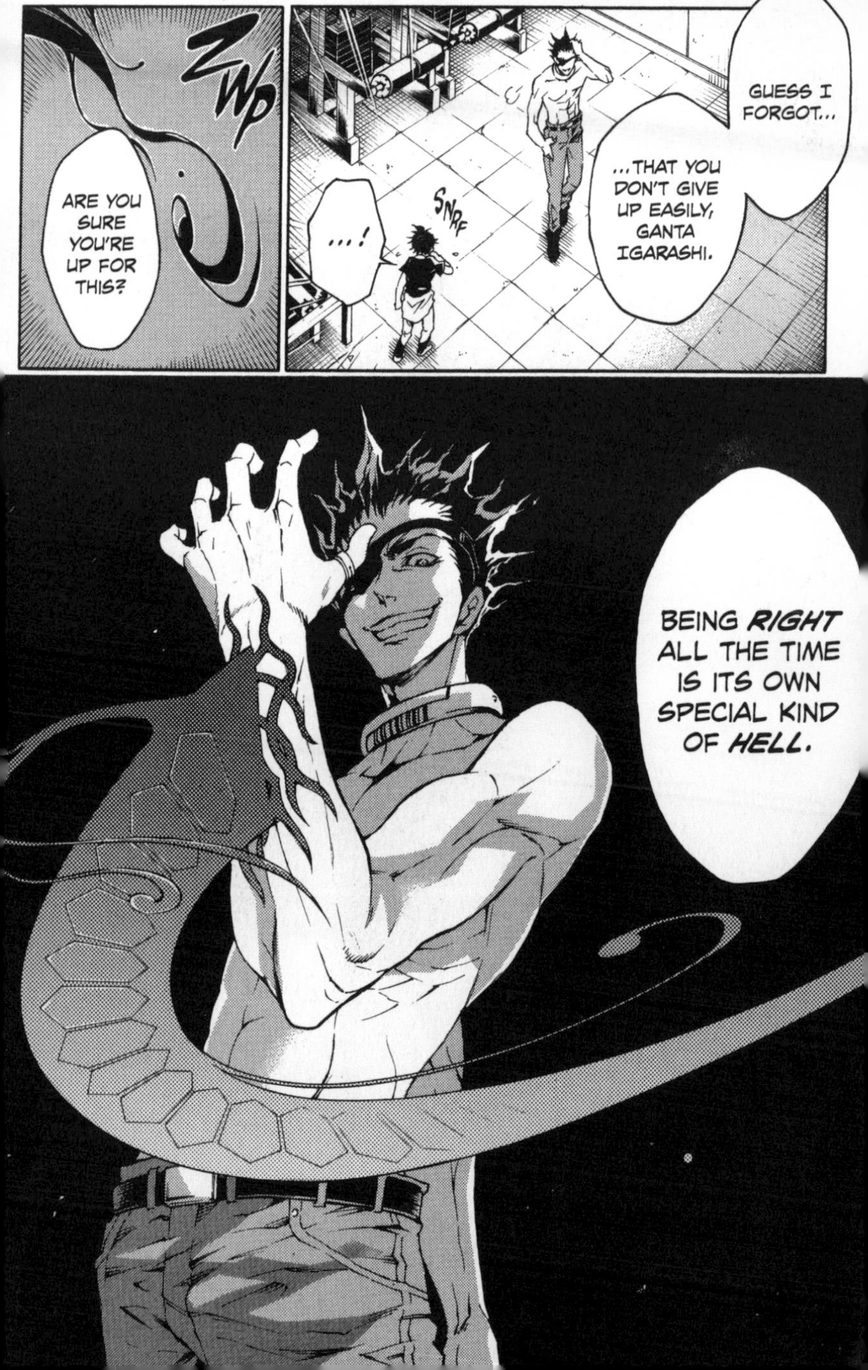
GUESS I FORGOT...
...THAT YOU DON'T GIVE UP EASILY, GANTA IGARASHI.
SNRF
...!
ZWP
ARE YOU SURE YOU'RE UP FOR THIS?
BEING RIGHT ALL THE TIME IS ITS OWN SPECIAL KIND OF HELL.

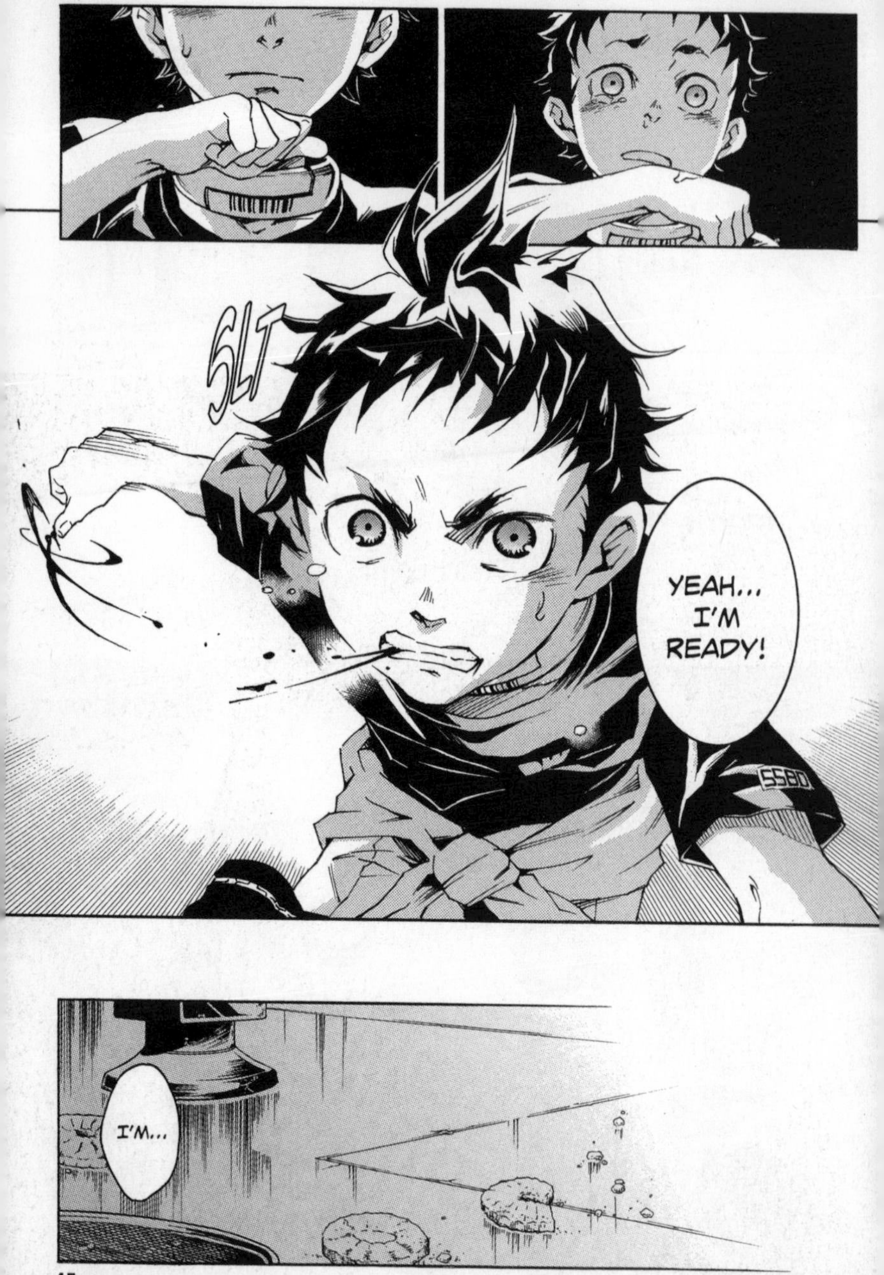
SLT
YEAH... I'M READY!
SSBD
I'M...

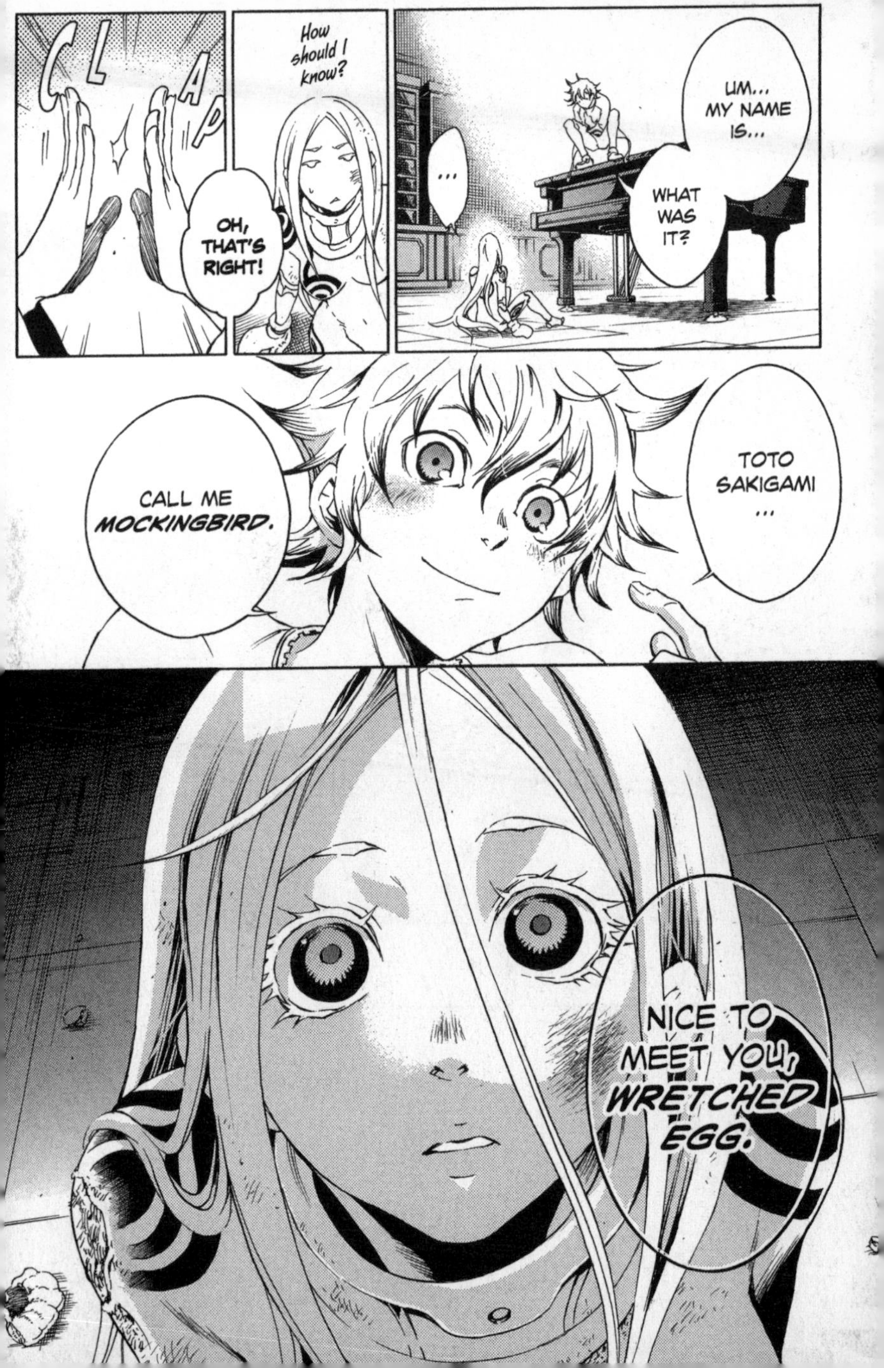
UM... MY NAME IS...
WHAT WAS IT?
...
How should I know?
OH, THAT'S RIGHT!
CLAP
TOTO SAKIGAMI ...
CALL ME *MOCKINGBIRD*.
NICE TO MEET YOU, *WRETCHED EGG*.

DEAD
MAN WONDER LAND

DEAD
MAN WONDER LAND

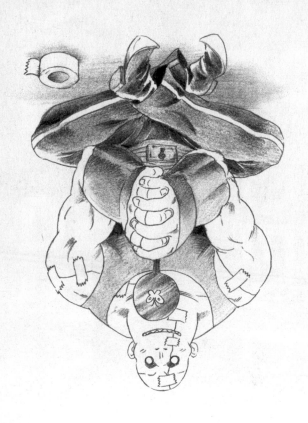

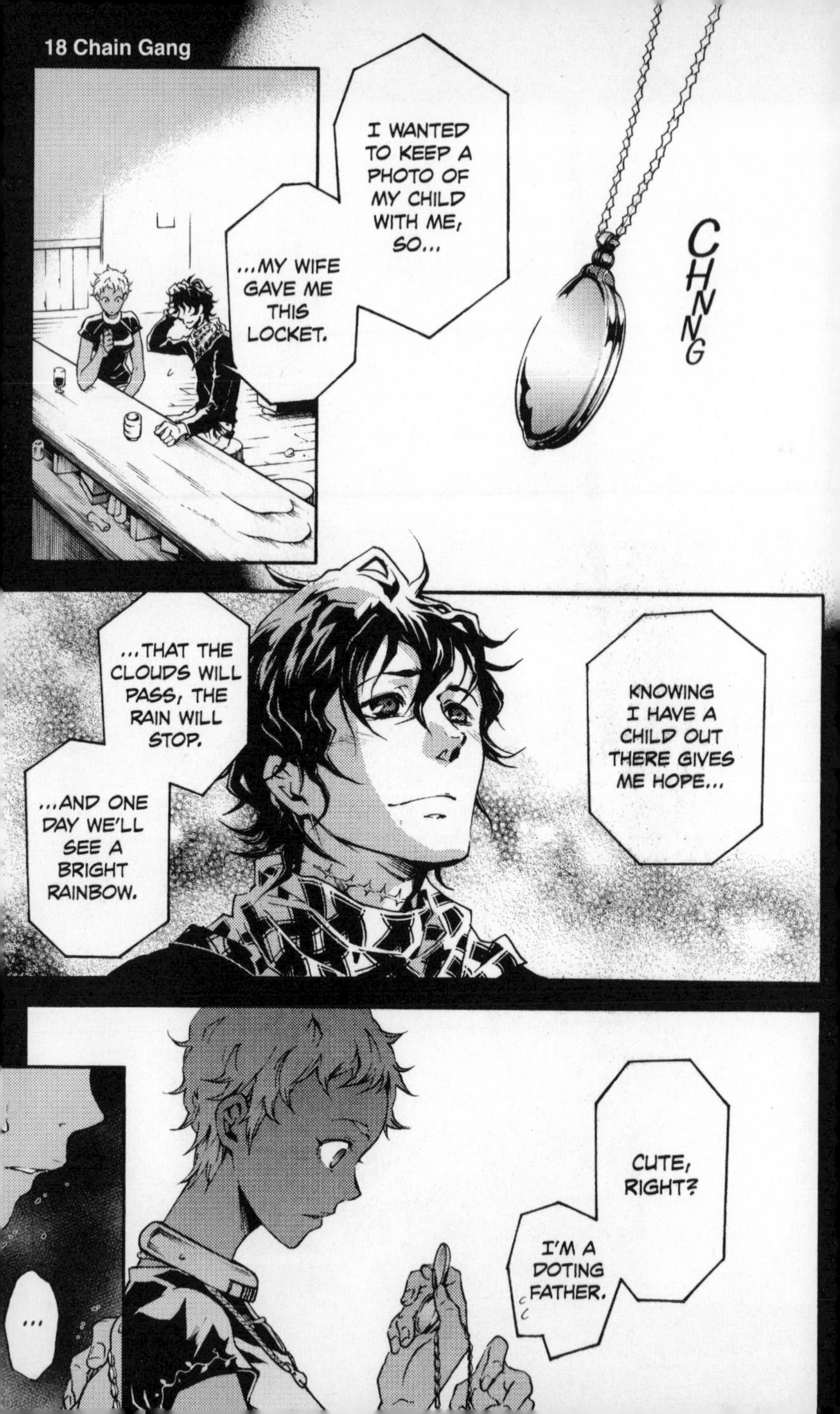
CHNNG
I WANTED TO KEEP A PHOTO OF MY CHILD WITH ME, SO...
...MY WIFE GAVE ME THIS LOCKET.
KNOWING I HAVE A CHILD OUT THERE GIVES ME HOPE...
...THAT THE CLOUDS WILL PASS, THE RAIN WILL STOP.
...AND ONE DAY WE'LL SEE A BRIGHT RAINBOW.
CUTE, RIGHT?
I'M A DOTING FATHER.
...

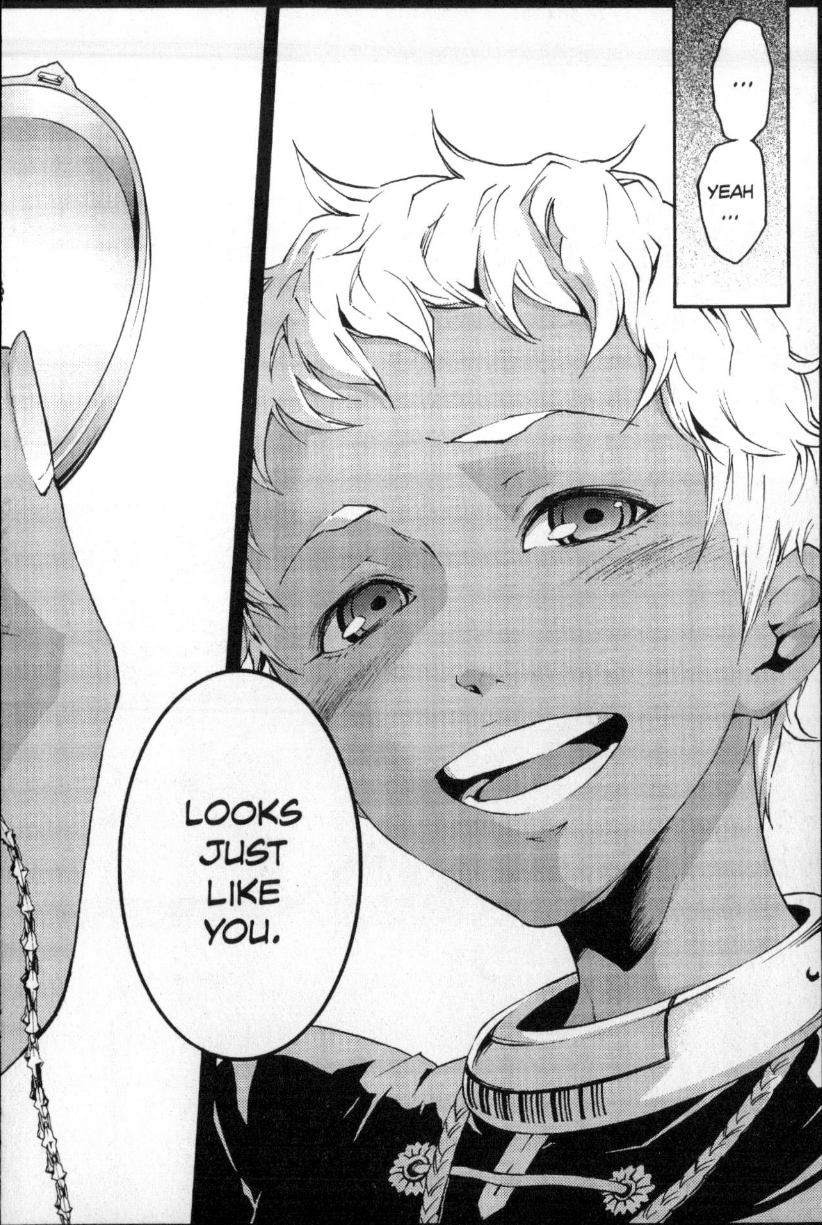
...
YEAH...
LOOKS JUST LIKE YOU.

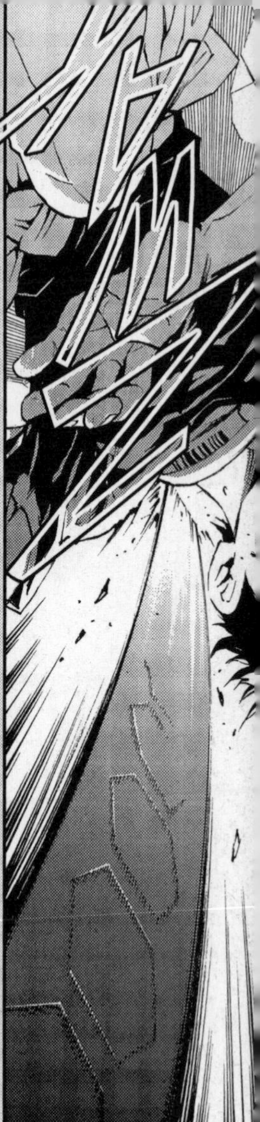
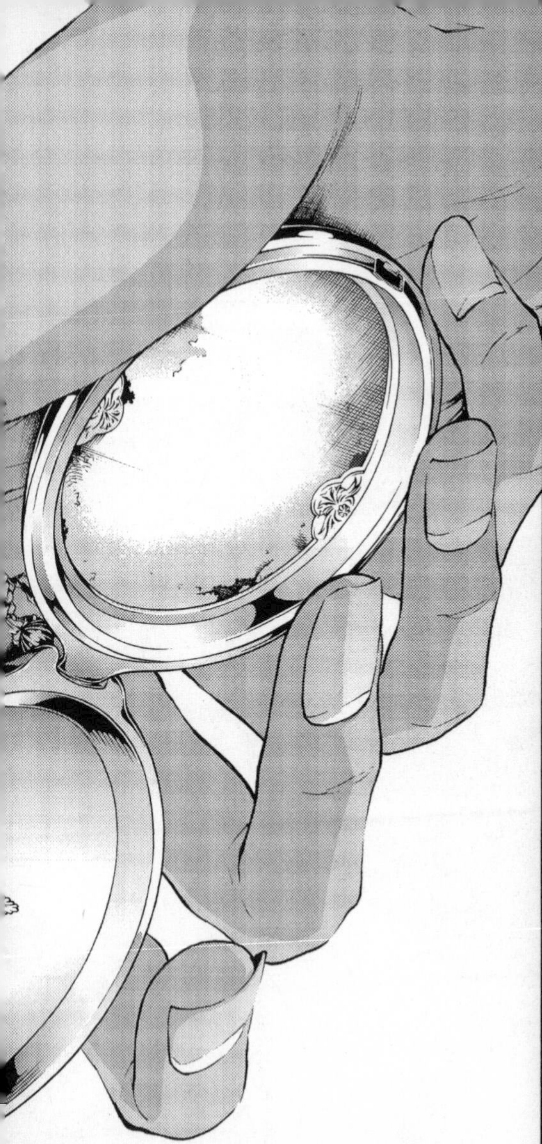

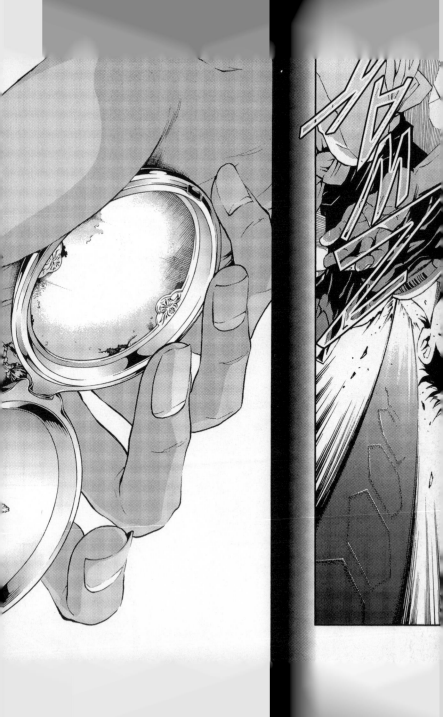

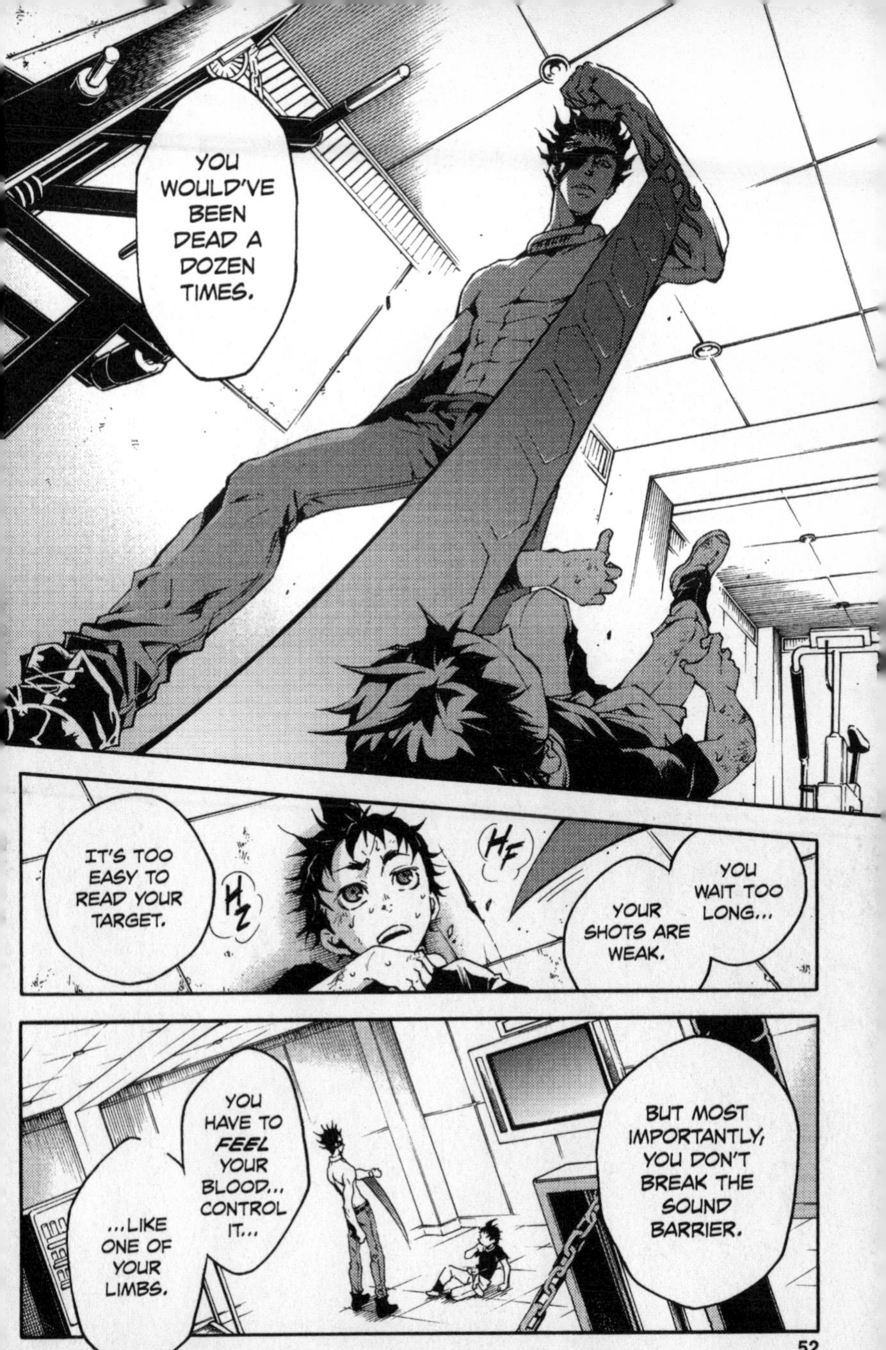
YOU WOULD'VE BEEN DEAD A DOZEN TIMES.
HF
YOU WAIT TOO LONG...
YOUR SHOTS ARE WEAK.
HZ
IT'S TOO EASY TO READ YOUR TARGET.
BUT MOST IMPORTANTLY, YOU DON'T BREAK THE SOUND BARRIER.
YOU HAVE TO *FEEL* YOUR BLOOD... CONTROL IT...
...LIKE ONE OF YOUR LIMBS.

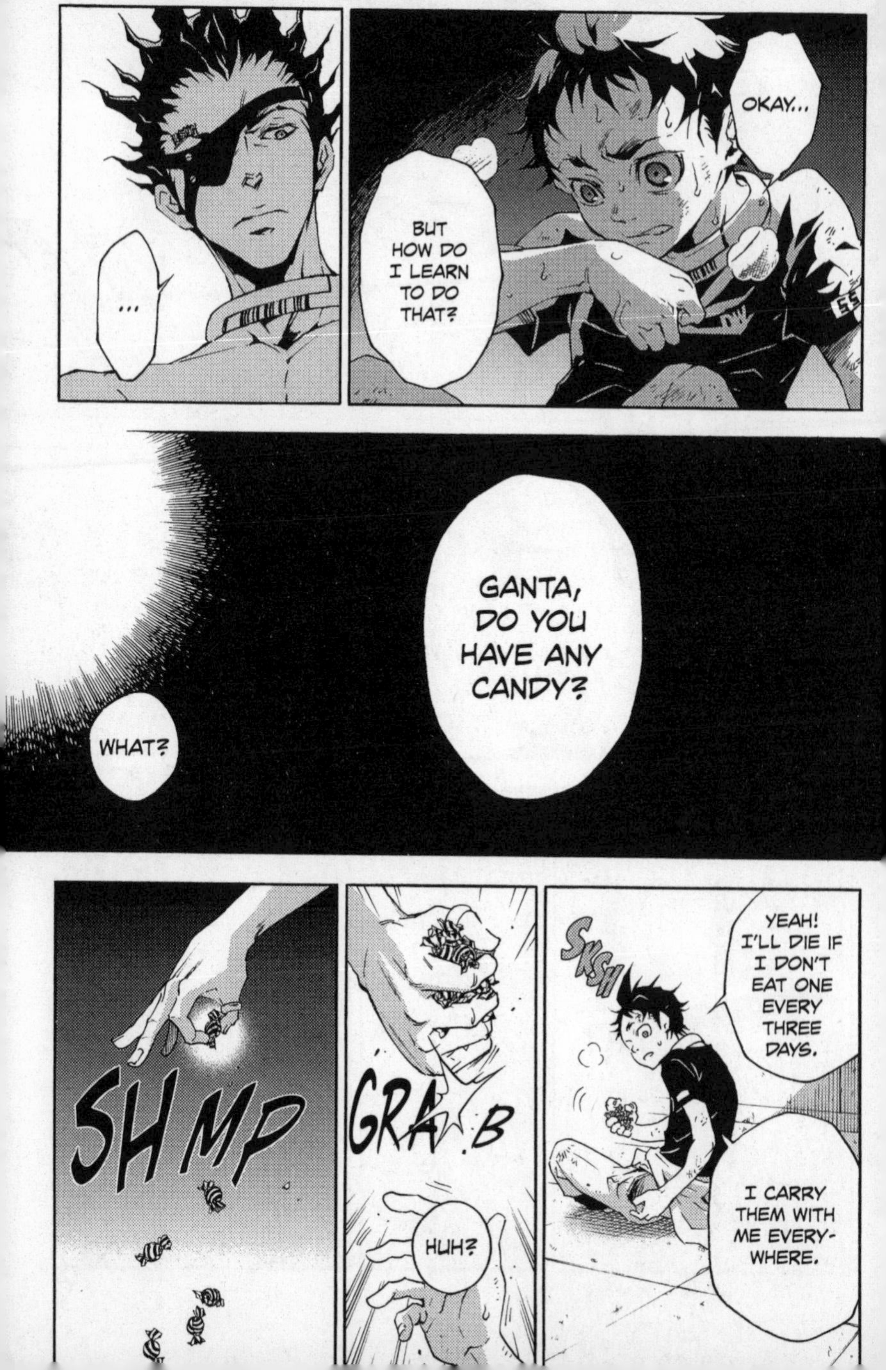
OKAY...
BUT HOW DO I LEARN TO DO THAT?
...
GANTA, DO YOU HAVE ANY CANDY?
WHAT?
YEAH! I'LL DIE IF I DON'T EAT ONE EVERY THREE DAYS.
SKSH
I CARRY THEM WITH ME EVERY-WHERE.
GRA.B
HUH?
SHMP

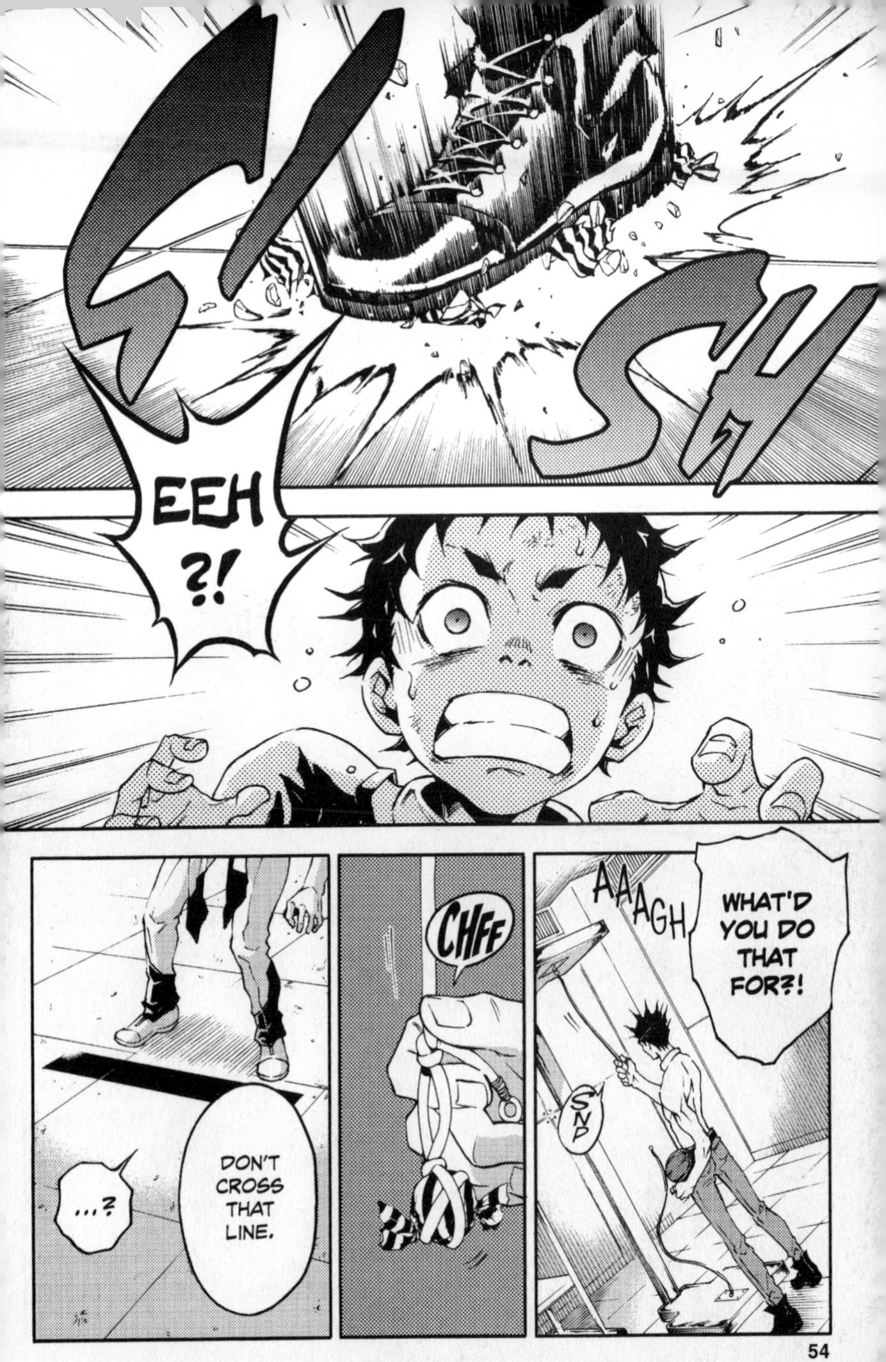
SMASH
EEH ?!
WHAT'D YOU DO THAT FOR?!
AAAAGH
SNP
CHFF
DON'T CROSS THAT LINE.
...?

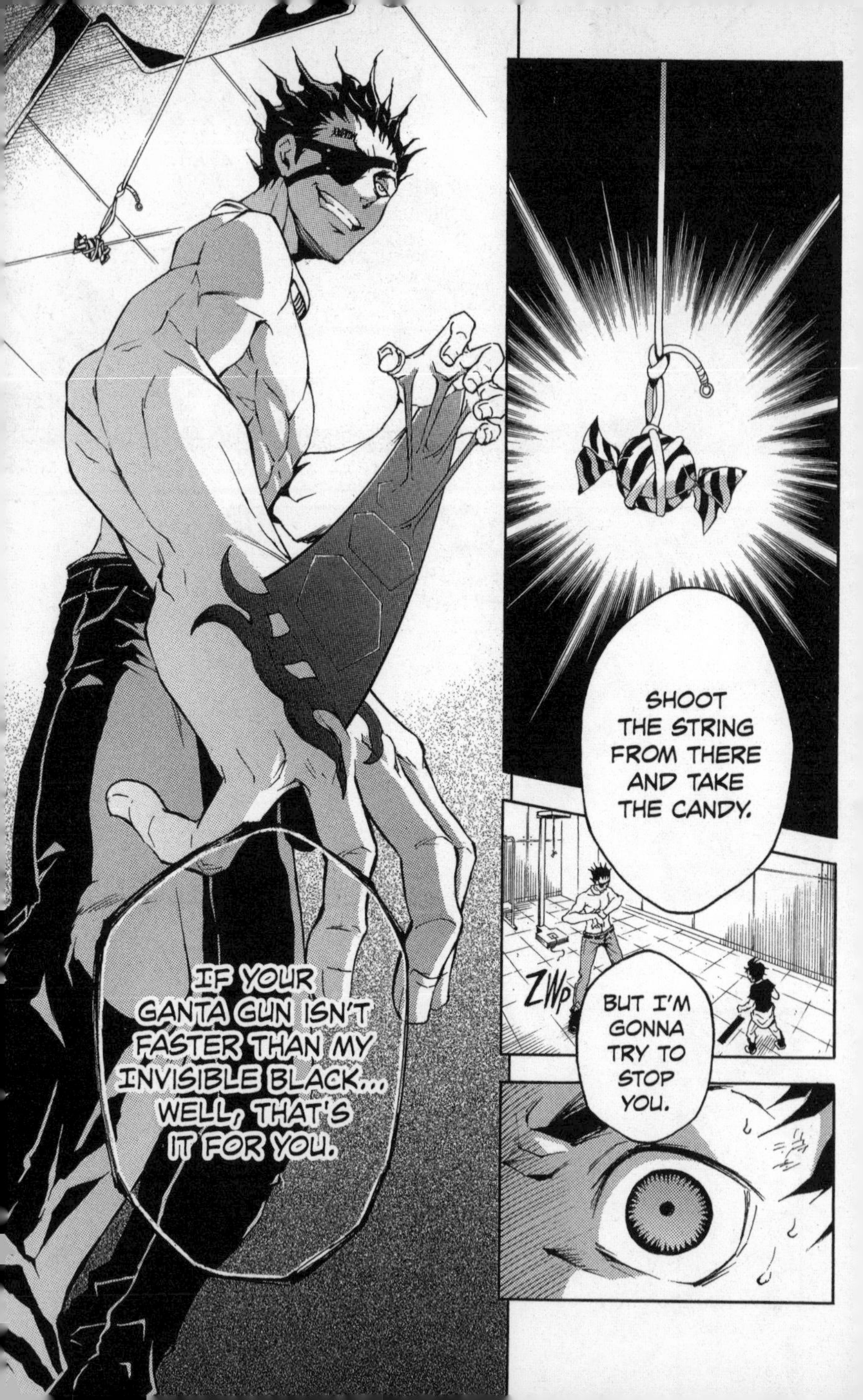
SHOOT THE STRING FROM THERE AND TAKE THE CANDY.
ZWP
BUT I'M GONNA TRY TO STOP YOU.
IF YOUR GANTA GUN ISN'T FASTER THAN MY INVISIBLE BLACK... WELL, THAT'S IT FOR YOU.

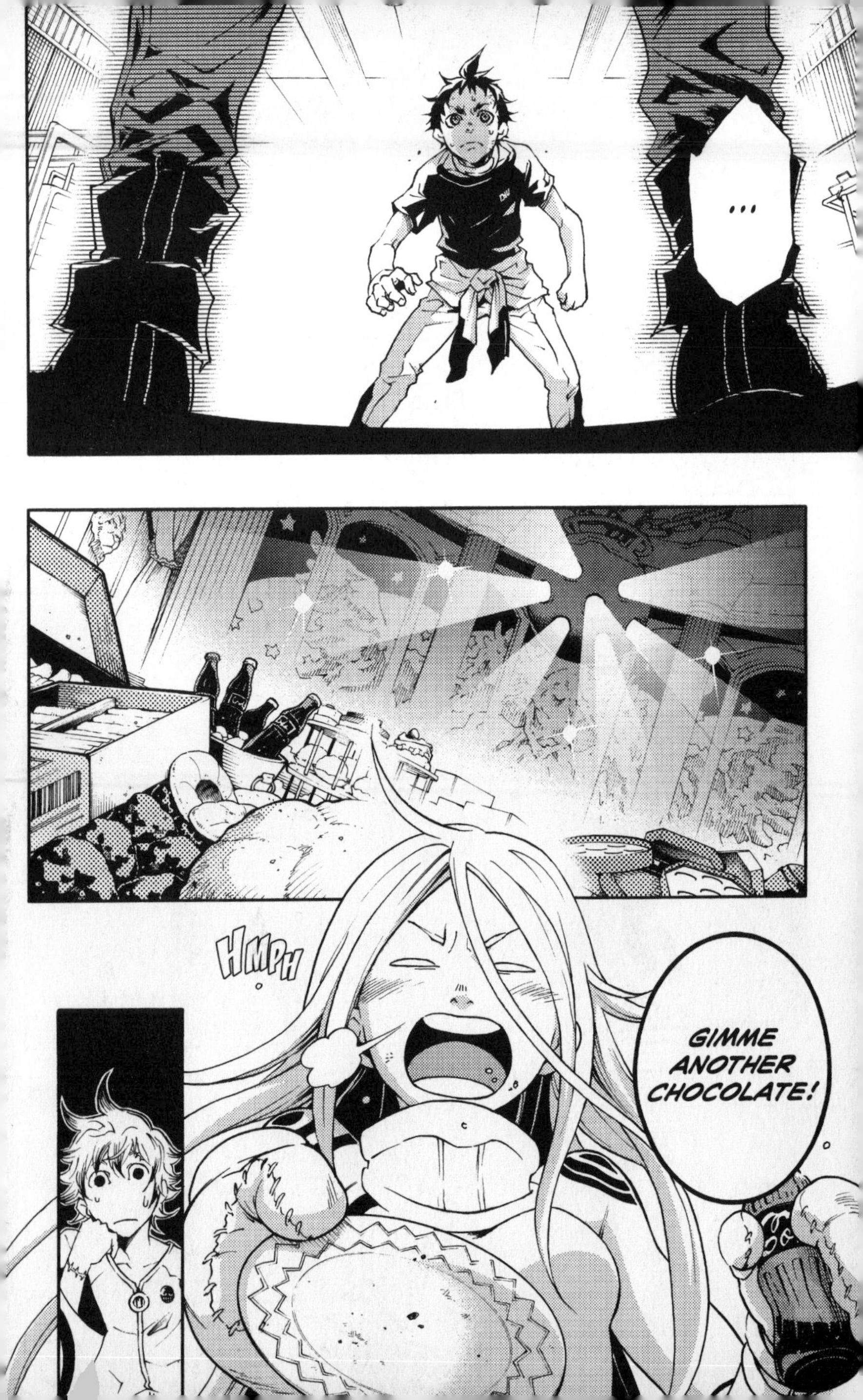
...
GIMME ANOTHER CHOCOLATE!
HMPH

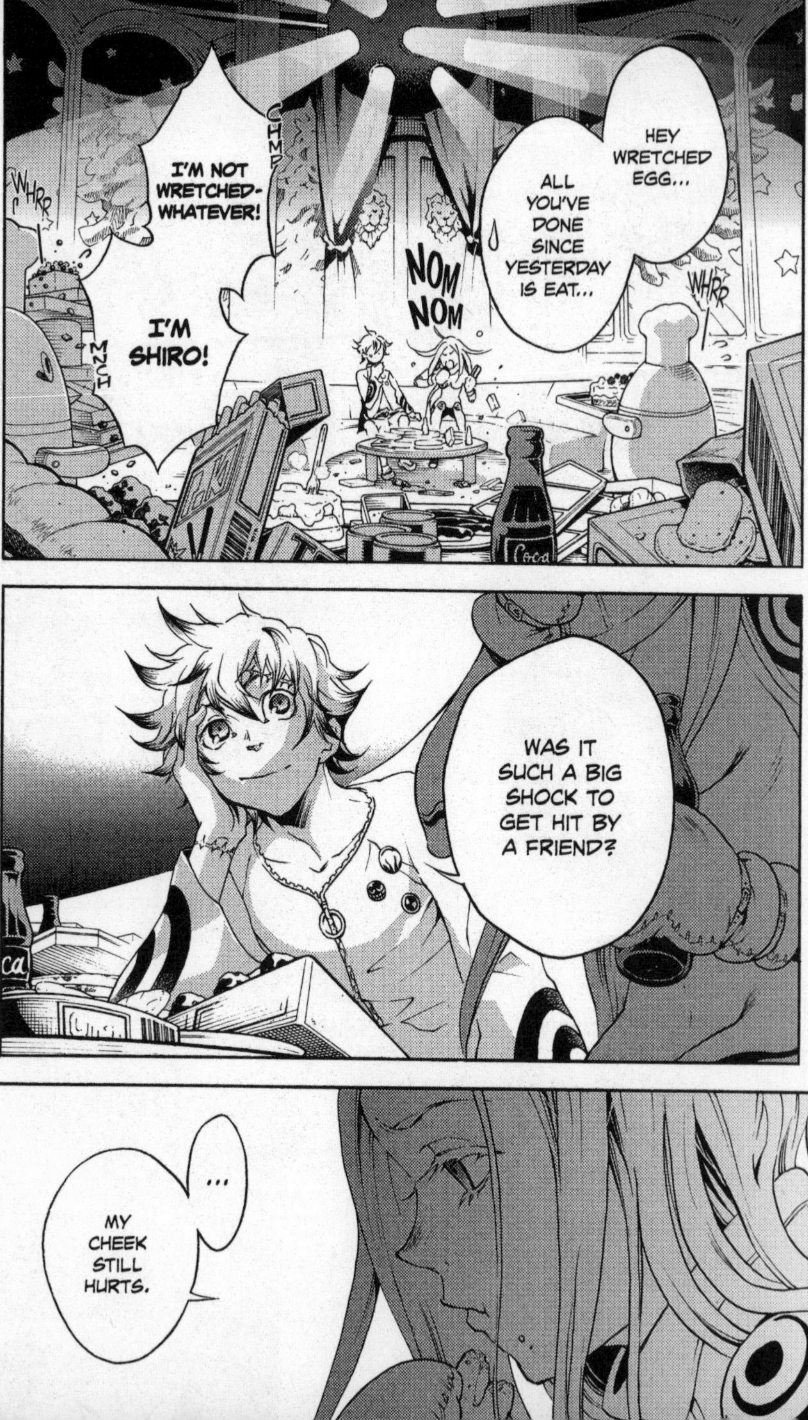
HEY WRETCHED EGG...
ALL YOU'VE DONE SINCE YESTERDAY IS EAT...
WHRR
NOM NOM
CHMP
I'M NOT WRETCHED-WHATEVER!
I'M SHIRO!
MNCH
WHRR
WAS IT SUCH A BIG SHOCK TO GET HIT BY A FRIEND?
...
MY CHEEK STILL HURTS.

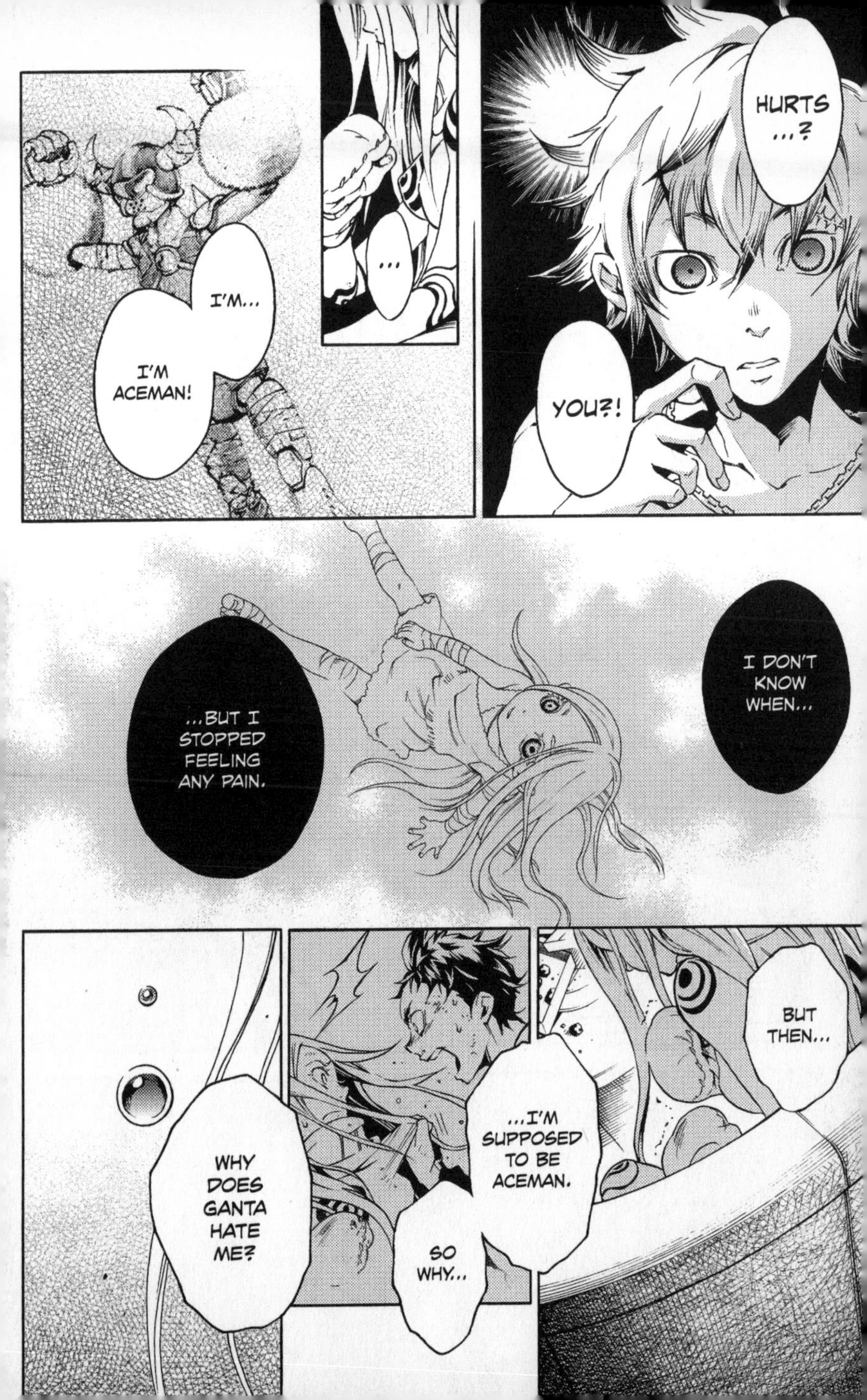
HURTS ...?
YOU?!
...
I'M...
I'M ACEMAN!
I DON'T KNOW WHEN...
...BUT I STOPPED FEELING ANY PAIN.
BUT THEN...
...I'M SUPPOSED TO BE ACEMAN.
SO WHY...
WHY DOES GANTA HATE ME?

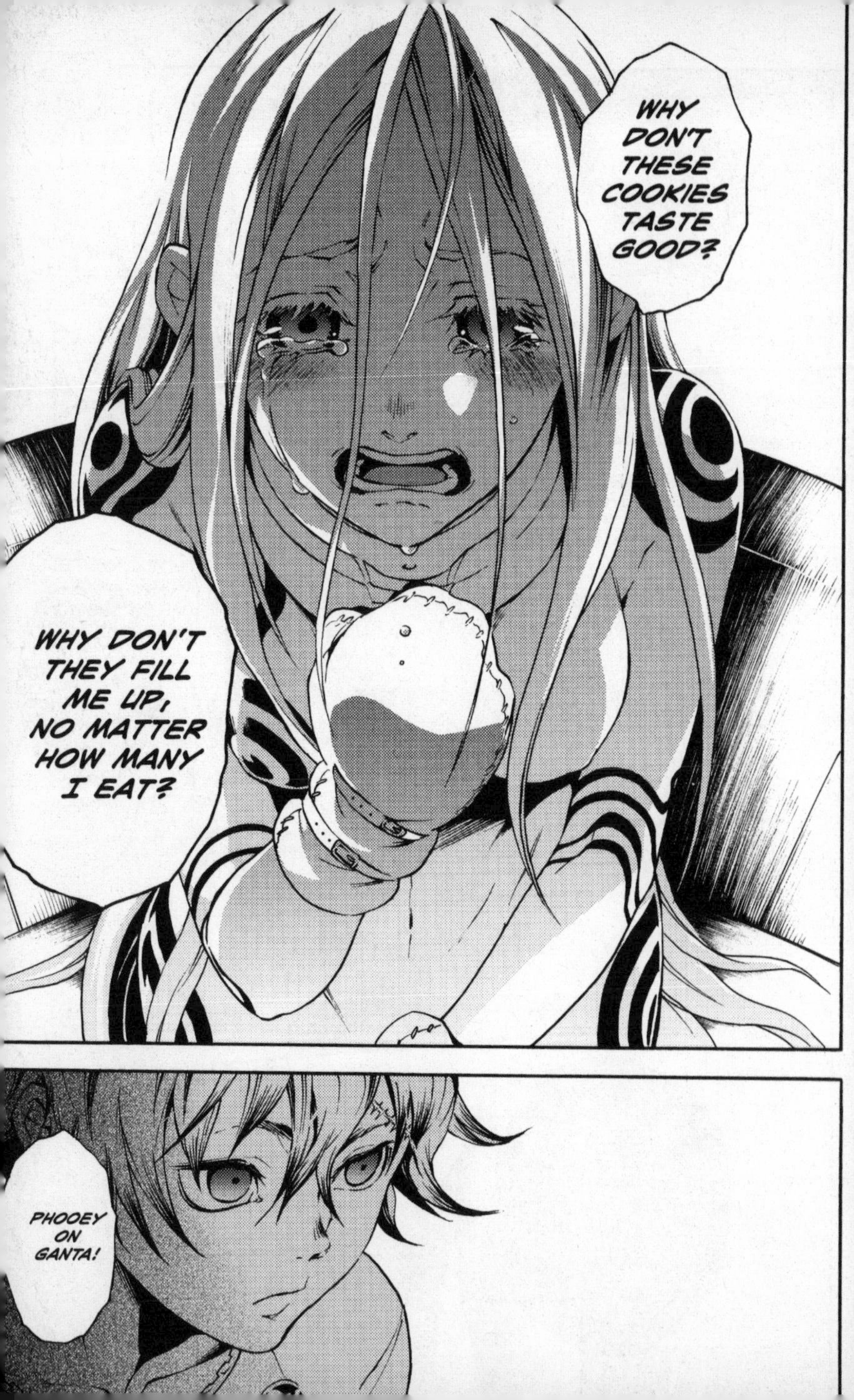
WHY DON'T THESE COOKIES TASTE GOOD?
WHY DON'T THEY FILL ME UP, NO MATTER HOW MANY I EAT?
PHOOEY ON GANTA!

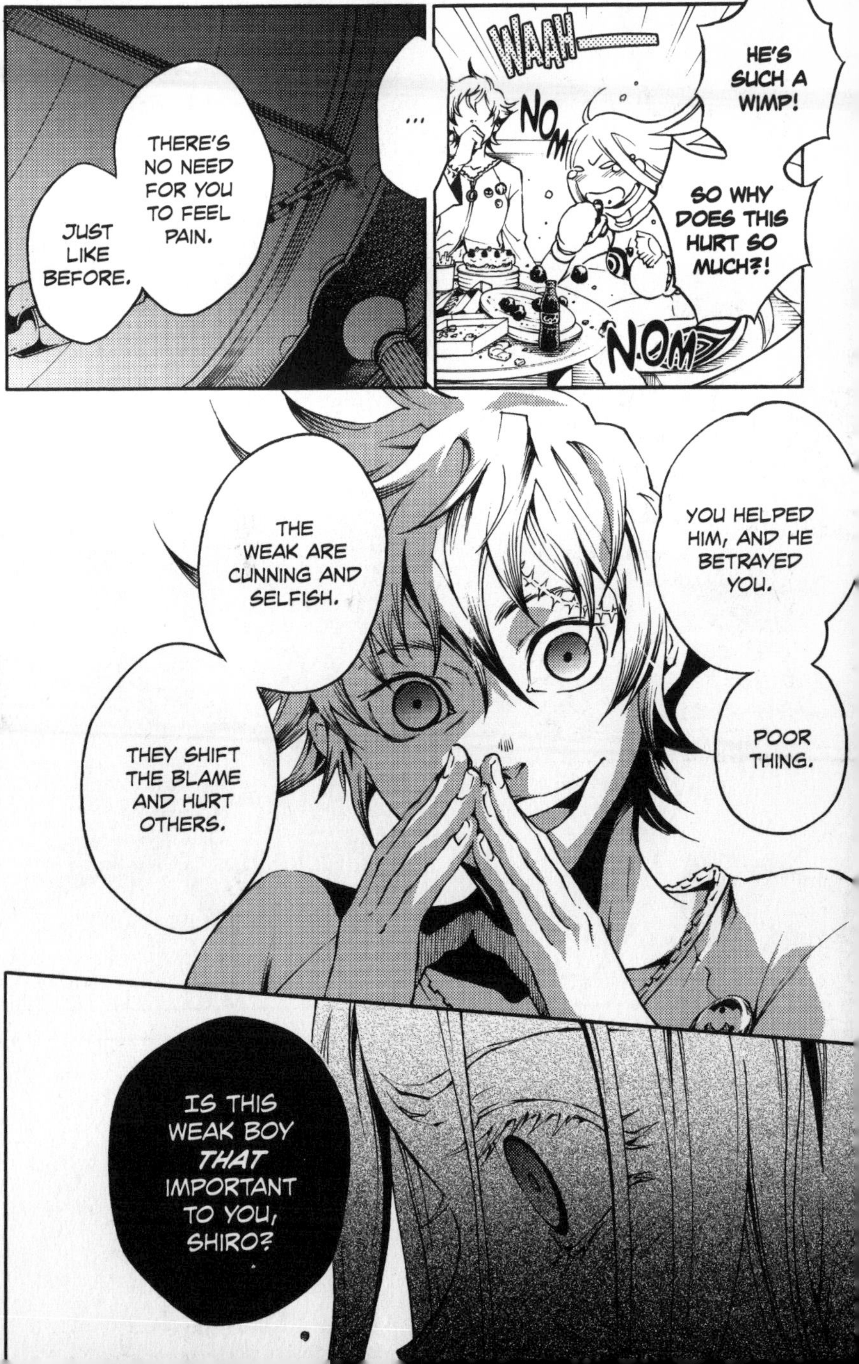
HE'S SUCH A WIMP!
WAAH—
NOM
SO WHY DOES THIS HURT SO MUCH?!
N.O.M
...
THERE'S NO NEED FOR YOU TO FEEL PAIN.
JUST LIKE BEFORE.
YOU HELPED HIM, AND HE BETRAYED YOU.
POOR THING.
THE WEAK ARE CUNNING AND SELFISH.
THEY SHIFT THE BLAME AND HURT OTHERS.
IS THIS WEAK BOY *THAT* IMPORTANT TO YOU, SHIRO?

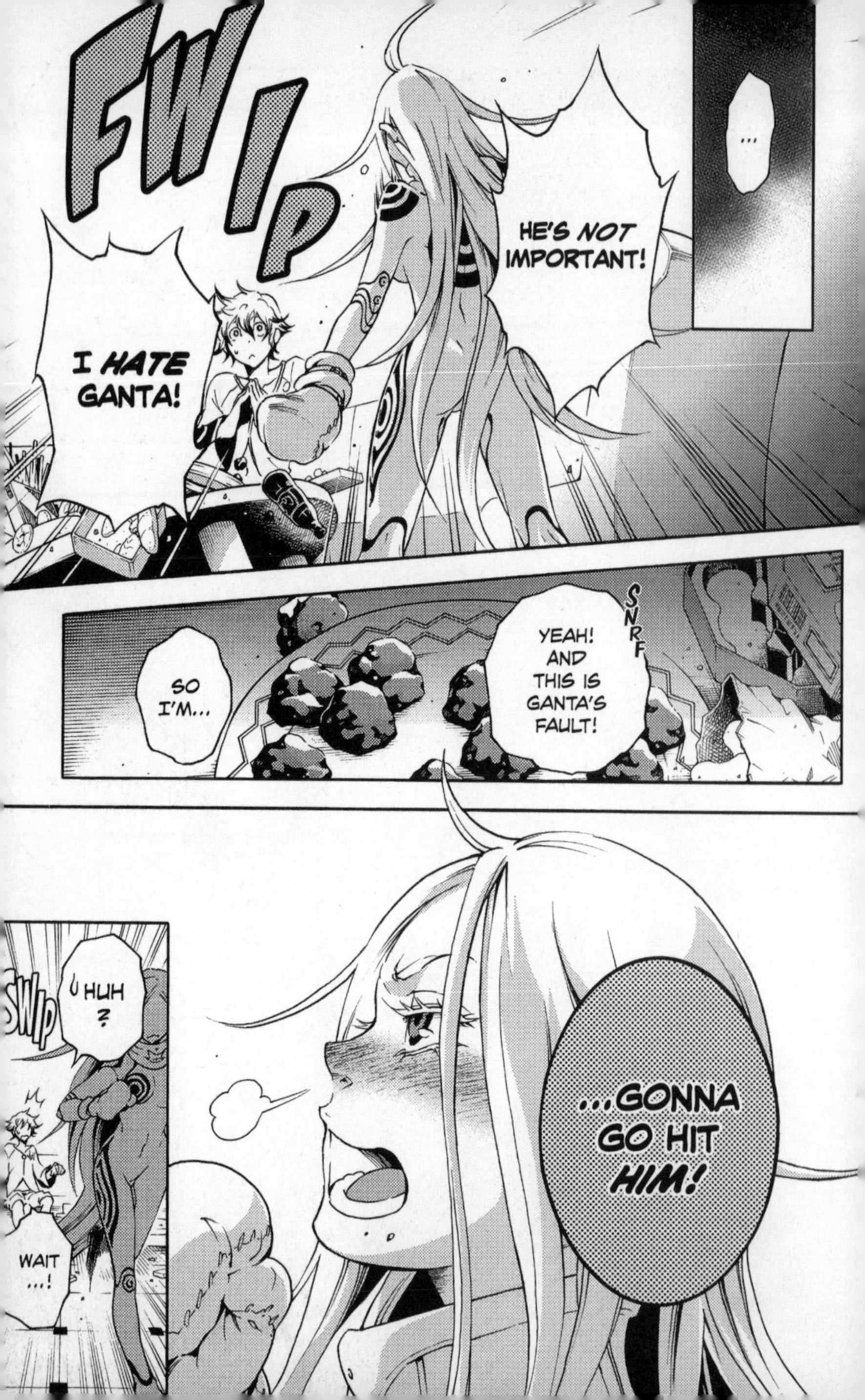
...
HE'S NOT IMPORTANT!
FWIP
I HATE GANTA!
SNRF
YEAH! AND THIS IS GANTA'S FAULT!
SO I'M...
...GONNA GO HIT HIM!
HUH?
SWIP
WAIT...!

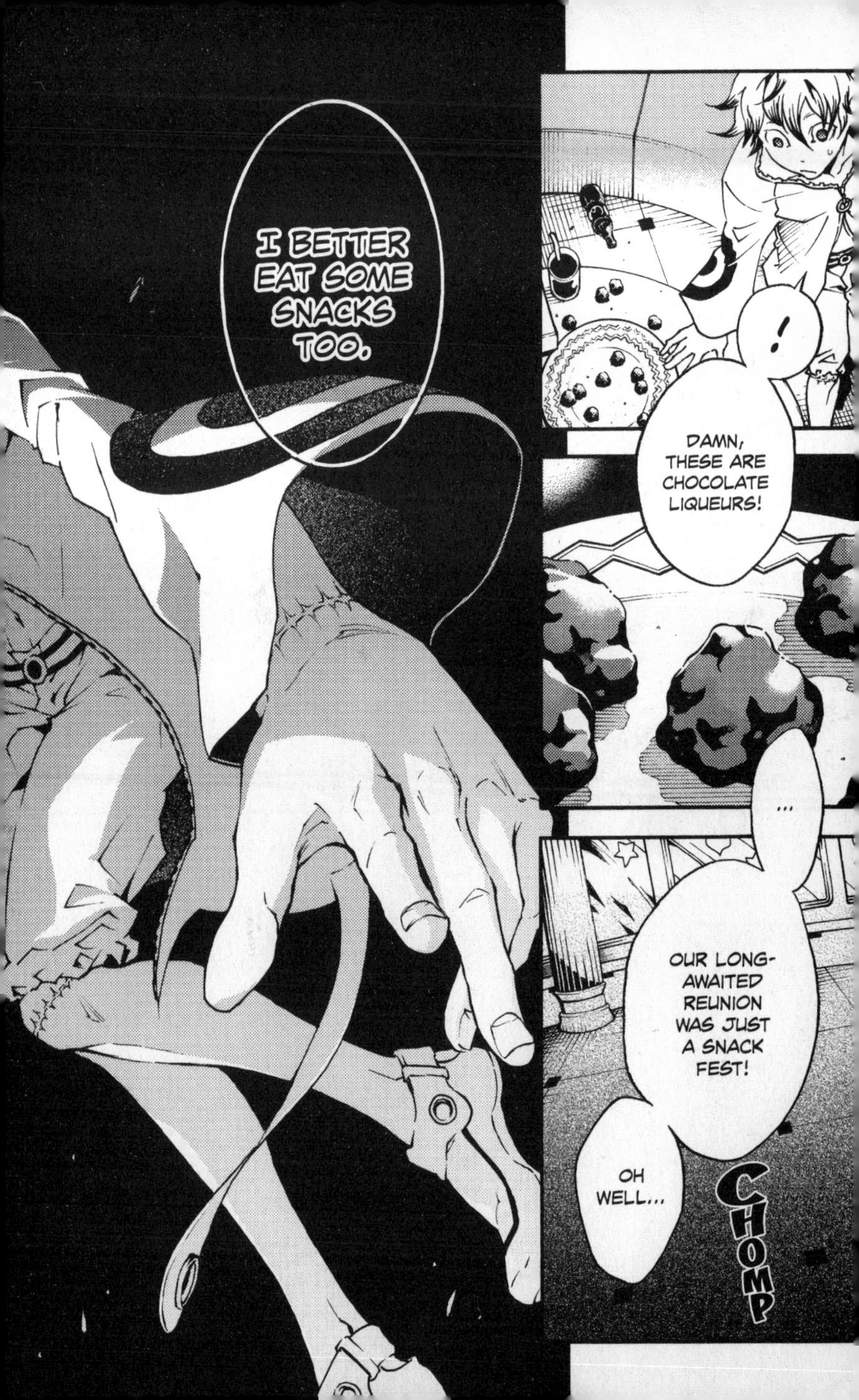
!
DAMN, THESE ARE CHOCOLATE LIQUEURS!
...
OUR LONG-AWAITED REUNION WAS JUST A SNACK FEST!
OH WELL...
CHOMP
I BETTER EAT SOME SNACKS TOO.

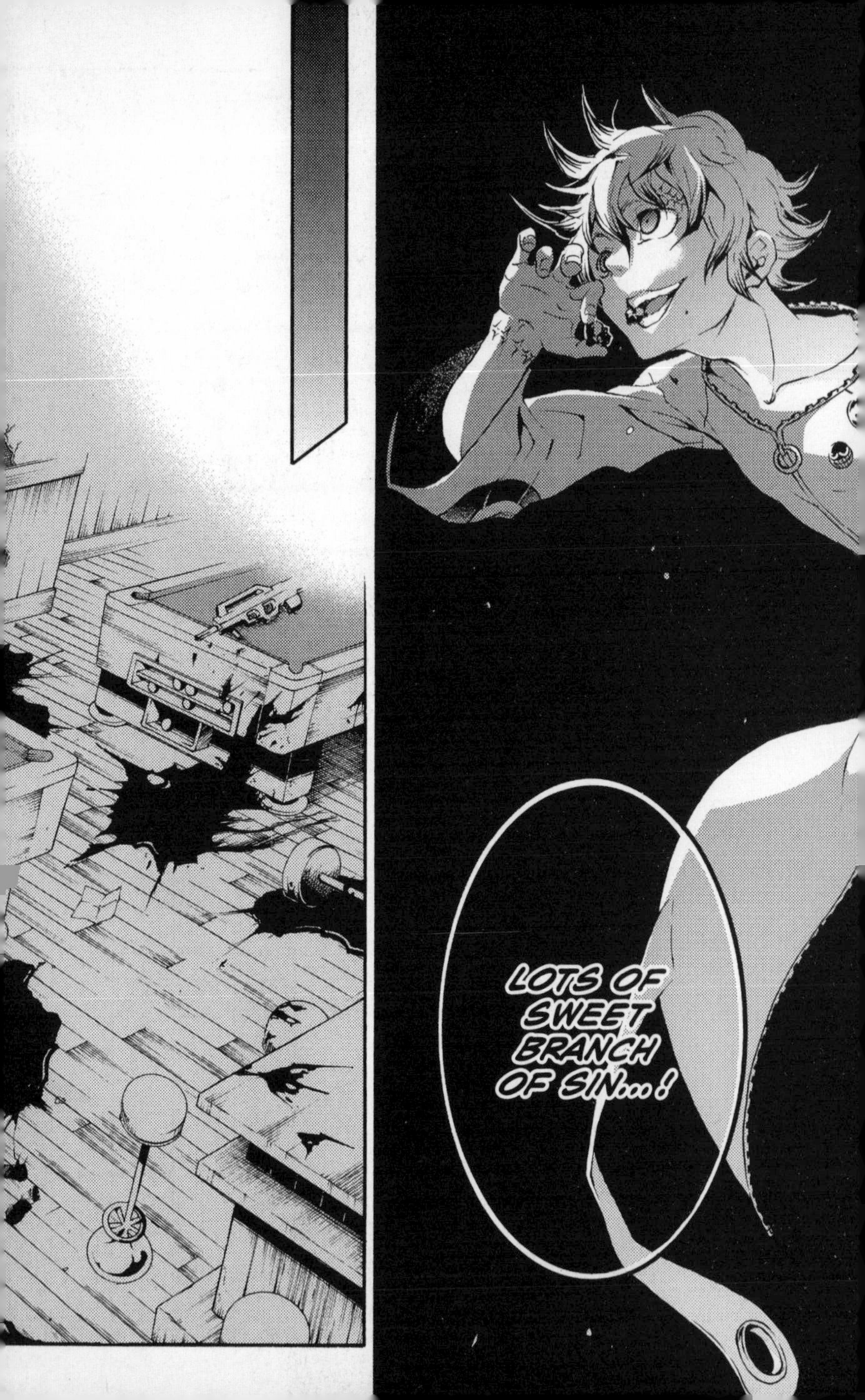
LOTS OF SWEET BRANCH OF SIN...!

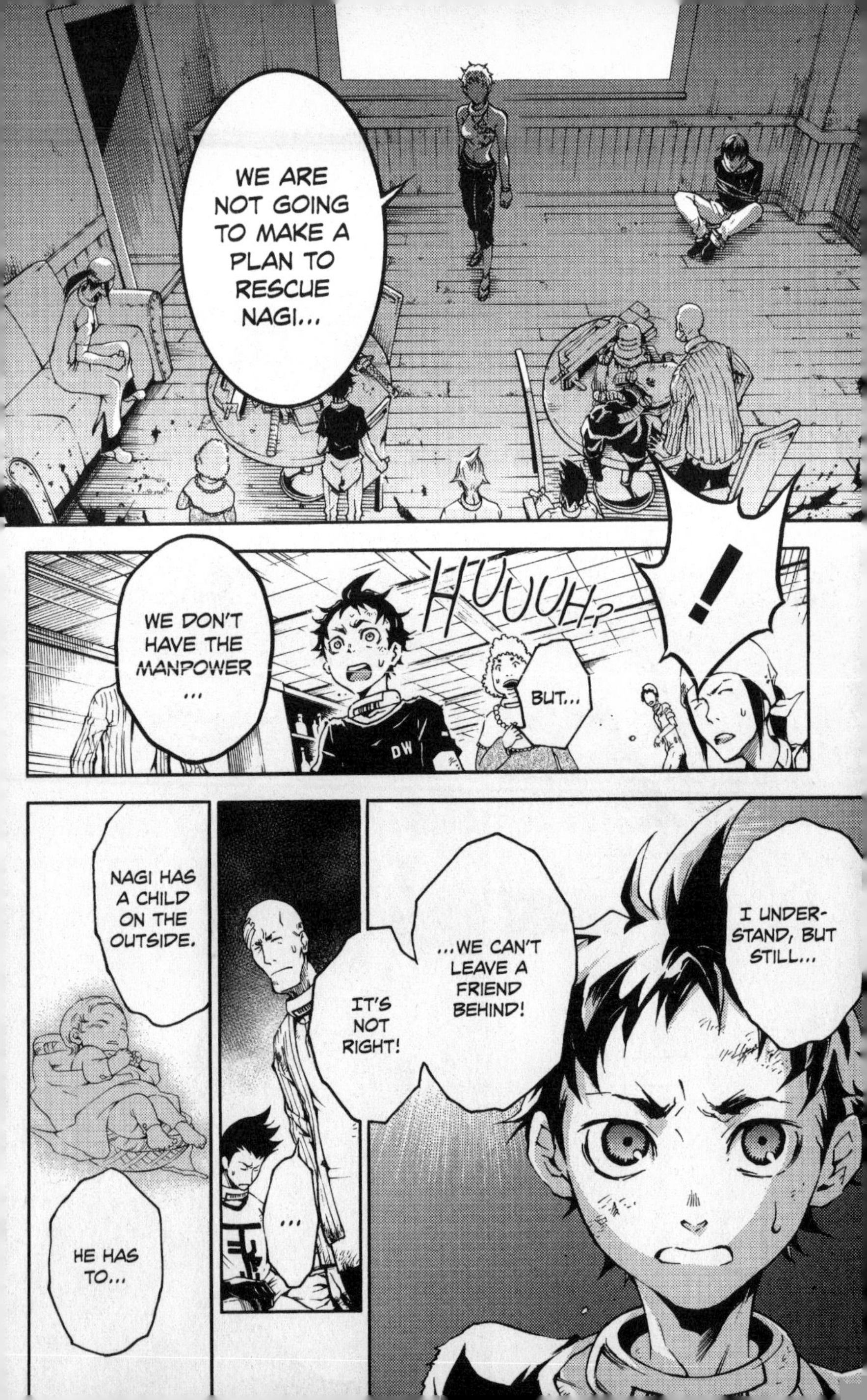
WE ARE NOT GOING TO MAKE A PLAN TO RESCUE NAGI...
!
HUUUH?
BUT...
WE DON'T HAVE THE MANPOWER ...
I UNDER-STAND, BUT STILL...
...WE CAN'T LEAVE A FRIEND BEHIND!
IT'S NOT RIGHT!
...
NAGI HAS A CHILD ON THE OUTSIDE.
HE HAS TO...

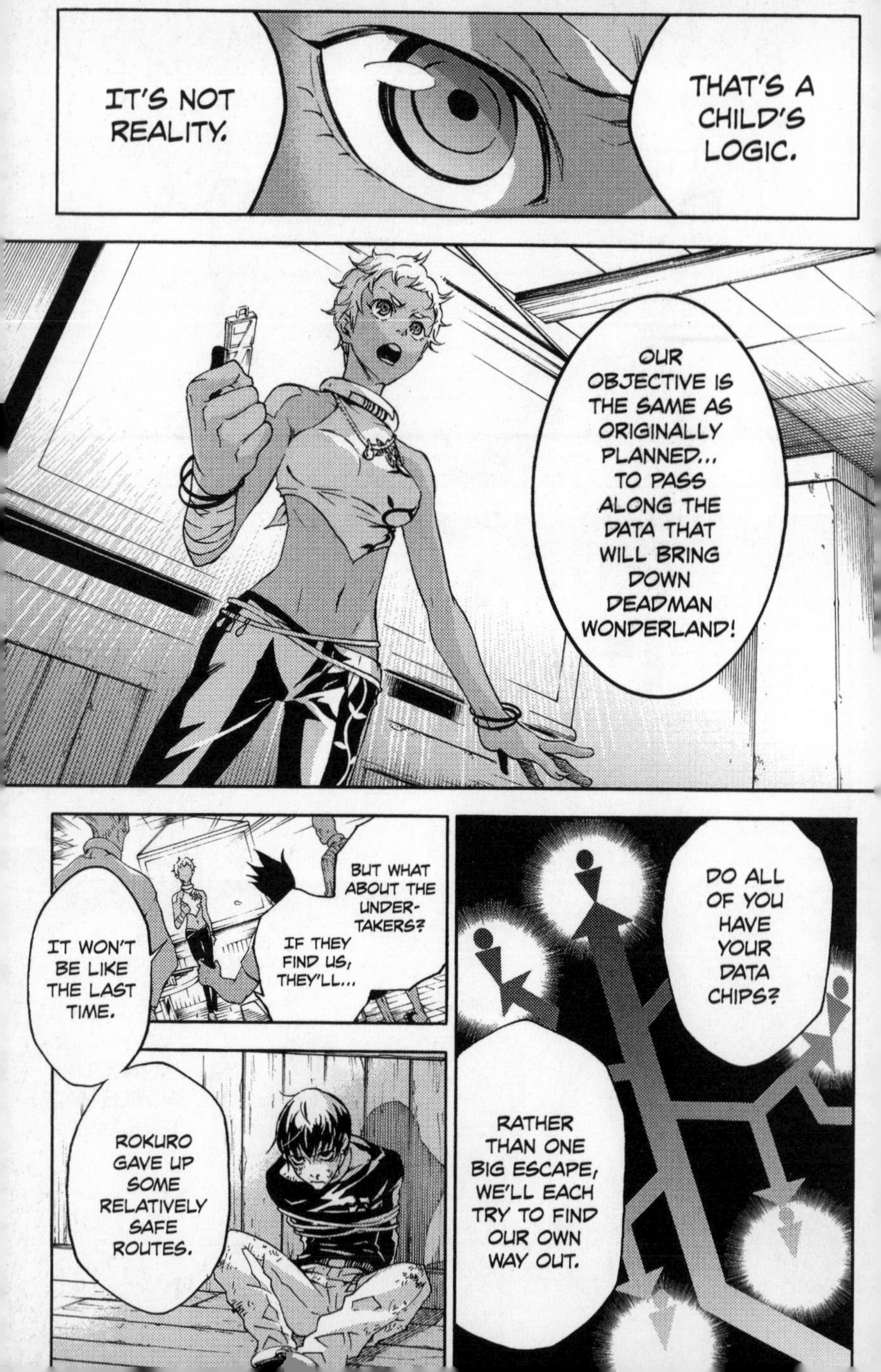
THAT'S A CHILD'S LOGIC.
IT'S NOT REALITY.
OUR OBJECTIVE IS THE SAME AS ORIGINALLY PLANNED... TO PASS ALONG THE DATA THAT WILL BRING DOWN DEADMAN WONDERLAND!
DO ALL OF YOU HAVE YOUR DATA CHIPS?
RATHER THAN ONE BIG ESCAPE, WE'LL EACH TRY TO FIND OUR OWN WAY OUT.
BUT WHAT ABOUT THE UNDER-TAKERS?
IF THEY FIND US, THEY'LL...
IT WON'T BE LIKE THE LAST TIME.
ROKURO GAVE UP SOME RELATIVELY SAFE ROUTES.

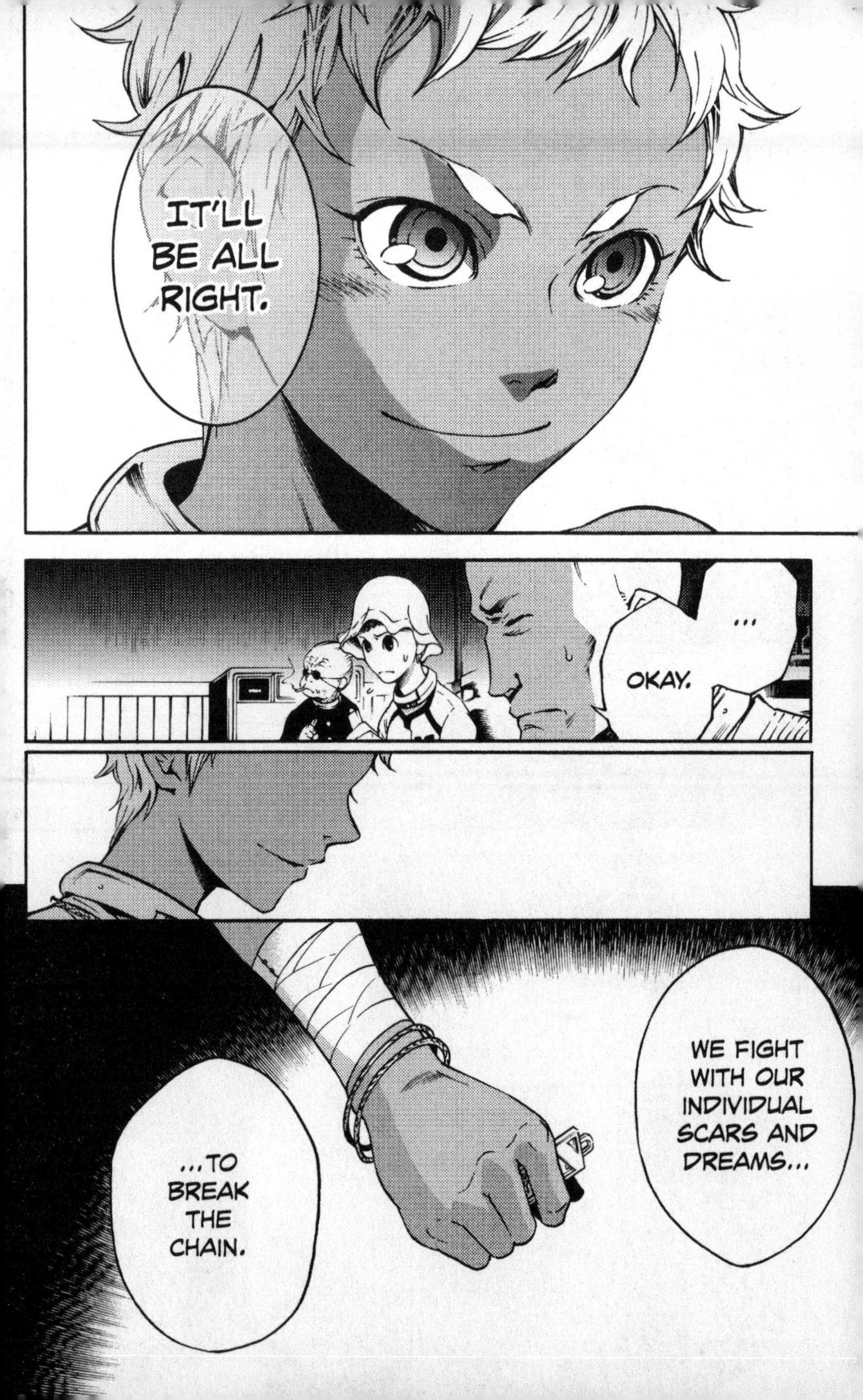
IT'LL BE ALL RIGHT.
...
OKAY.
WE FIGHT WITH OUR INDIVIDUAL SCARS AND DREAMS...
...TO BREAK THE CHAIN.

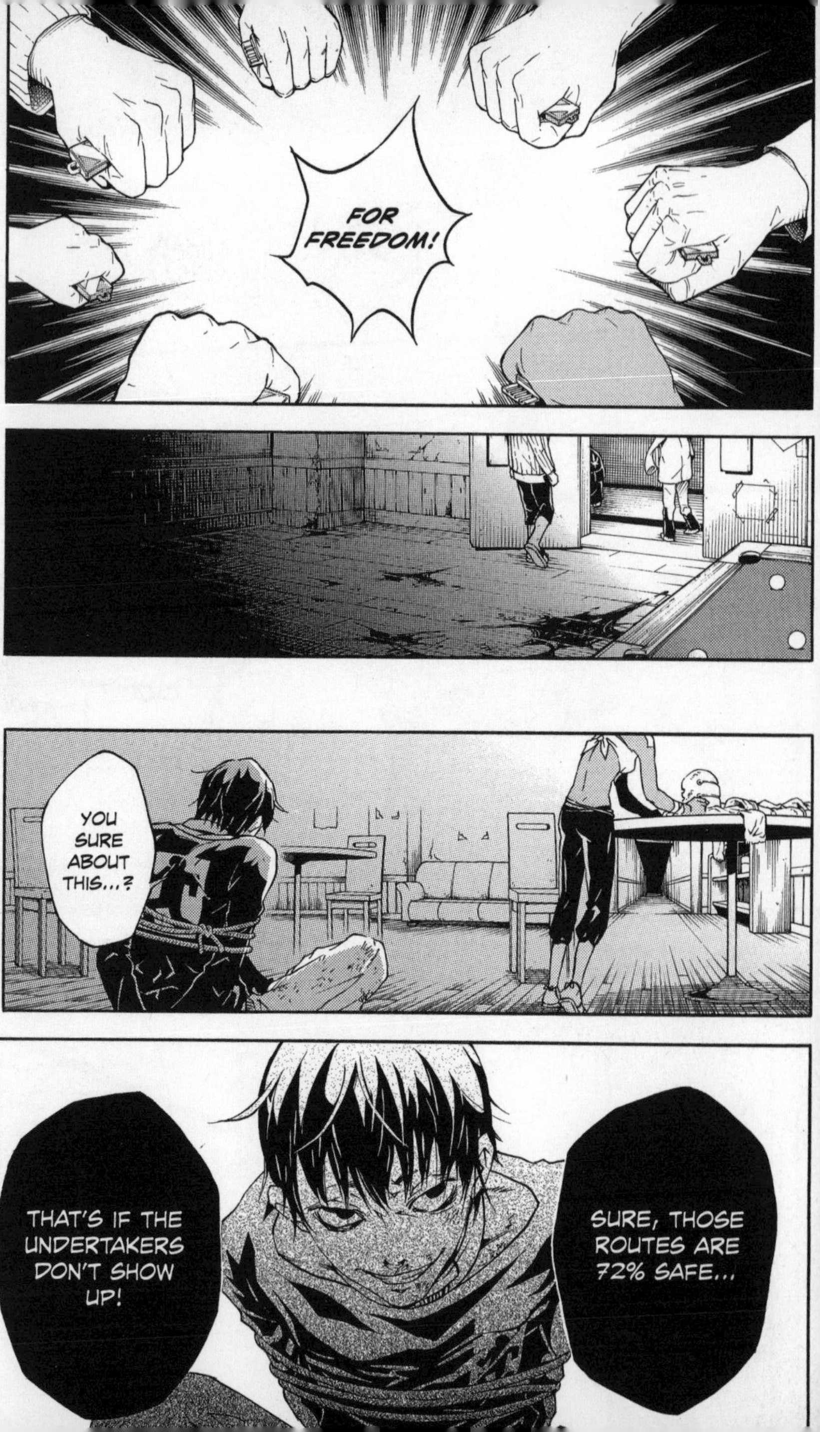
FOR FREEDOM!
YOU SURE ABOUT THIS...?
SURE, THOSE ROUTES ARE 72% SAFE...
THAT'S IF THE UNDERTAKERS DON'T SHOW UP!

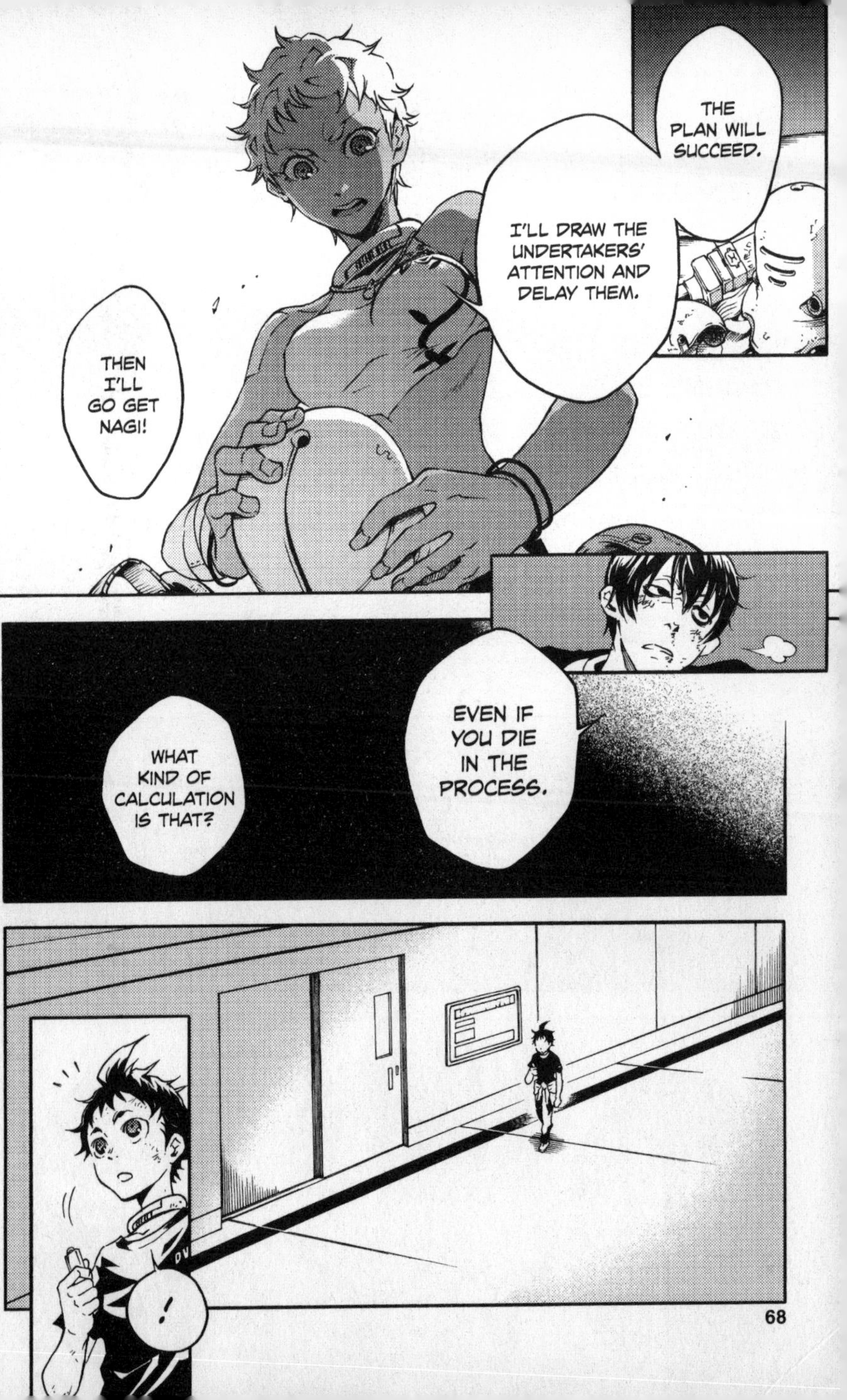
THE PLAN WILL SUCCEED.
I'LL DRAW THE UNDERTAKERS' ATTENTION AND DELAY THEM.
THEN I'LL GO GET NAGI!
EVEN IF YOU DIE IN THE PROCESS.
WHAT KIND OF CALCULATION IS THAT?
!

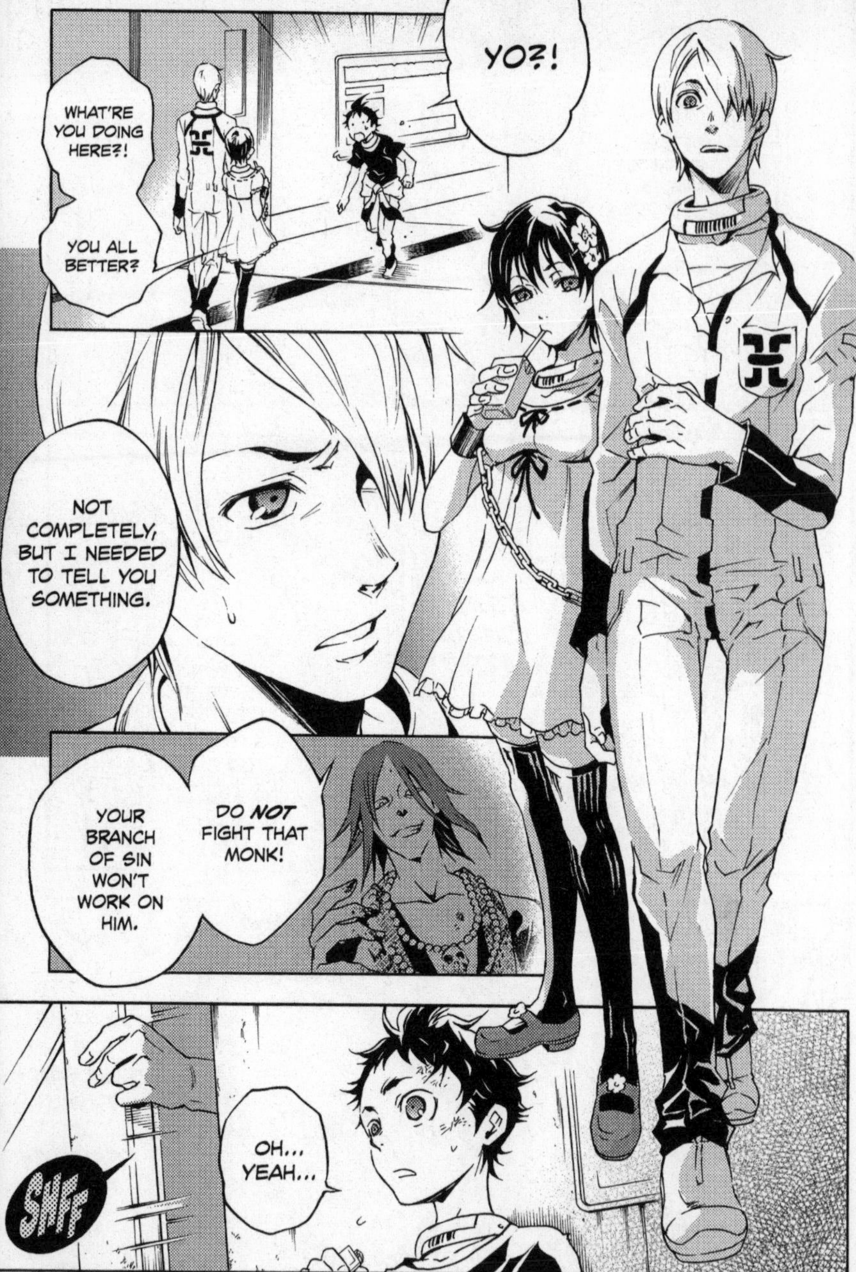
YO?!
WHAT'RE YOU DOING HERE?!
YOU ALL BETTER?
NOT COMPLETELY, BUT I NEEDED TO TELL YOU SOMETHING.
DO *NOT* FIGHT THAT MONK!
YOUR BRANCH OF SIN WON'T WORK ON HIM.
OH... YEAH...
SHFF

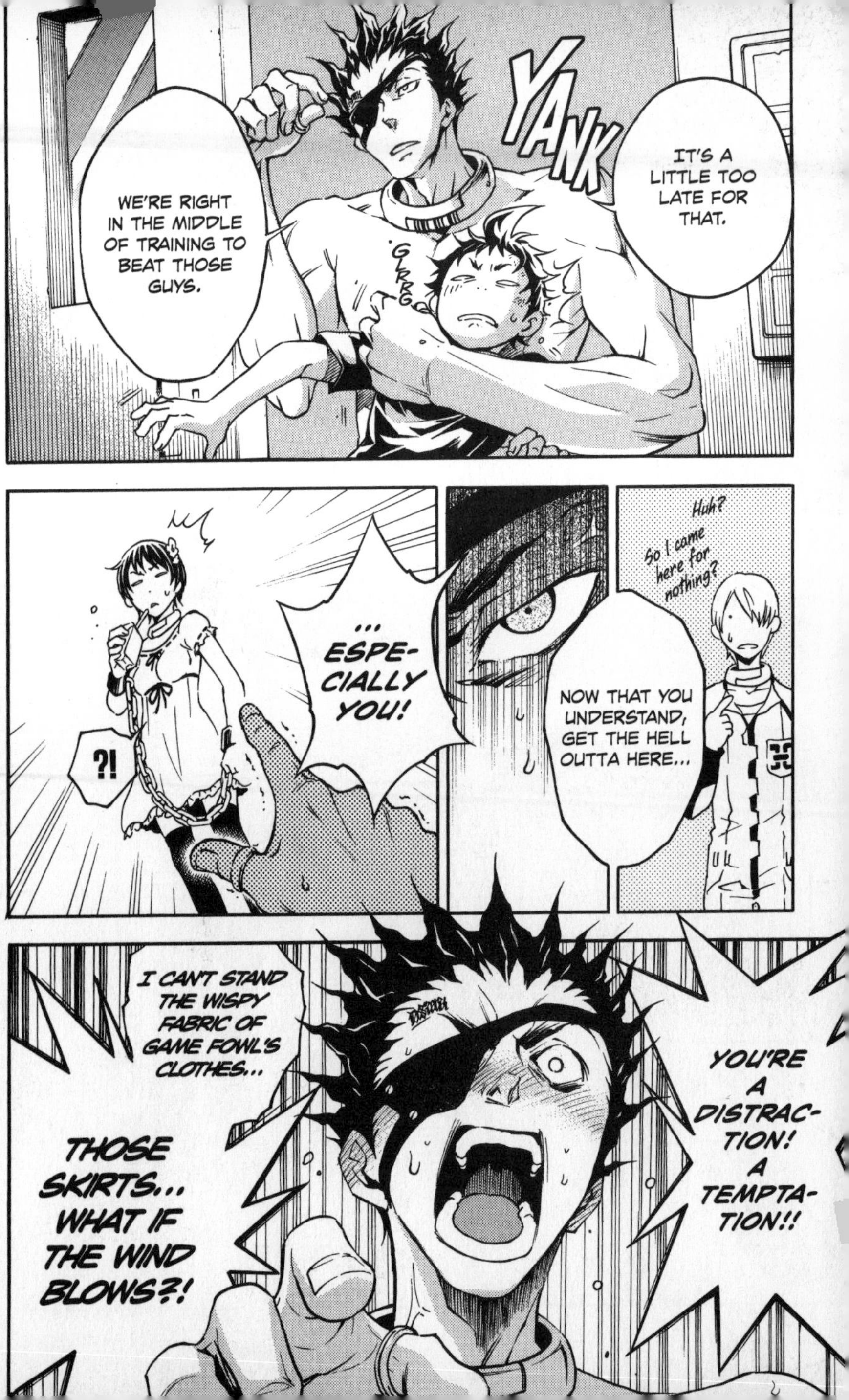
IT'S A LITTLE TOO LATE FOR THAT.
YANK
WE'RE RIGHT IN THE MIDDLE OF TRAINING TO BEAT THOSE GUYS.
GLRRG
Huh? So I came here for nothing?
NOW THAT YOU UNDERSTAND, GET THE HELL OUTTA HERE...
... ESPE-CIALLY YOU!
?!
YOU'RE A DISTRAC-TION! A TEMPTA-TION!!
I CAN'T STAND THE WISPY FABRIC OF GAME FOWL'S CLOTHES...
THOSE SKIRTS... WHAT IF THE WIND BLOWS?!

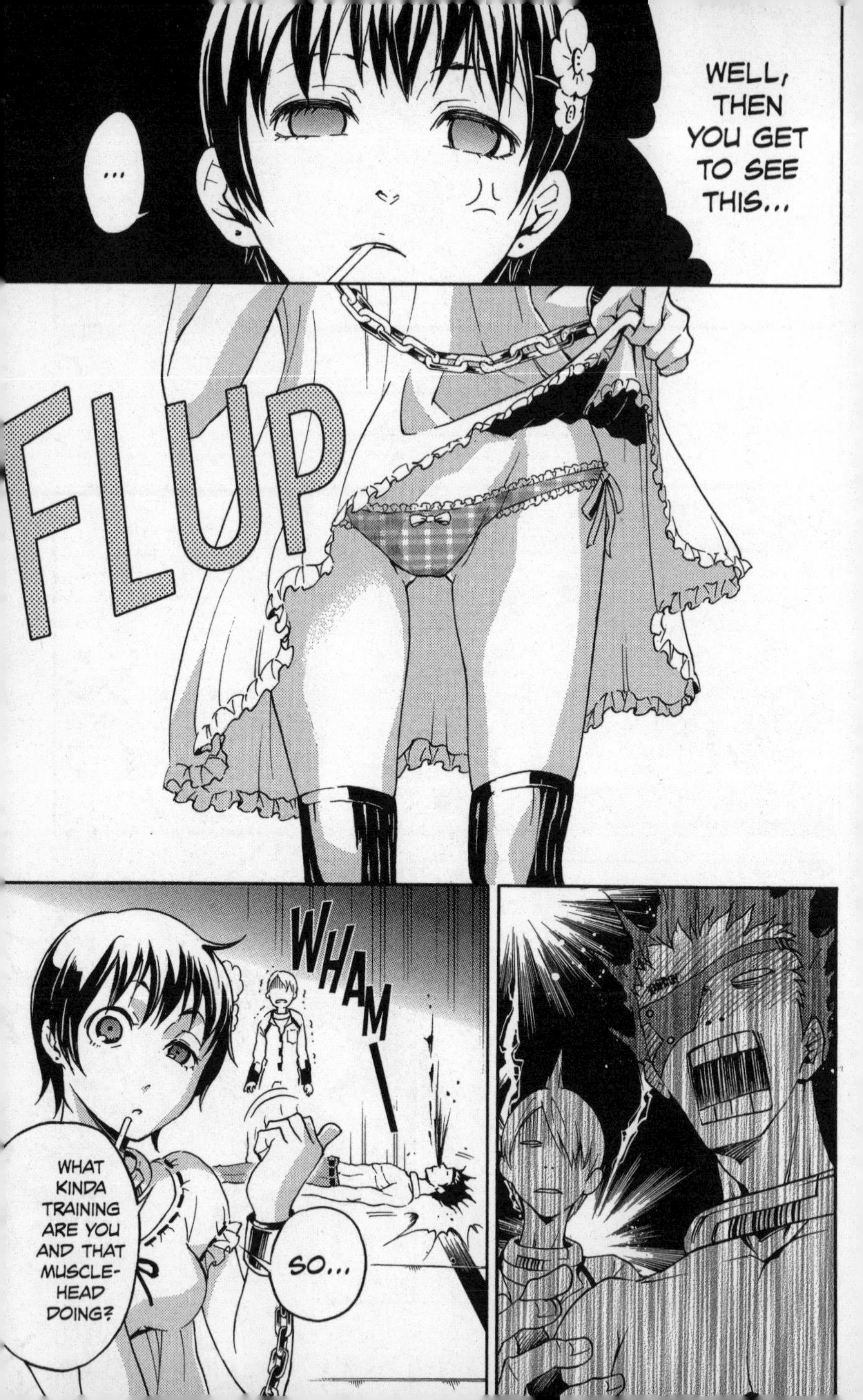
WELL, THEN YOU GET TO SEE THIS...
...
FLUP
WHAM
SO...
WHAT KINDA TRAINING ARE YOU AND THAT MUSCLE-HEAD DOING?

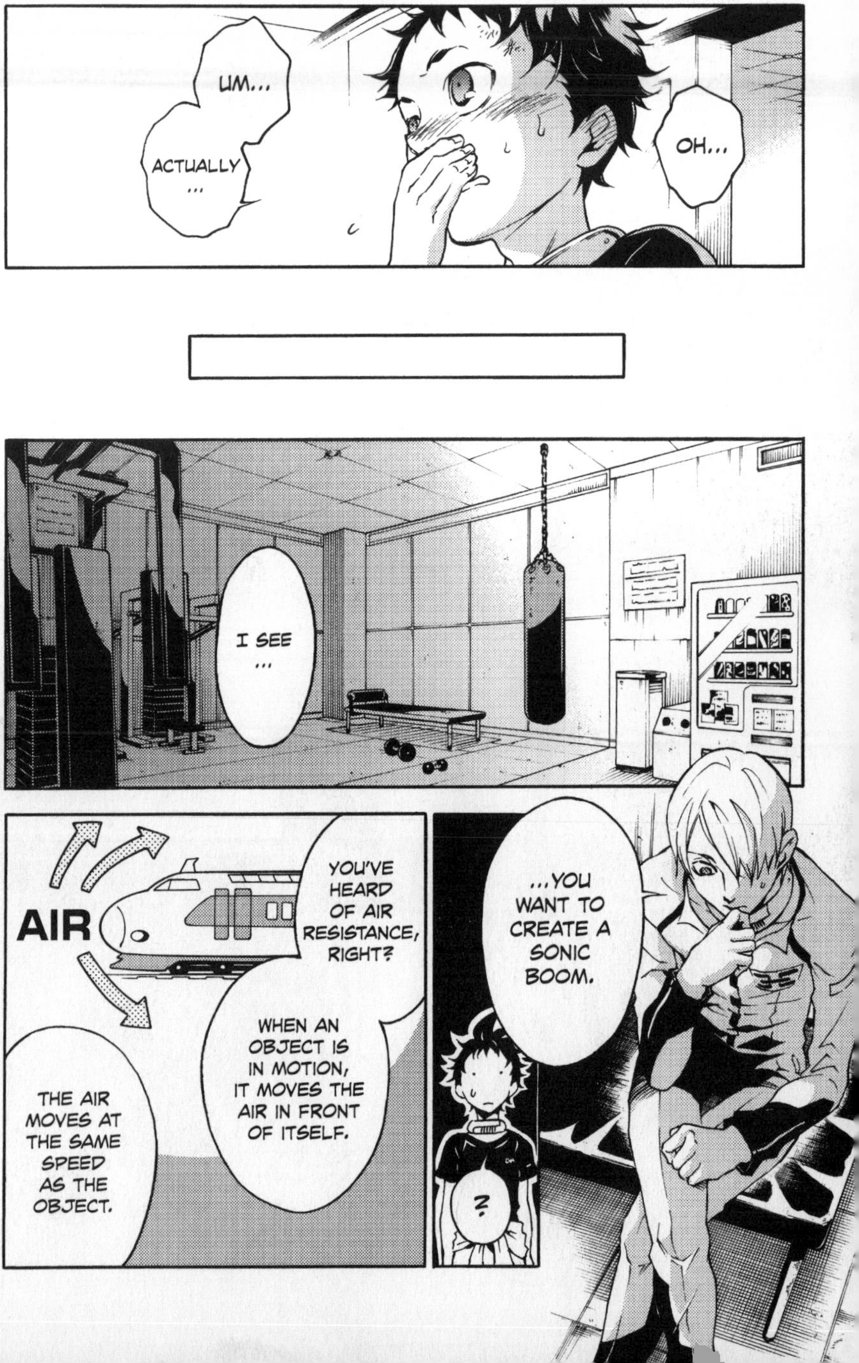
OH...
UM...
ACTUALLY ...
I SEE ...
...YOU WANT TO CREATE A SONIC BOOM.
?
YOU'VE HEARD OF AIR RESISTANCE, RIGHT?
AIR
WHEN AN OBJECT IS IN MOTION, IT MOVES THE AIR IN FRONT OF ITSELF.
THE AIR MOVES AT THE SAME SPEED AS THE OBJECT.

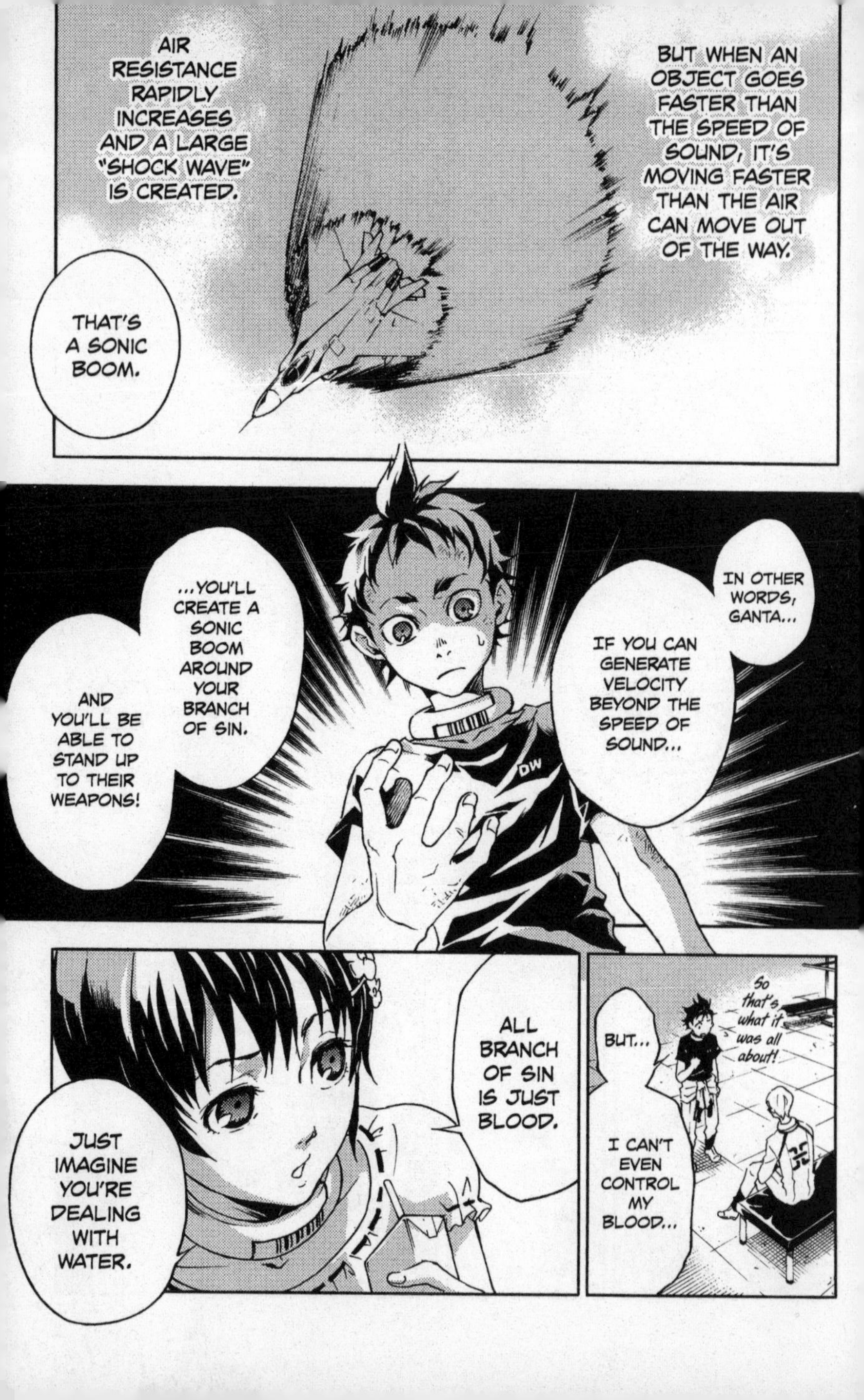
BUT WHEN AN OBJECT GOES FASTER THAN THE SPEED OF SOUND, IT'S MOVING FASTER THAN THE AIR CAN MOVE OUT OF THE WAY.
AIR RESISTANCE RAPIDLY INCREASES AND A LARGE "SHOCK WAVE" IS CREATED.
THAT'S A SONIC BOOM.
IN OTHER WORDS, GANTA...
IF YOU CAN GENERATE VELOCITY BEYOND THE SPEED OF SOUND...
...YOU'LL CREATE A SONIC BOOM AROUND YOUR BRANCH OF SIN.
AND YOU'LL BE ABLE TO STAND UP TO THEIR WEAPONS!
So that's what it was all about!
BUT...
I CAN'T EVEN CONTROL MY BLOOD...
ALL BRANCH OF SIN IS JUST BLOOD.
JUST IMAGINE YOU'RE DEALING WITH WATER.

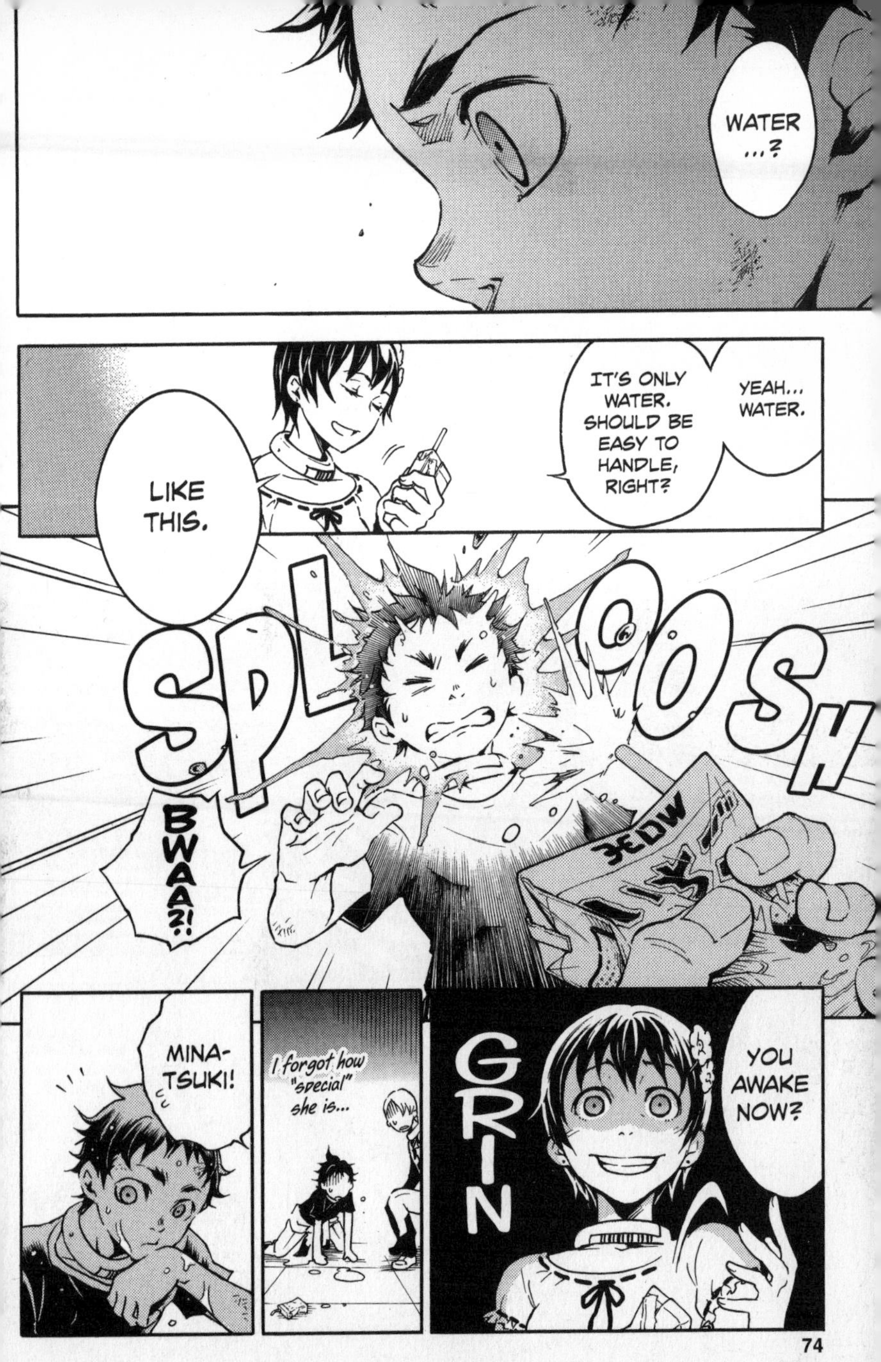
WATER ...?
YEAH... WATER.
IT'S ONLY WATER. SHOULD BE EASY TO HANDLE, RIGHT?
LIKE THIS.
SPLOOSH
BWAA?!
YOU AWAKE NOW?
GRIN
I forgot how "special" she is...
MINA-TSUKI!

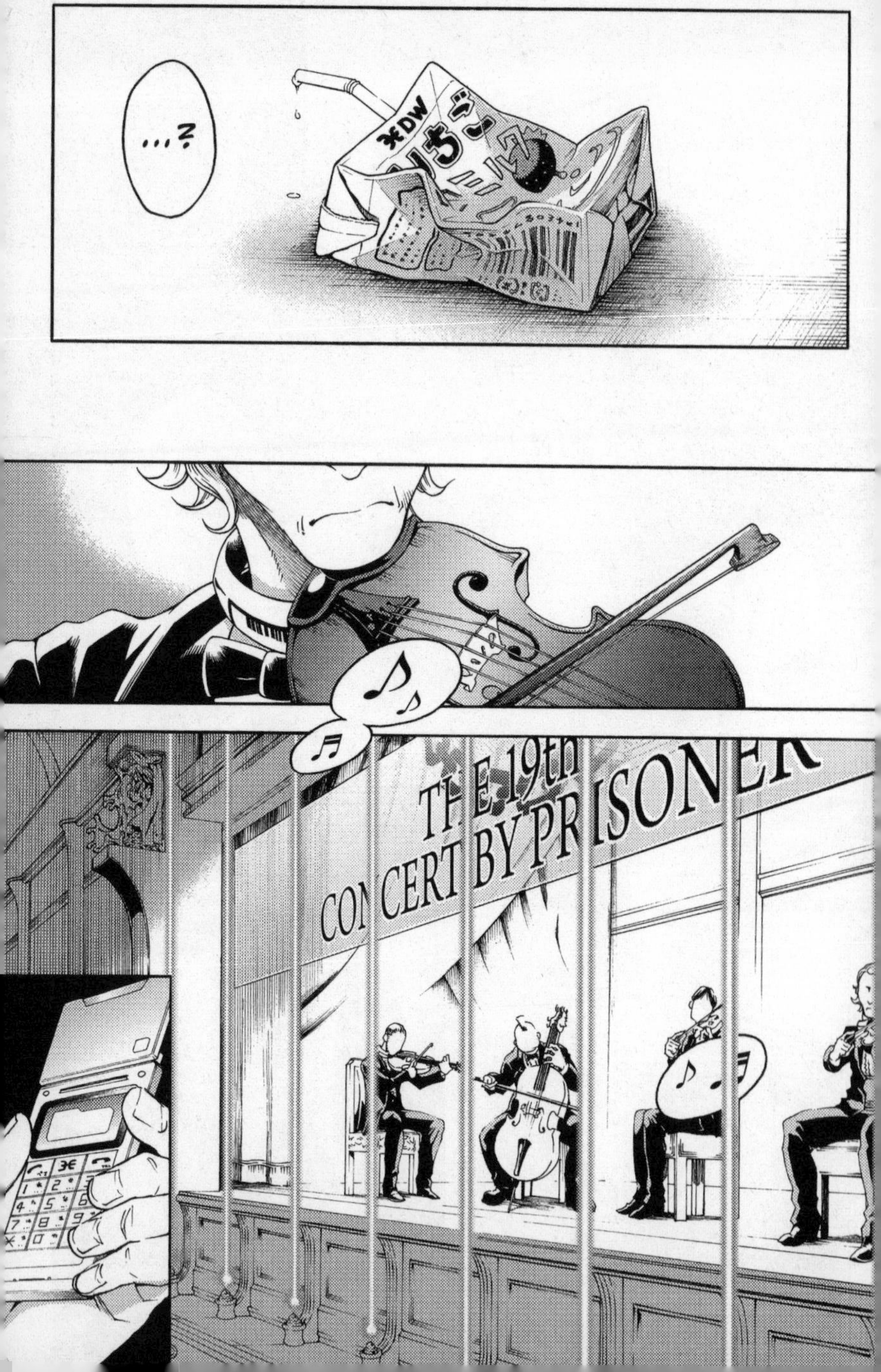
N...?
THE 19th
CONCERT BY PRISONER

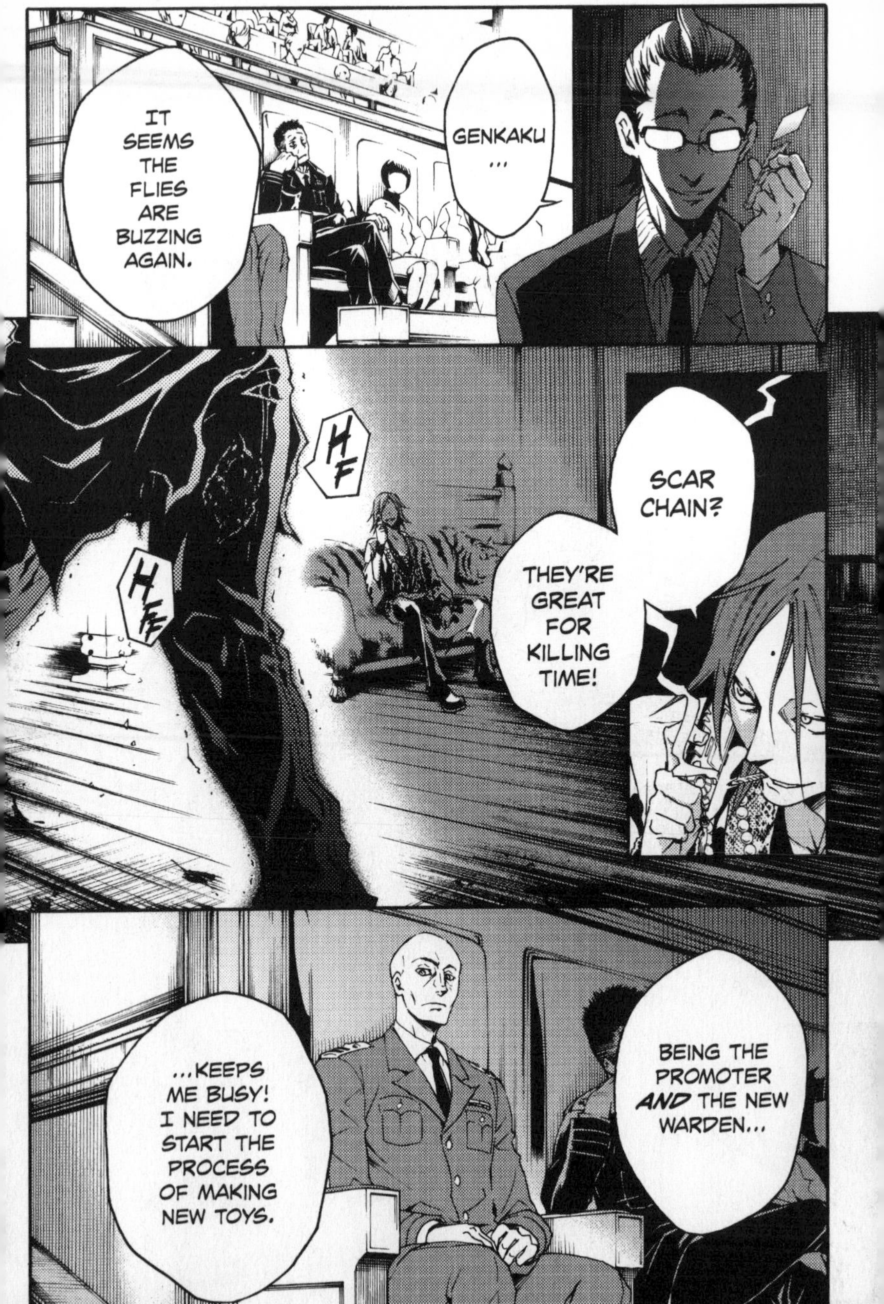
GENKAKU ...
IT SEEMS THE FLIES ARE BUZZING AGAIN.
SCAR CHAIN?
THEY'RE GREAT FOR KILLING TIME!
HF
HFF
BEING THE PROMOTER AND THE NEW WARDEN...
...KEEPS ME BUSY! I NEED TO START THE PROCESS OF MAKING NEW TOYS.

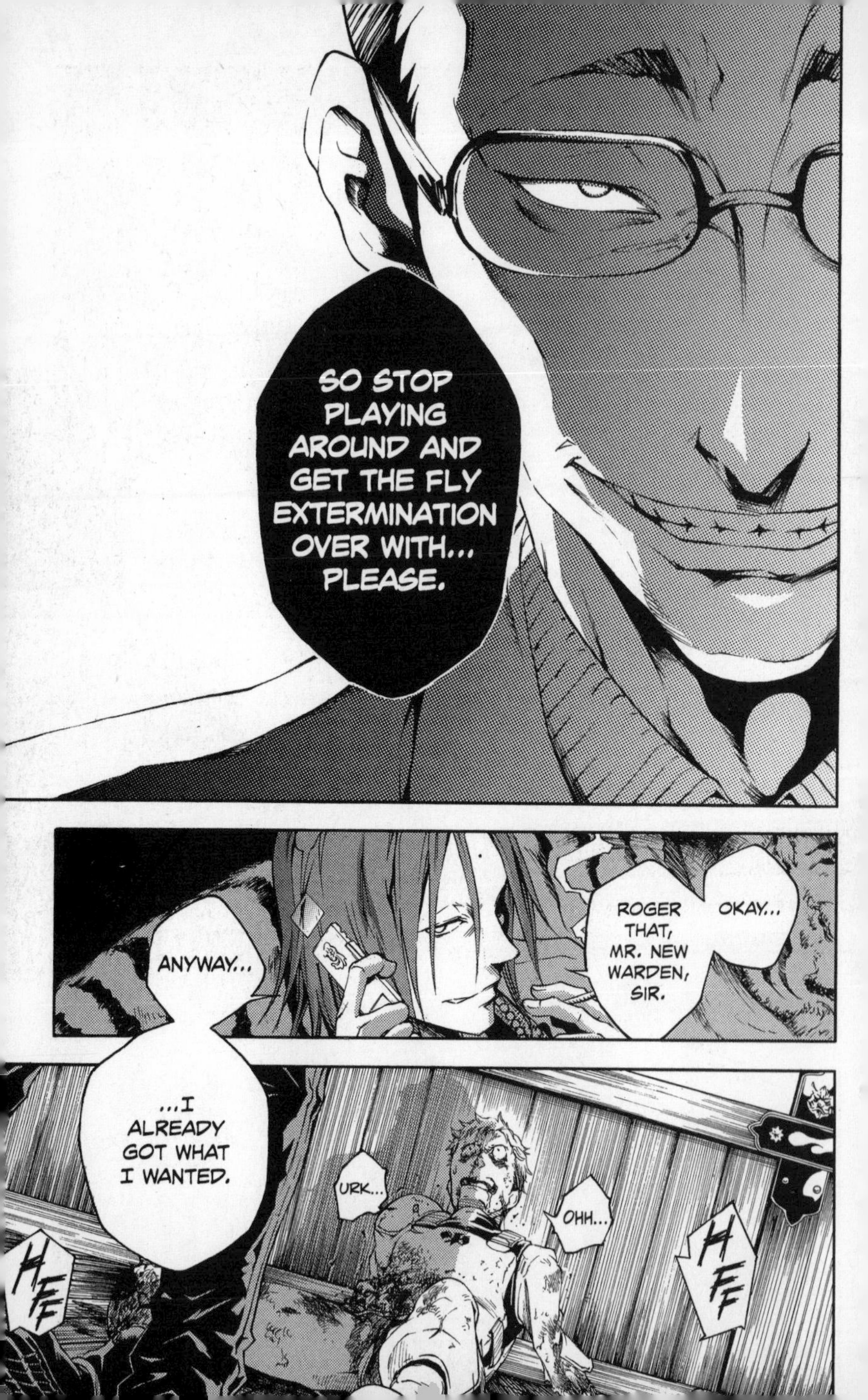
SO STOP PLAYING AROUND AND GET THE FLY EXTERMINATION OVER WITH... PLEASE.
OKAY...
ROGER THAT, MR. NEW WARDEN, SIR.
ANYWAY...
...I ALREADY GOT WHAT I WANTED.
HFF
OHH...
URK...
HFF

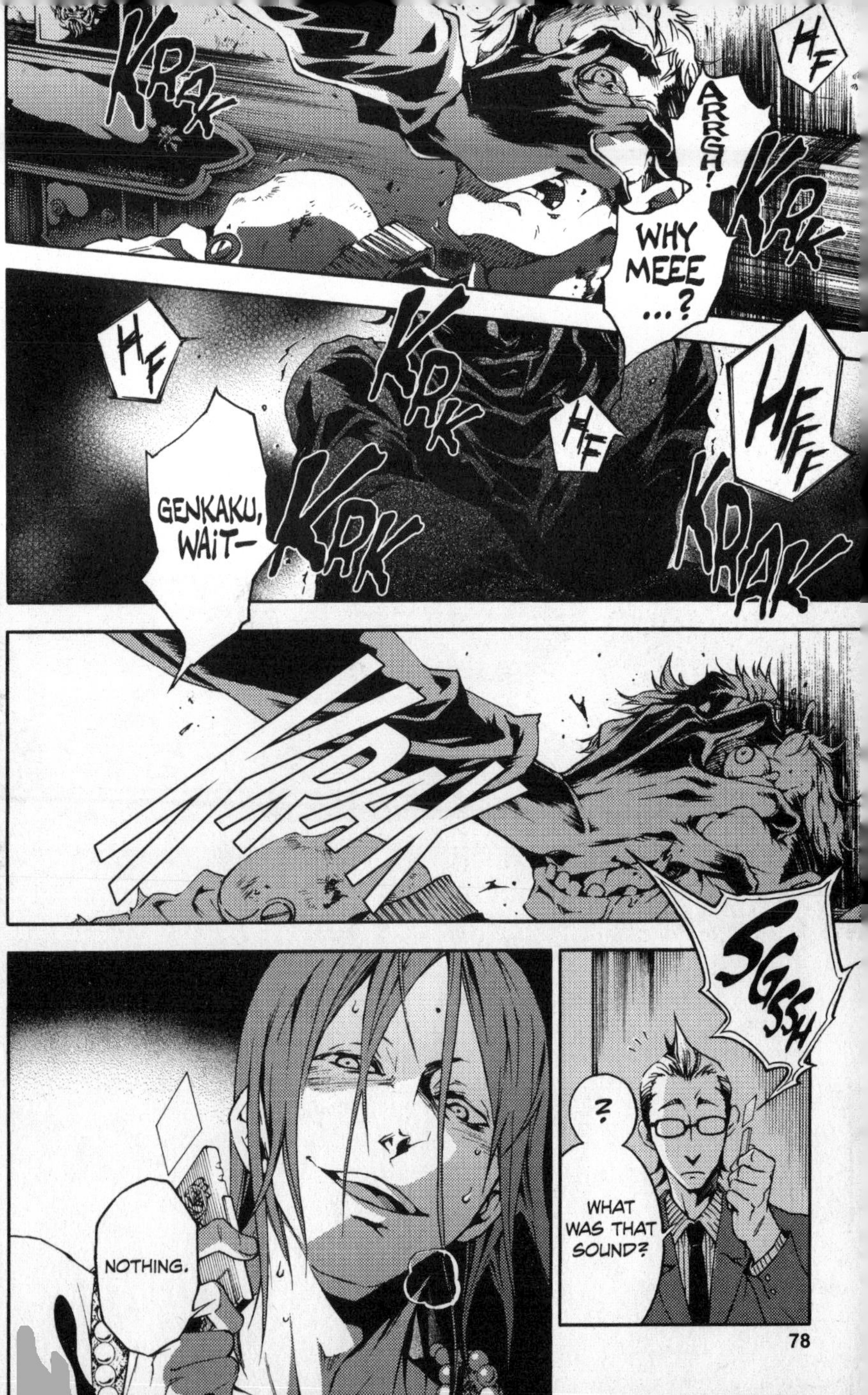
HF
ARRGH!
KRK
WHY MEEE ...?
KRAK
HEFF
KRAK
HF
KRK
HF
KRK
GENKAKU, WAIT—
KRAK
SGSSH
?
WHAT WAS THAT SOUND?
NOTHING.

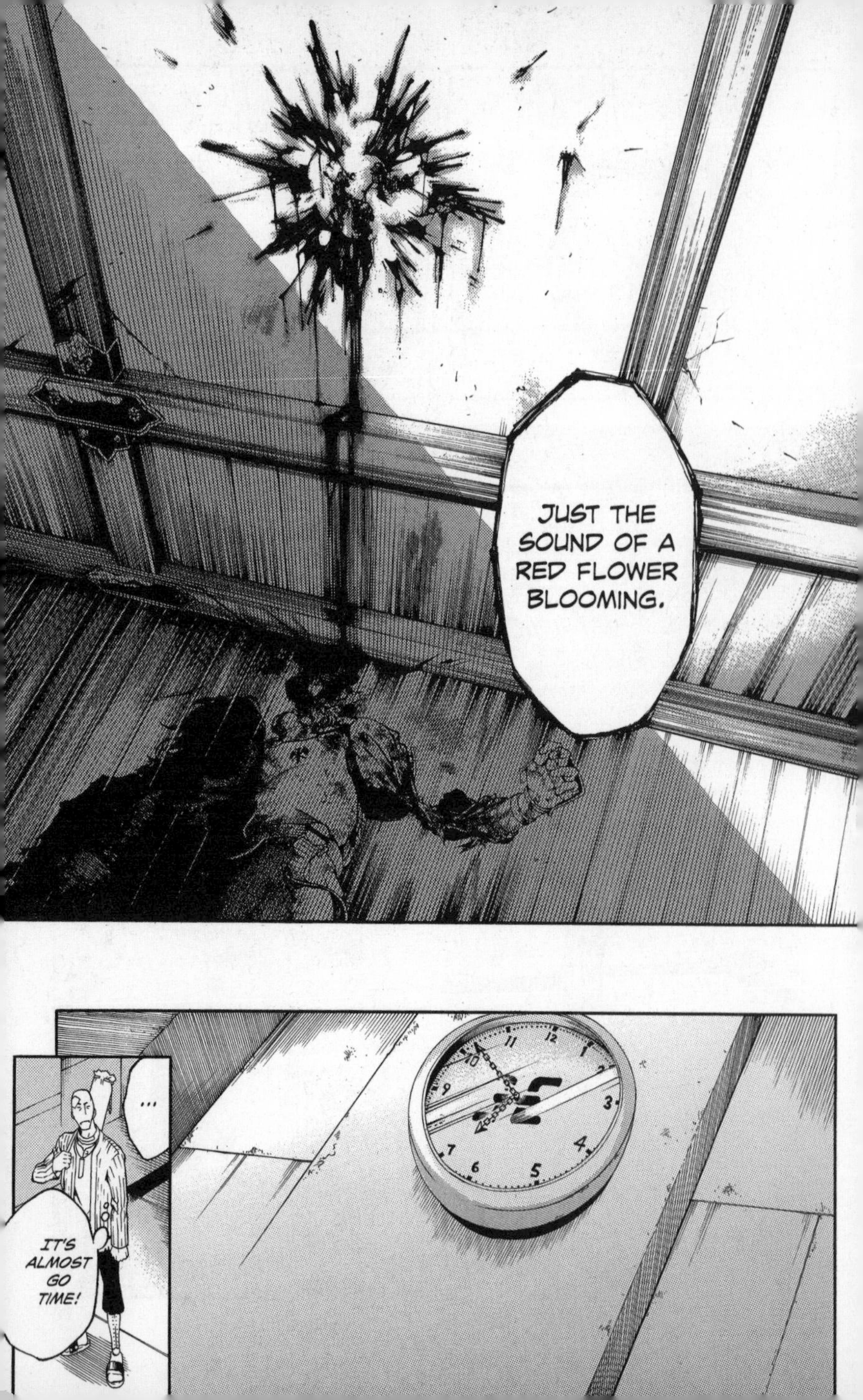
JUST THE SOUND OF A RED FLOWER BLOOMING.
...
IT'S ALMOST GO TIME!

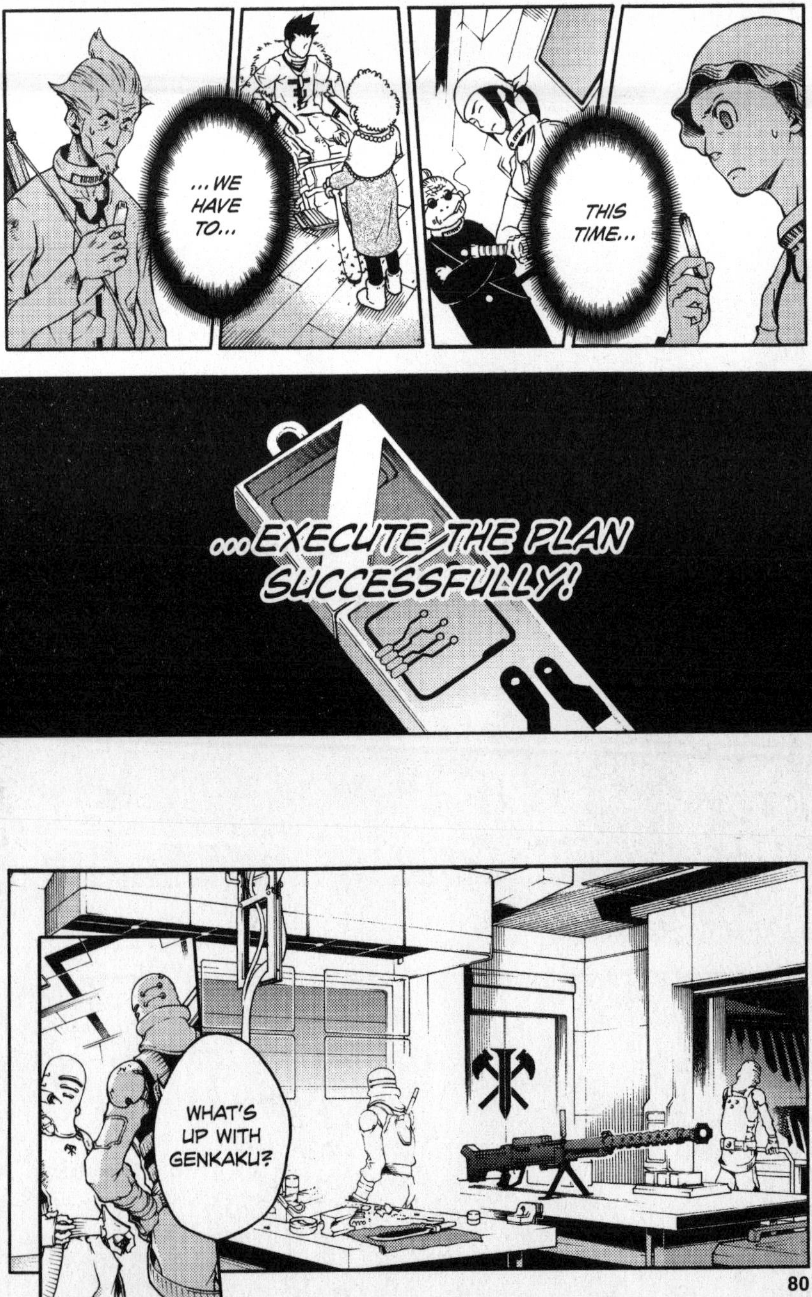
THIS TIME...
...WE HAVE TO...
...EXECUTE THE PLAN SUCCESSFULLY!
WHAT'S UP WITH GENKAKU?

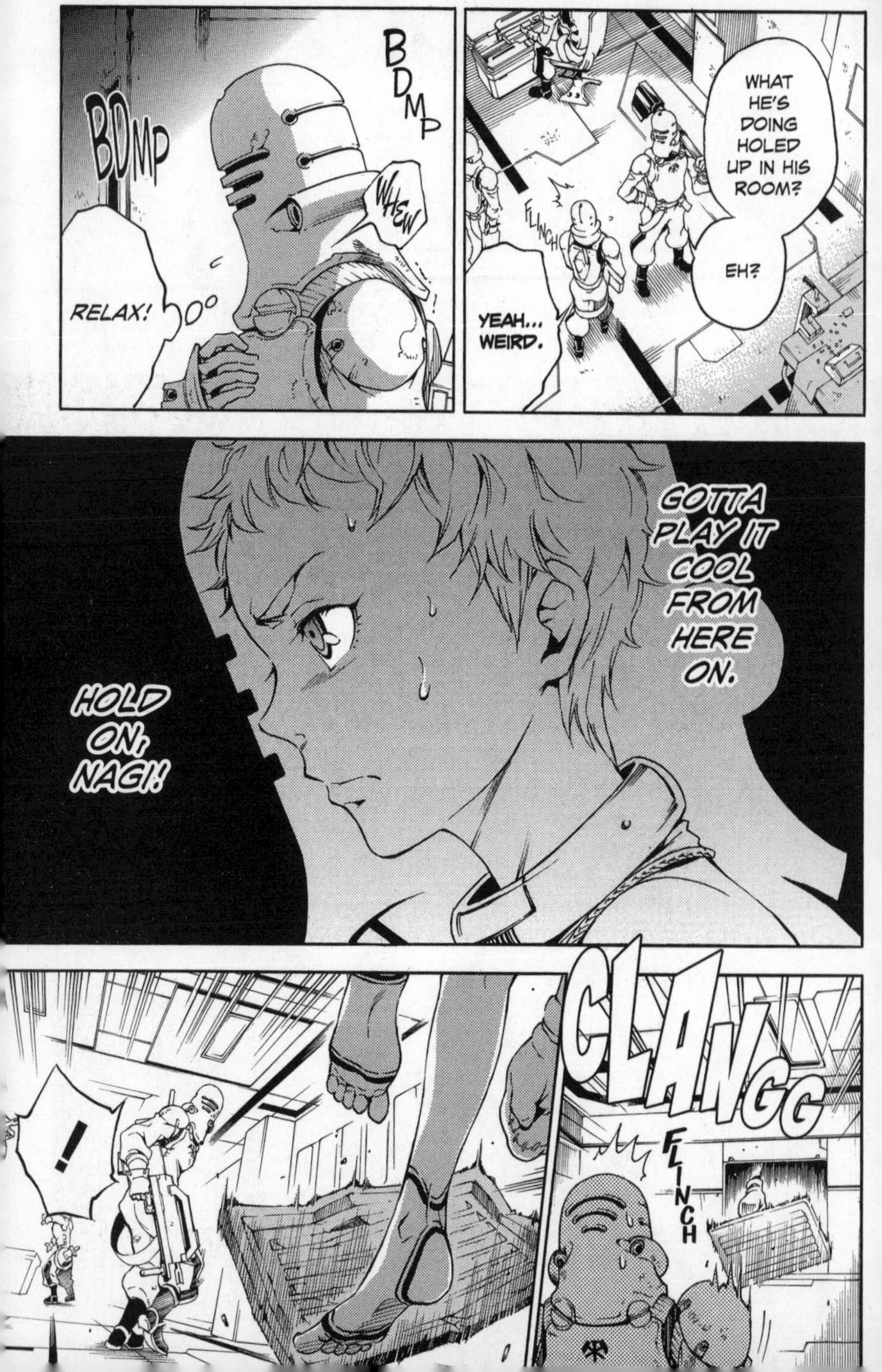
WHAT HE'S DOING HOLED UP IN HIS ROOM?
EH?
FLINCH
YEAH... WEIRD.
BDMP
BDMP
WHEW
RELAX!
GOTTA PLAY IT COOL FROM HERE ON.
HOLD ON, NAGI!
CLANGG
FLINCH
!

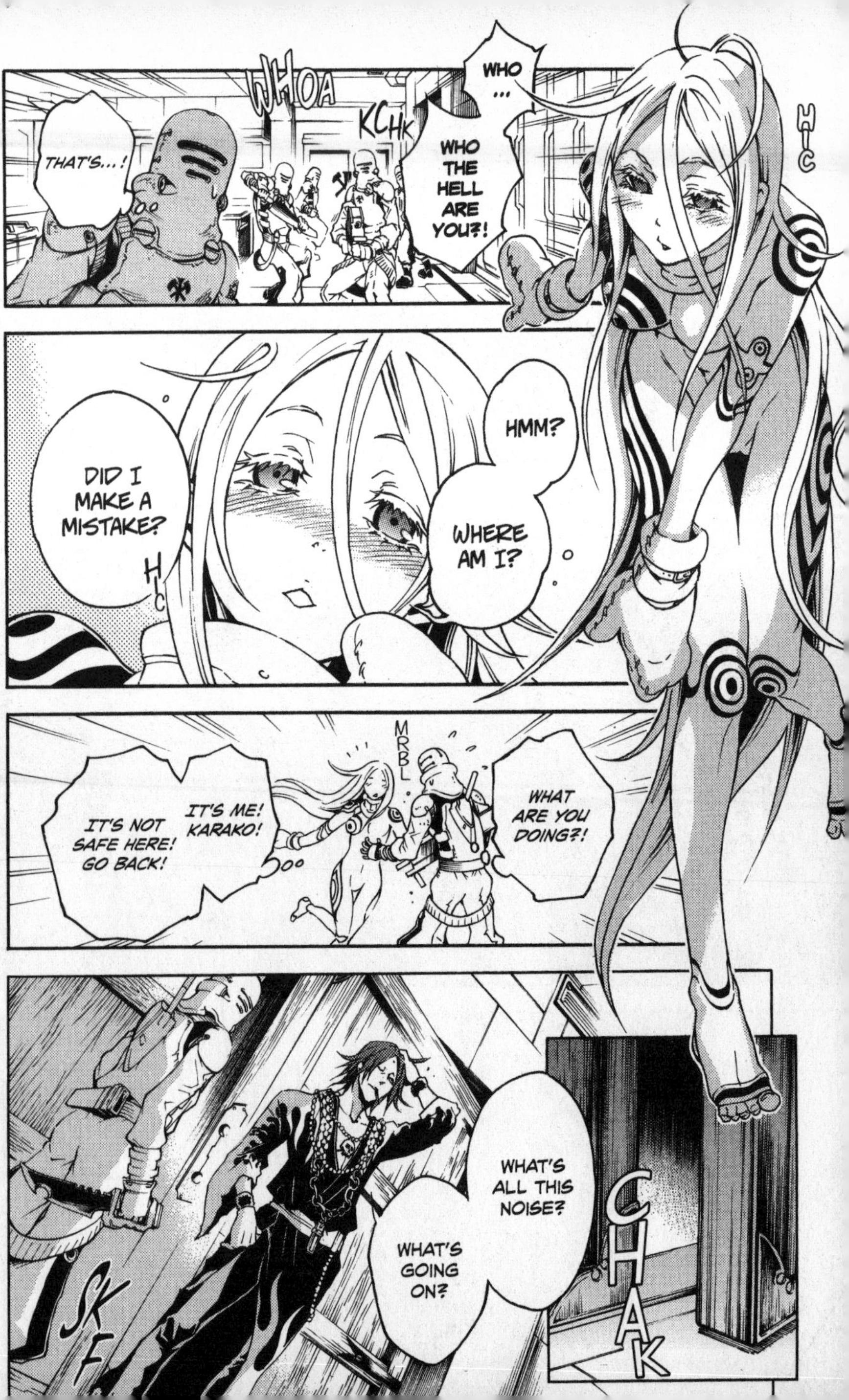
HIC
WHO …
WHO THE HELL ARE YOU?!
KCHK
WHOA
THAT'S…!
HMM?
WHERE AM I?
DID I MAKE A MISTAKE?
HIC
WHAT ARE YOU DOING?!
MRBL
IT'S ME! KARAKO!
IT'S NOT SAFE HERE! GO BACK!
CHAK
WHAT'S ALL THIS NOISE?
WHAT'S GOING ON?
SKF

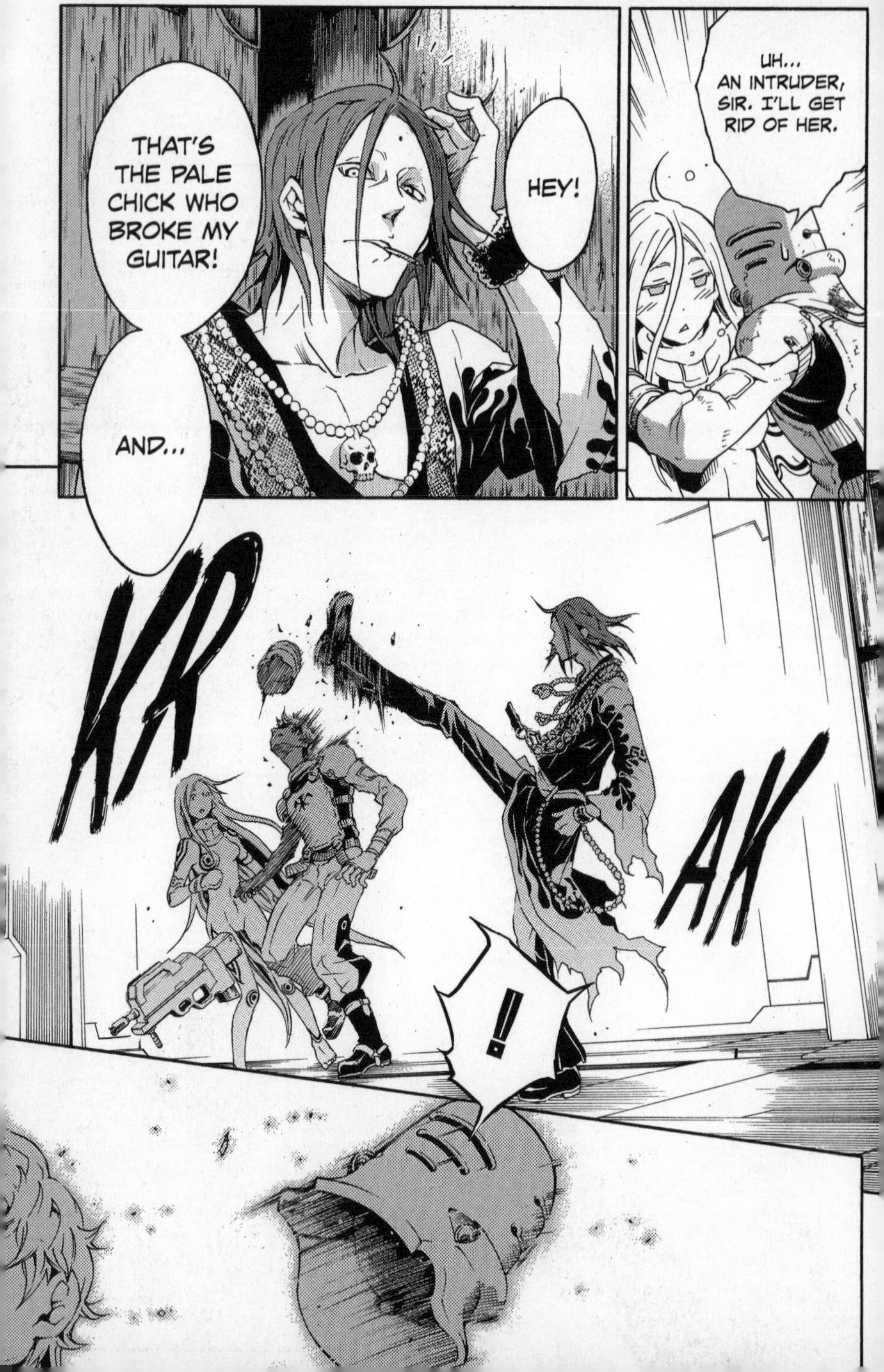
UH... AN INTRUDER, SIR. I'LL GET RID OF HER.
HEY!
THAT'S THE PALE CHICK WHO BROKE MY GUITAR!
AND...
KR
AK
!

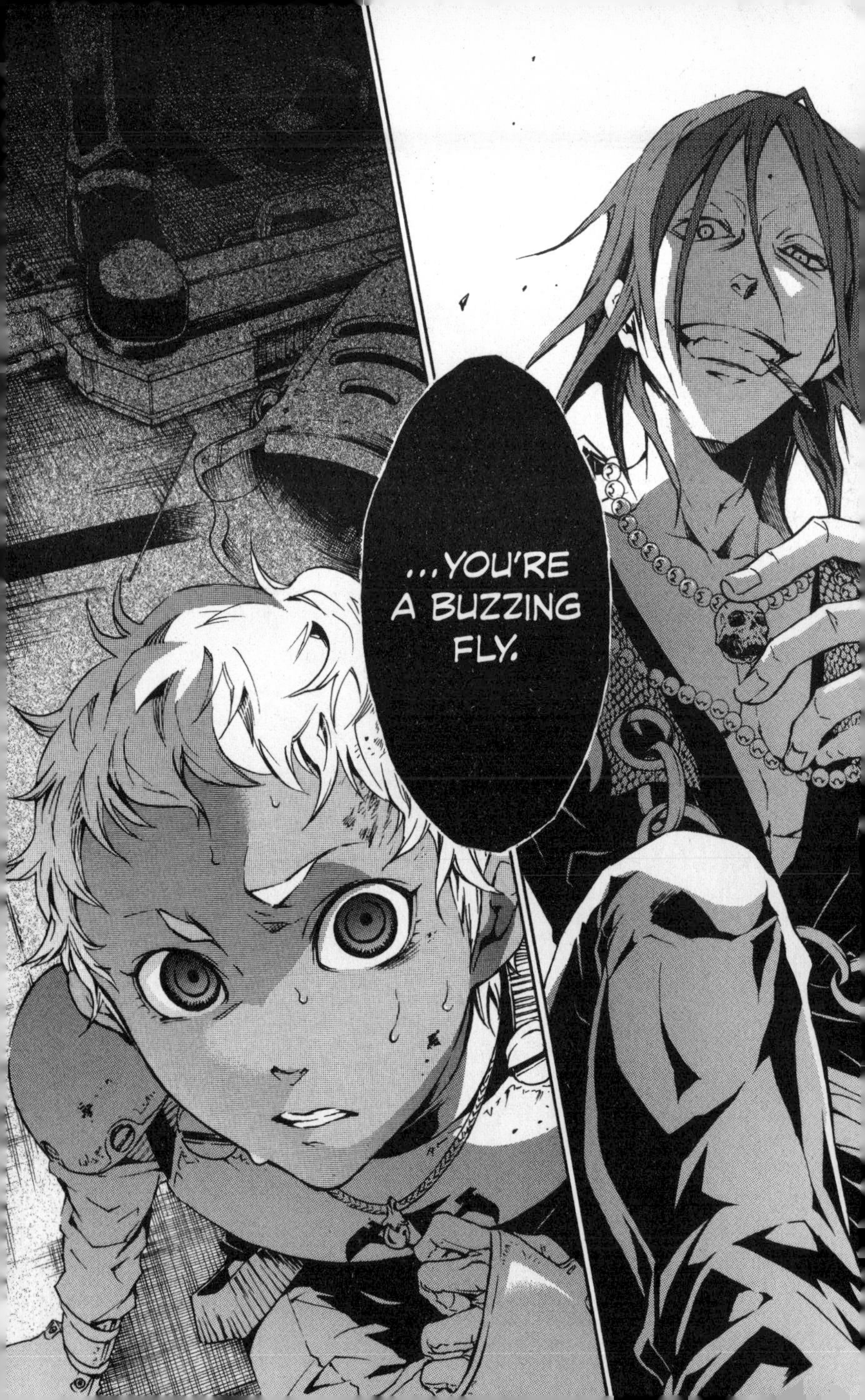
...YOU'RE A BUZZING FLY.

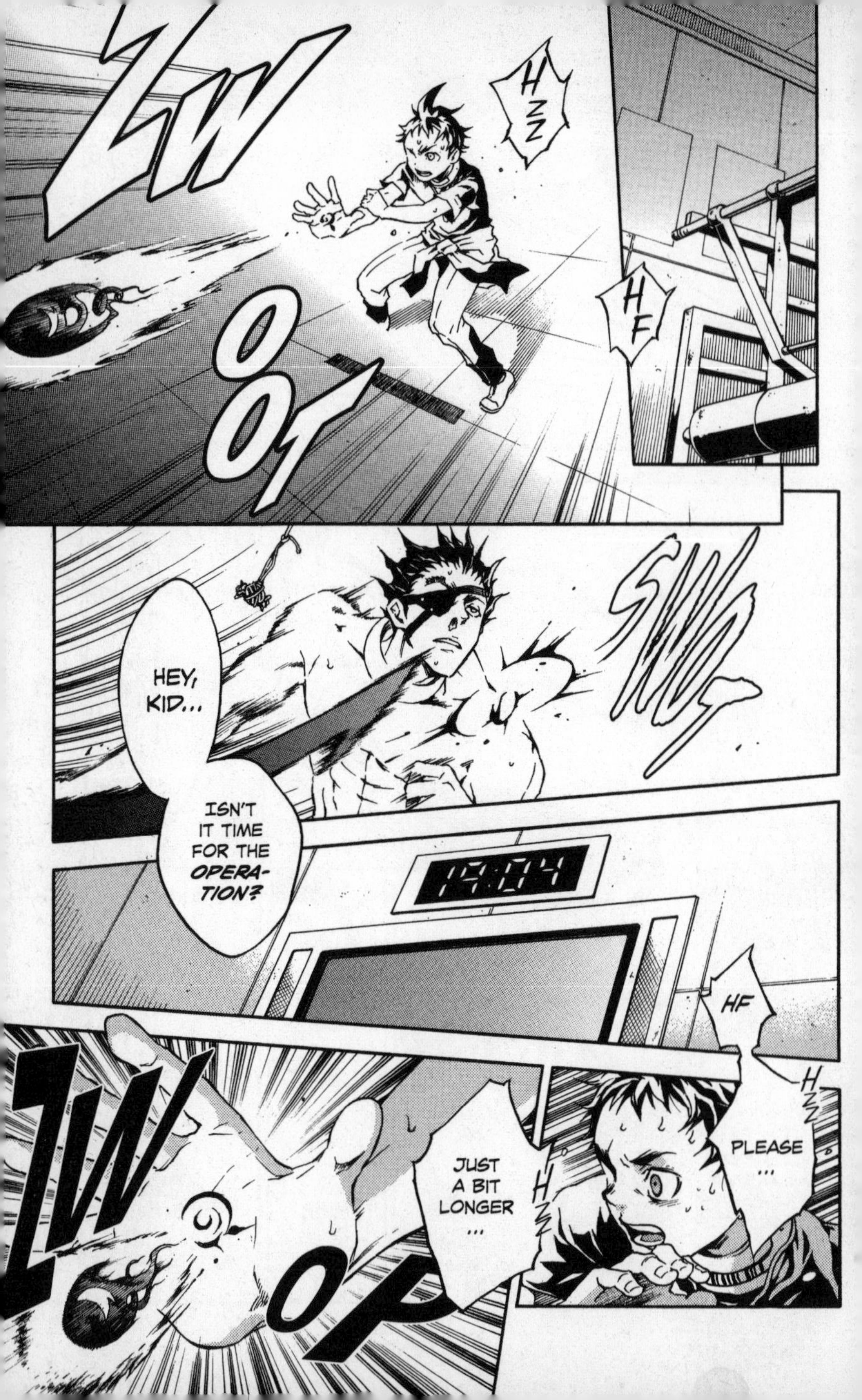
HF
HZZ
ZWOOP
SWOP
HEY, KID...
ISN'T IT TIME FOR THE *OPERATION?*
19:04
HF
HZZ
PLEASE...
HZZ
JUST A BIT LONGER...
ZWOP

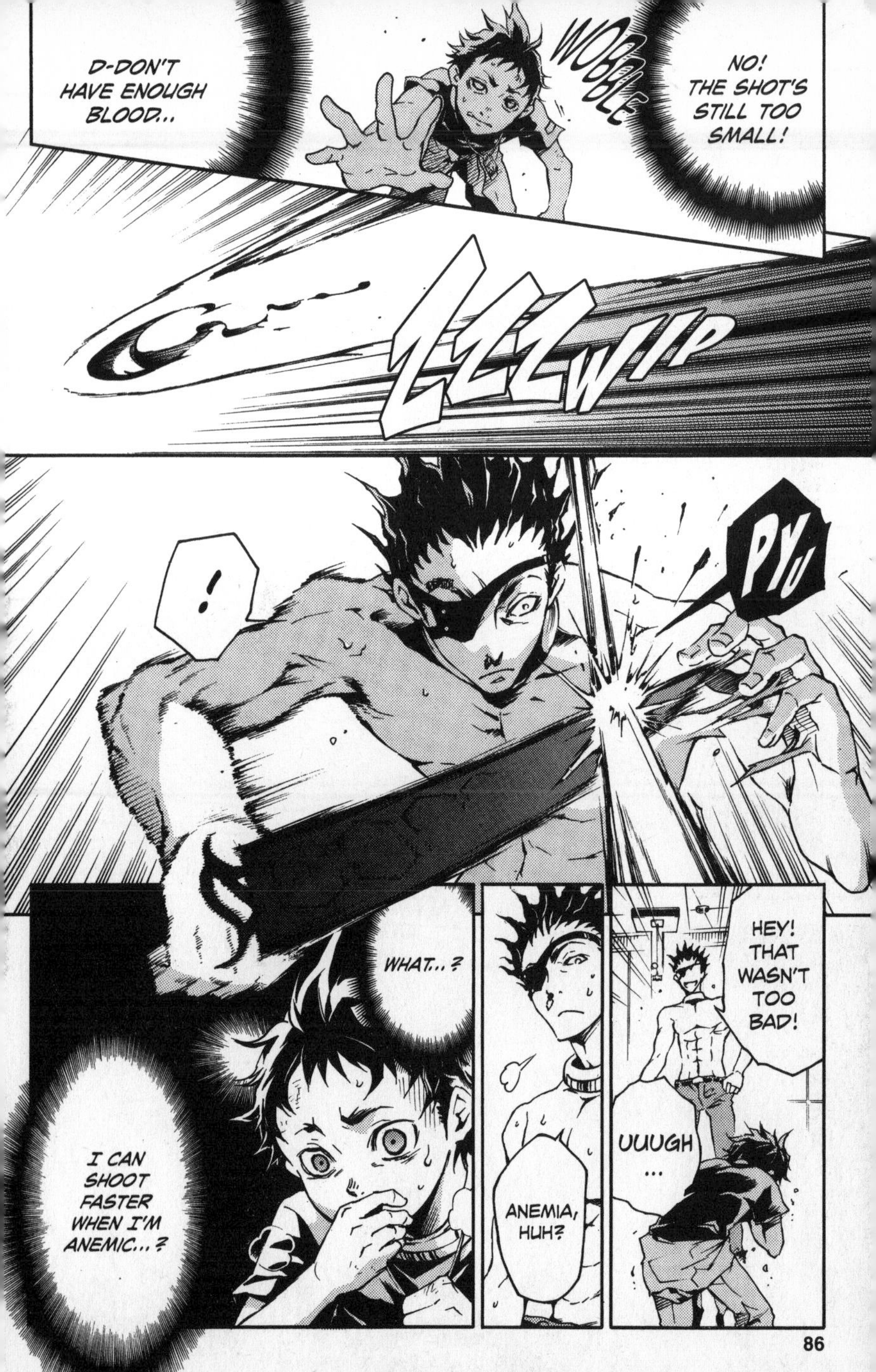
NO! THE SHOT'S STILL TOO SMALL!
WOBBLE
D-DON'T HAVE ENOUGH BLOOD...
ZZZWIP
PYU
!
HEY! THAT WASN'T TOO BAD!
UUUGH ...
ANEMIA, HUH?
WHAT...?
I CAN SHOOT FASTER WHEN I'M ANEMIC...?

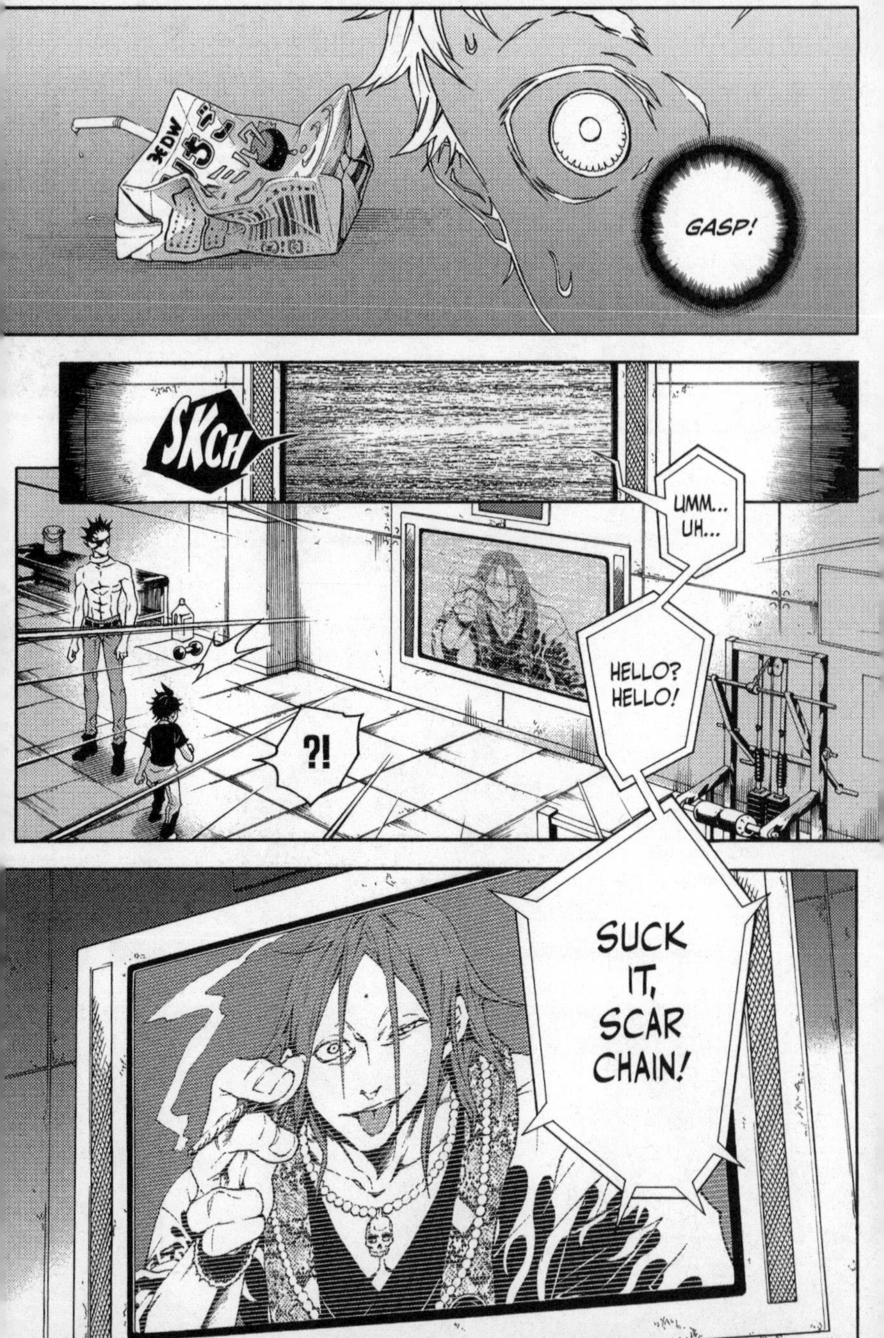
GASP!
UMM... UH...
SKCH
HELLO? HELLO!
?!
SUCK IT, SCAR CHAIN!

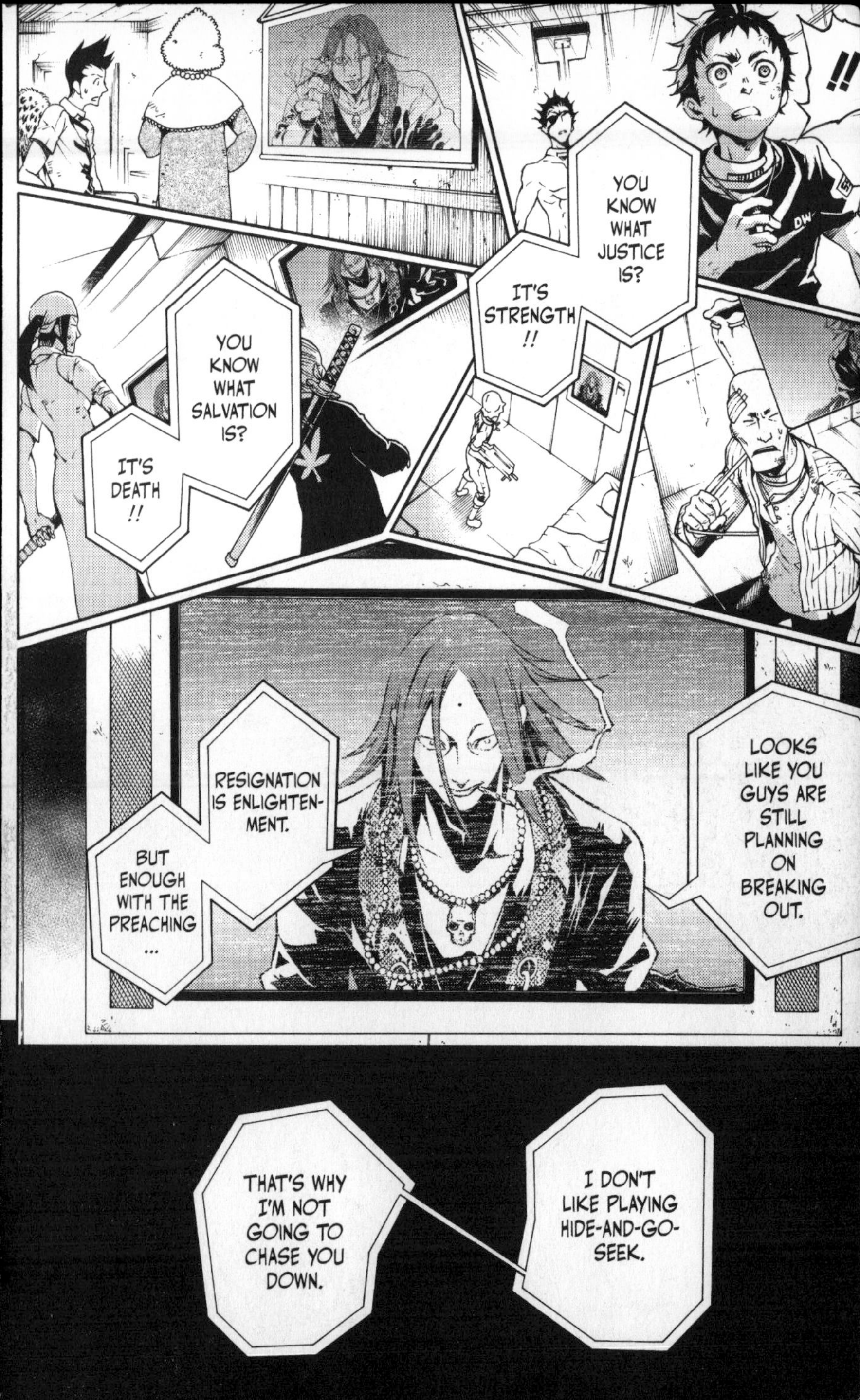
!!
YOU KNOW WHAT JUSTICE IS?
IT'S STRENGTH!!
YOU KNOW WHAT SALVATION IS?
IT'S DEATH!!
LOOKS LIKE YOU GUYS ARE STILL PLANNING ON BREAKING OUT.
RESIGNATION IS ENLIGHTENMENT.
BUT ENOUGH WITH THE PREACHING...
I DON'T LIKE PLAYING HIDE-AND-GO-SEEK.
THAT'S WHY I'M NOT GOING TO CHASE YOU DOWN.

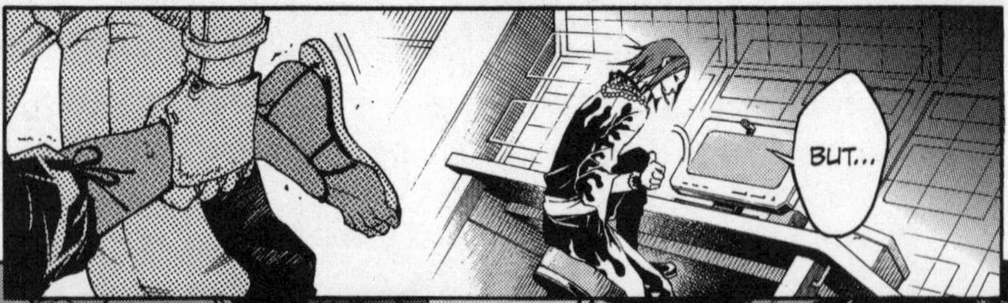
BUT...

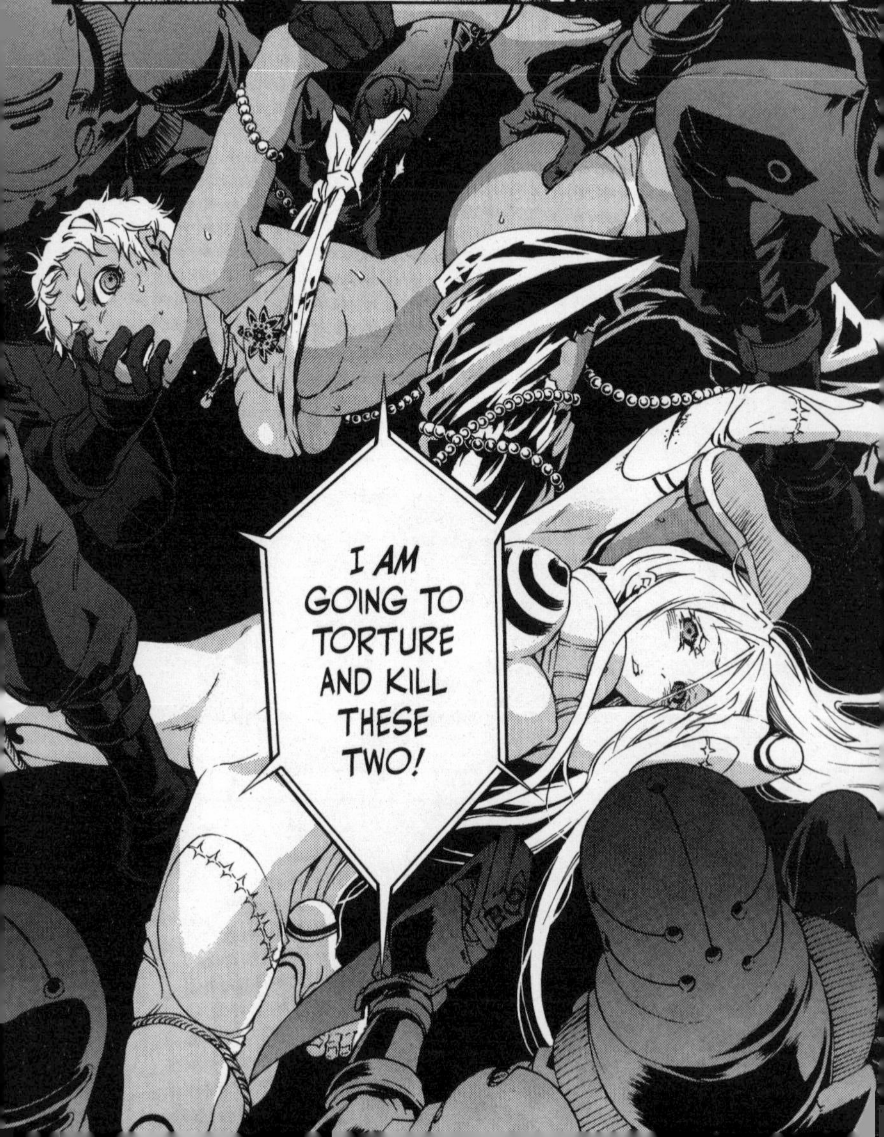
I AM GOING TO TORTURE AND KILL THESE TWO!

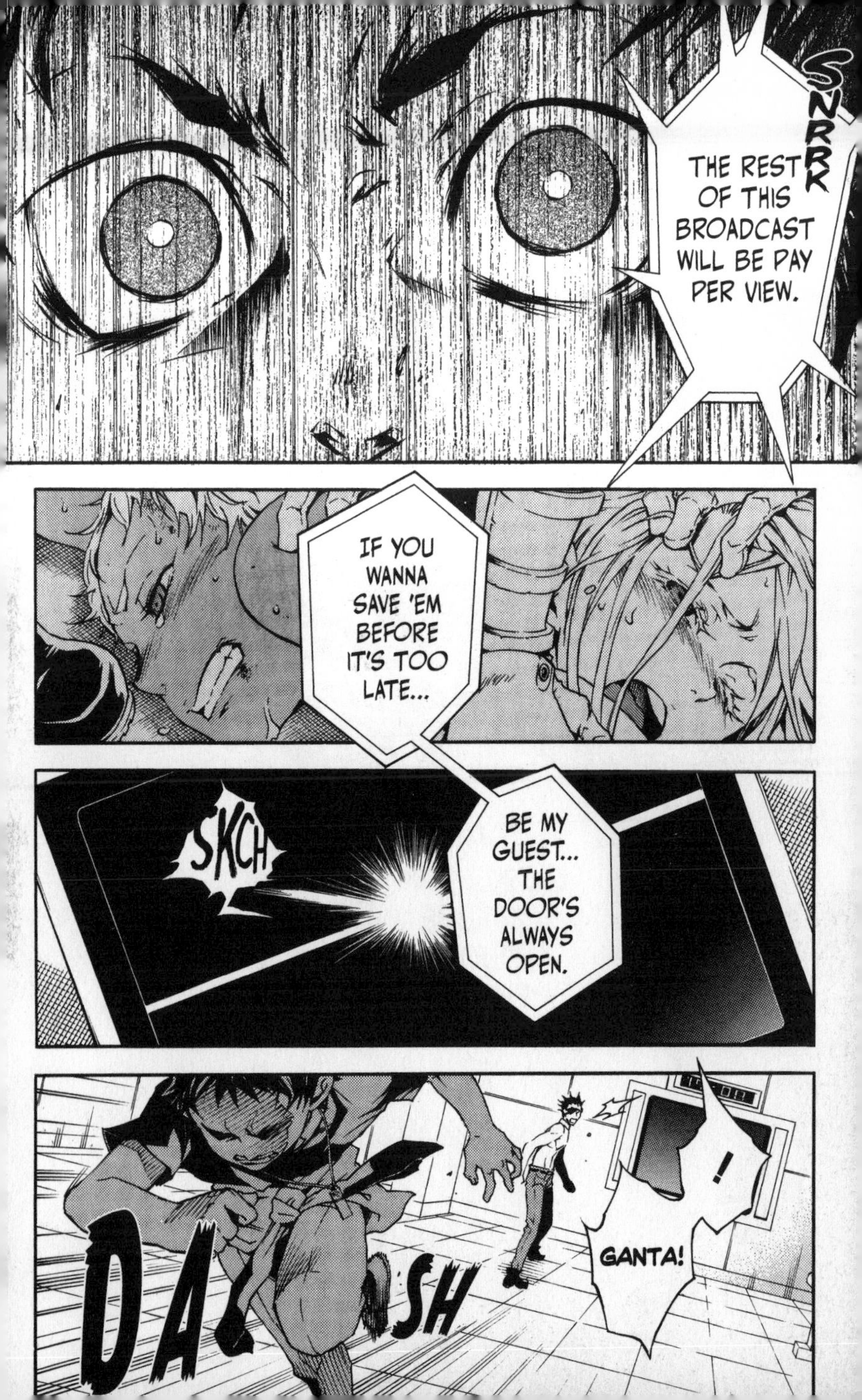
SNRRK
THE REST OF THIS BROADCAST WILL BE PAY PER VIEW.
IF YOU WANNA SAVE 'EM BEFORE IT'S TOO LATE...
BE MY GUEST... THE DOOR'S ALWAYS OPEN.
SKCH
!
GANTA!
DA SH

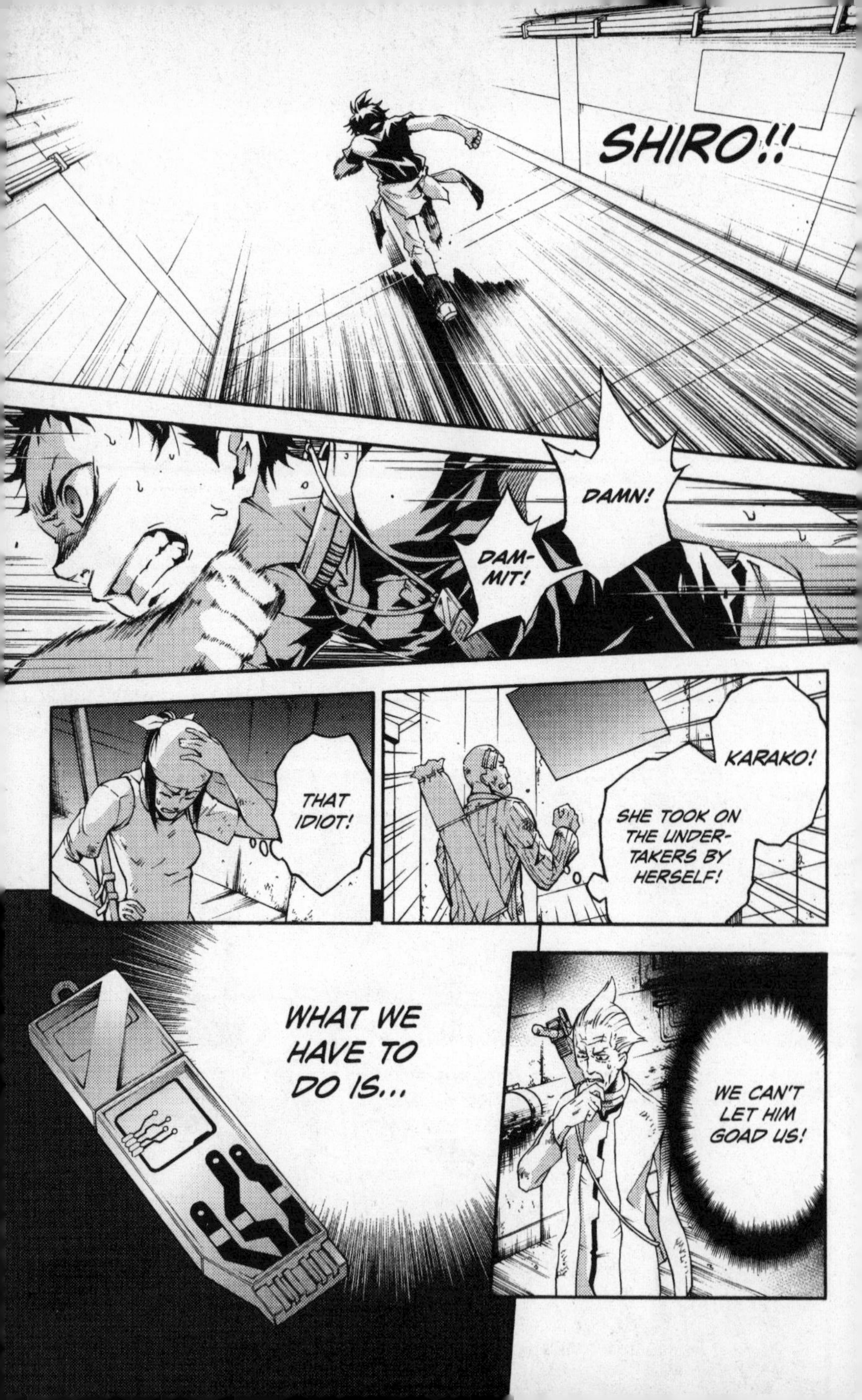
SHIRO!!
DAMN!
DAM-MIT!
KARAKO!
SHE TOOK ON THE UNDER-TAKERS BY HERSELF!
THAT IDIOT!
WE CAN'T LET HIM GOAD US!
WHAT WE HAVE TO DO IS...

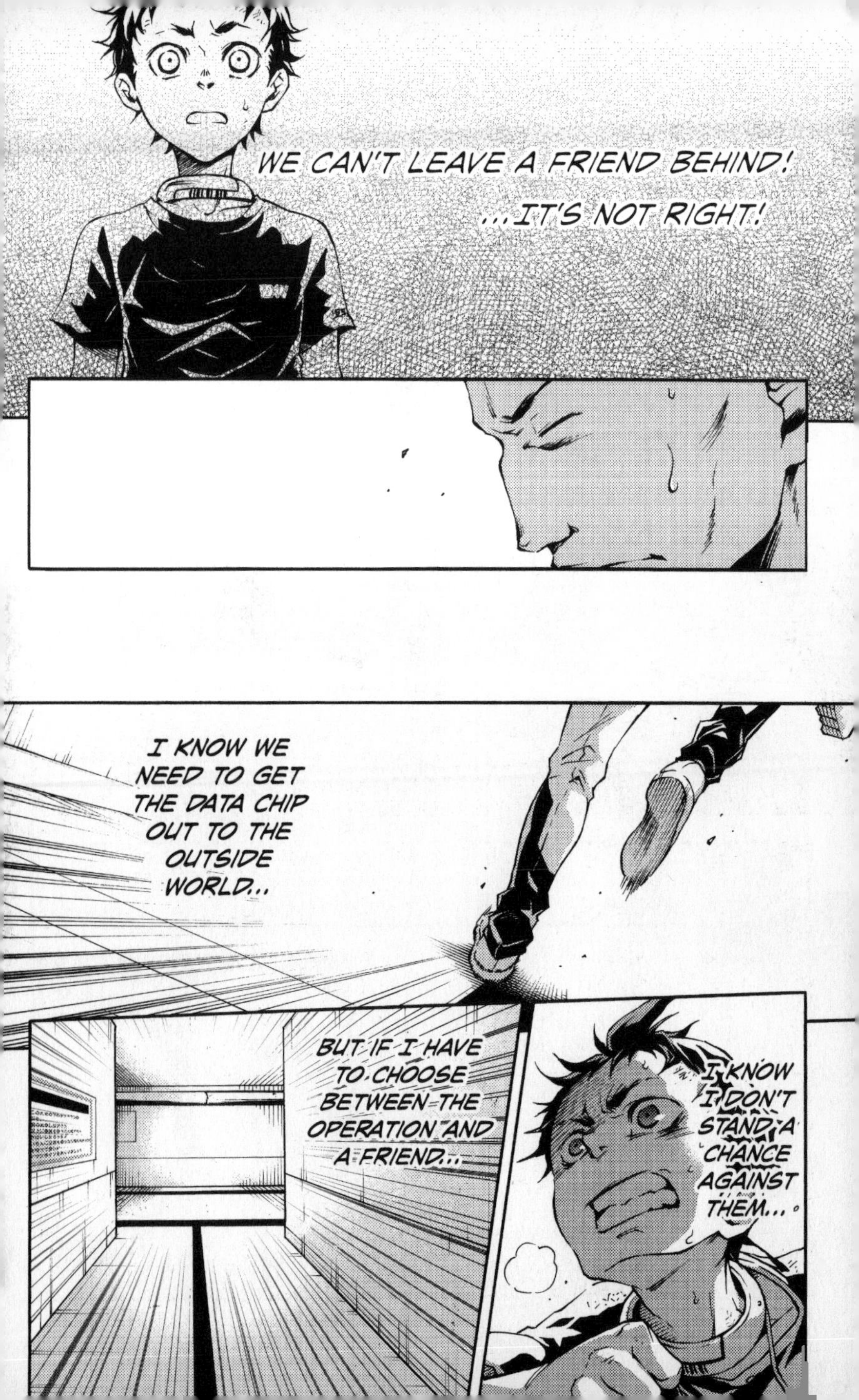
WE CAN'T LEAVE A FRIEND BEHIND!
...IT'S NOT RIGHT!
I KNOW WE NEED TO GET THE DATA CHIP OUT TO THE OUTSIDE WORLD...
I KNOW I DON'T STAND A CHANCE AGAINST THEM...
BUT IF I HAVE TO CHOOSE BETWEEN THE OPERATION AND A FRIEND...

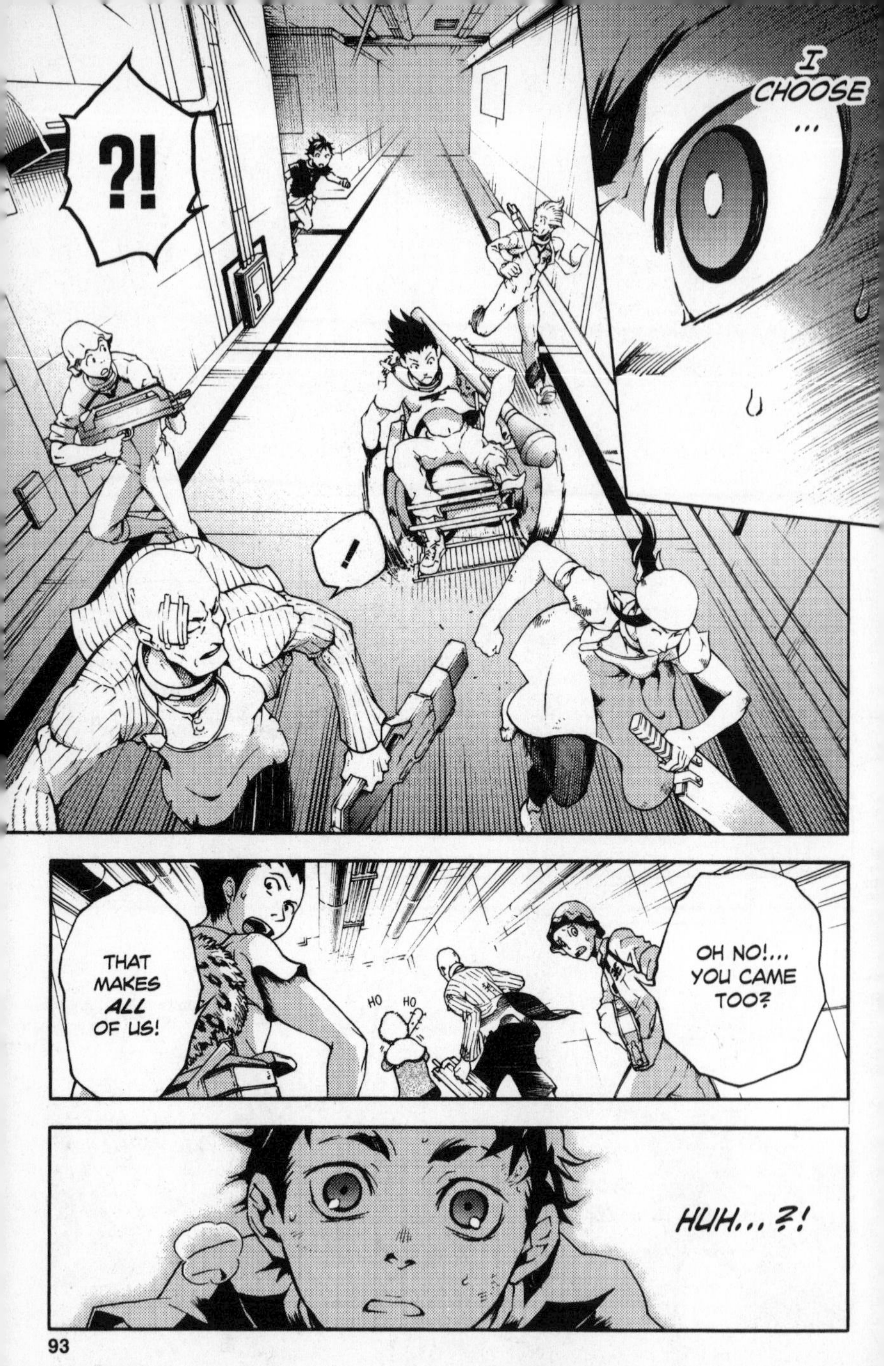
I CHOOSE ...
?!
!
OH NO!... YOU CAME TOO?
HO HO
THAT MAKES ALL OF US!
HUH... ?!

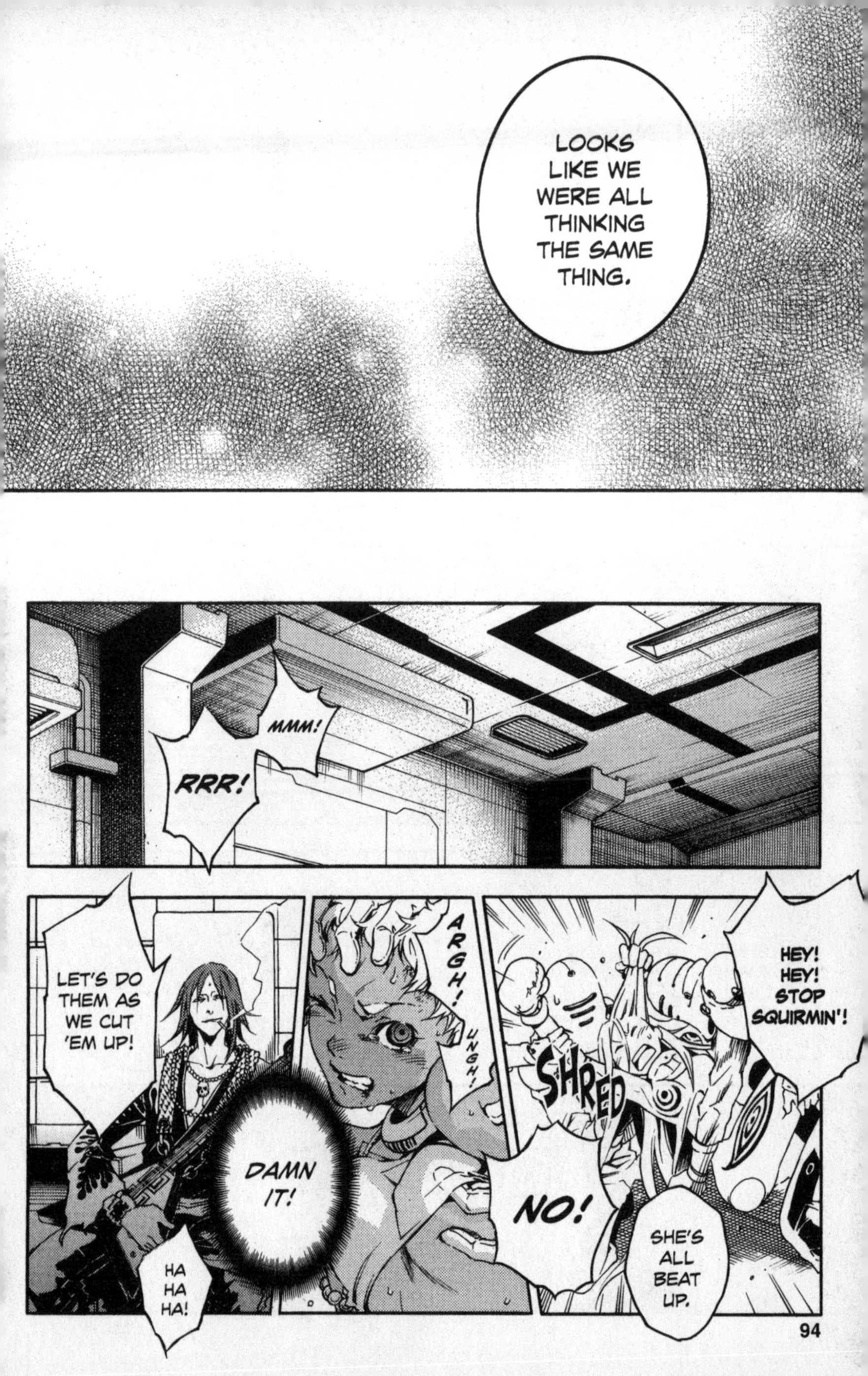
LOOKS LIKE WE WERE ALL THINKING THE SAME THING.
MMM!
RRR!
HEY! HEY! STOP SQUIRMIN'!
SHRED
SHE'S ALL BEAT UP.
NO!
ARGH!
UNGH!
LET'S DO THEM AS WE CUT 'EM UP!
DAMN IT!
HA HA HA!

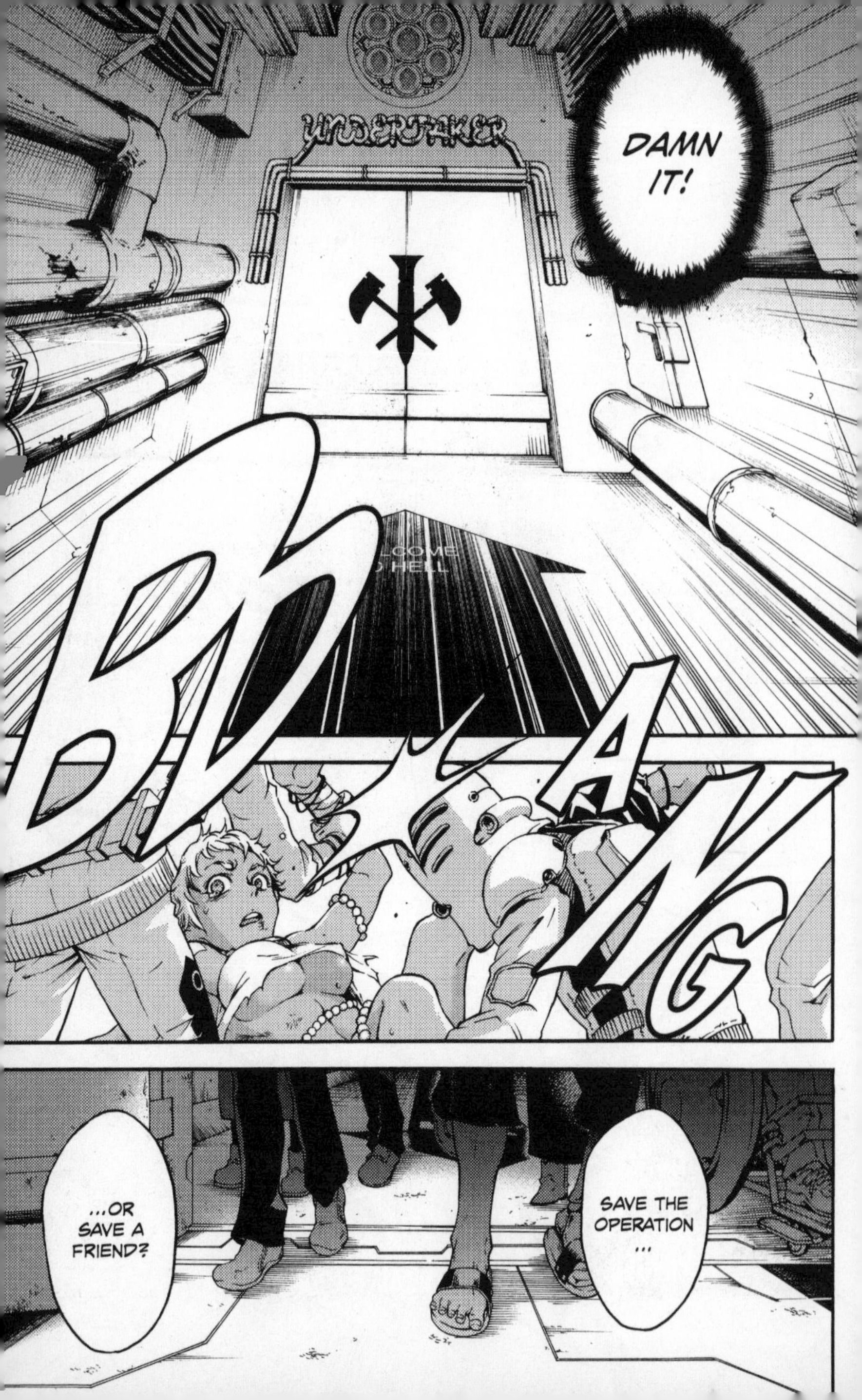
UNDERTAKER
DAMN IT!
BLAM
...LCOME ...O HELL
BANG
SAVE THE OPERATION ...
...OR SAVE A FRIEND?

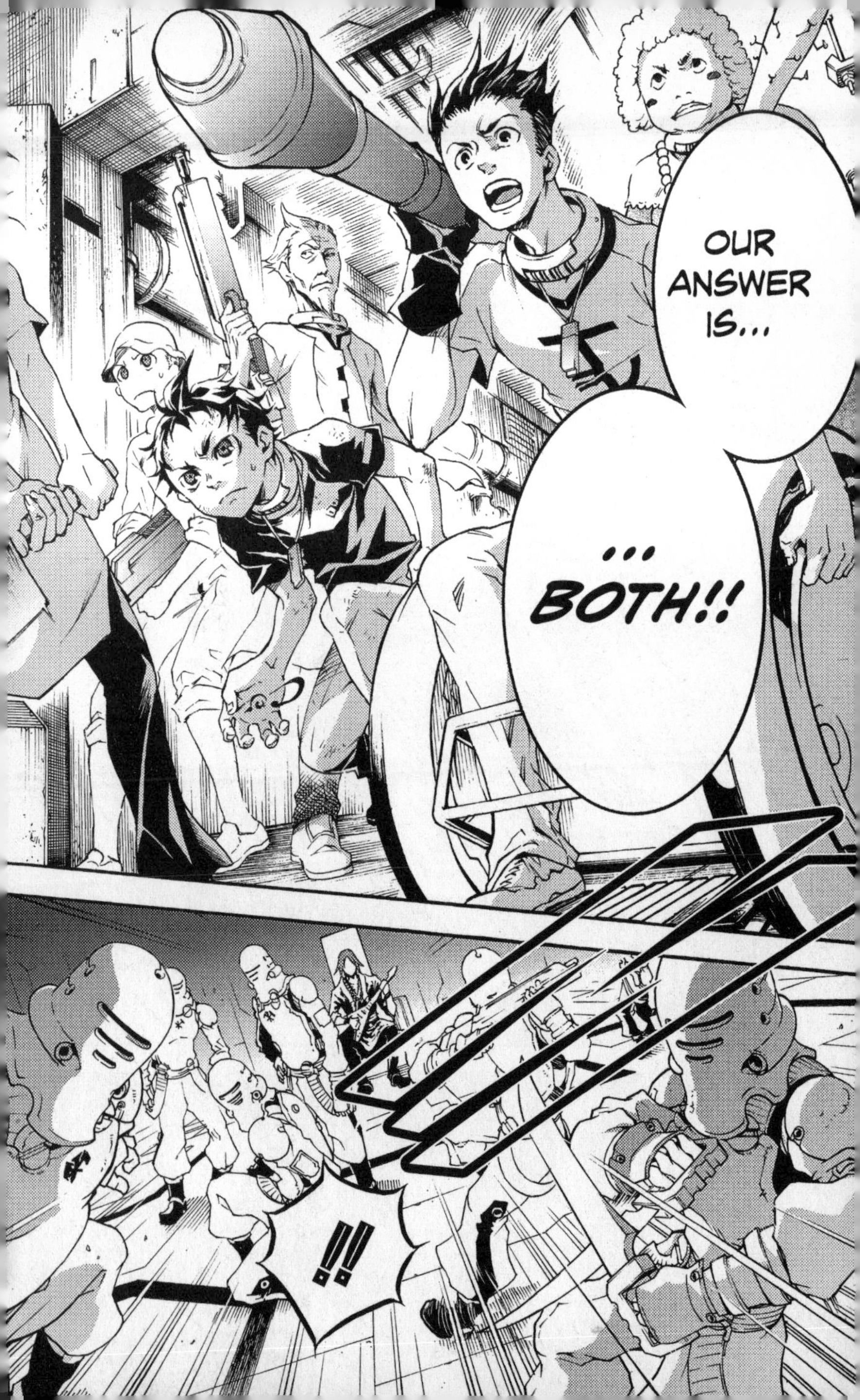
OUR ANSWER IS...
...BOTH!!
!!

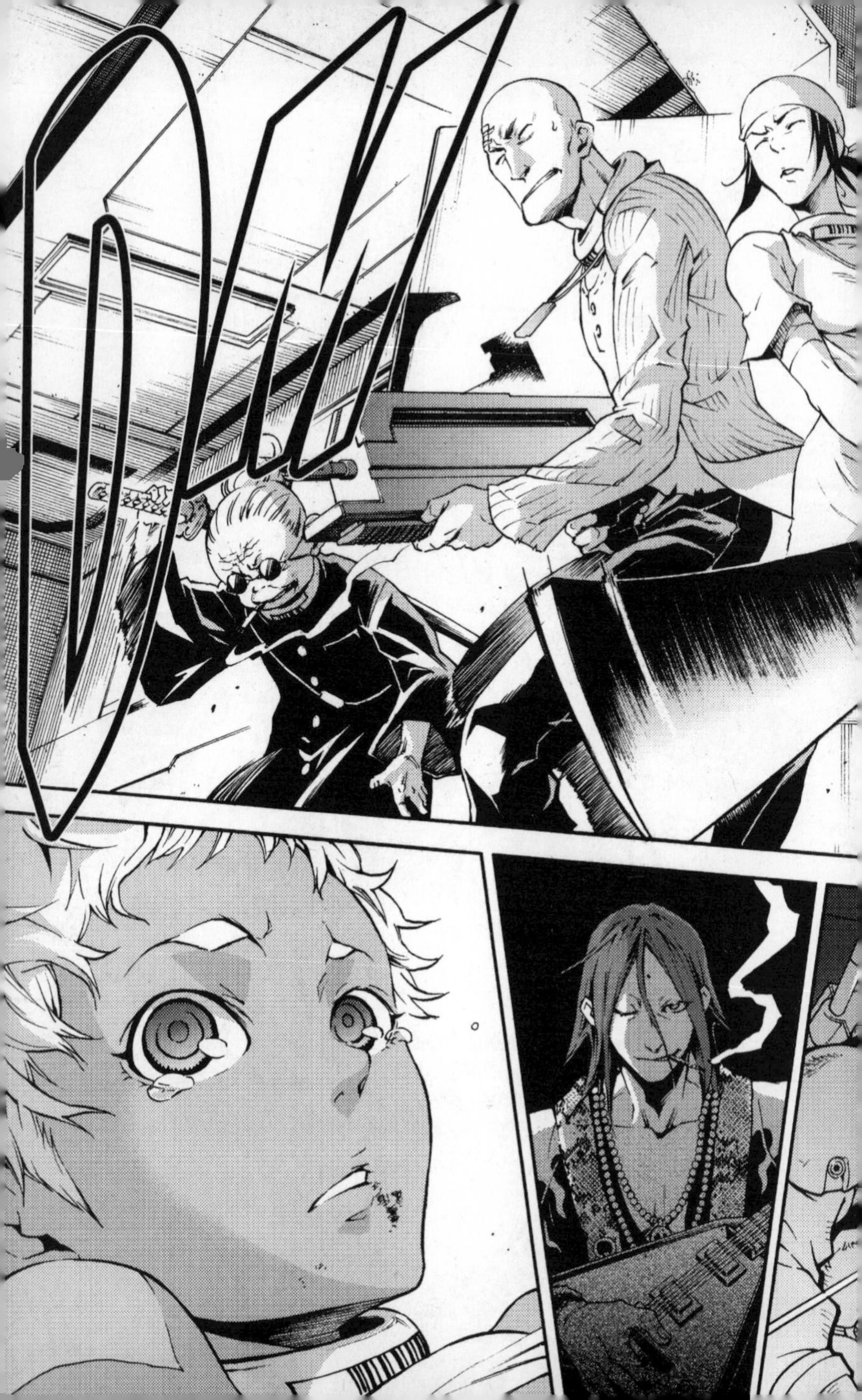

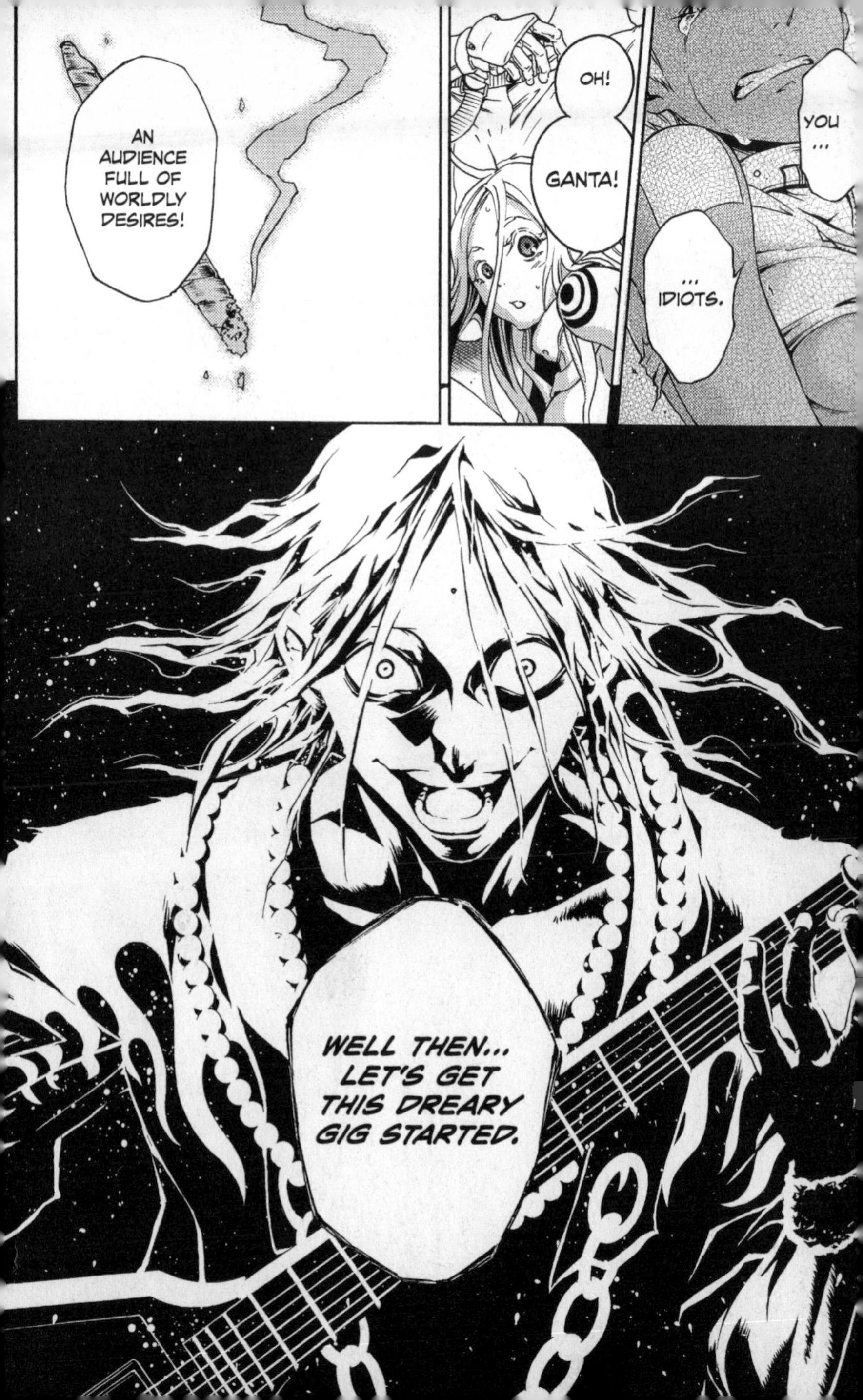
YOU ...
... IDIOTS.
OH!
GANTA!
AN AUDIENCE FULL OF WORLDLY DESIRES!
WELL THEN... LET'S GET THIS DREARY GIG STARTED.

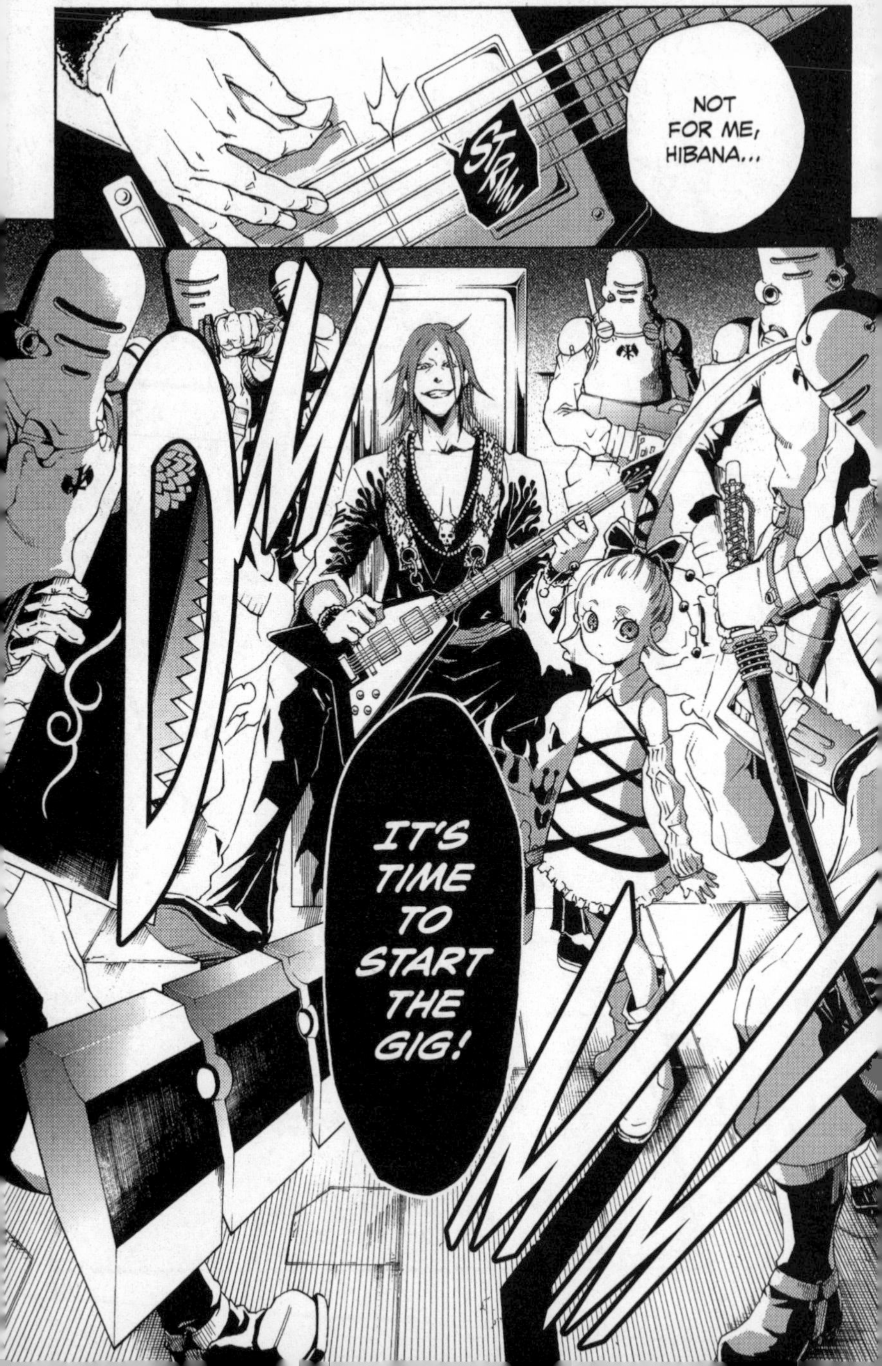
NOT FOR ME, HIBANA...
STRMM
IT'S TIME TO START THE GIG!

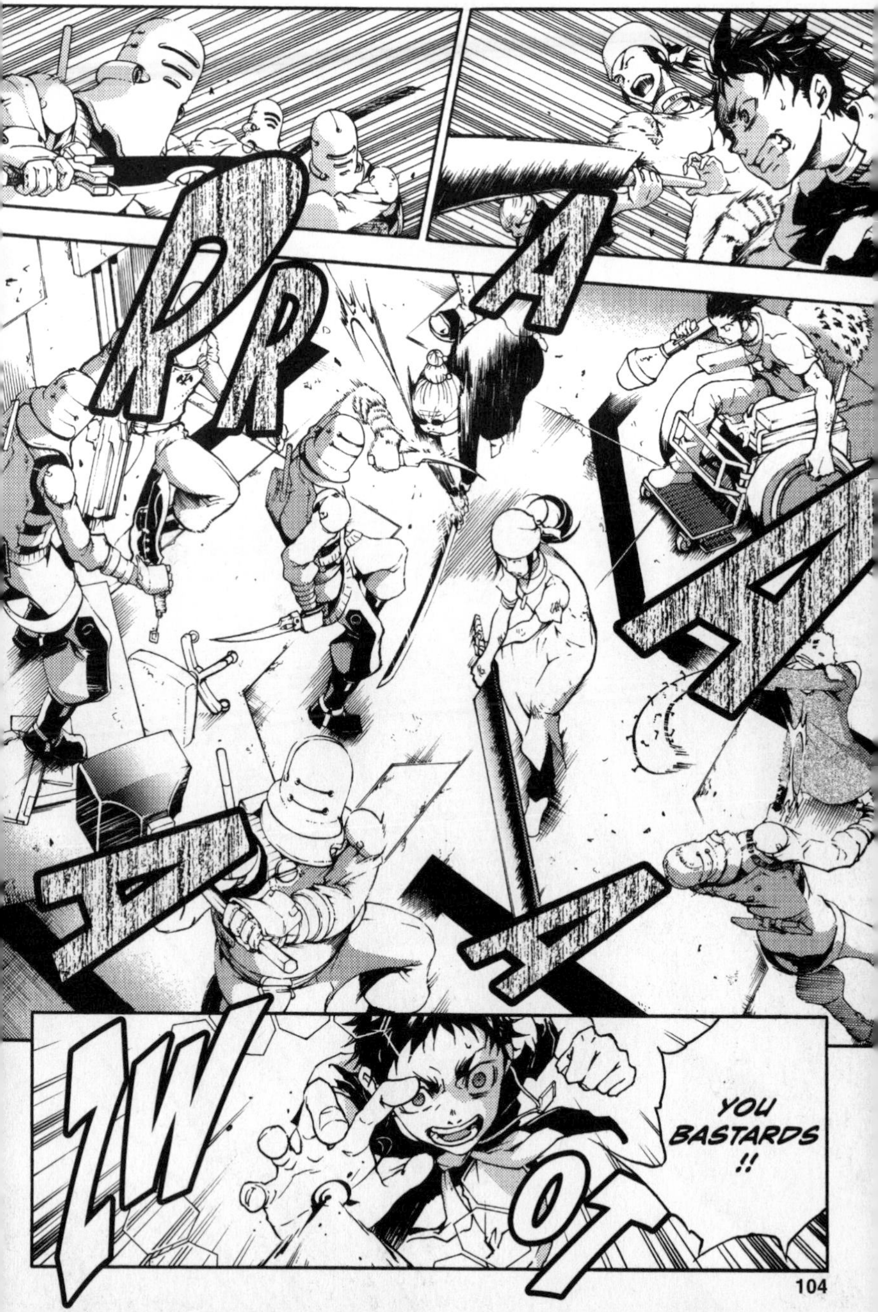

RR
A
ZZ
ZZ
A
YOU BASTARDS !!
ZW
OT

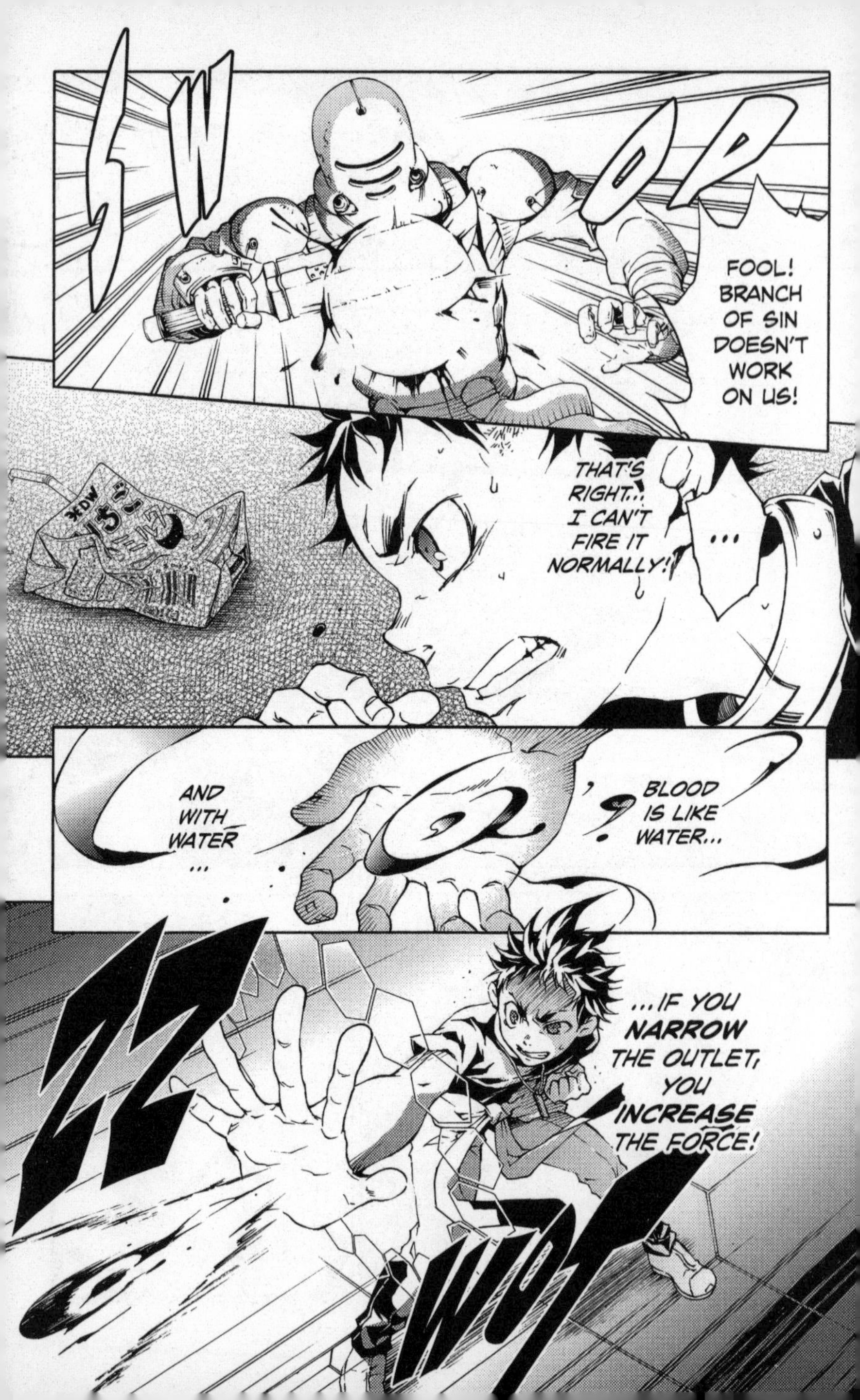
SW
OP
FOOL! BRANCH OF SIN DOESN'T WORK ON US!
THAT'S RIGHT... I CAN'T FIRE IT NORMALLY!
...
BLOOD IS LIKE WATER...
AND WITH WATER ...
...IF YOU **NARROW** THE OUTLET, YOU **INCREASE** THE FORCE!

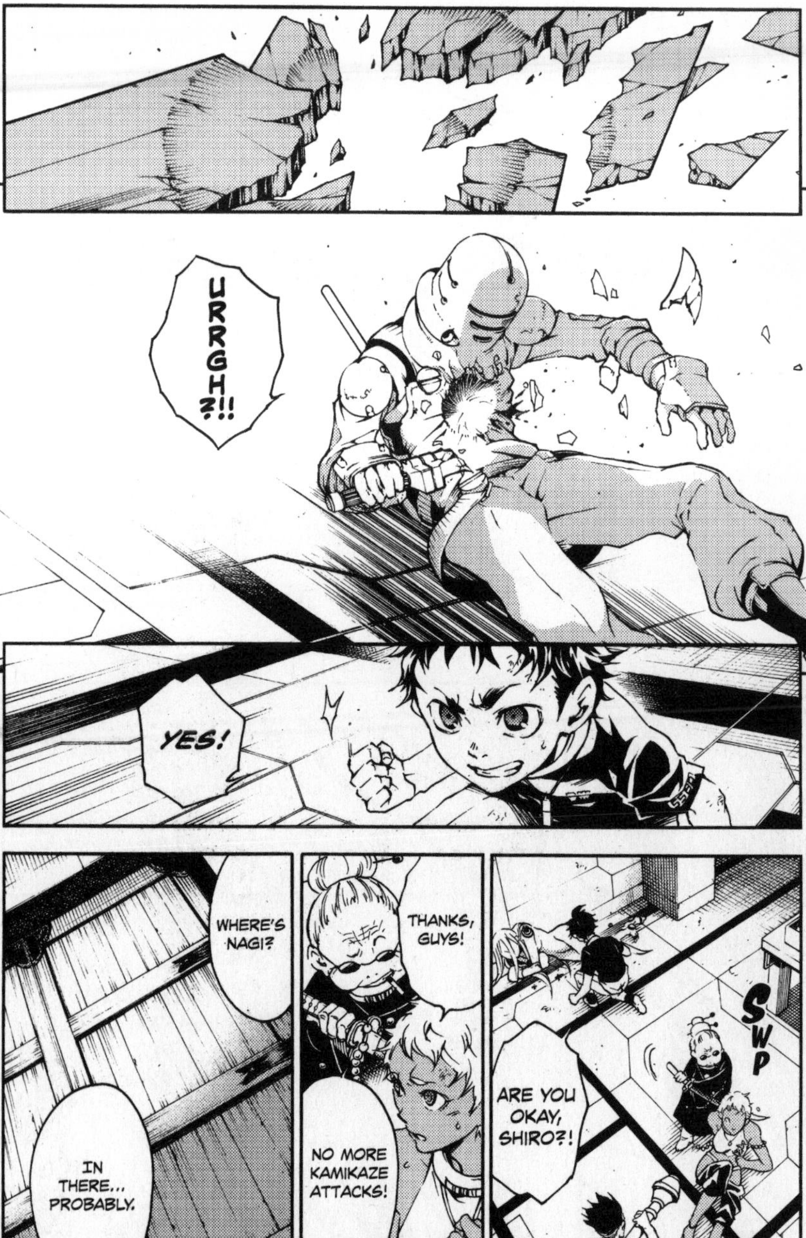
URRGH?!!
YES!
ARE YOU OKAY, SHIRO?!
SWP
THANKS, GUYS!
NO MORE KAMIKAZE ATTACKS!
WHERE'S NAGI?
IN THERE... PROBABLY.

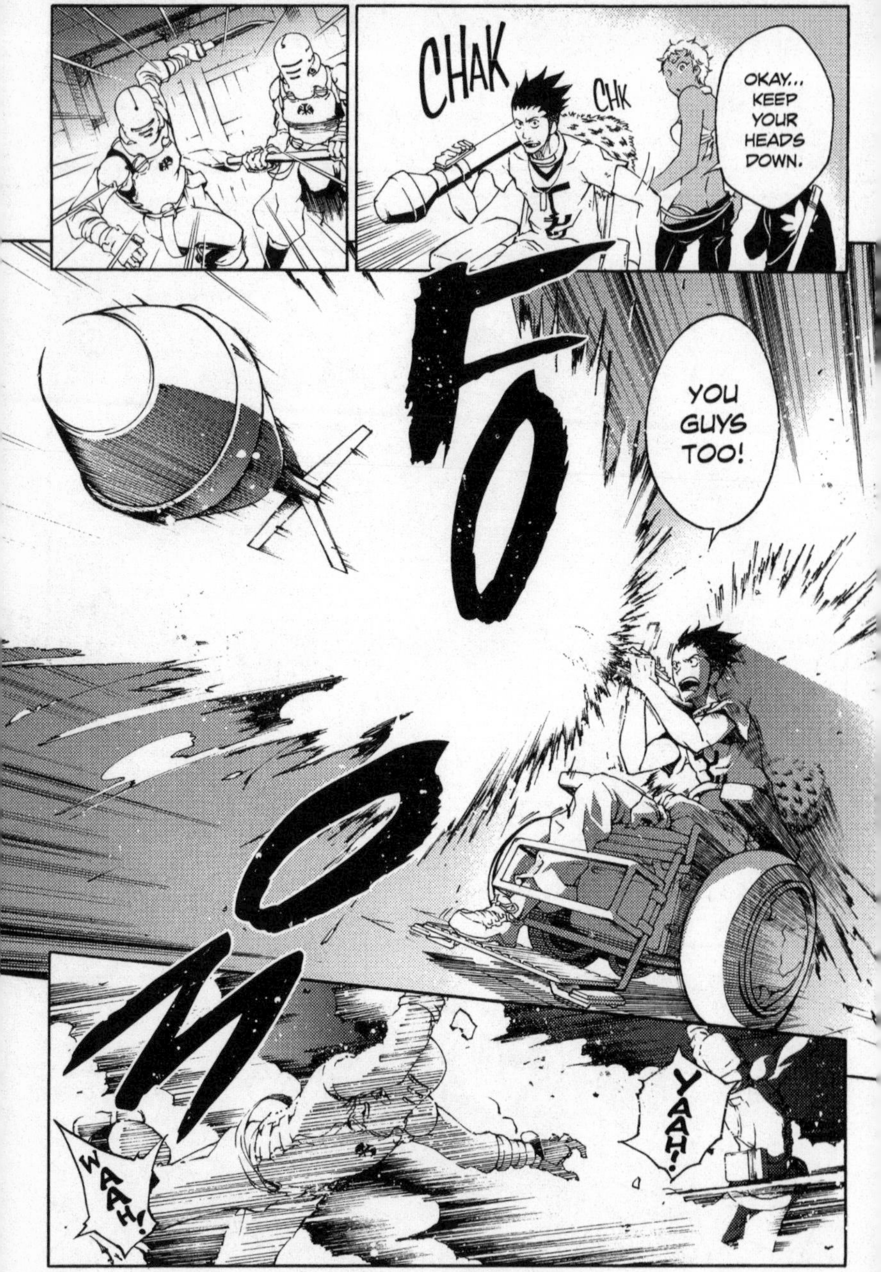
OKAY... KEEP YOUR HEADS DOWN.
CHAK
CHK
YOU GUYS TOO!
5
O
O
M
YAAH!
WAAH!

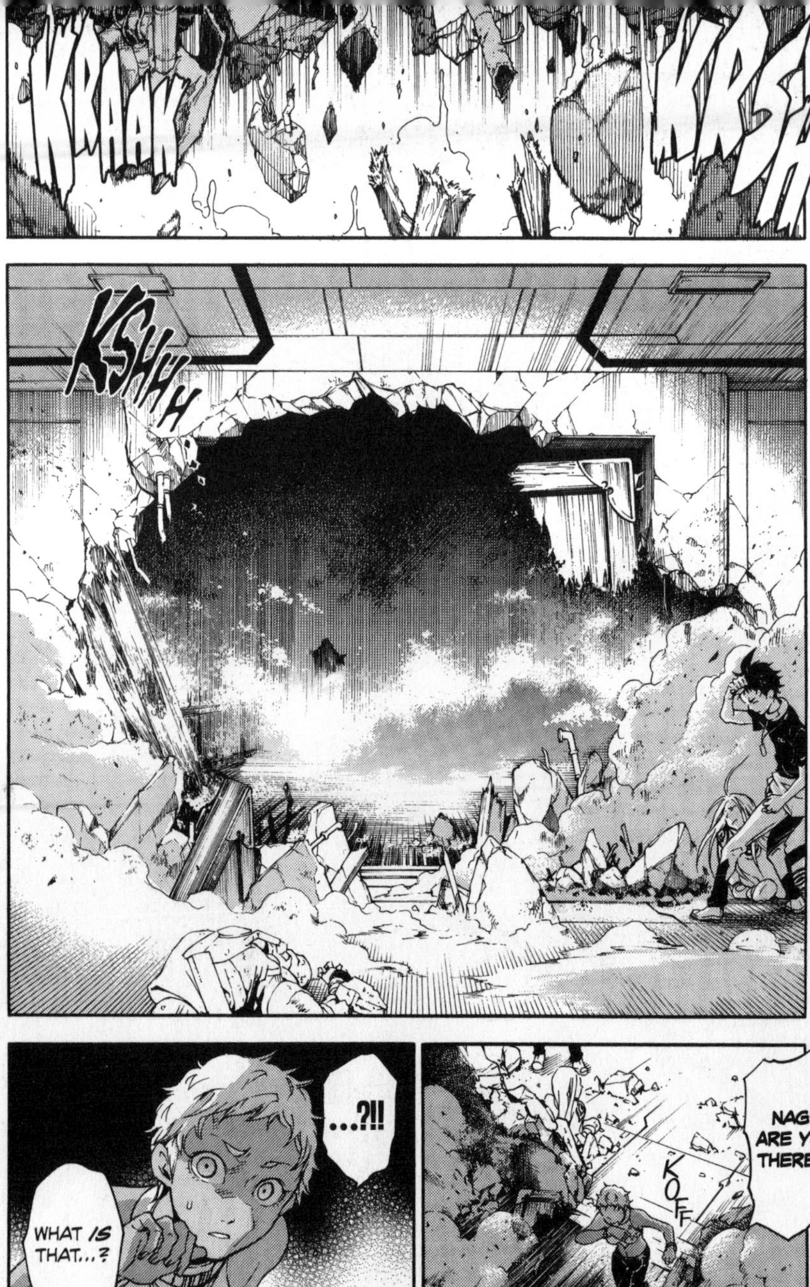
KRSH
KRAAK
KSHHH
NAGI! ARE YOU THERE?!
KOFF
...?!!
WHAT IS THAT...?

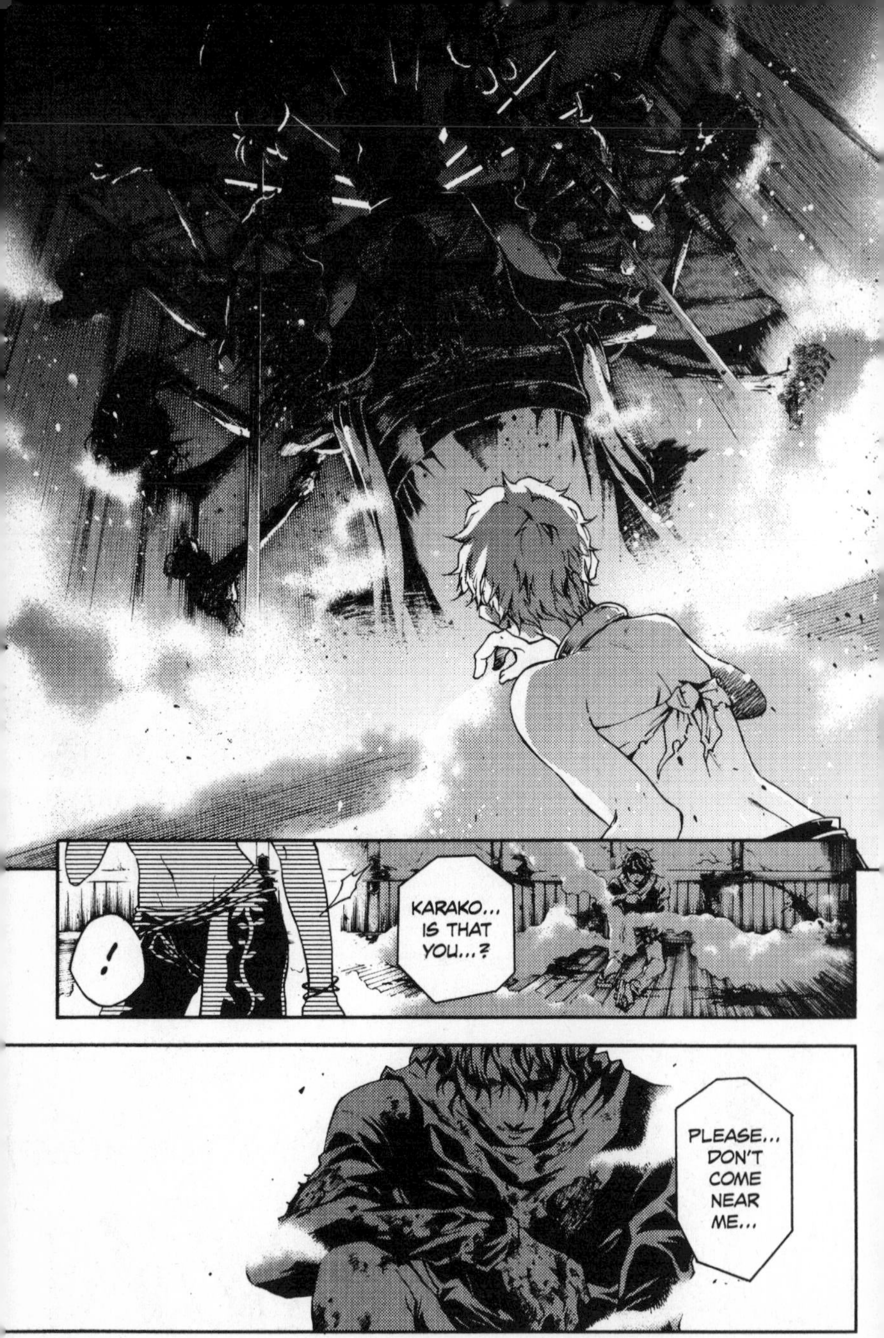
KARAKO... IS THAT YOU...?
!
PLEASE... DON'T COME NEAR ME...

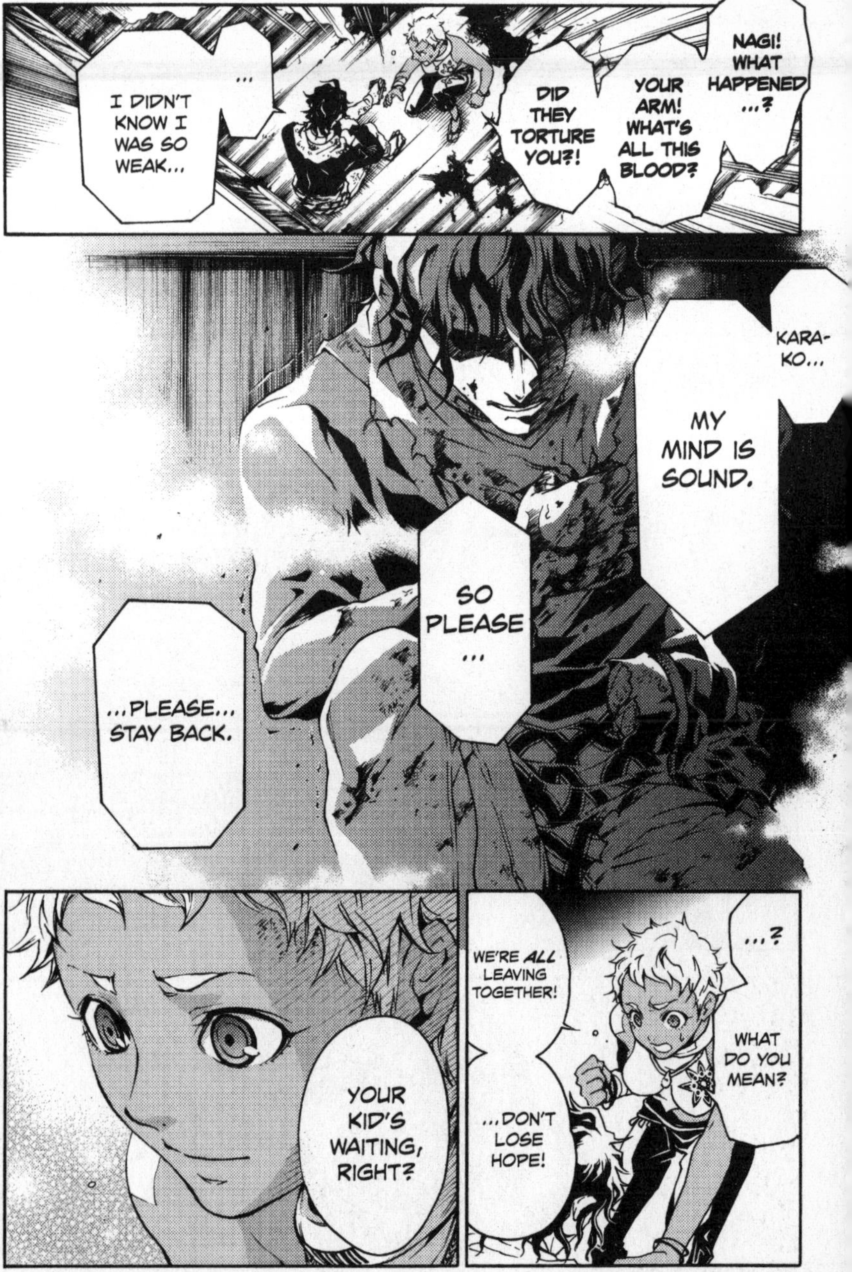
NAGI! WHAT HAPPENED ...?
YOUR ARM! WHAT'S ALL THIS BLOOD?
DID THEY TORTURE YOU?!
...
I DIDN'T KNOW I WAS SO WEAK...
KARA-KO...
MY MIND IS SOUND.
SO PLEASE ...
...PLEASE... STAY BACK.
...?
WHAT DO YOU MEAN?
WE'RE ALL LEAVING TOGETHER!
...DON'T LOSE HOPE!
YOUR KID'S WAITING, RIGHT?

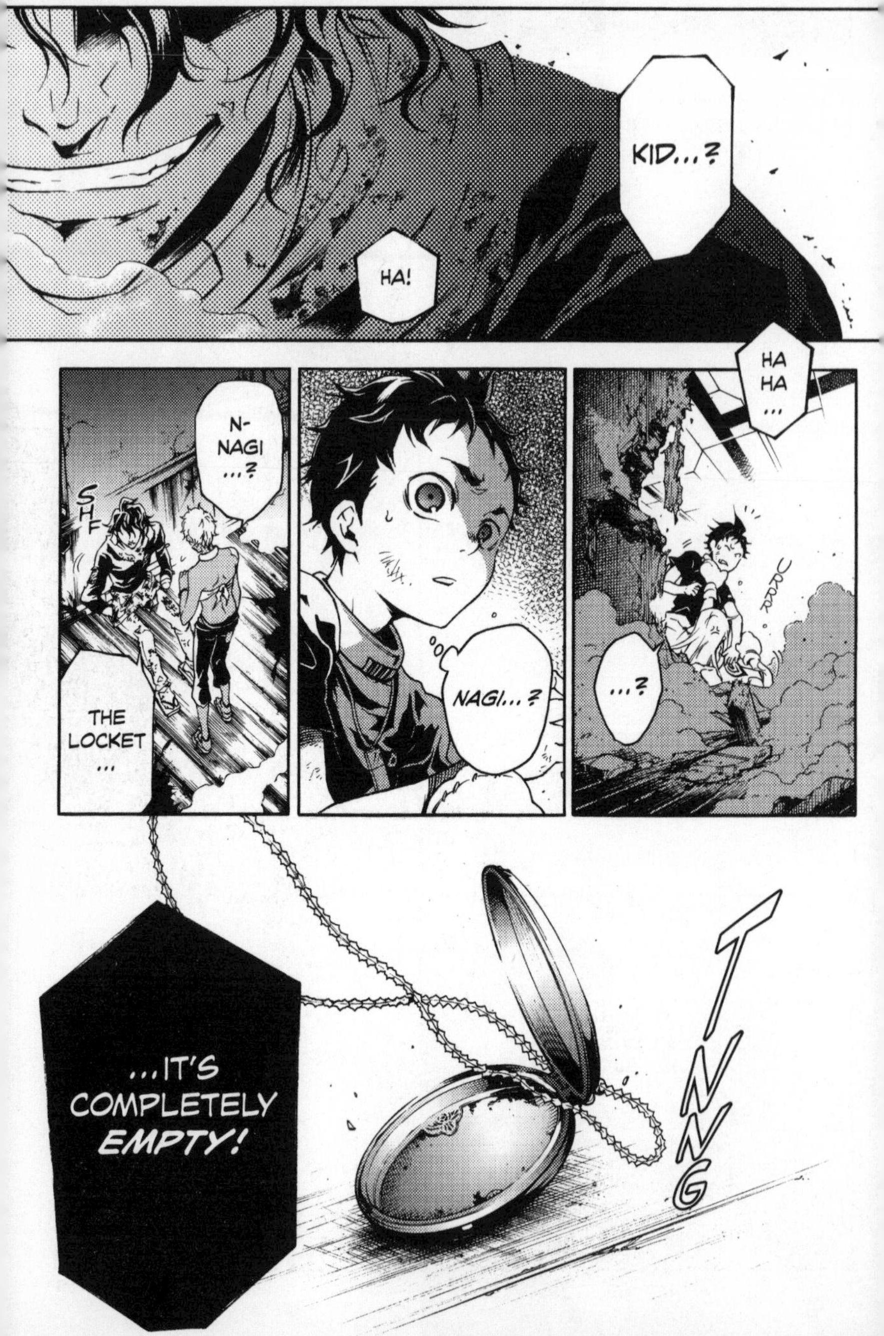
KID...?
HA!
HA HA ...
URRR
...?
NAGI...?
N-NAGI ...?
SHF
THE LOCKET ...
...IT'S COMPLETELY EMPTY!
TINNG

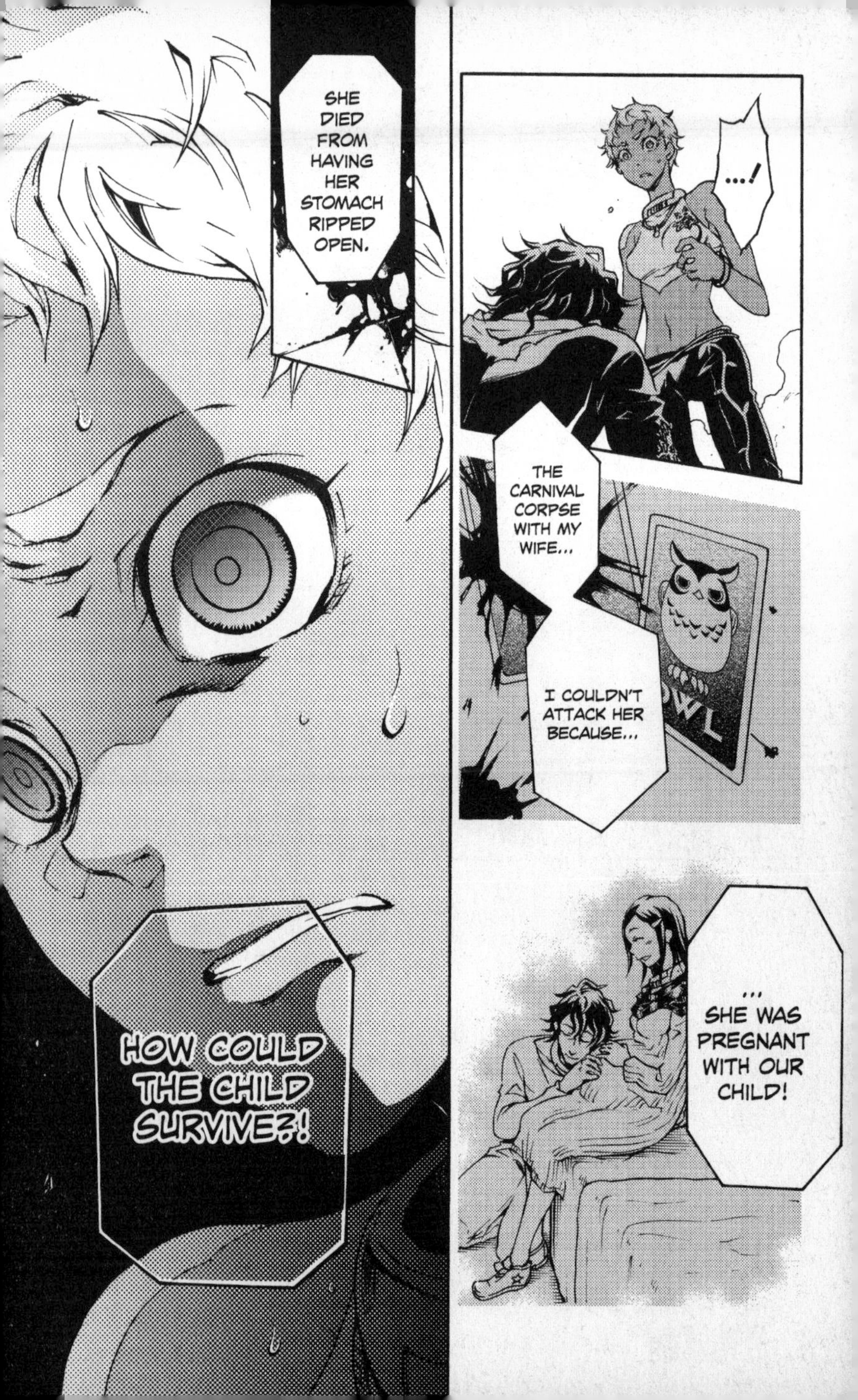
...!
THE CARNIVAL CORPSE WITH MY WIFE...
I COULDN'T ATTACK HER BECAUSE...
... SHE WAS PREGNANT WITH OUR CHILD!
SHE DIED FROM HAVING HER STOMACH RIPPED OPEN.
HOW COULD THE CHILD SURVIVE?!

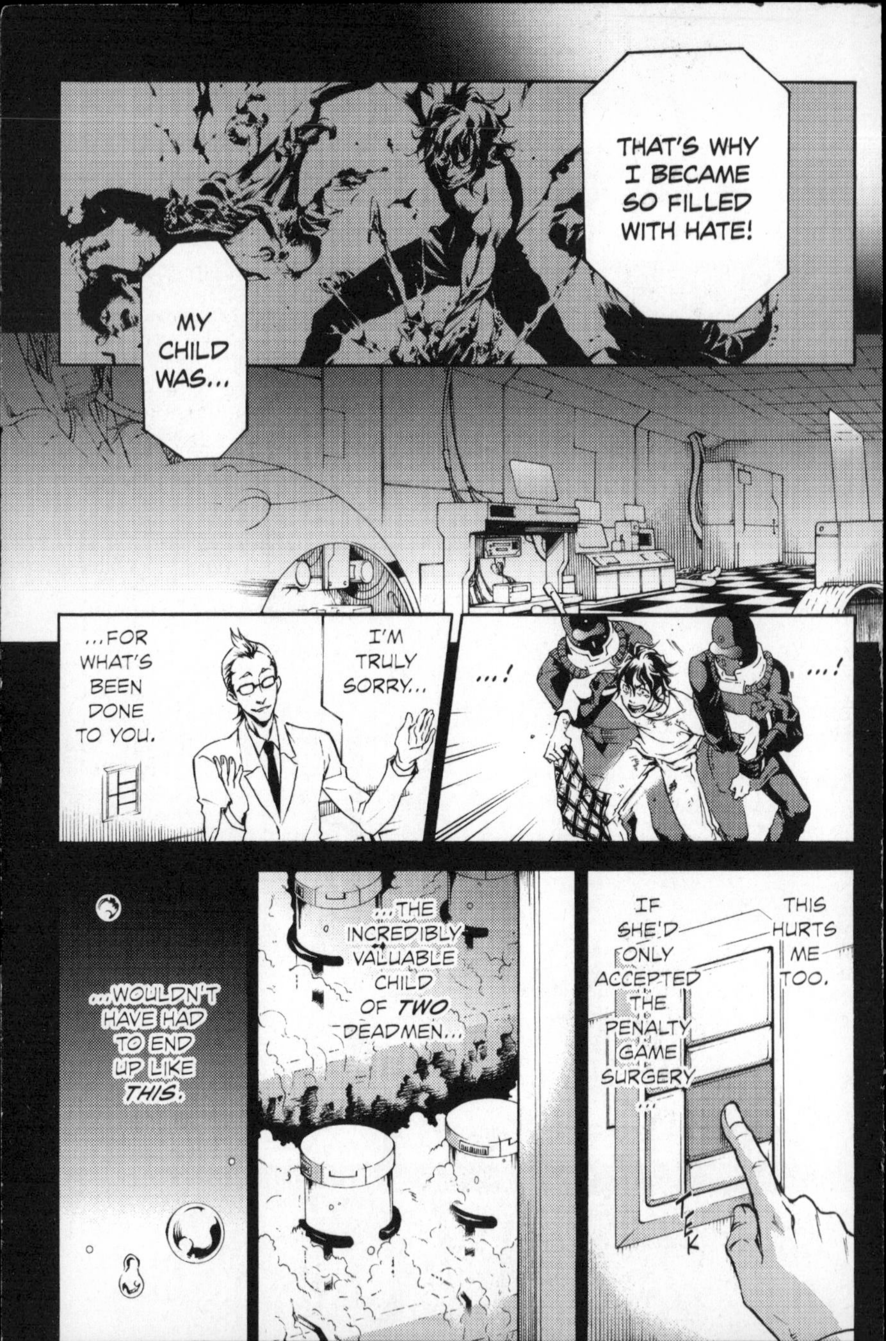
THAT'S WHY I BECAME SO FILLED WITH HATE!
MY CHILD WAS...
...!
...!
I'M TRULY SORRY...
...FOR WHAT'S BEEN DONE TO YOU.
THIS HURTS ME TOO.
IF SHE'D ONLY ACCEPTED THE PENALTY GAME SURGERY...
TEK
...THE INCREDIBLY VALUABLE CHILD OF TWO DEADMEN...
...WOULDN'T HAVE HAD TO END UP LIKE THIS.

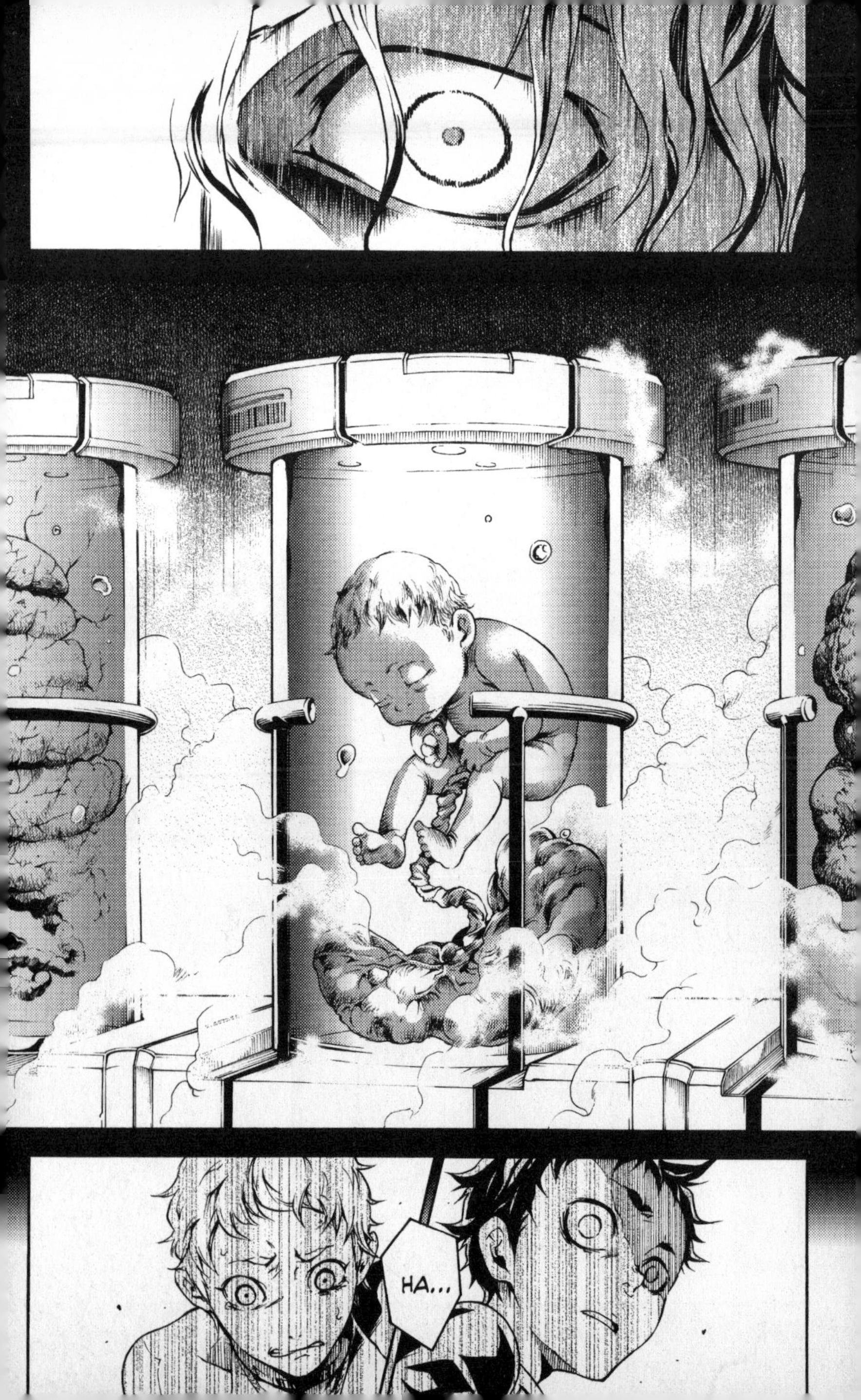
HA...

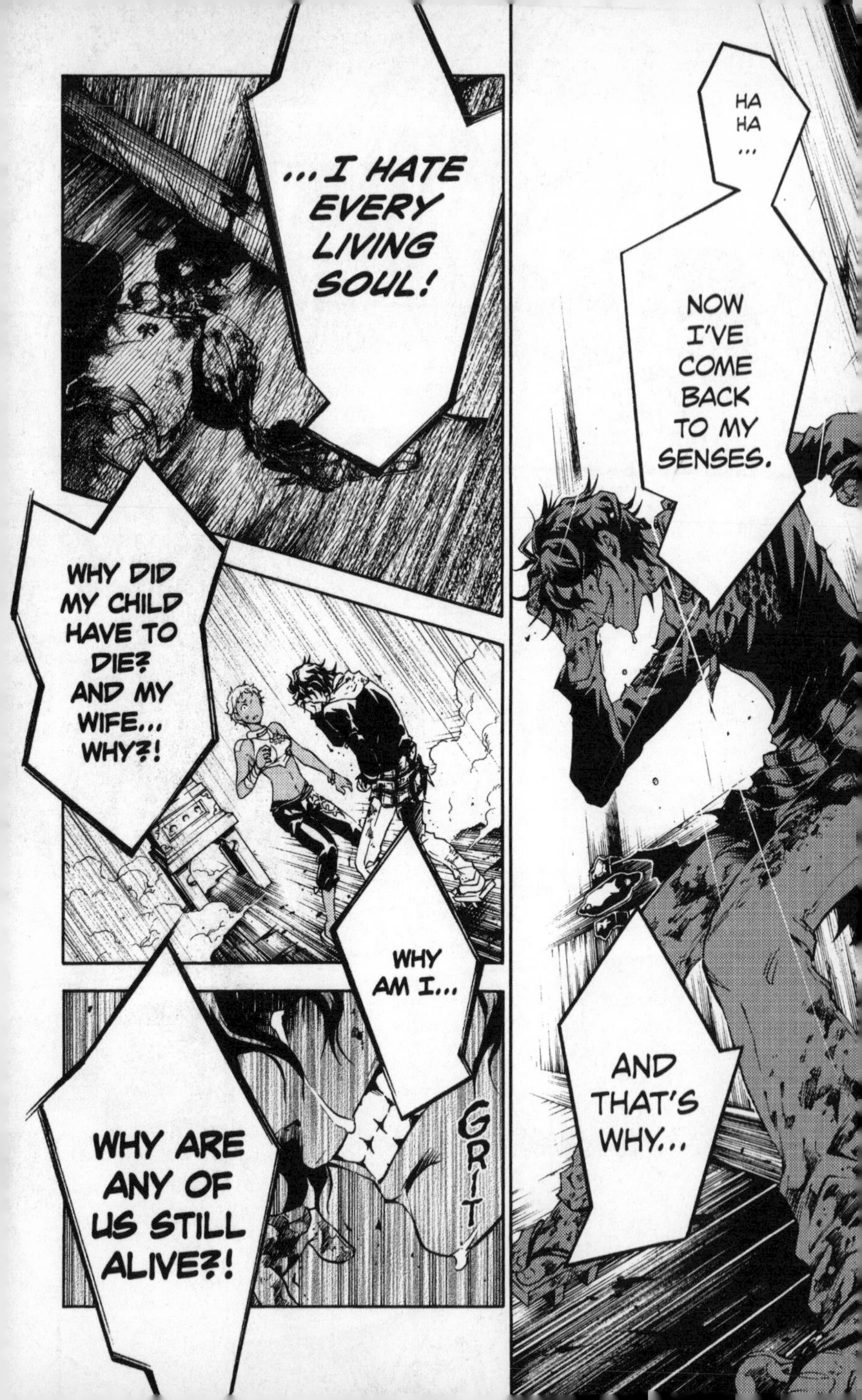
HA HA ...
NOW I'VE COME BACK TO MY SENSES.
AND THAT'S WHY...
...I HATE EVERY LIVING SOUL!
WHY DID MY CHILD HAVE TO DIE? AND MY WIFE... WHY?!
WHY AM I...
GRIT
WHY ARE ANY OF US STILL ALIVE?!

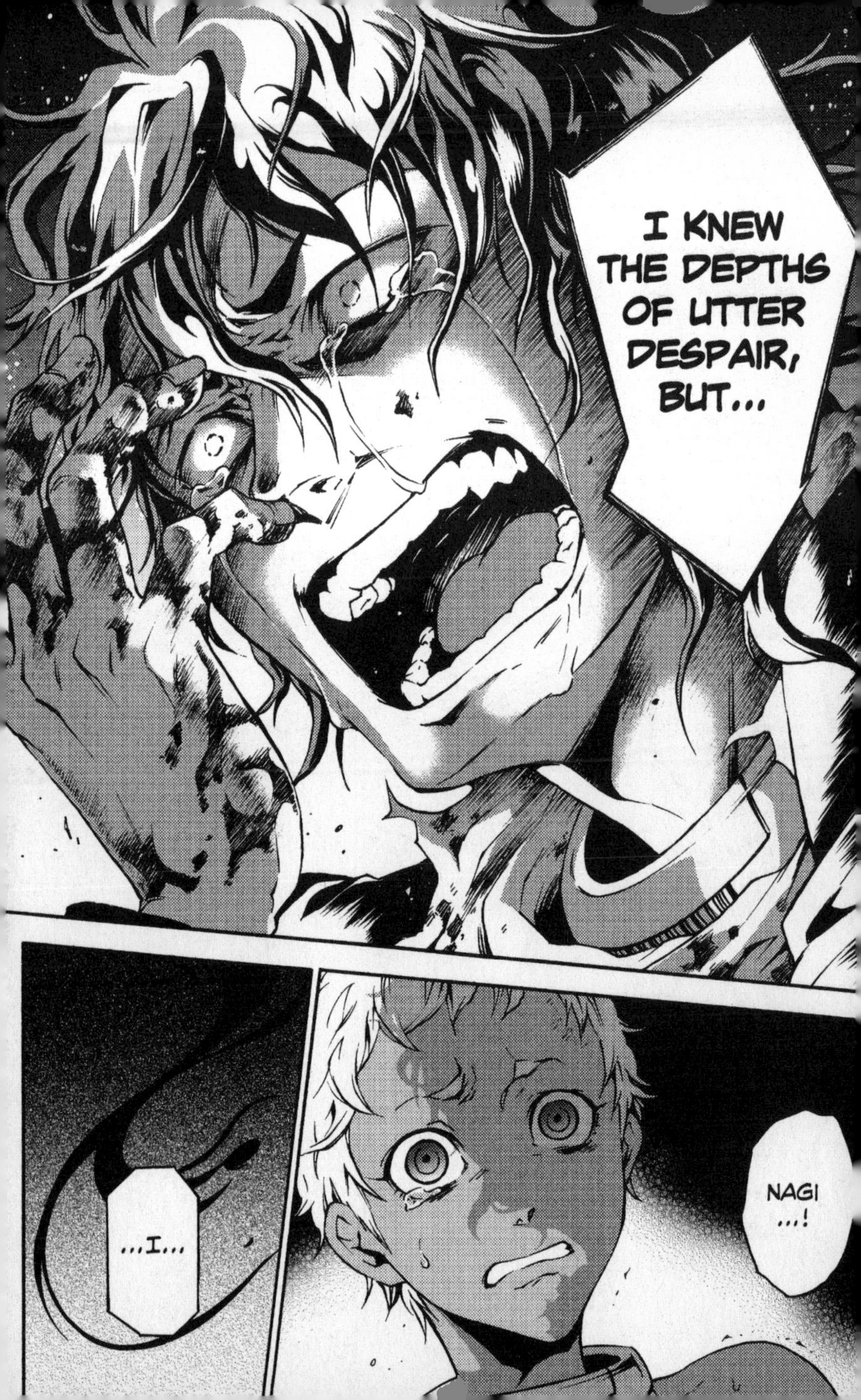
I KNEW THE DEPTHS OF UTTER DESPAIR, BUT...
NAGI ...!
...I...

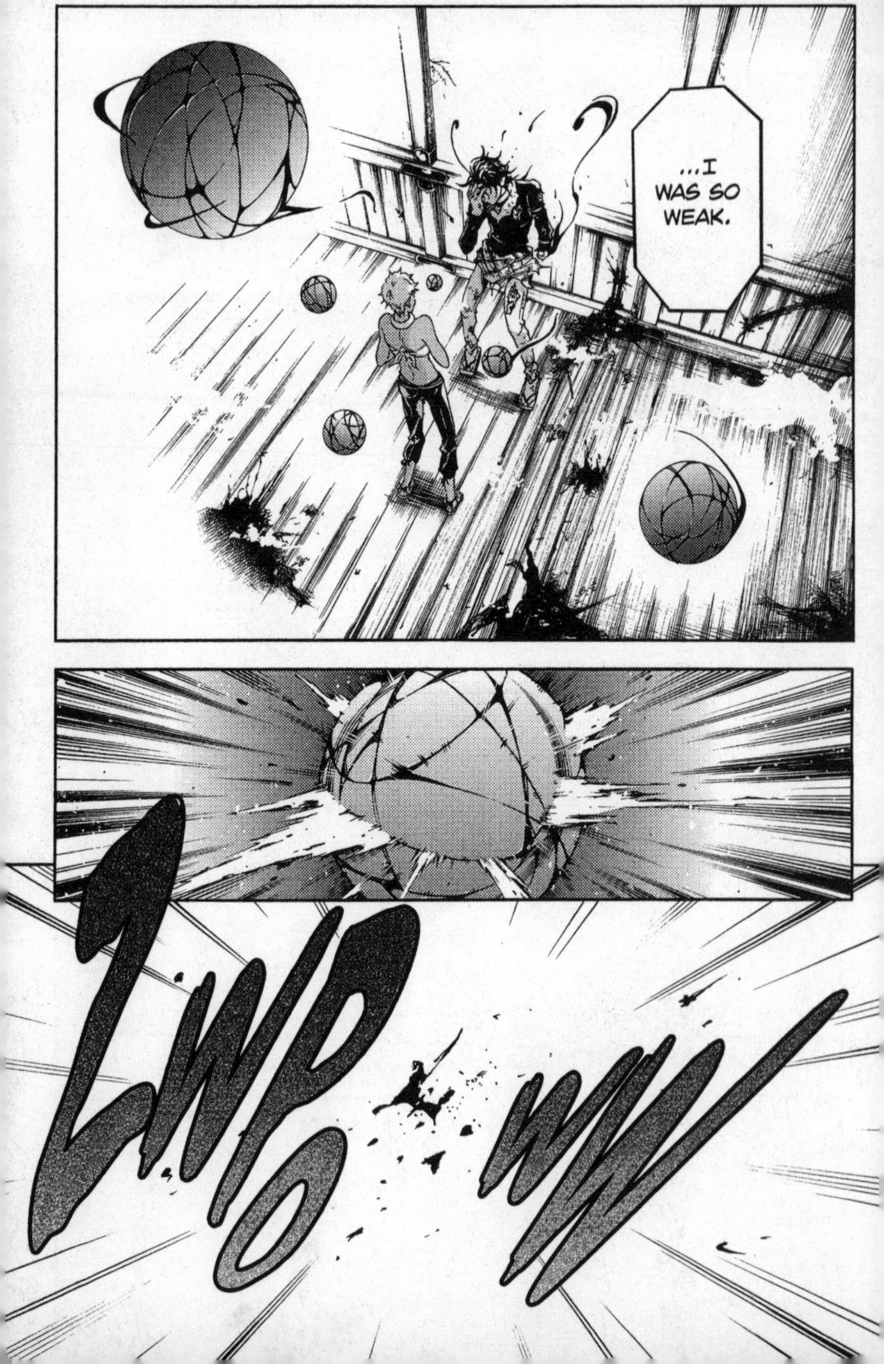
...I WAS SO WEAK.

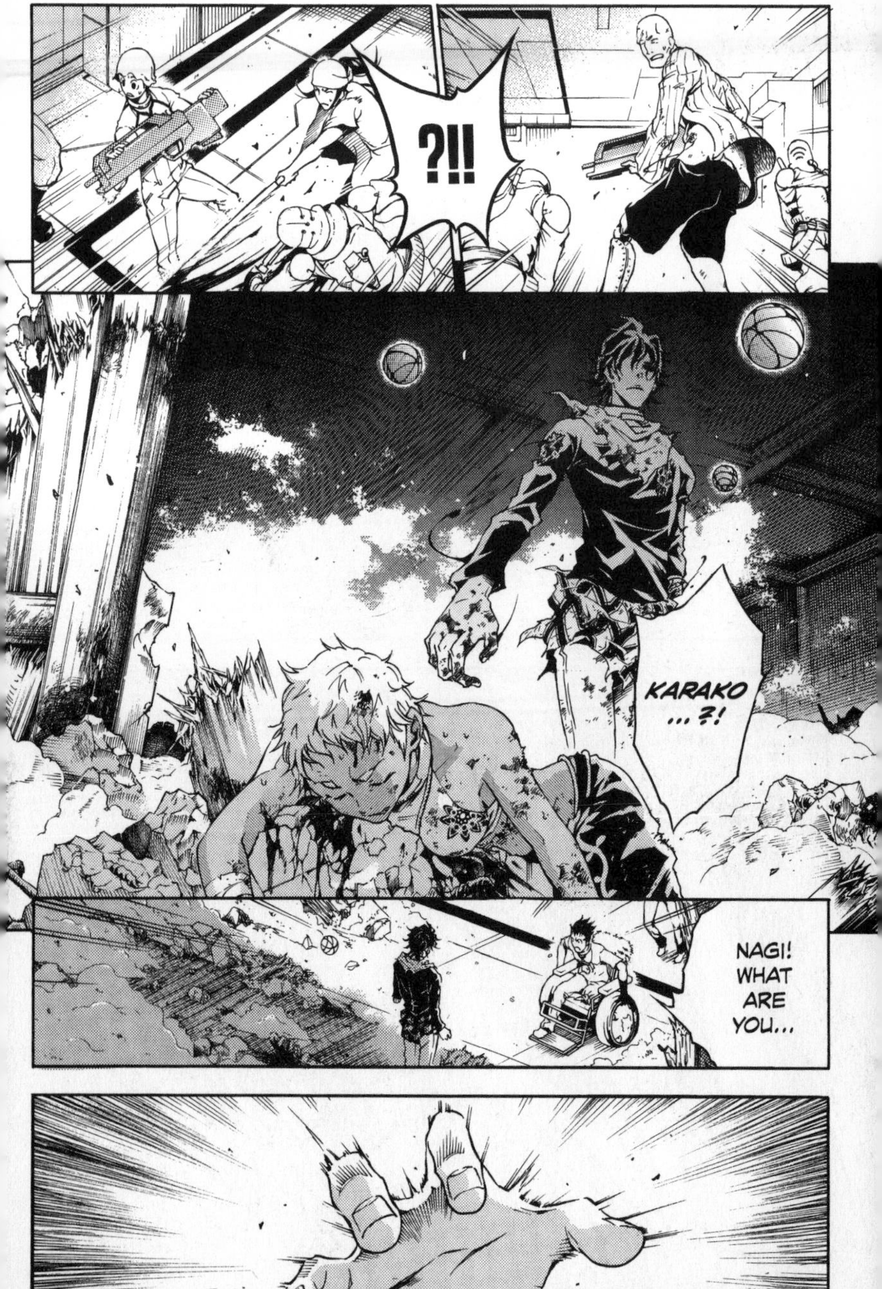
?!!
KARAKO ...?!
NAGI! WHAT ARE YOU...

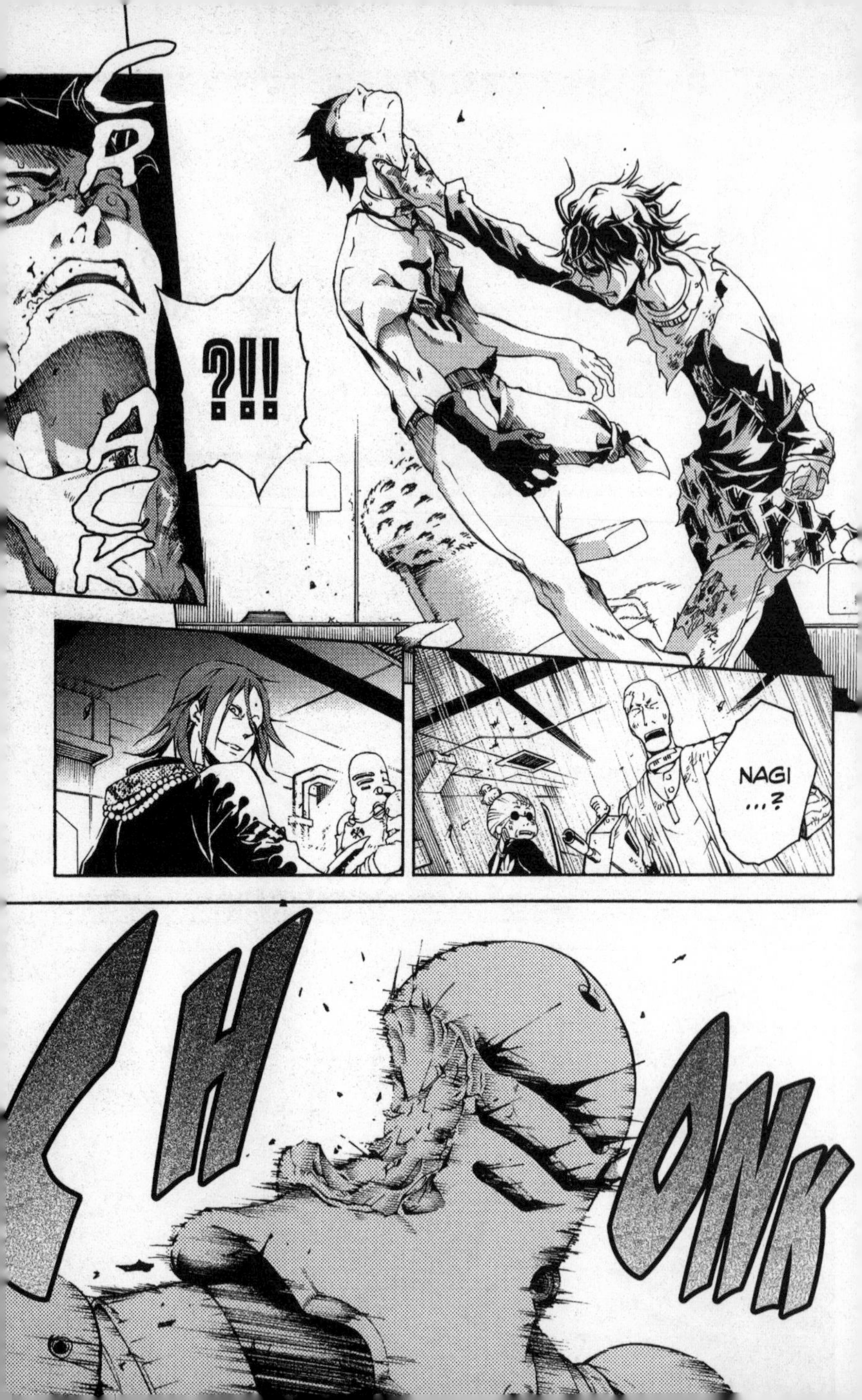
?!!
CRACK
NAGI ...?
CHONK

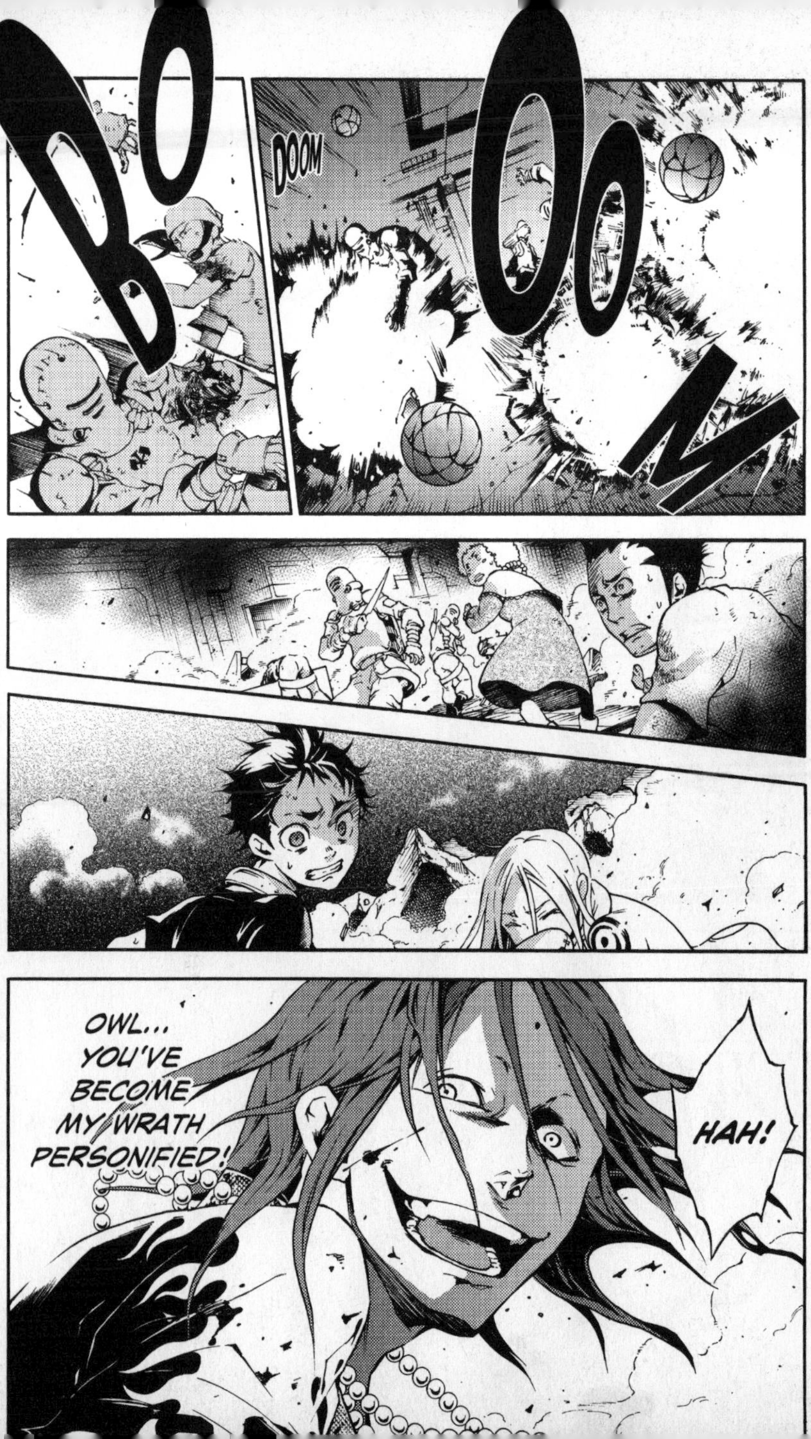
BOOOM
DOOM
HAH!
OWL... YOU'VE BECOME MY WRATH PERSONIFIED!

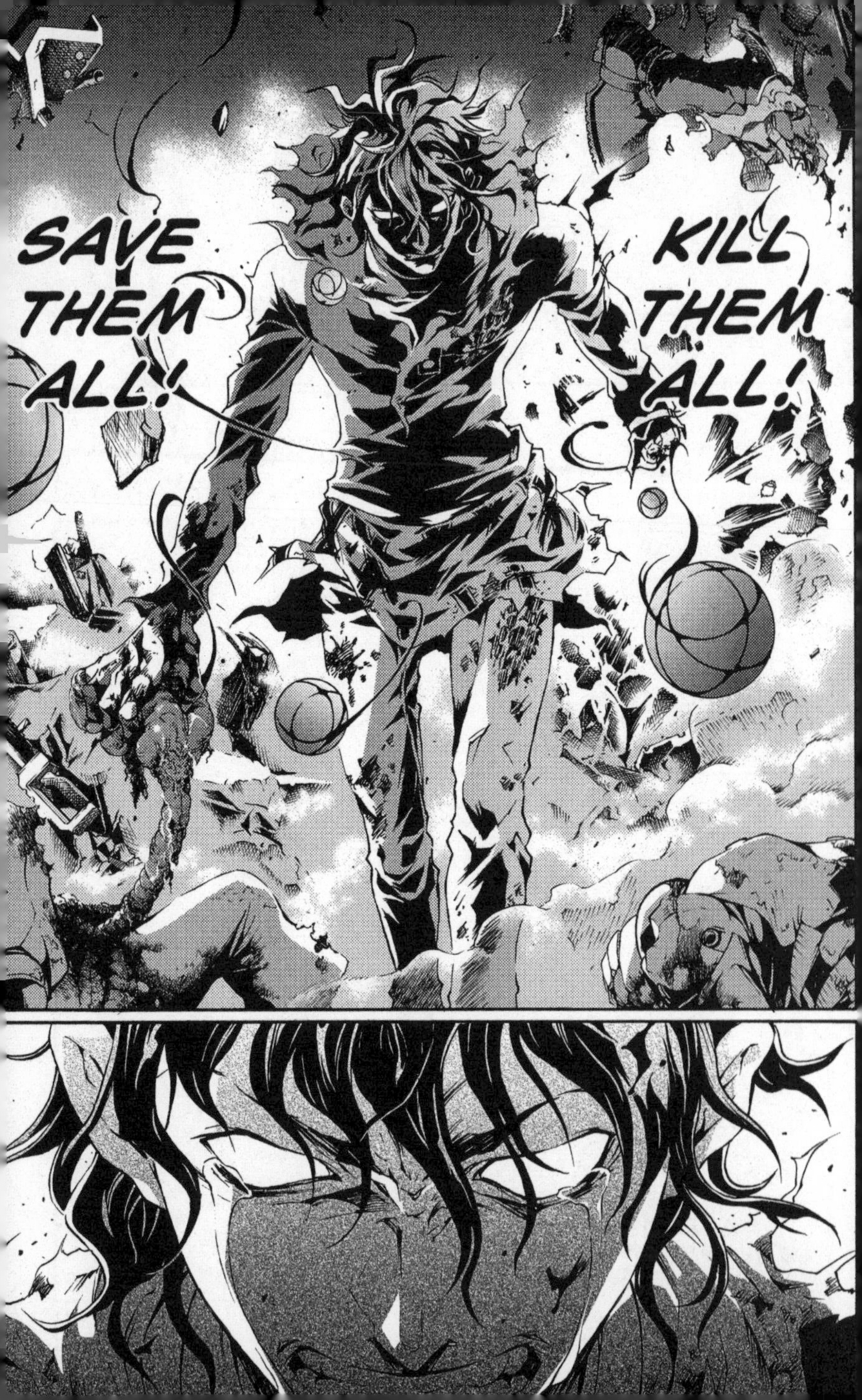
KILL THEM ALL!
SAVE THEM ALL!

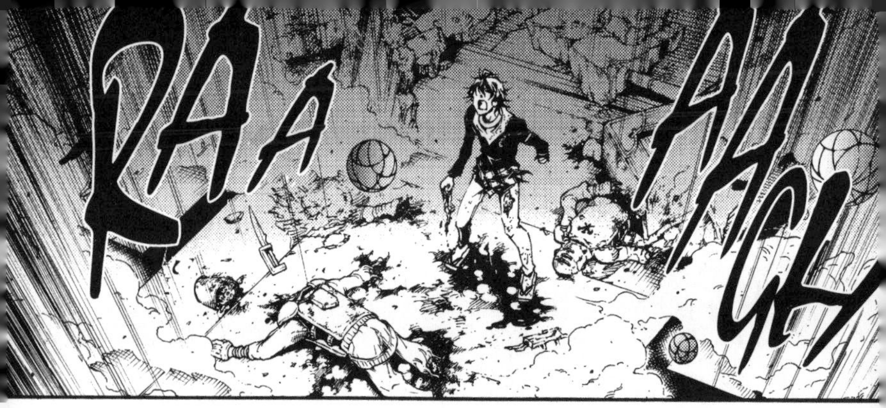
RAAAAAGH

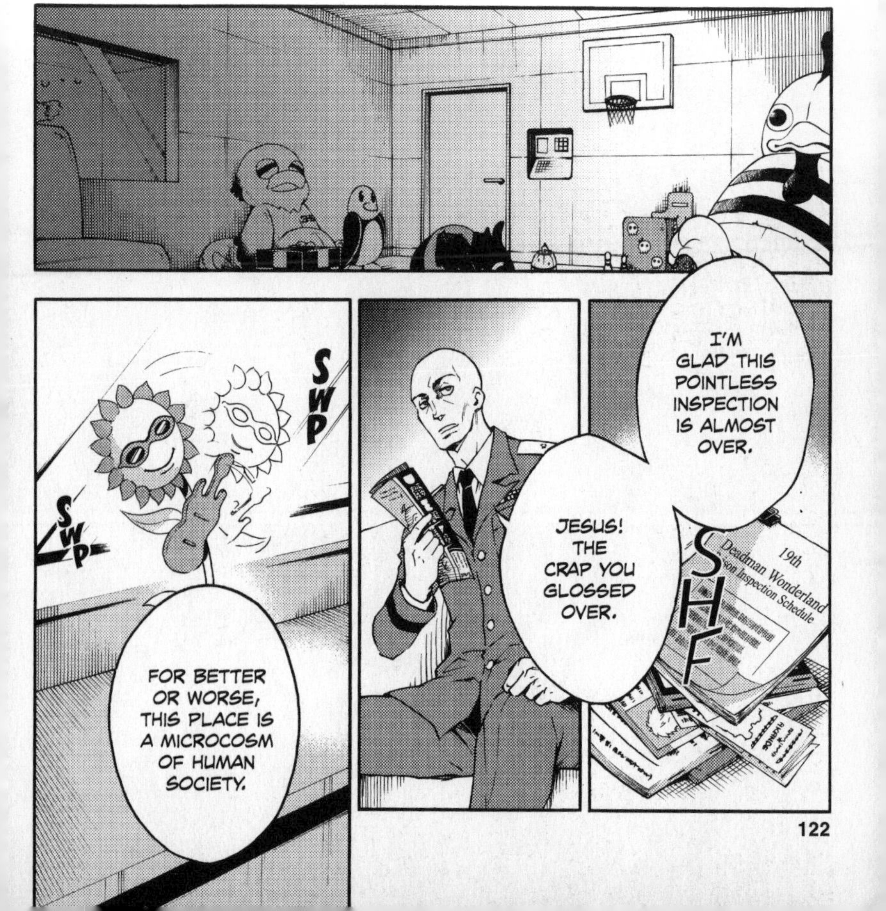
I'M GLAD THIS POINTLESS INSPECTION IS ALMOST OVER.
19th Deadman Wonderland ...son Inspection Schedule
SHF
JESUS! THE CRAP YOU GLOSSED OVER.
SWP
SWP
FOR BETTER OR WORSE, THIS PLACE IS A MICROCOSM OF HUMAN SOCIETY.

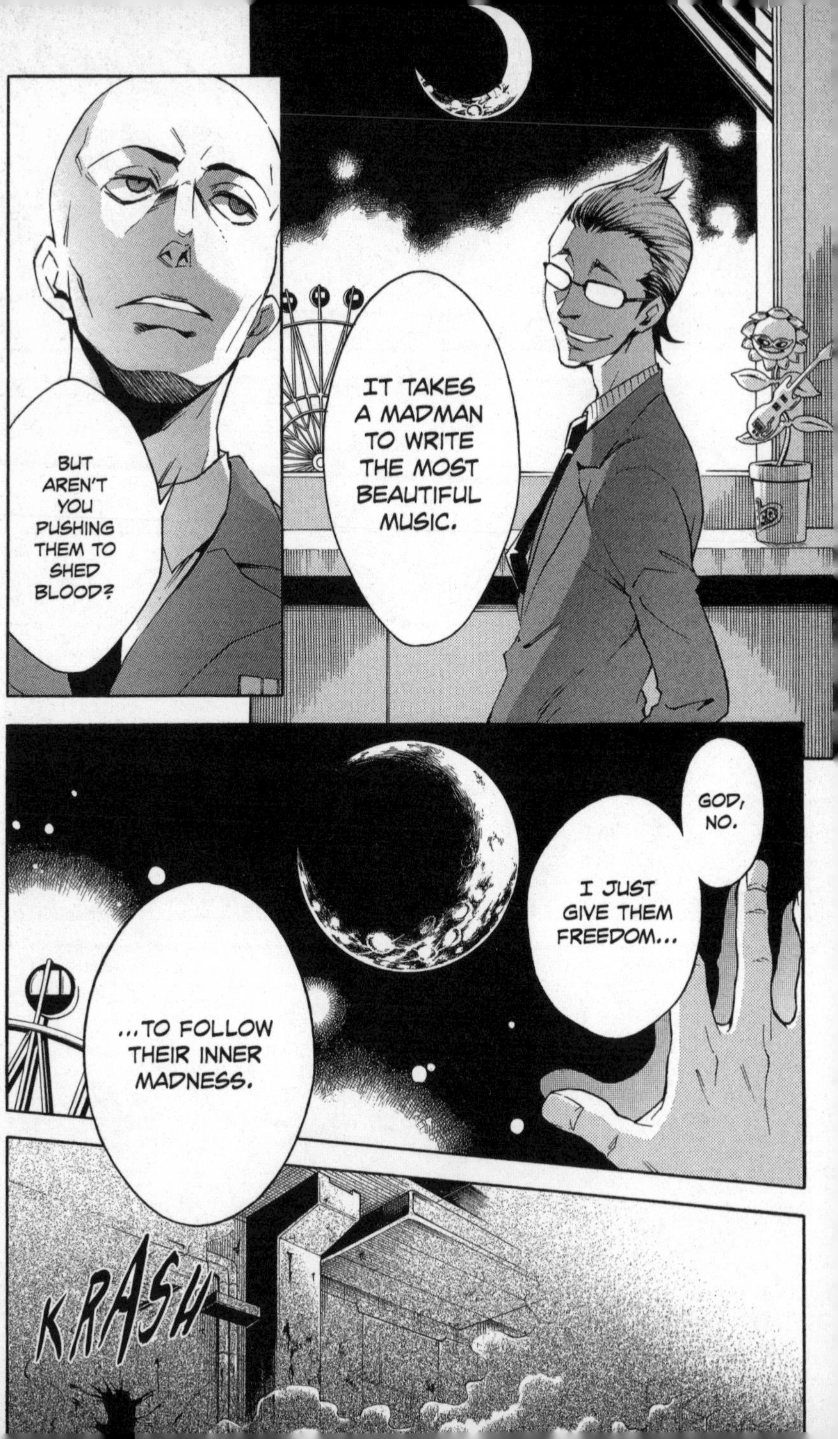
IT TAKES A MADMAN TO WRITE THE MOST BEAUTIFUL MUSIC.
BUT AREN'T YOU PUSHING THEM TO SHED BLOOD?
GOD, NO.
I JUST GIVE THEM FREEDOM...
...TO FOLLOW THEIR INNER MADNESS.
KRASH

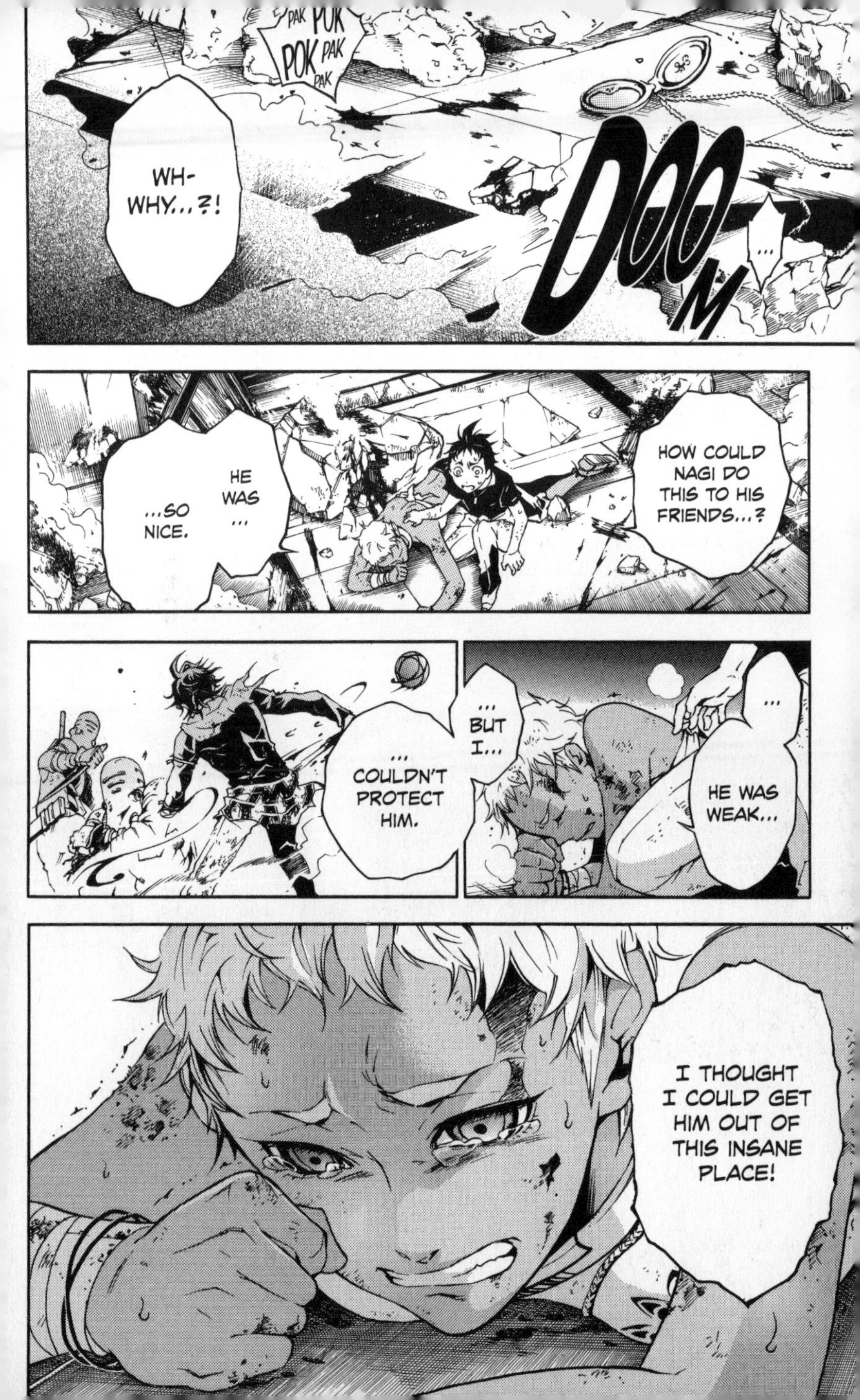
...
DOOOM
PUK PAK POK PAK PAK
WH- WHY...?!
HOW COULD NAGI DO THIS TO HIS FRIENDS...?
HE WAS ...
...SO NICE.
...
HE WAS WEAK...
... BUT I...
... COULDN'T PROTECT HIM.
I THOUGHT I COULD GET HIM OUT OF THIS INSANE PLACE!

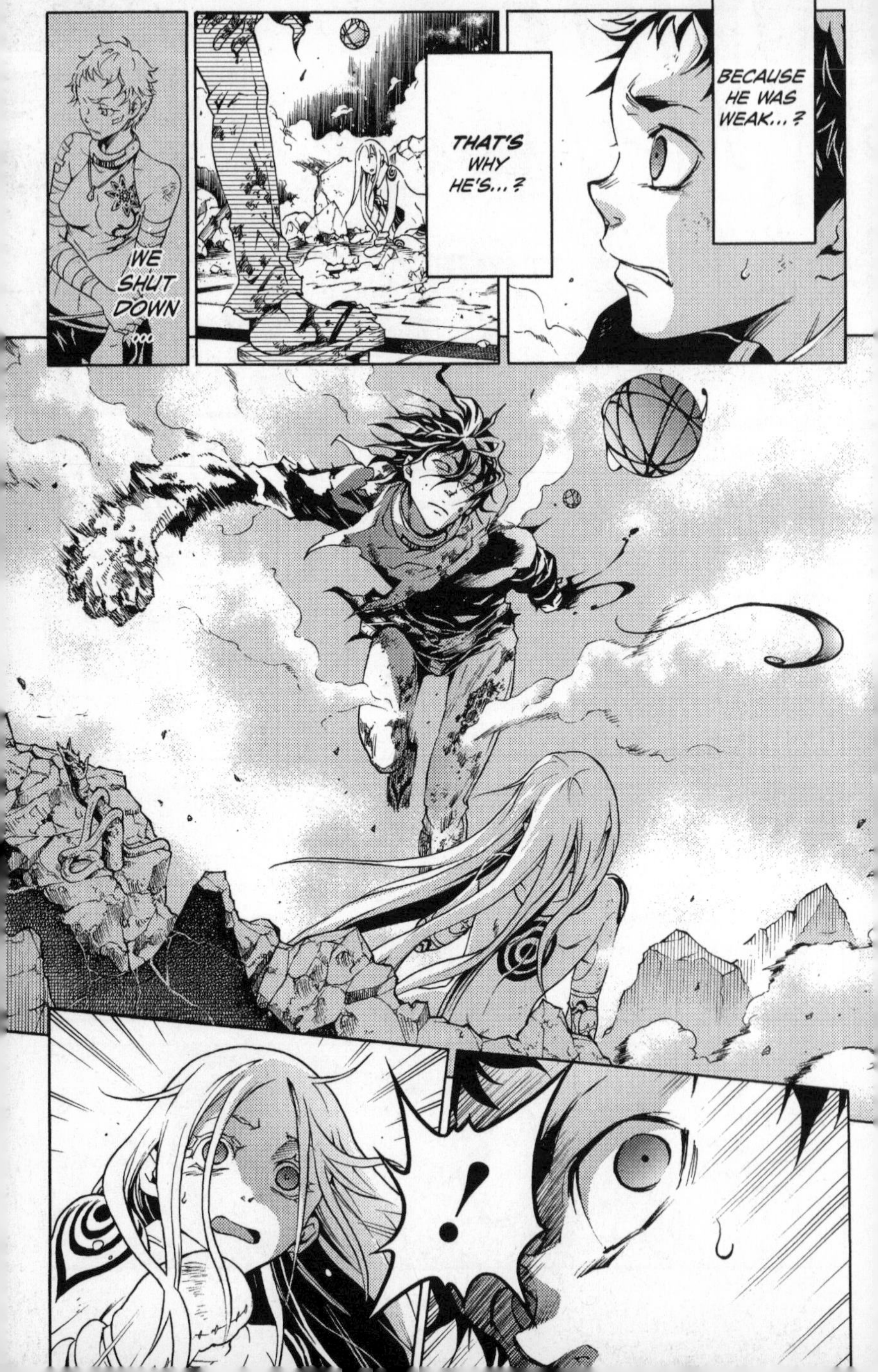
BECAUSE HE WAS WEAK...?
THAT'S WHY HE'S...?
WE SHUT DOWN...
!

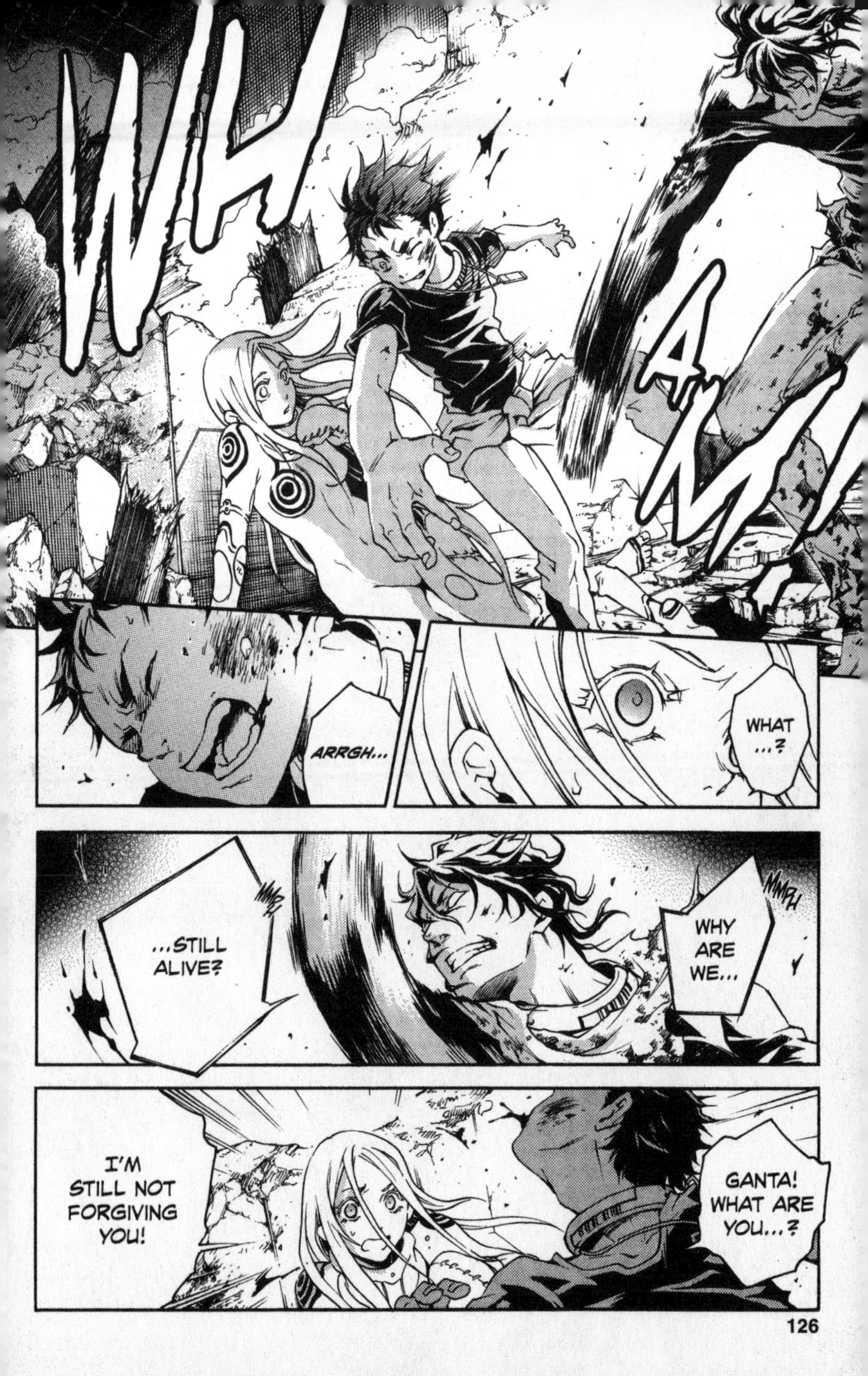
WHAM
WHAT ...?
ARRGH...
MMPH
WHY ARE WE...
MMPH
...STILL ALIVE?
GANTA! WHAT ARE YOU...?
I'M STILL NOT FORGIVING YOU!

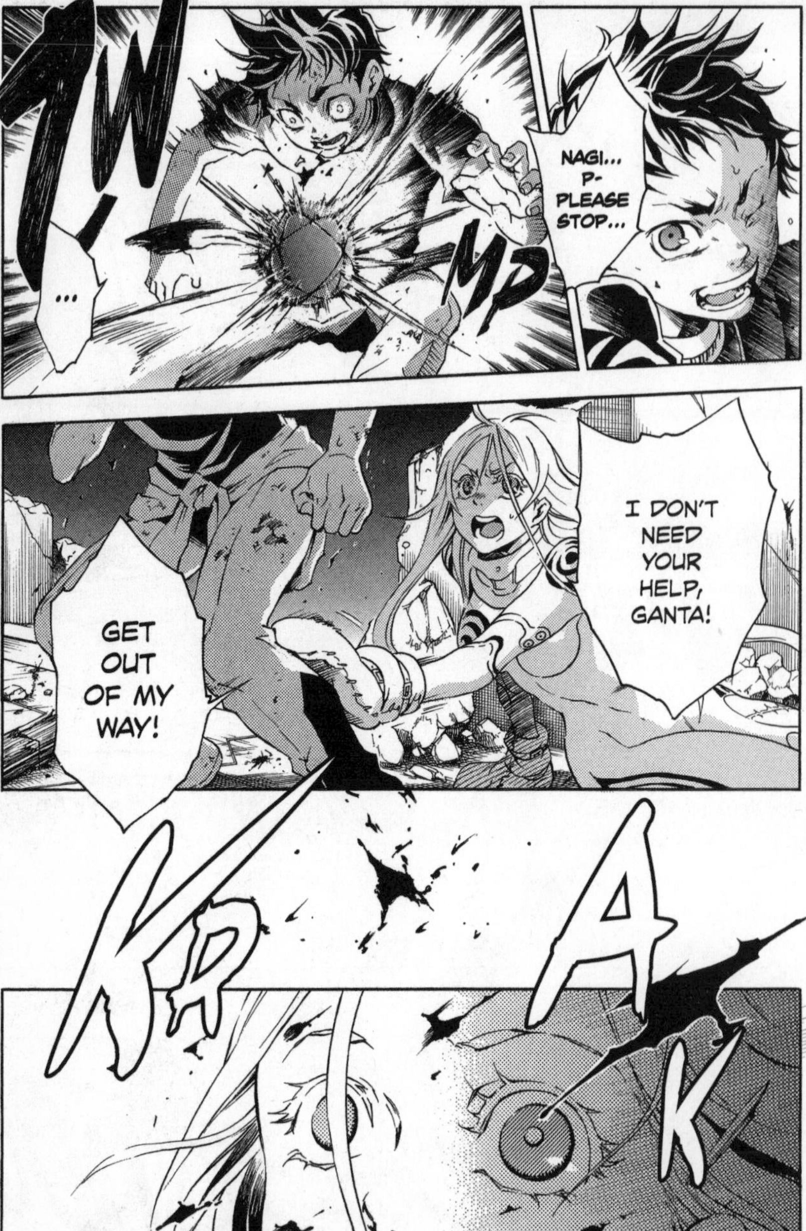
NAGI... P-PLEASE STOP...
THWMP
...
I DON'T NEED YOUR HELP, GANTA!
GET OUT OF MY WAY!
KRAAK

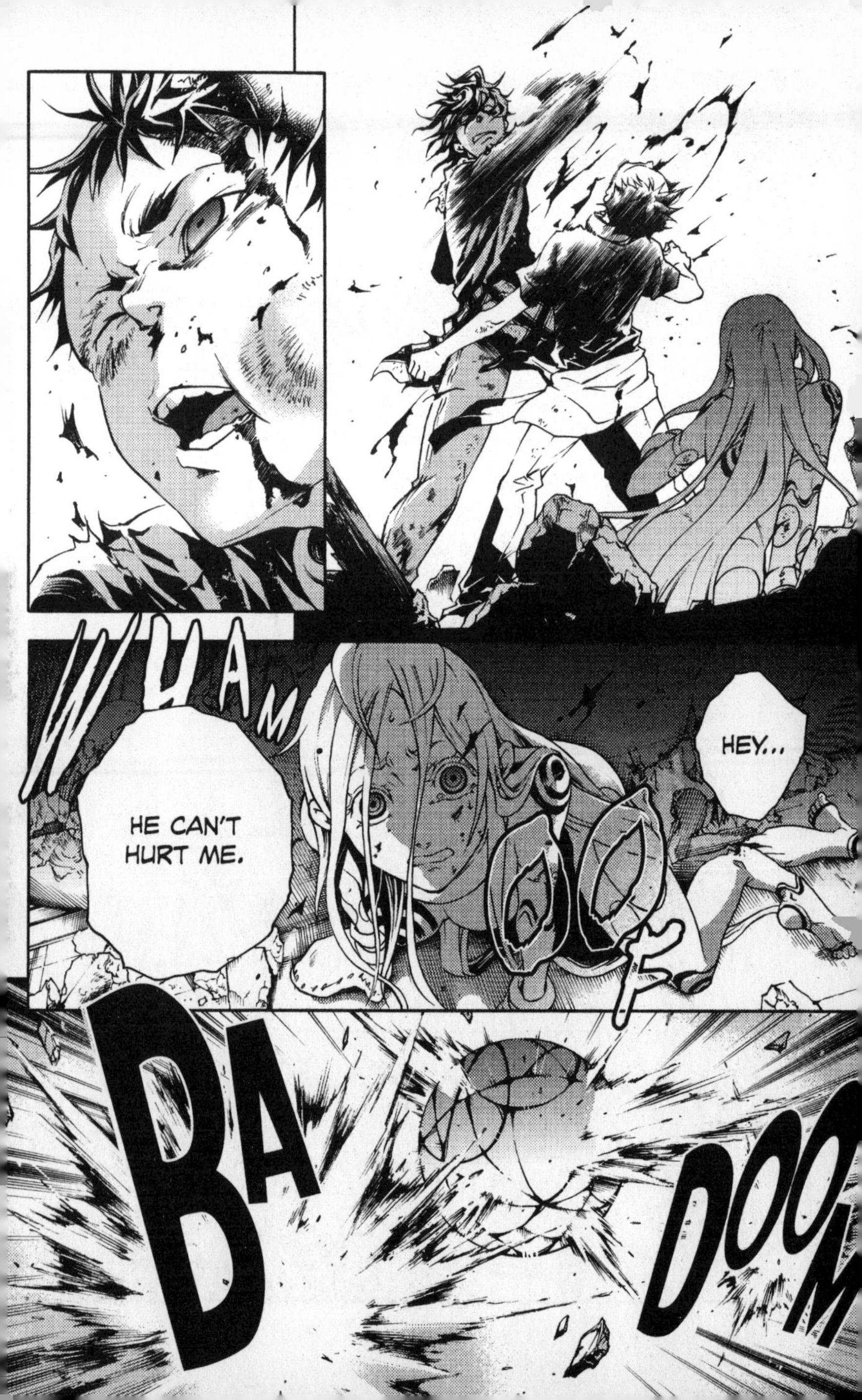
HEY...
HE CAN'T HURT ME.
WHAM
BA DOOM

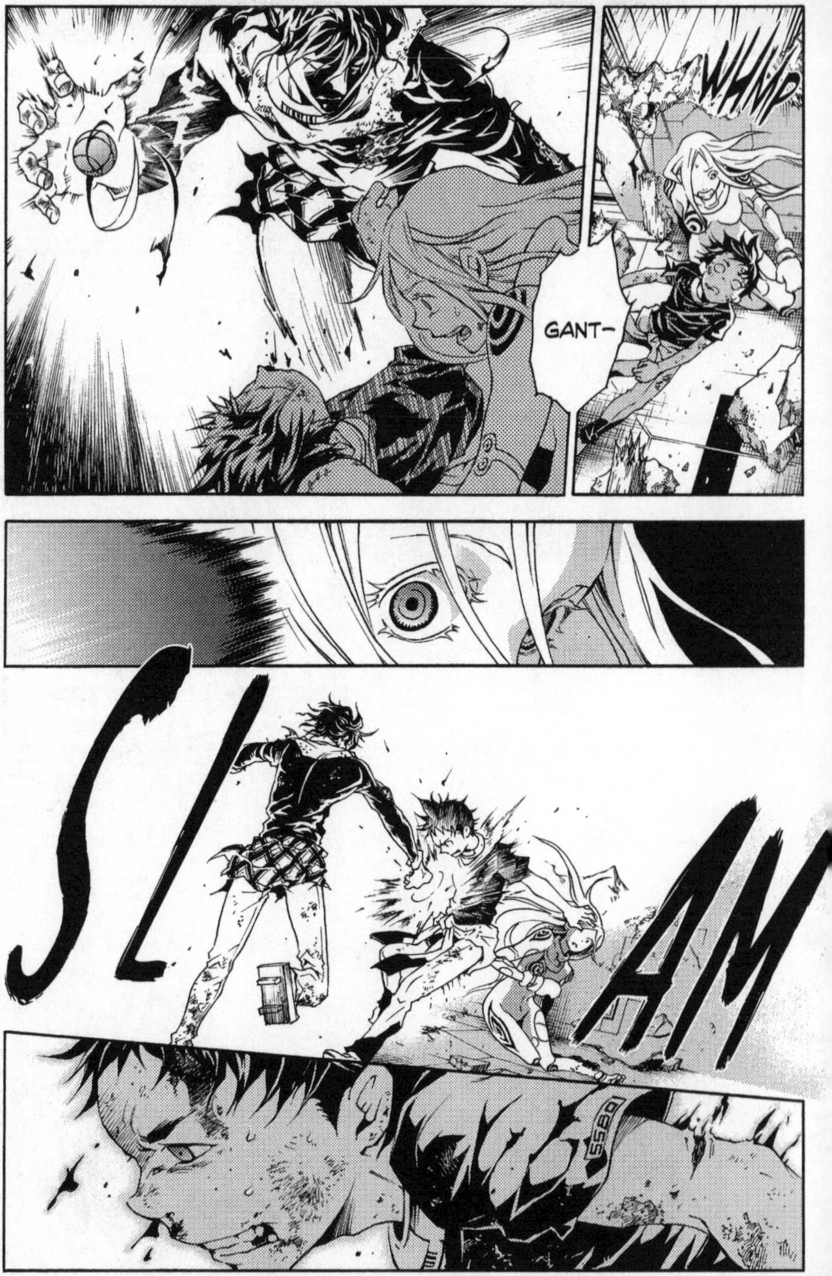
WHMP
GANT-
SLAM

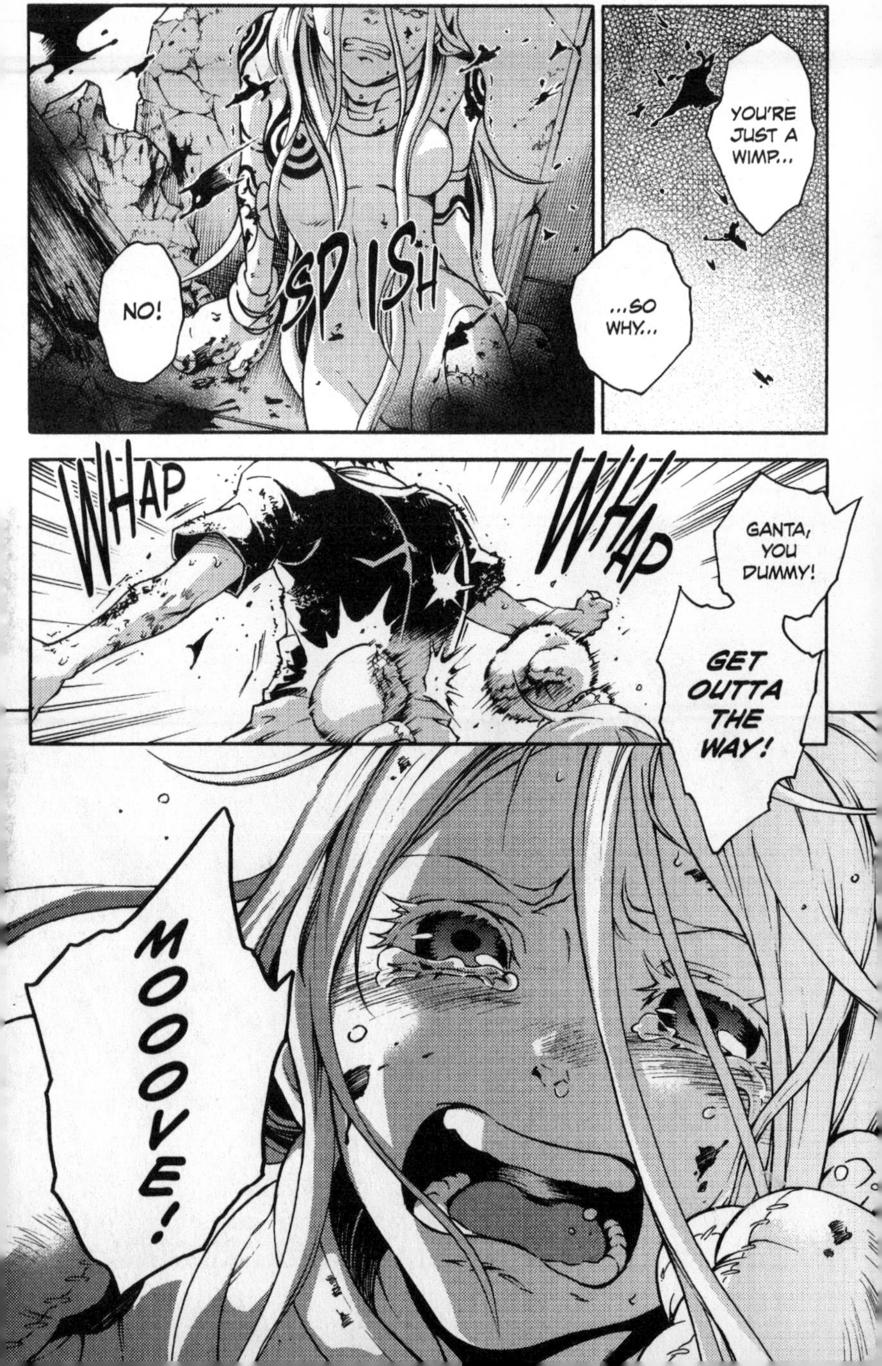
YOU'RE JUST A WIMP...
...SO WHY...
SPISH
NO!
GANTA, YOU DUMMY!
WHAP
WHAP
GET OUTTA THE WAY!
MOOOOVE!

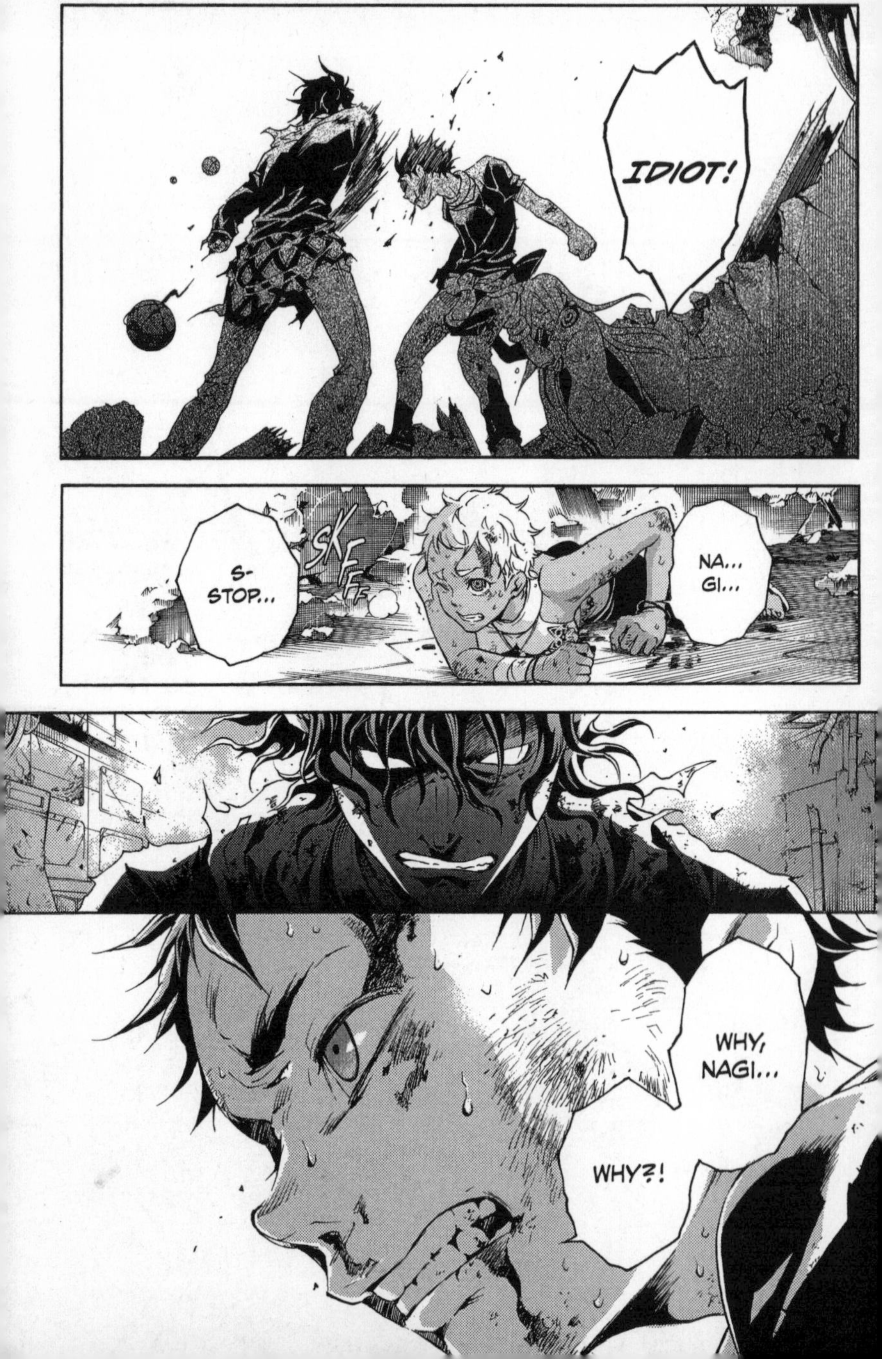
IDIOT!
NA... GI...
SKFFF
S- STOP...
WHY, NAGI...
WHY?!

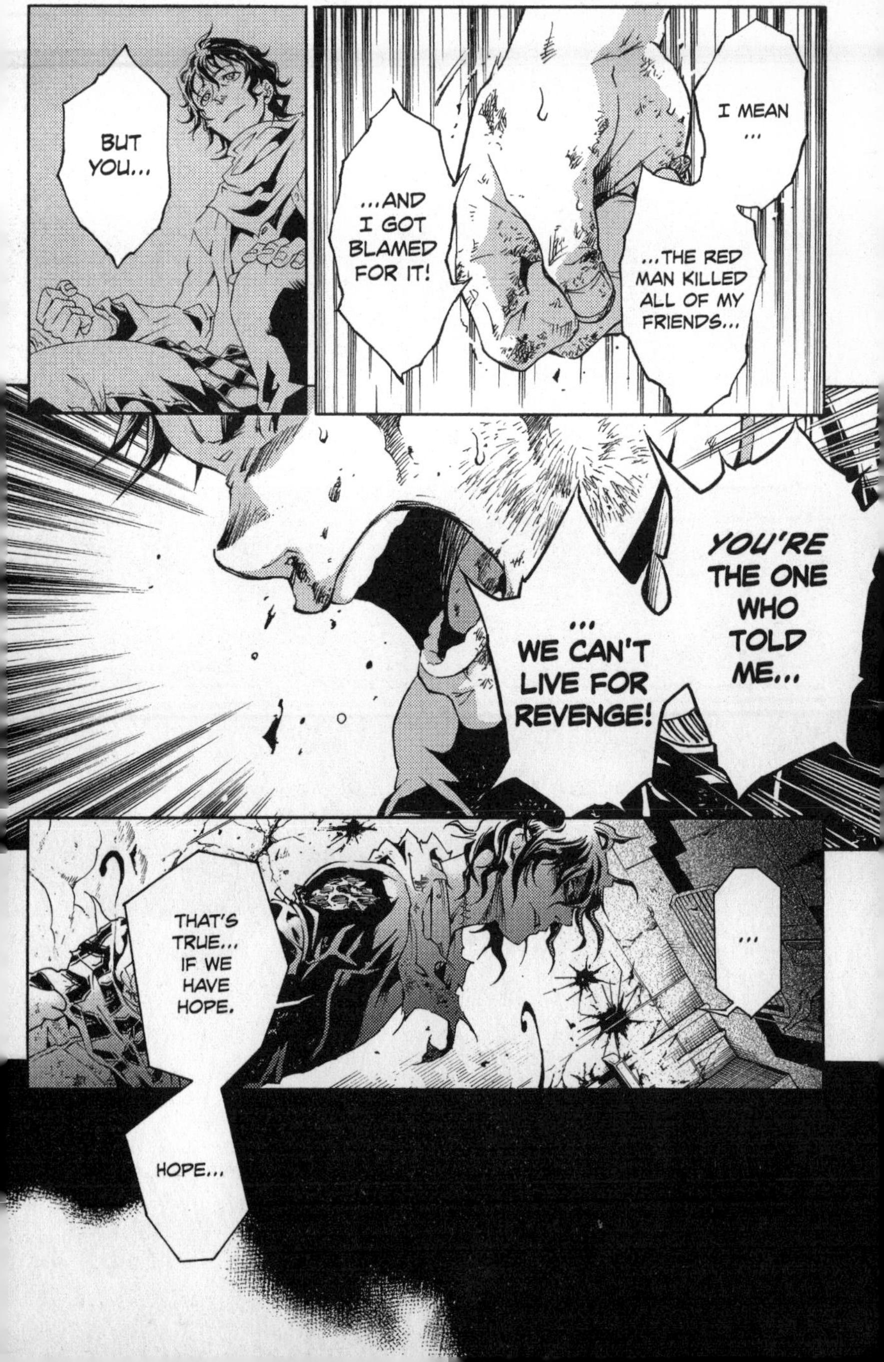
I MEAN ...
...THE RED MAN KILLED ALL OF MY FRIENDS...
...AND I GOT BLAMED FOR IT!
BUT YOU...
YOU'RE THE ONE WHO TOLD ME...
... WE CAN'T LIVE FOR REVENGE!
...
THAT'S TRUE... IF WE HAVE HOPE.
HOPE...

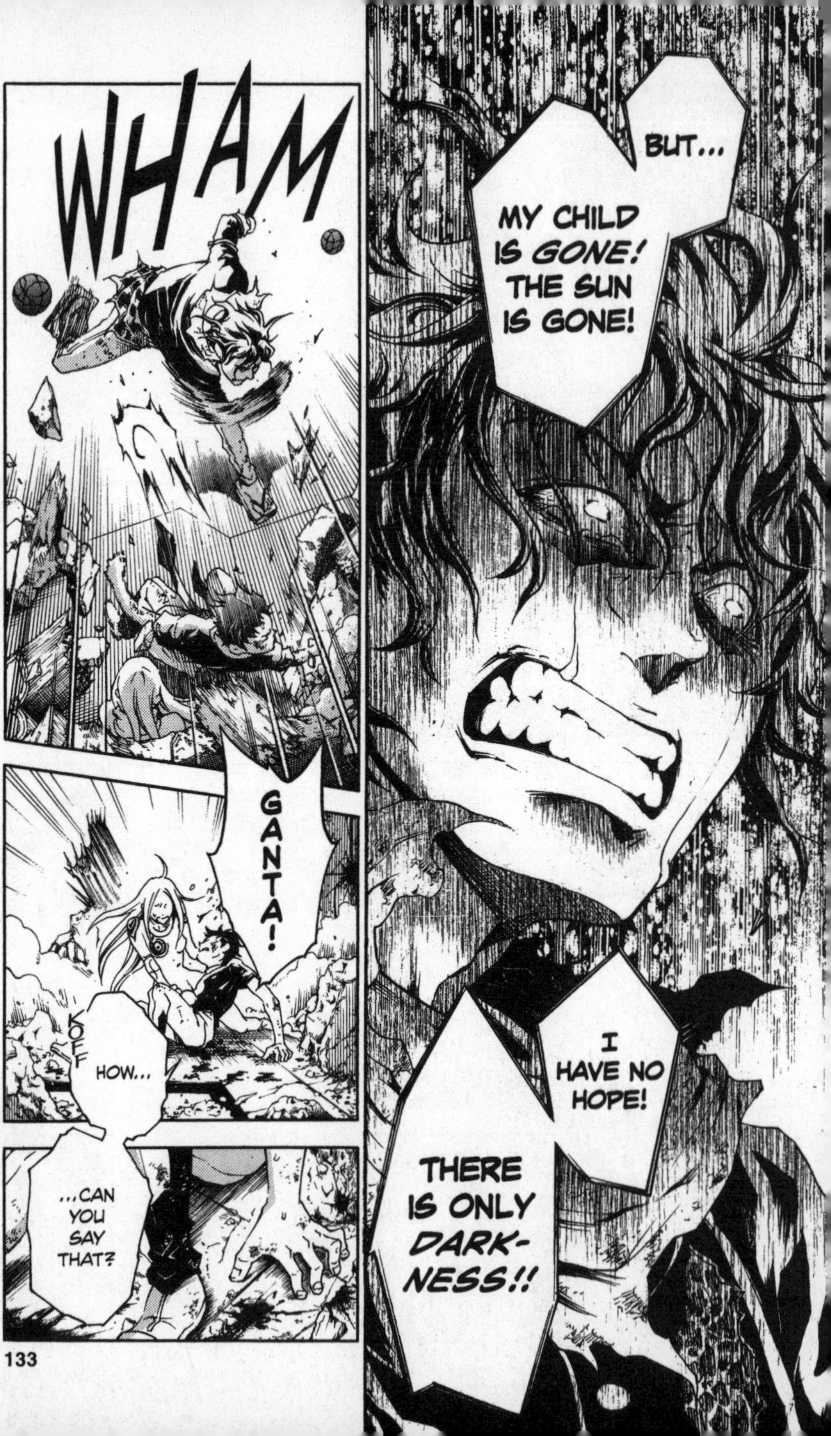
BUT...
MY CHILD IS *GONE!* THE SUN IS GONE!
I HAVE NO HOPE!
THERE IS ONLY *DARKNESS!!*
WHAM
GANTA!
KOFF
HOW...
...CAN YOU SAY THAT?

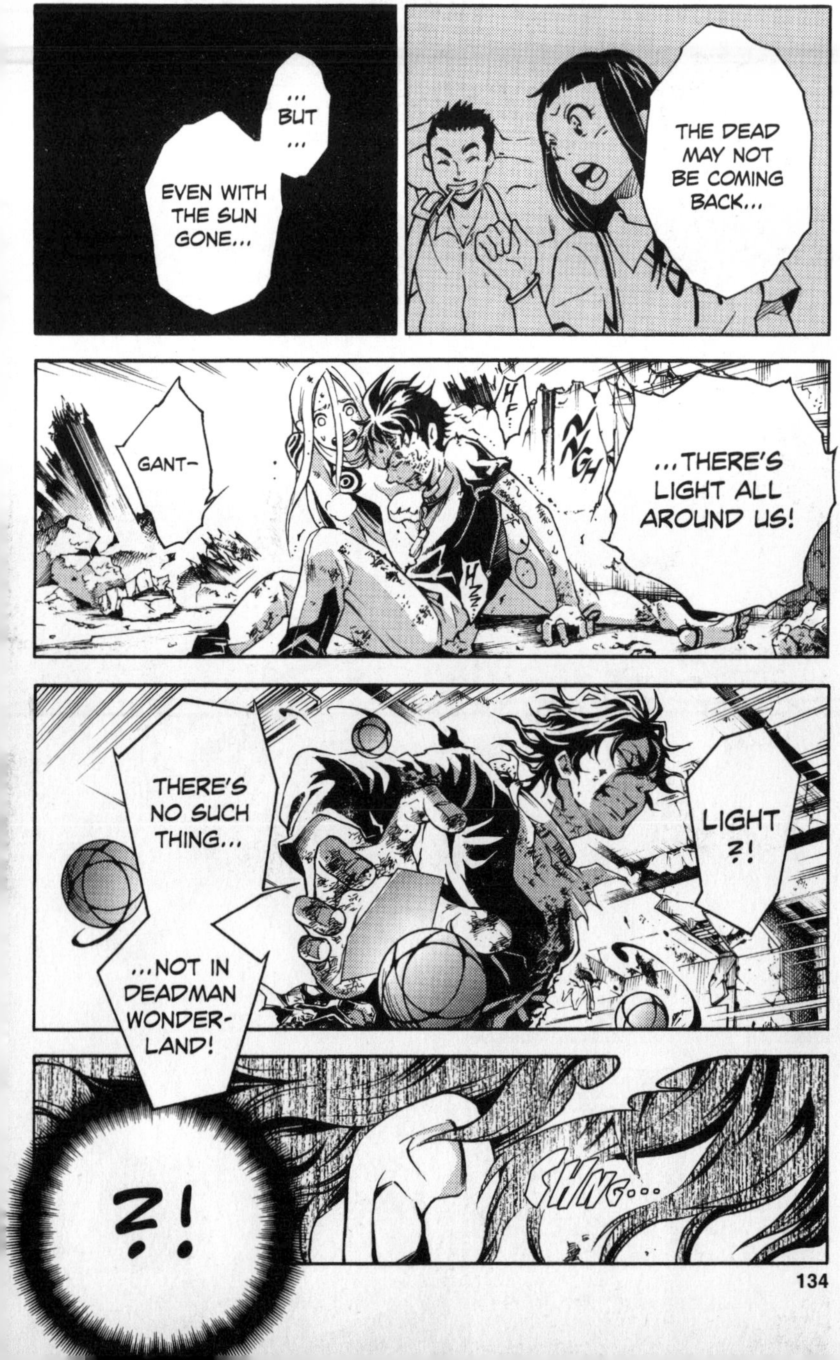
THE DEAD MAY NOT BE COMING BACK...
...BUT...
EVEN WITH THE SUN GONE...
...THERE'S LIGHT ALL AROUND US!
HF...
NNGH
HZZ
GANT-
LIGHT ?!
THERE'S NO SUCH THING...
...NOT IN DEADMAN WONDERLAND!
SHNG...
?!

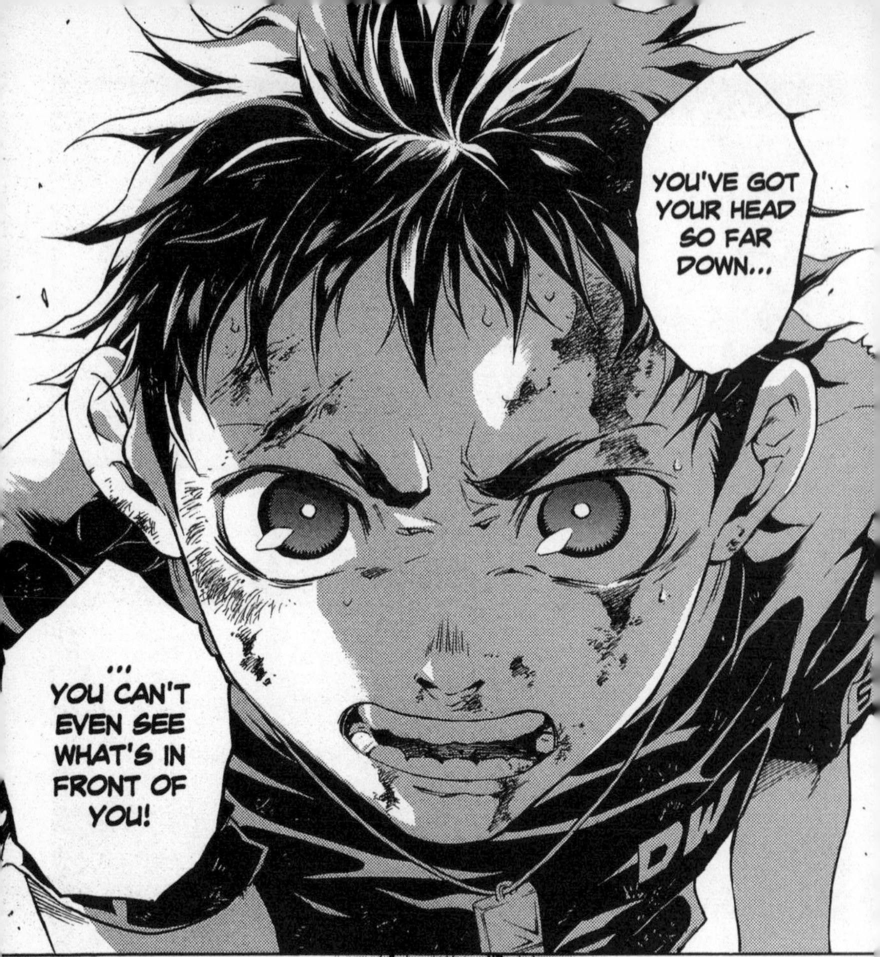
YOU'VE GOT YOUR HEAD SO FAR DOWN...
...YOU CAN'T EVEN SEE WHAT'S IN FRONT OF YOU!
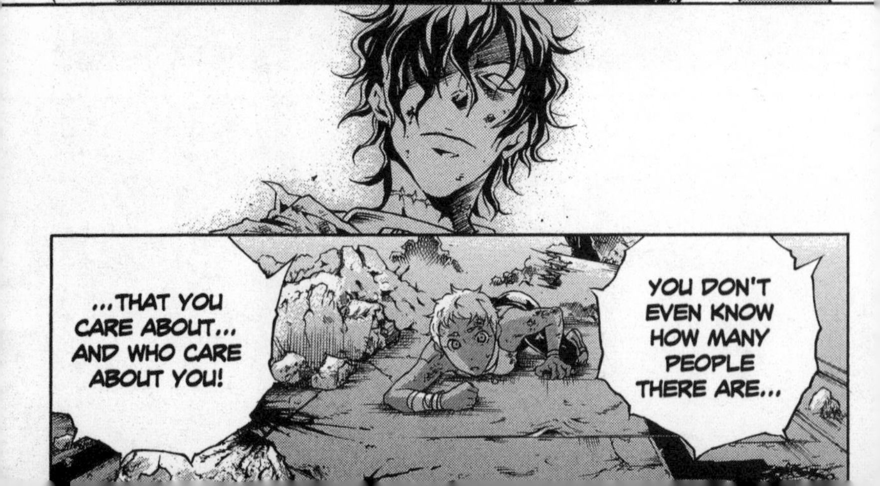
YOU DON'T EVEN KNOW HOW MANY PEOPLE THERE ARE...
...THAT YOU CARE ABOUT... AND WHO CARE ABOUT YOU!

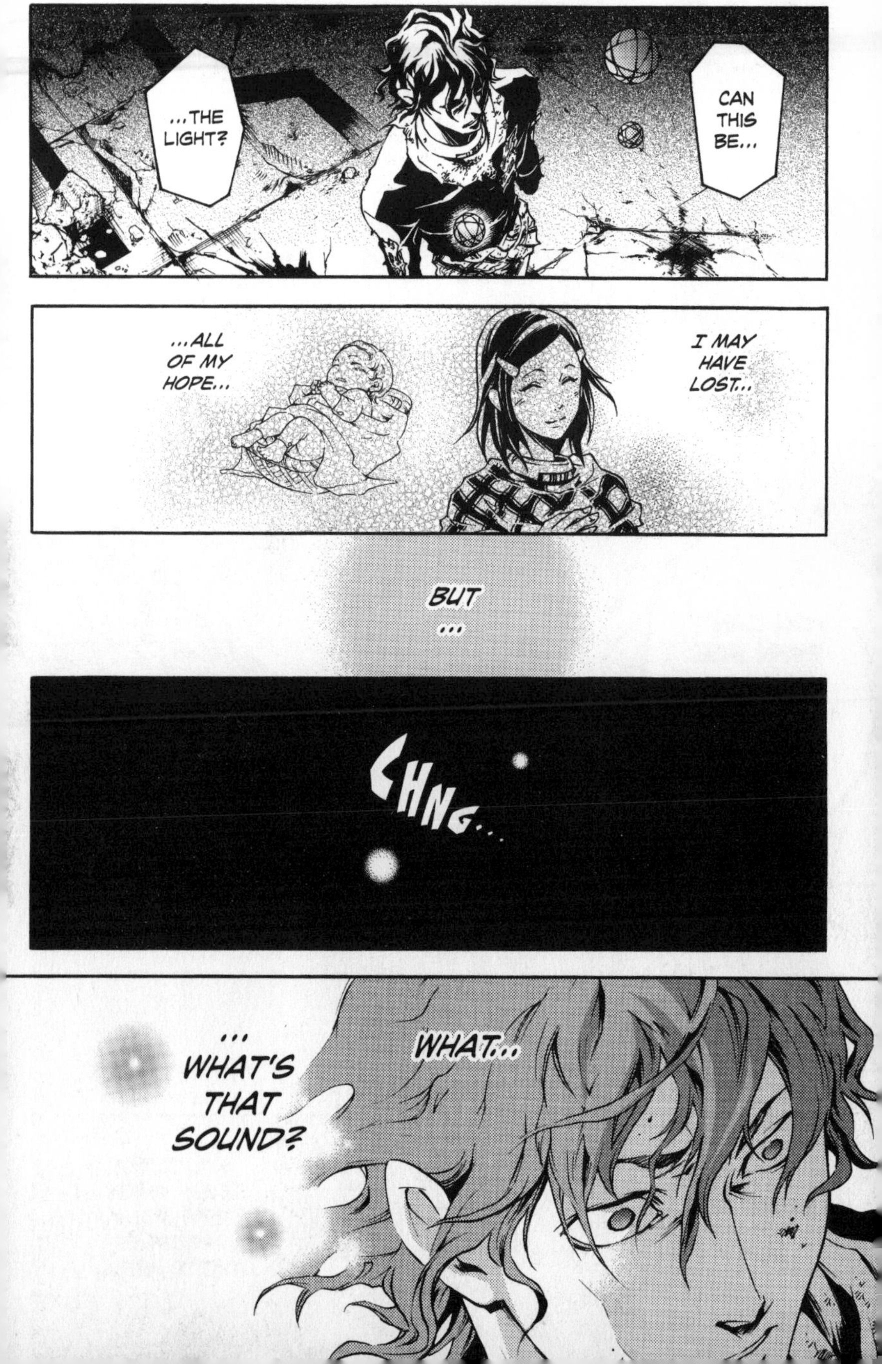

CAN THIS BE...
...THE LIGHT?
I MAY HAVE LOST...
...ALL OF MY HOPE...
BUT ...
CHNG...
WHAT...
... WHAT'S THAT SOUND?

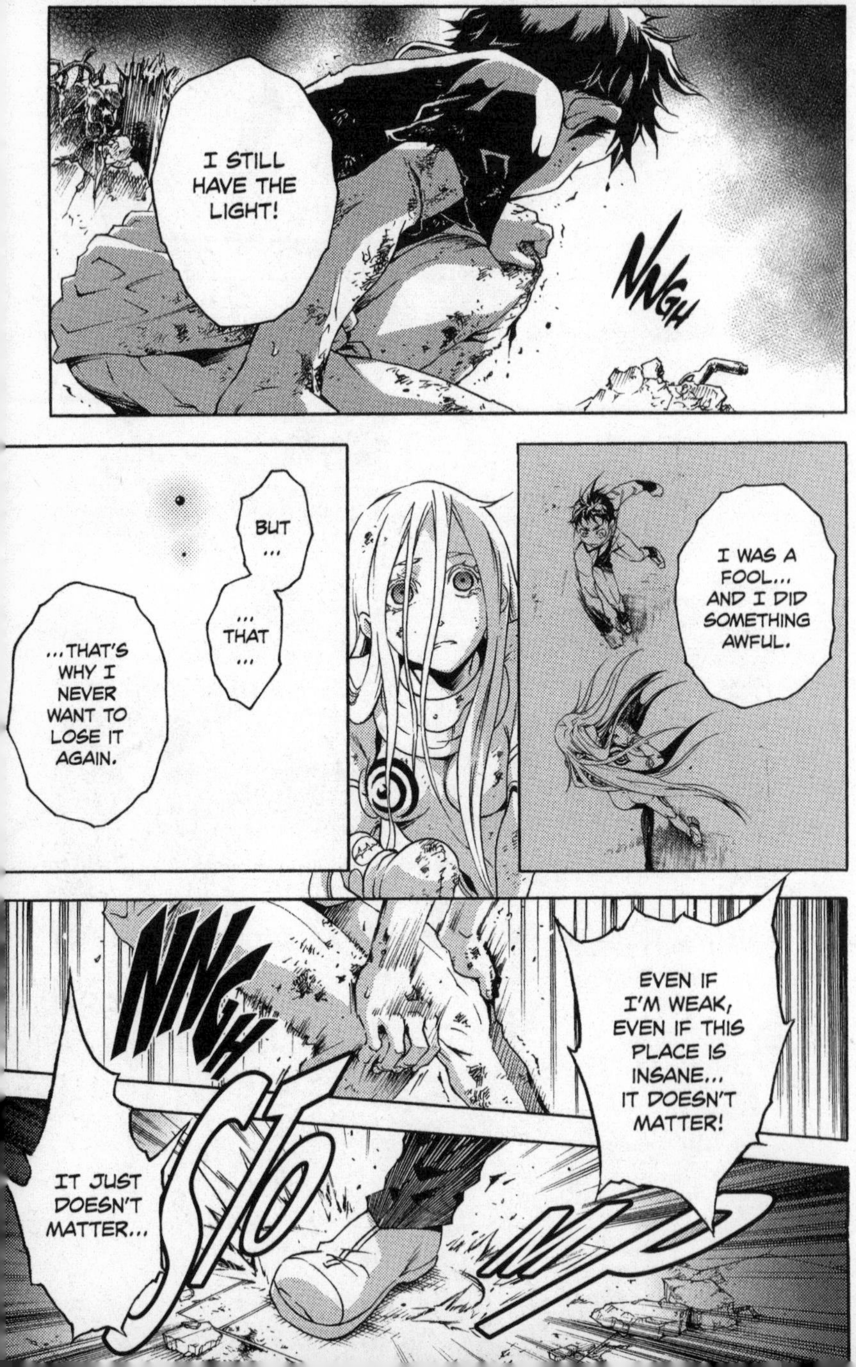
I STILL HAVE THE LIGHT!
NNGH
I WAS A FOOL... AND I DID SOMETHING AWFUL.
BUT ...
... THAT ...
...THAT'S WHY I NEVER WANT TO LOSE IT AGAIN.
EVEN IF I'M WEAK, EVEN IF THIS PLACE IS INSANE... IT DOESN'T MATTER!
NNGH
STOMP
IT JUST DOESN'T MATTER...

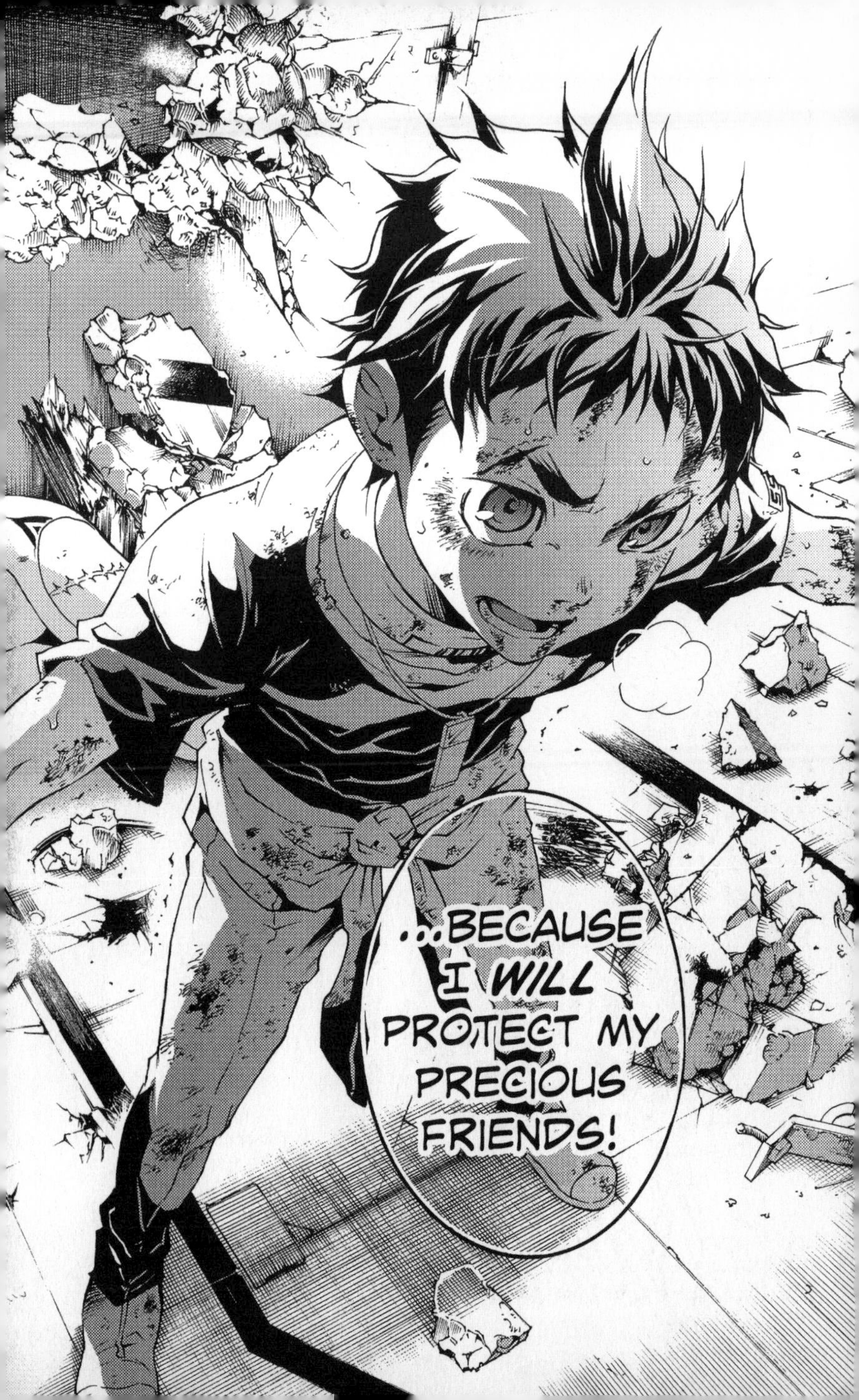
...BECAUSE I *WILL* PROTECT MY PRECIOUS FRIENDS!

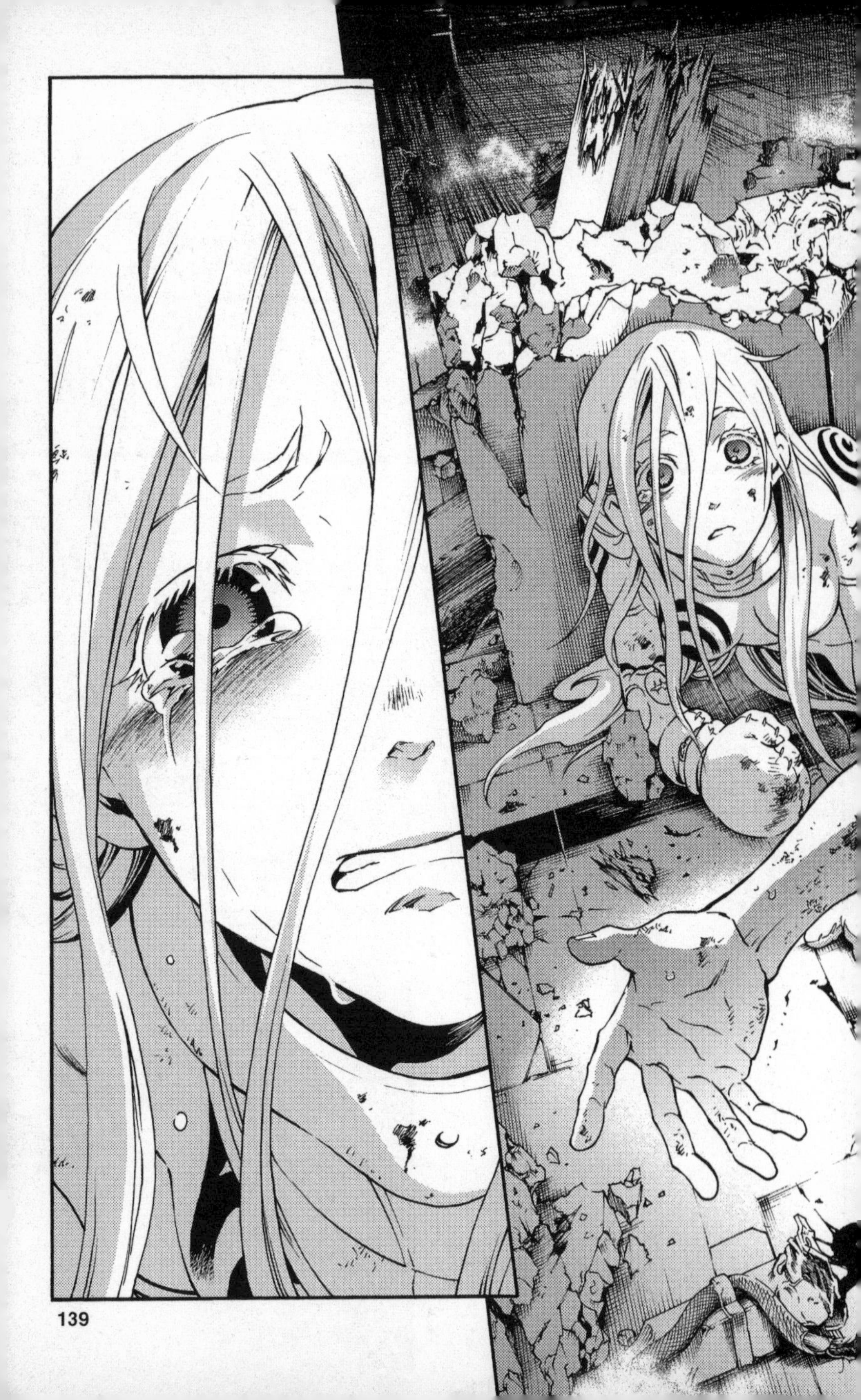

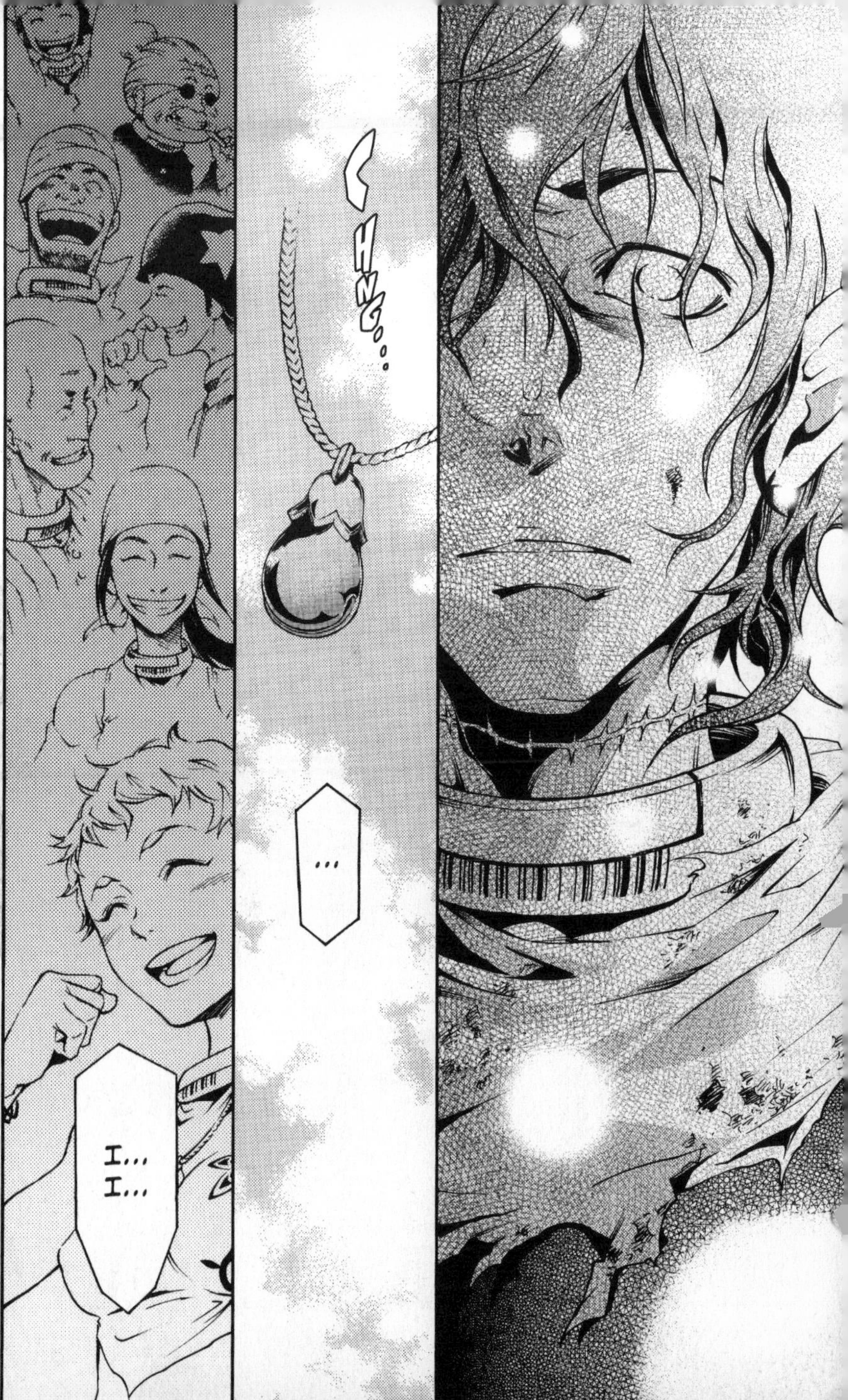
CHNG...
...
I...
I...

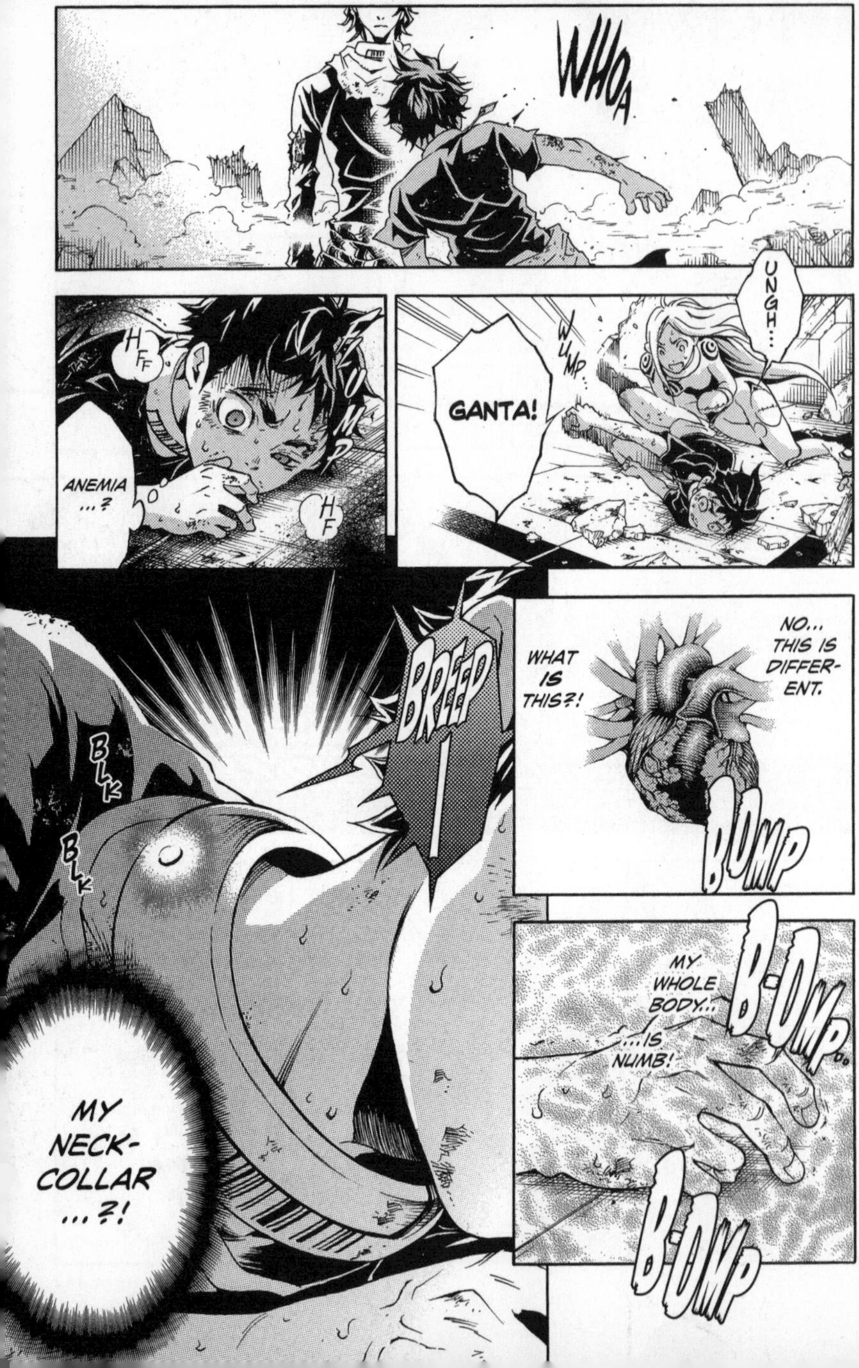
WHOA
UNGH...
WUMP
GANTA!
HFF
FUMP
ANEMIA ...?
HF
NO... THIS IS DIFFER-ENT.
WHAT IS THIS?!
B-OMP
BREEP
BLK
BLK
MY WHOLE BODY...
...IS NUMB!
B-OMP
B-OMP
MY NECK-COLLAR ...?!

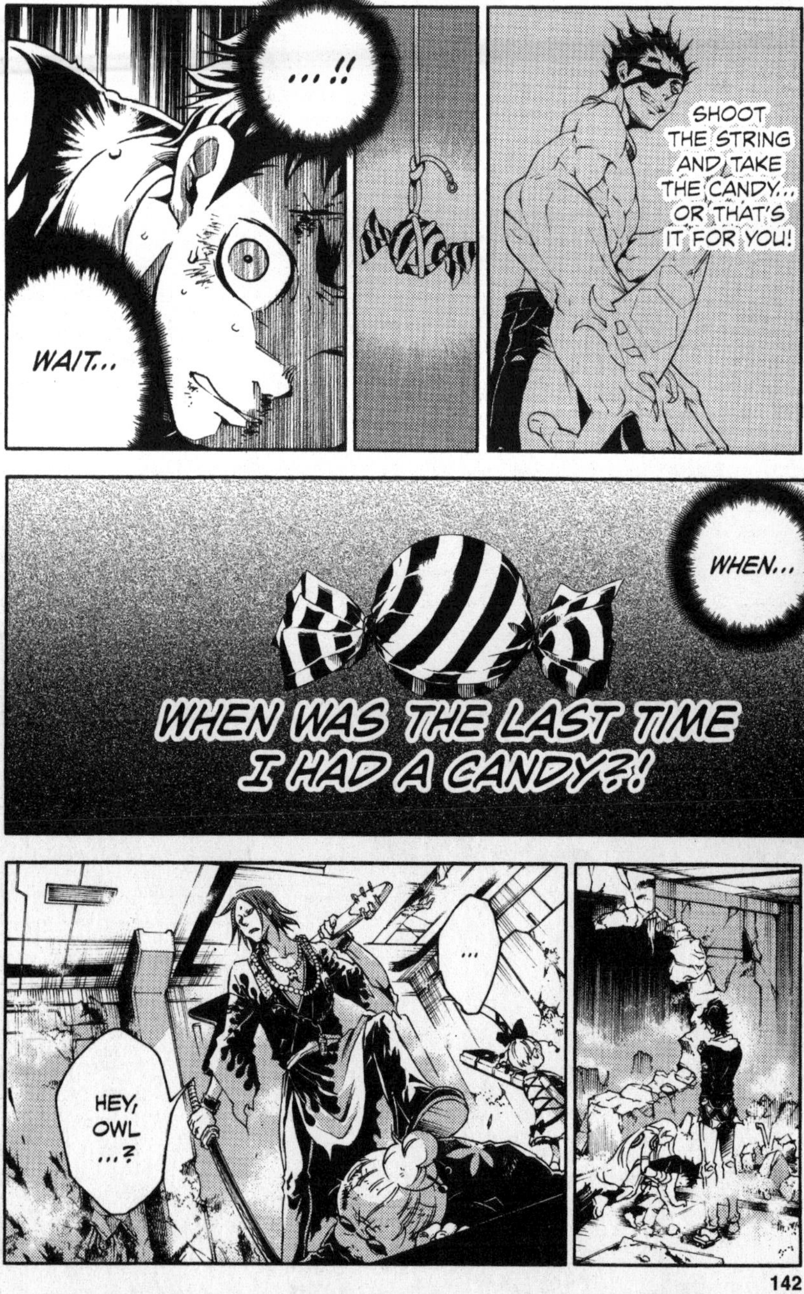
SHOOT THE STRING AND TAKE THE CANDY... OR THAT'S IT FOR YOU!
...!!
WAIT...
WHEN...
WHEN WAS THE LAST TIME I HAD A CANDY?!
HEY, OWL ...?
...

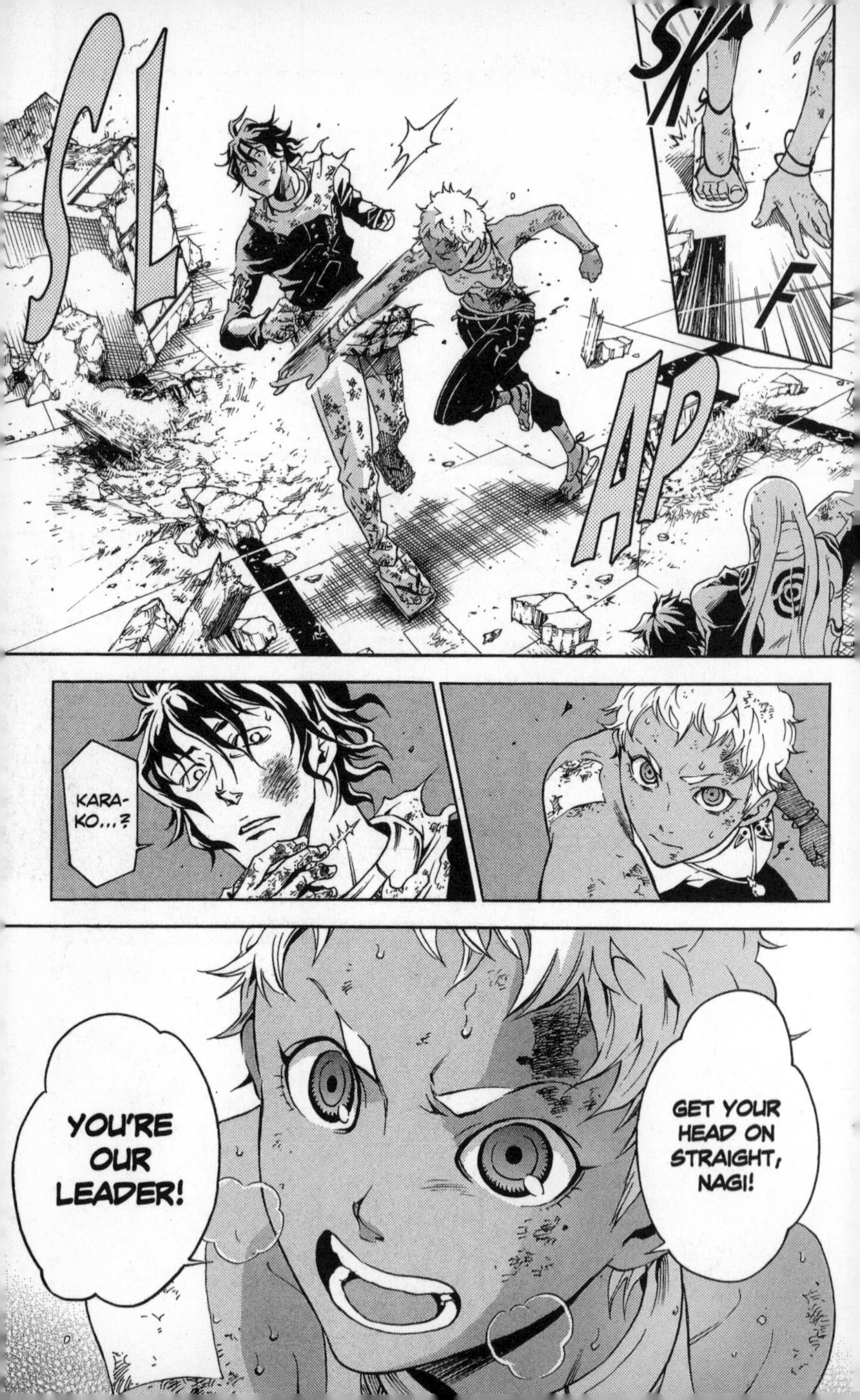
SK
F
SLAP
KARA-KO...?
GET YOUR HEAD ON STRAIGHT, NAGI!
YOU'RE OUR LEADER!

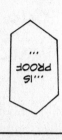

CHNG...
THE SOUND OF THAT BELL...
...IS PROOF...
...THAT I HAVE PRECIOUS FRIENDS TOO.

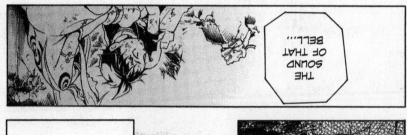

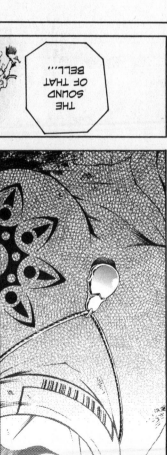

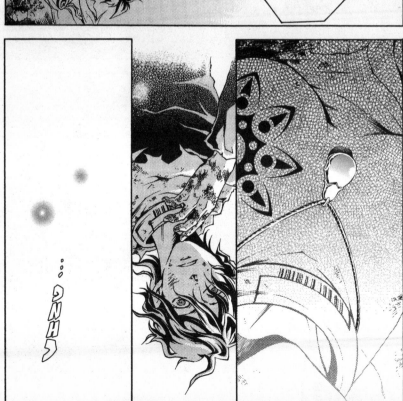

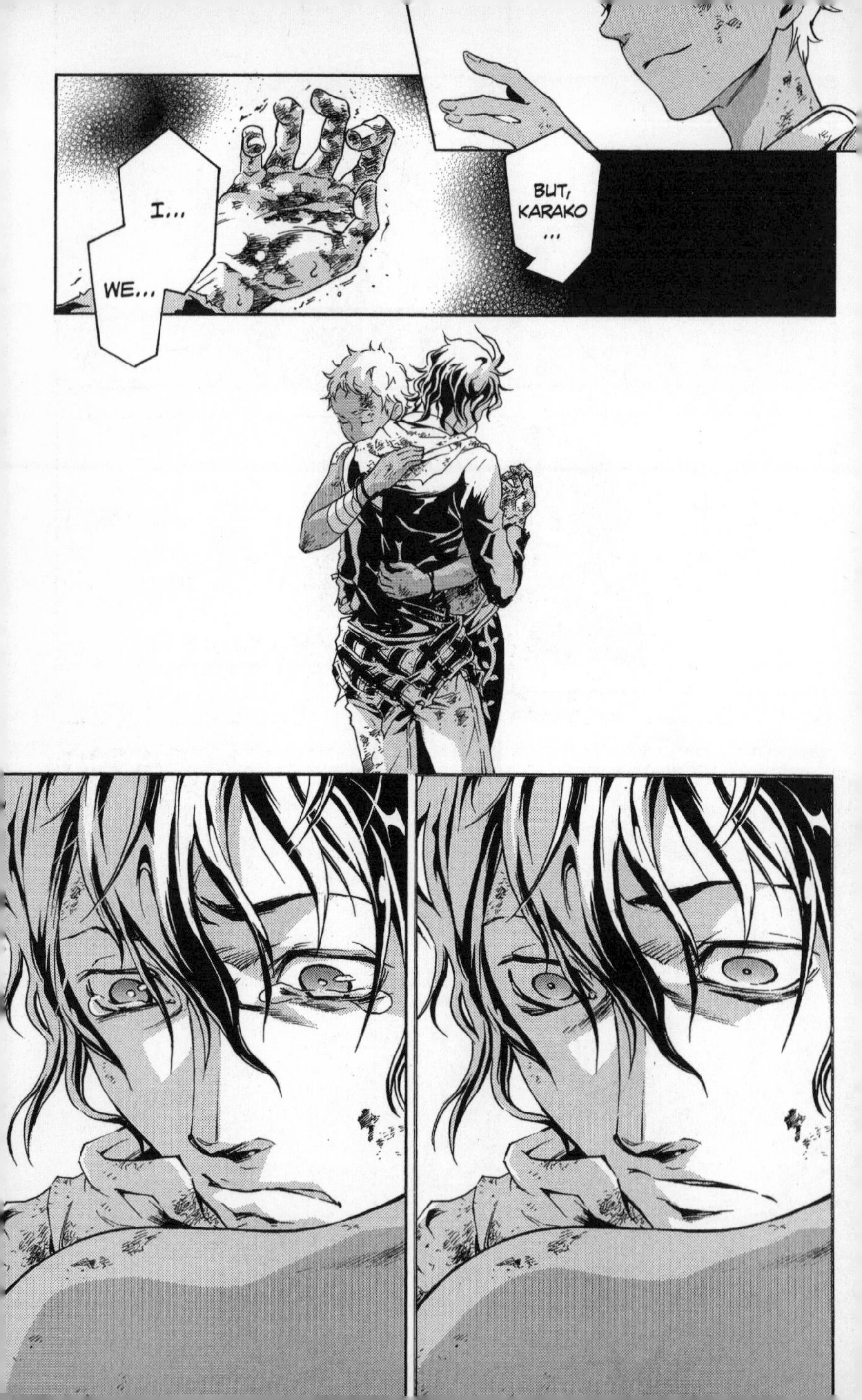
BUT, KARAKO ...
I...
WE...

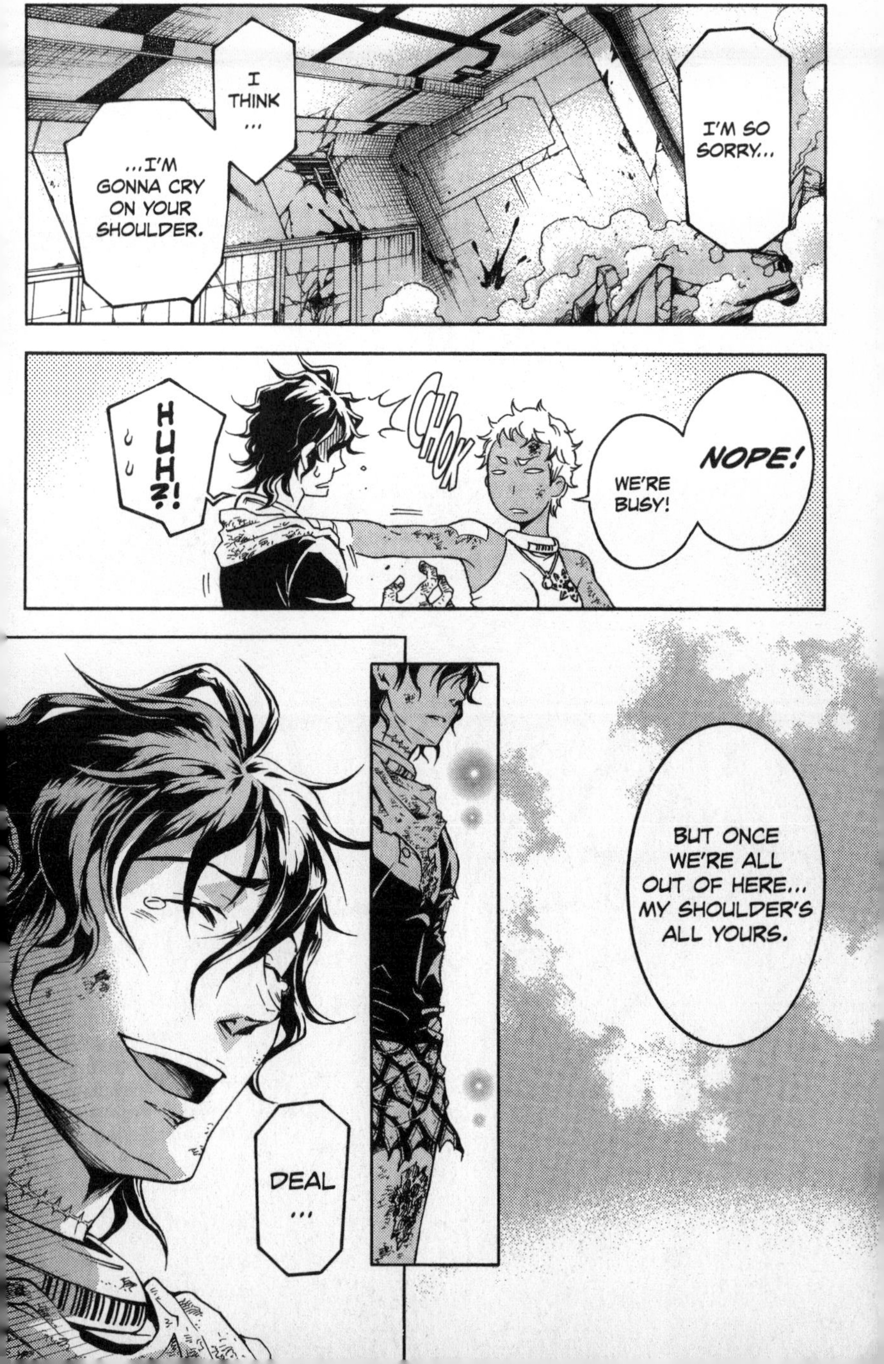
I'M SO SORRY...
I THINK...
...I'M GONNA CRY ON YOUR SHOULDER.
NOPE!
WE'RE BUSY!
CHOK
HUH?!
BUT ONCE WE'RE ALL OUT OF HERE... MY SHOULDER'S ALL YOURS.
DEAL...

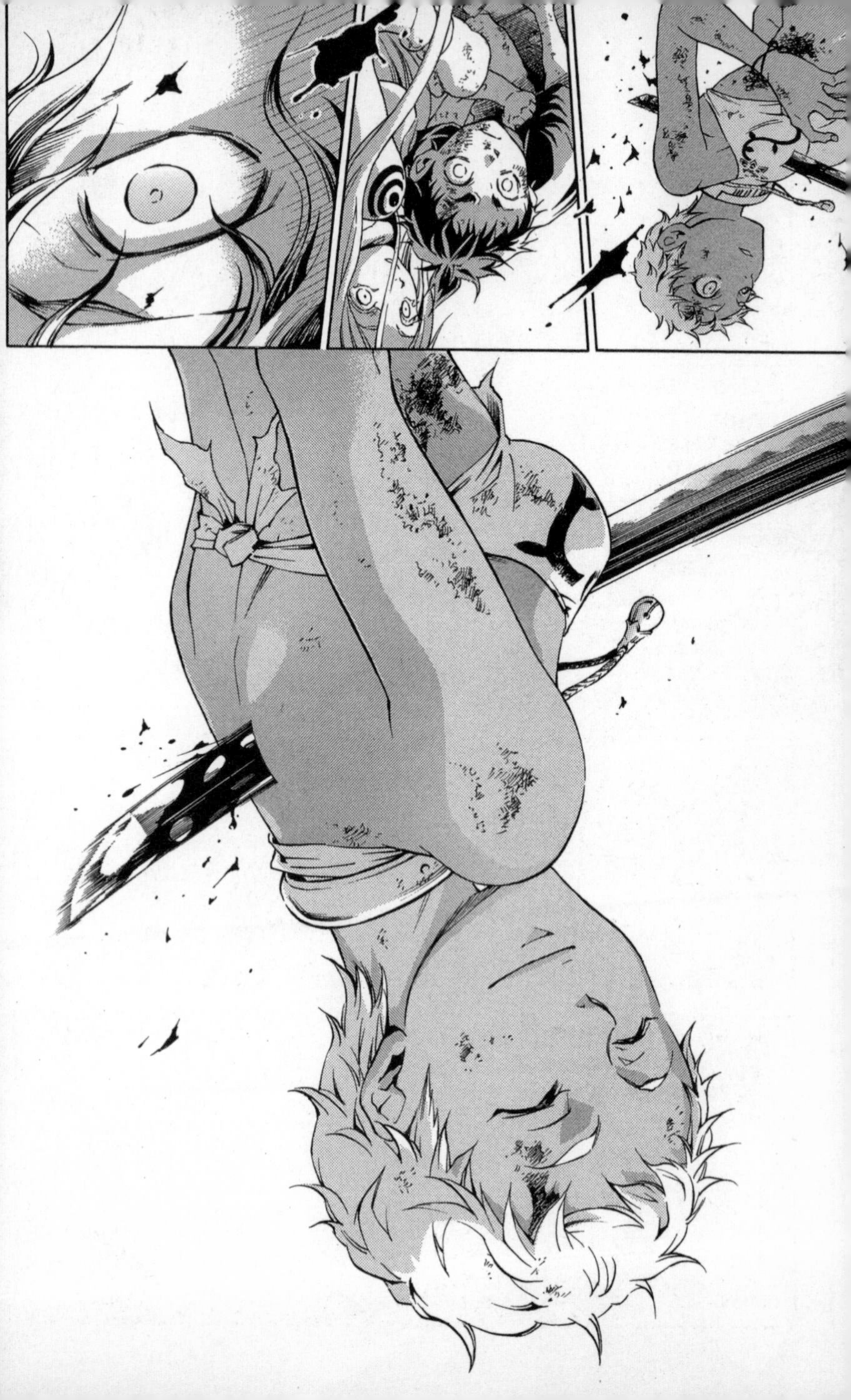

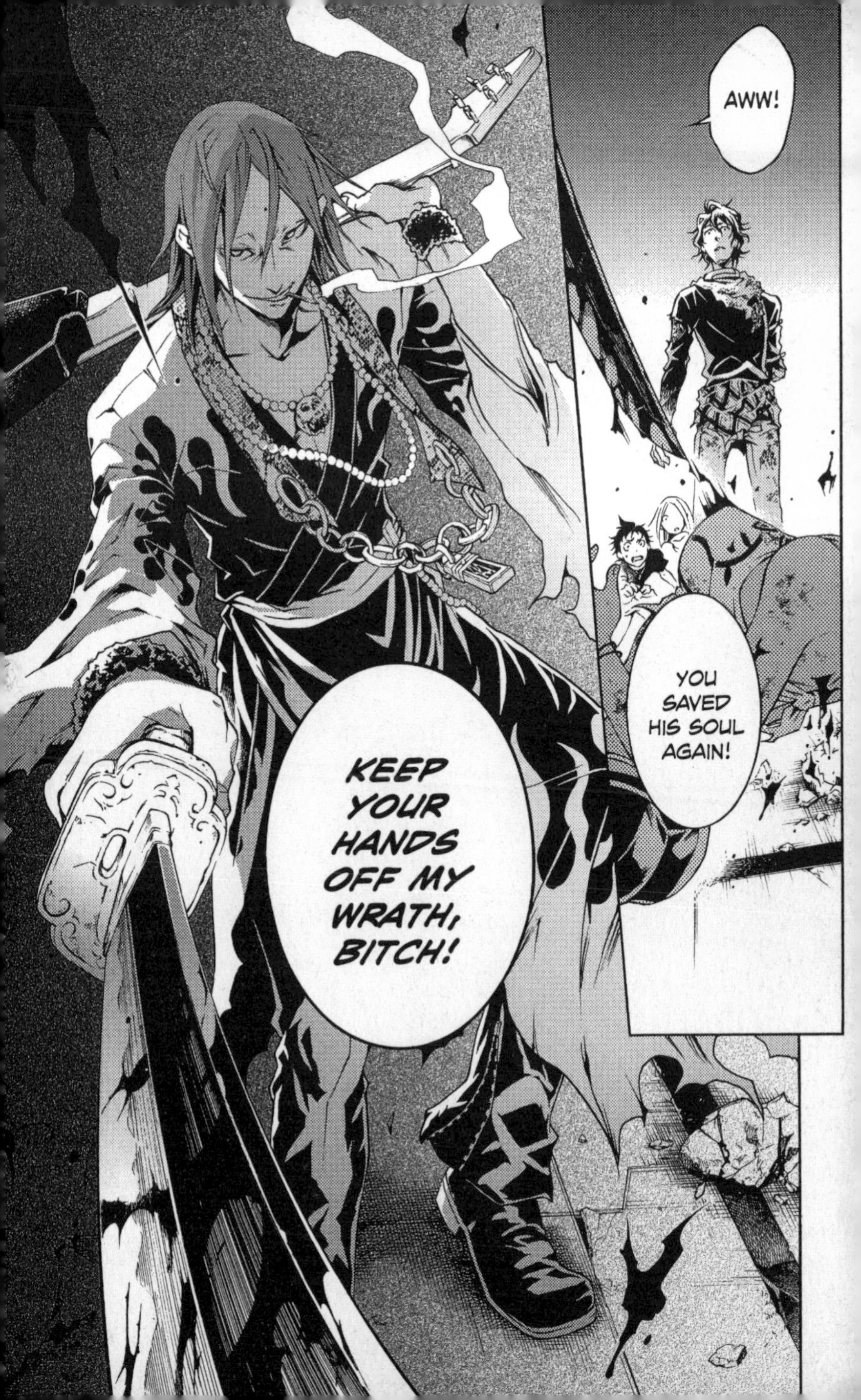
AWW!
YOU SAVED HIS SOUL AGAIN!
KEEP YOUR HANDS OFF MY WRATH, BITCH!

DEADMAU

WONDERLAND

WONDER

DEADMAU

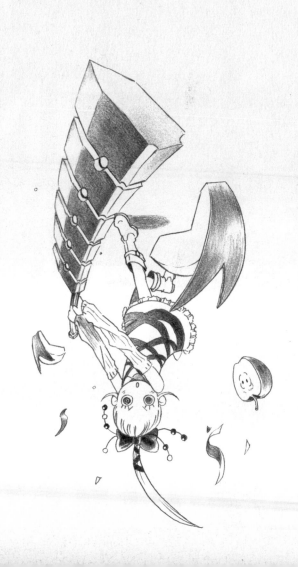

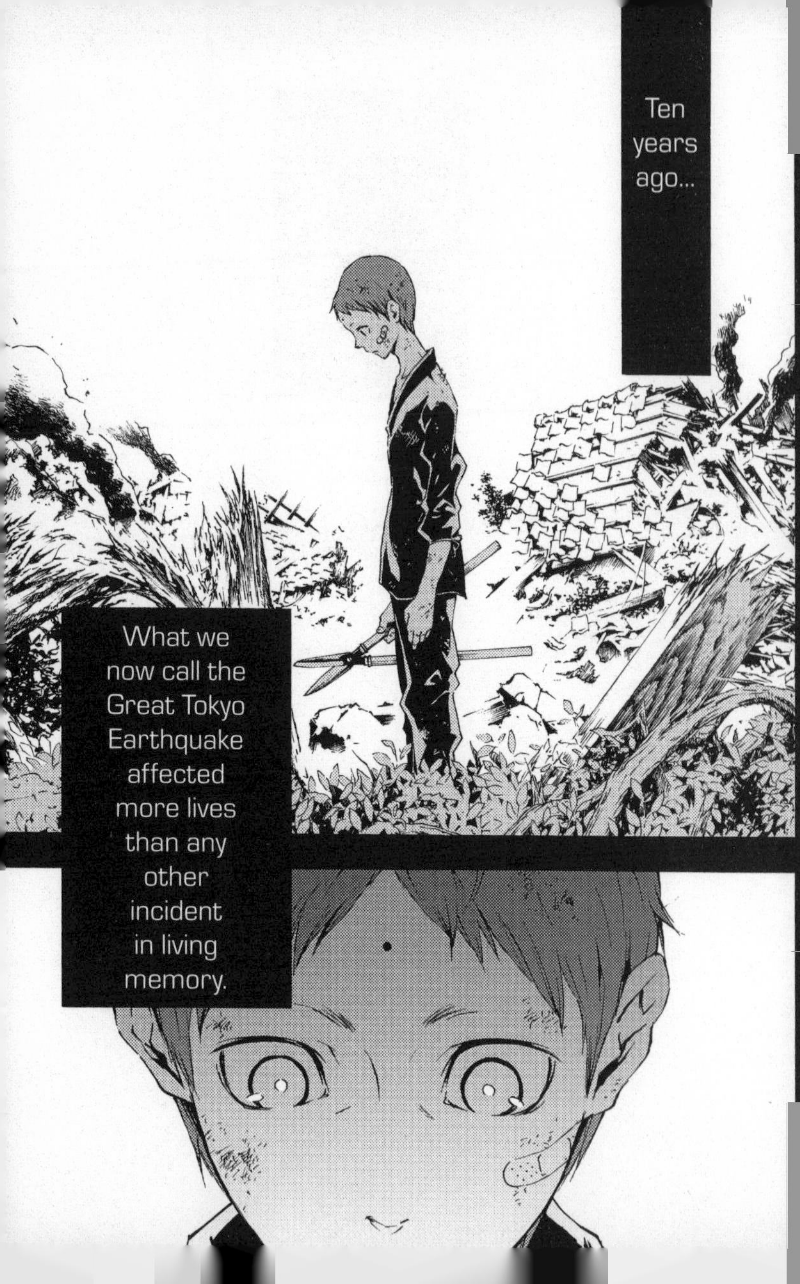
Ten years ago...
What we now call the Great Tokyo Earthquake affected more lives than any other incident in living memory.

Leaving only death in its wake.

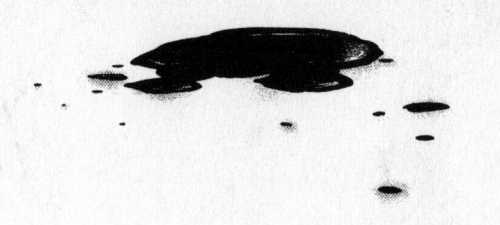

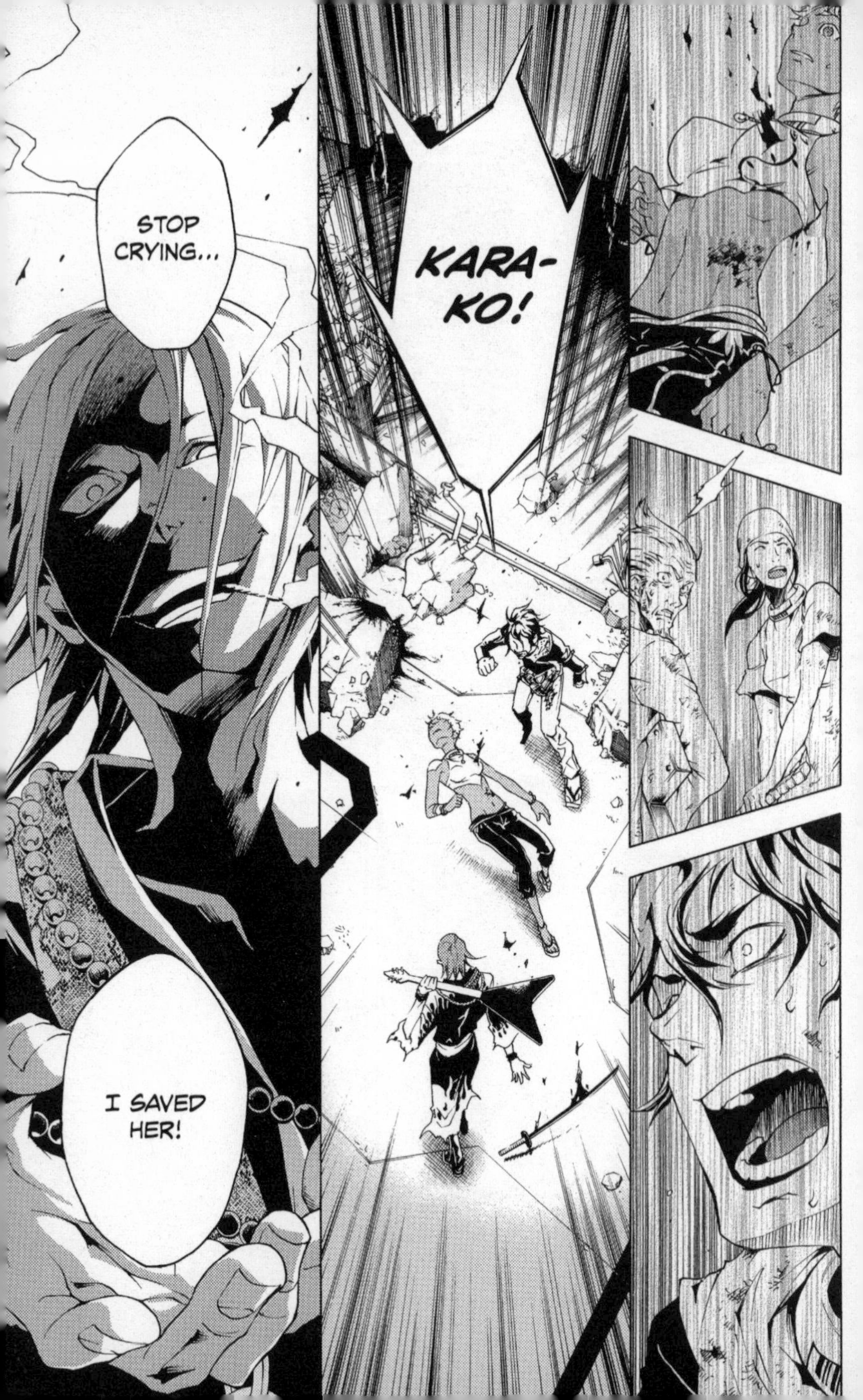
KARA-KO!
STOP CRYING...
I SAVED HER!

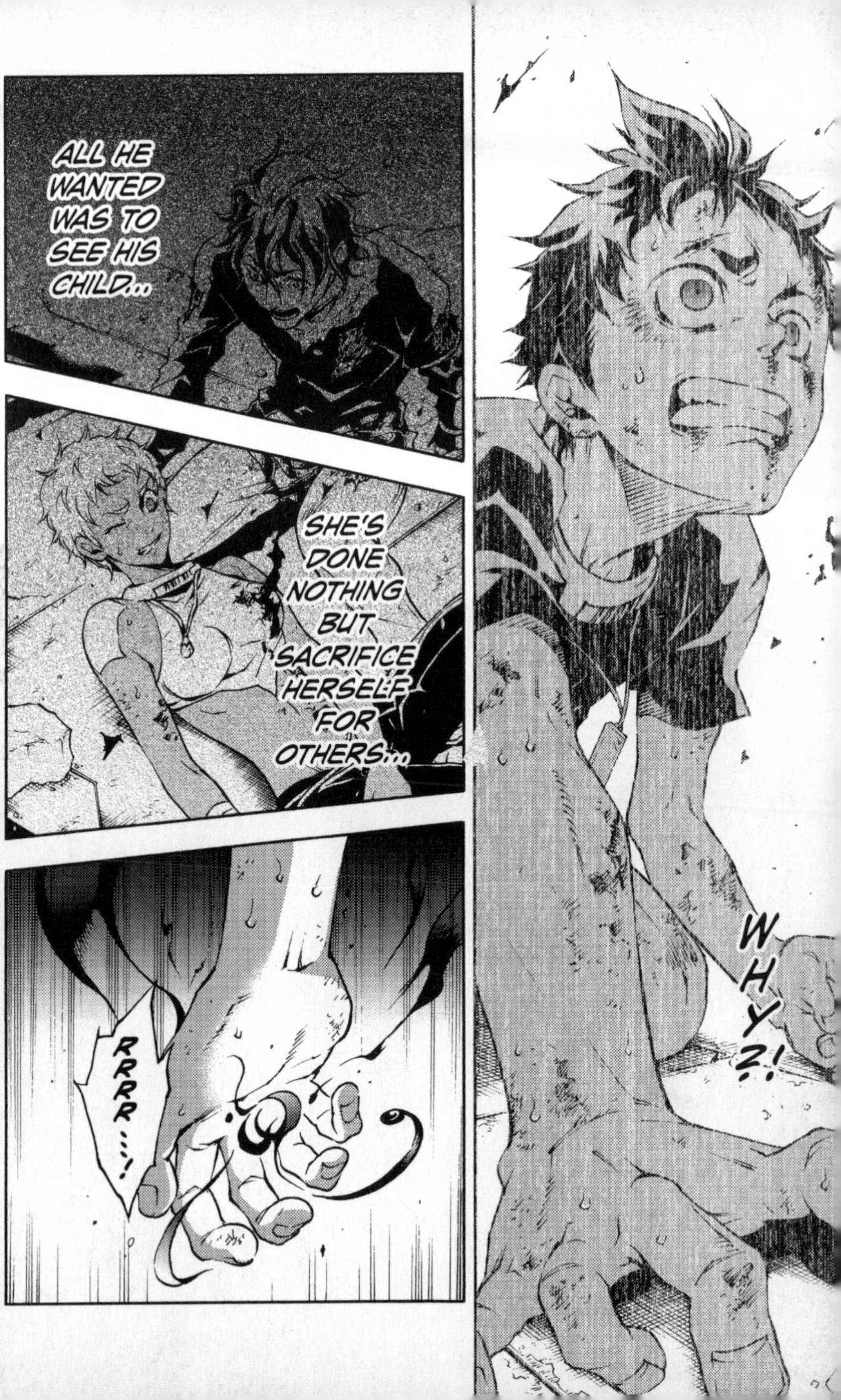
WHY?!
ALL HE WANTED WAS TO SEE HIS CHILD...
SHE'S DONE NOTHING BUT SACRIFICE HERSELF FOR OTHERS...
RRRR...!

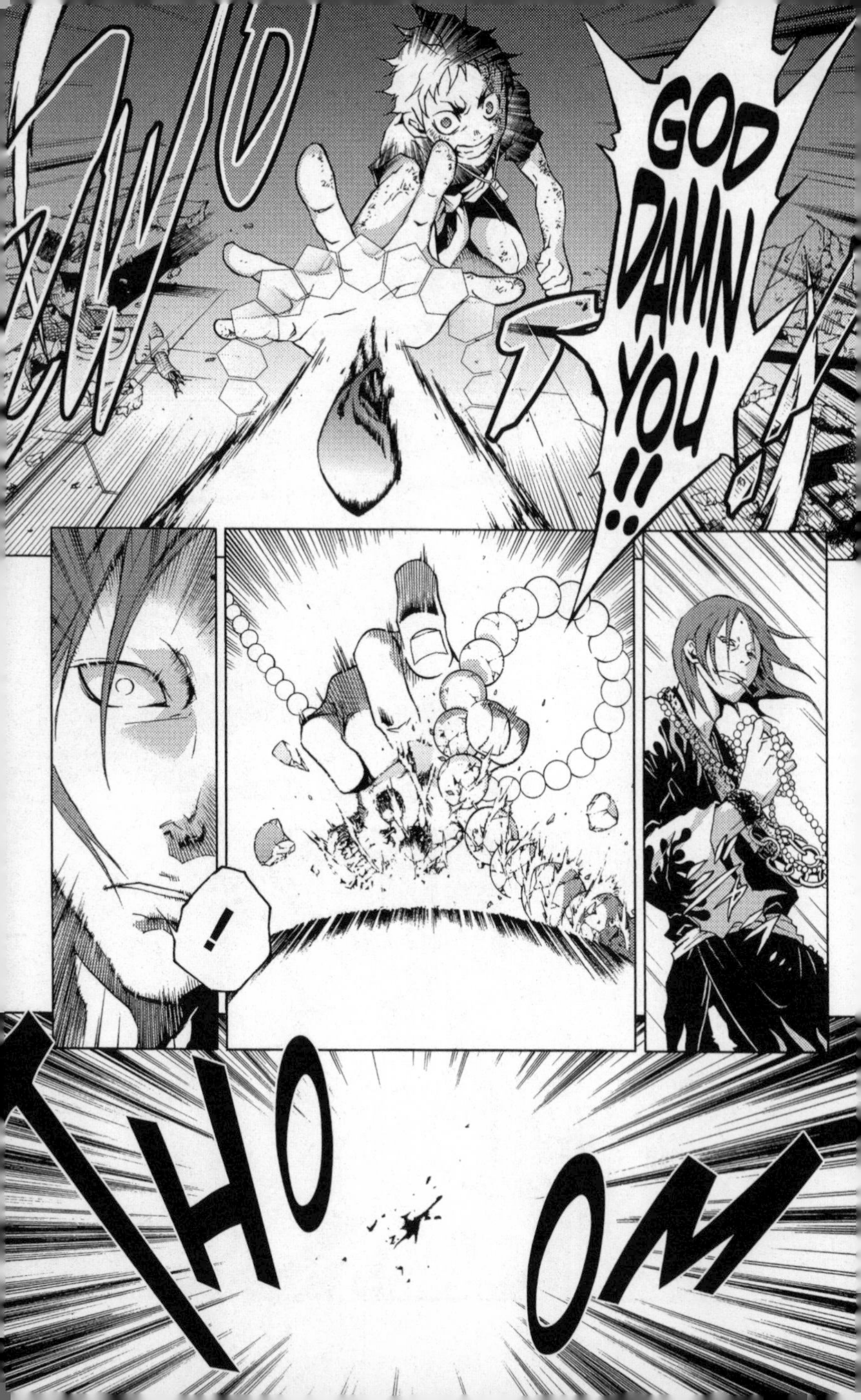
GOD DAMN YOU!!
!
THOOM

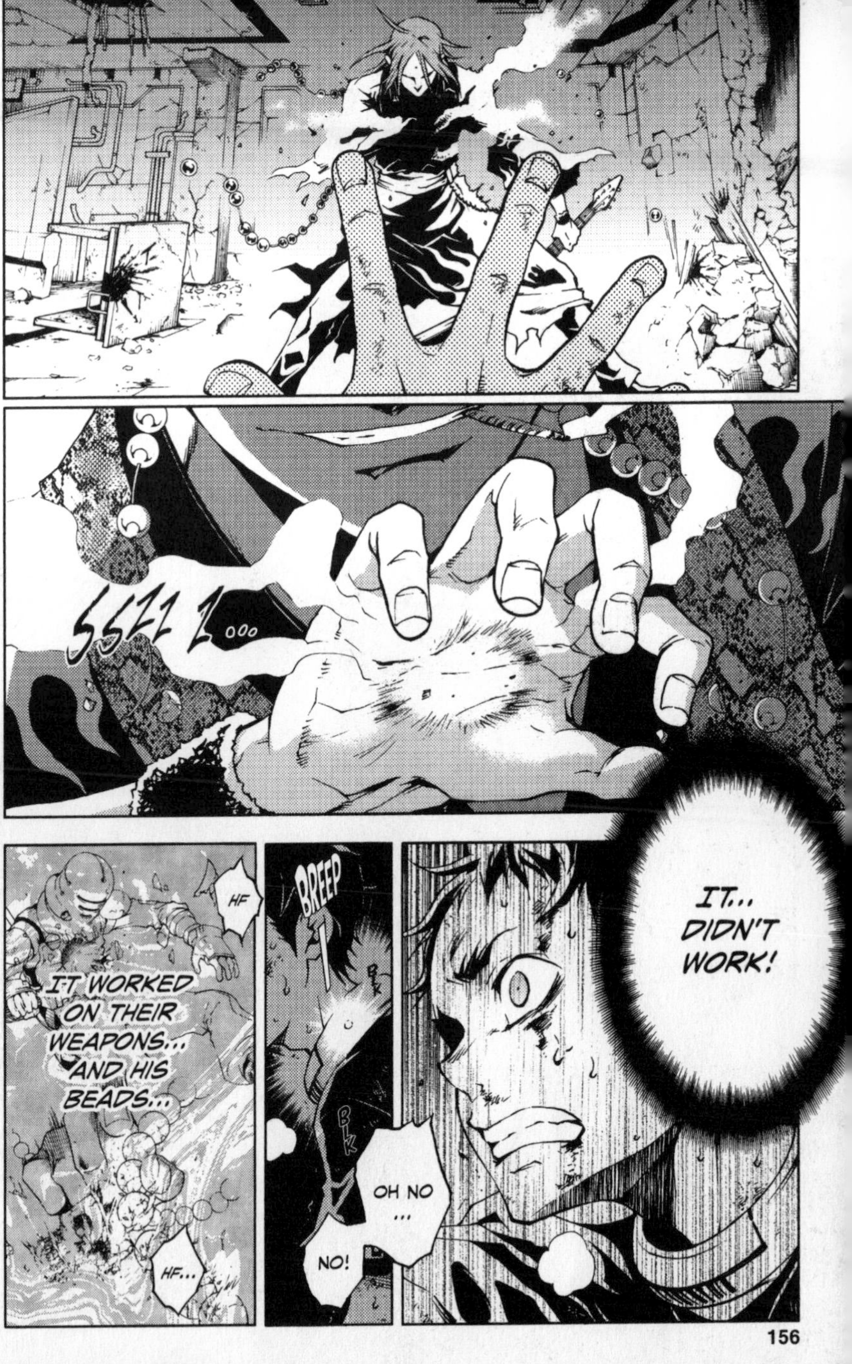
SSZZ Z...
IT... DIDN'T WORK!
BREEP
BLK
OH NO ...
NO!
BLK
HF
IT WORKED ON THEIR WEAPONS... AND HIS BEADS...
HF...

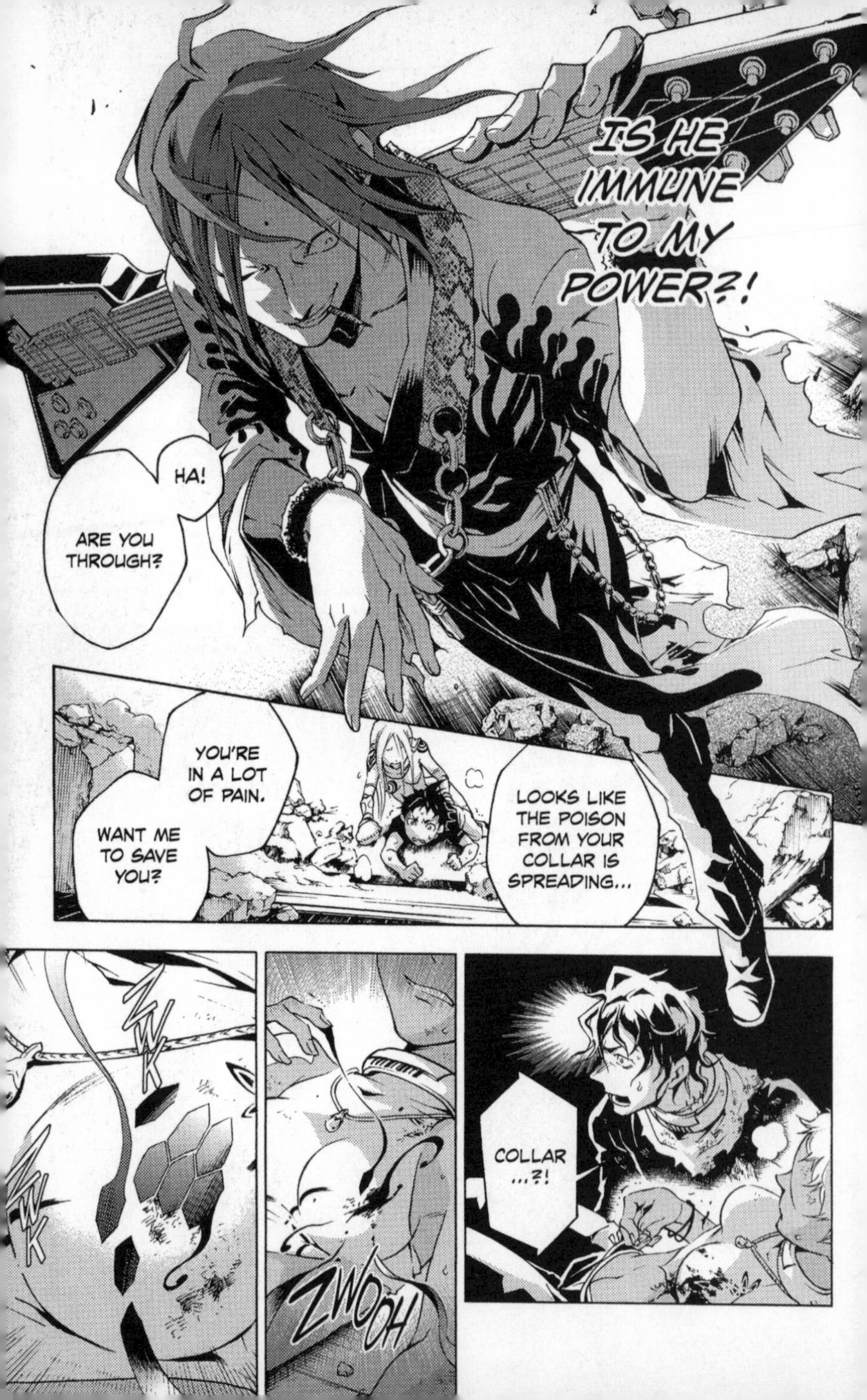
IS HE IMMUNE TO MY POWER?!
HA!
ARE YOU THROUGH?
LOOKS LIKE THE POISON FROM YOUR COLLAR IS SPREADING...
YOU'RE IN A LOT OF PAIN.
WANT ME TO SAVE YOU?
COLLAR ...?!
ZWOOH
NWK
NWK

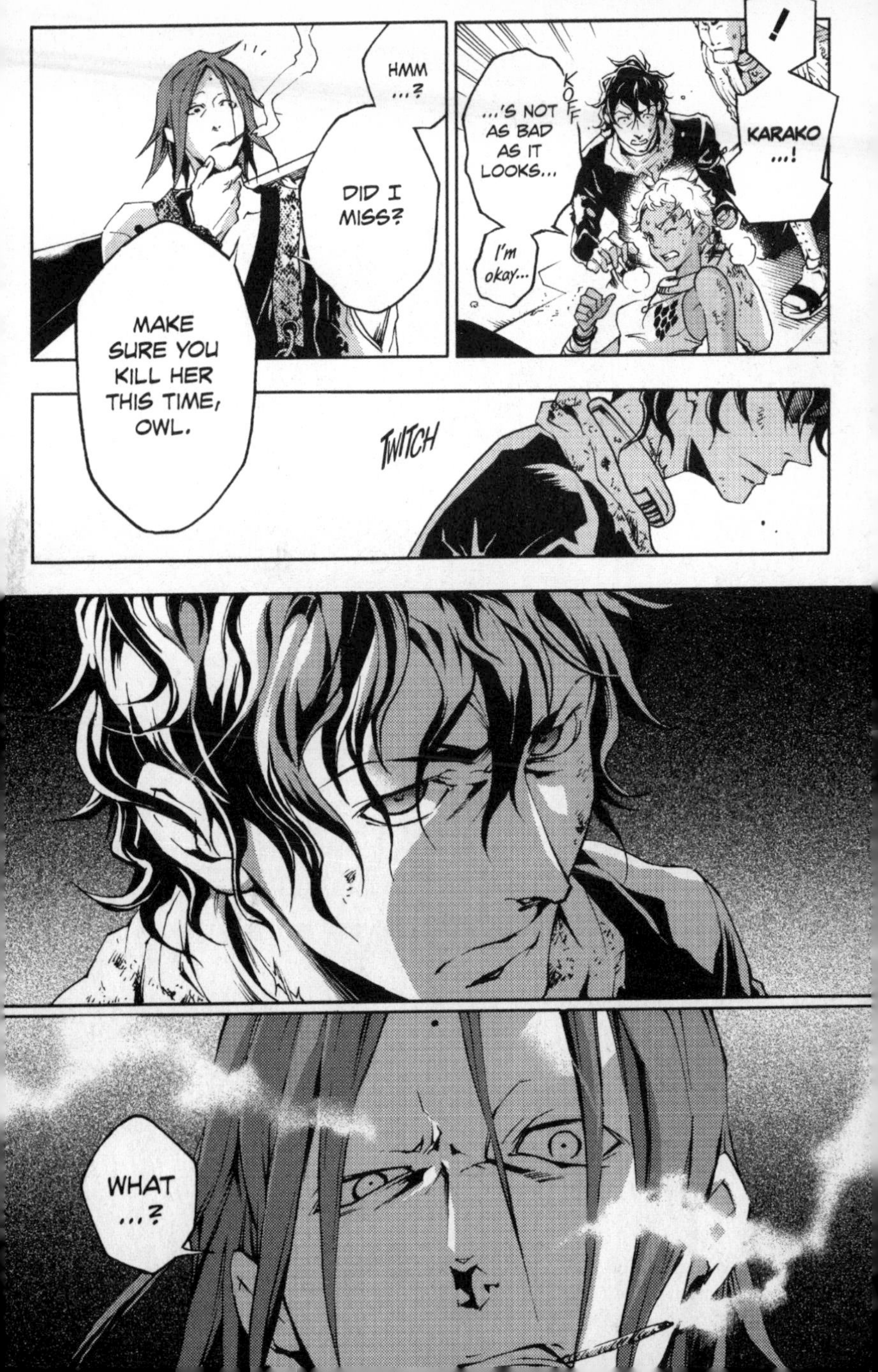
!
KARAKO ...!
KOFF
...'S NOT AS BAD AS IT LOOKS...
I'm okay...
HMM ...?
DID I MISS?
MAKE SURE YOU KILL HER THIS TIME, OWL.
TWITCH
WHAT ...?

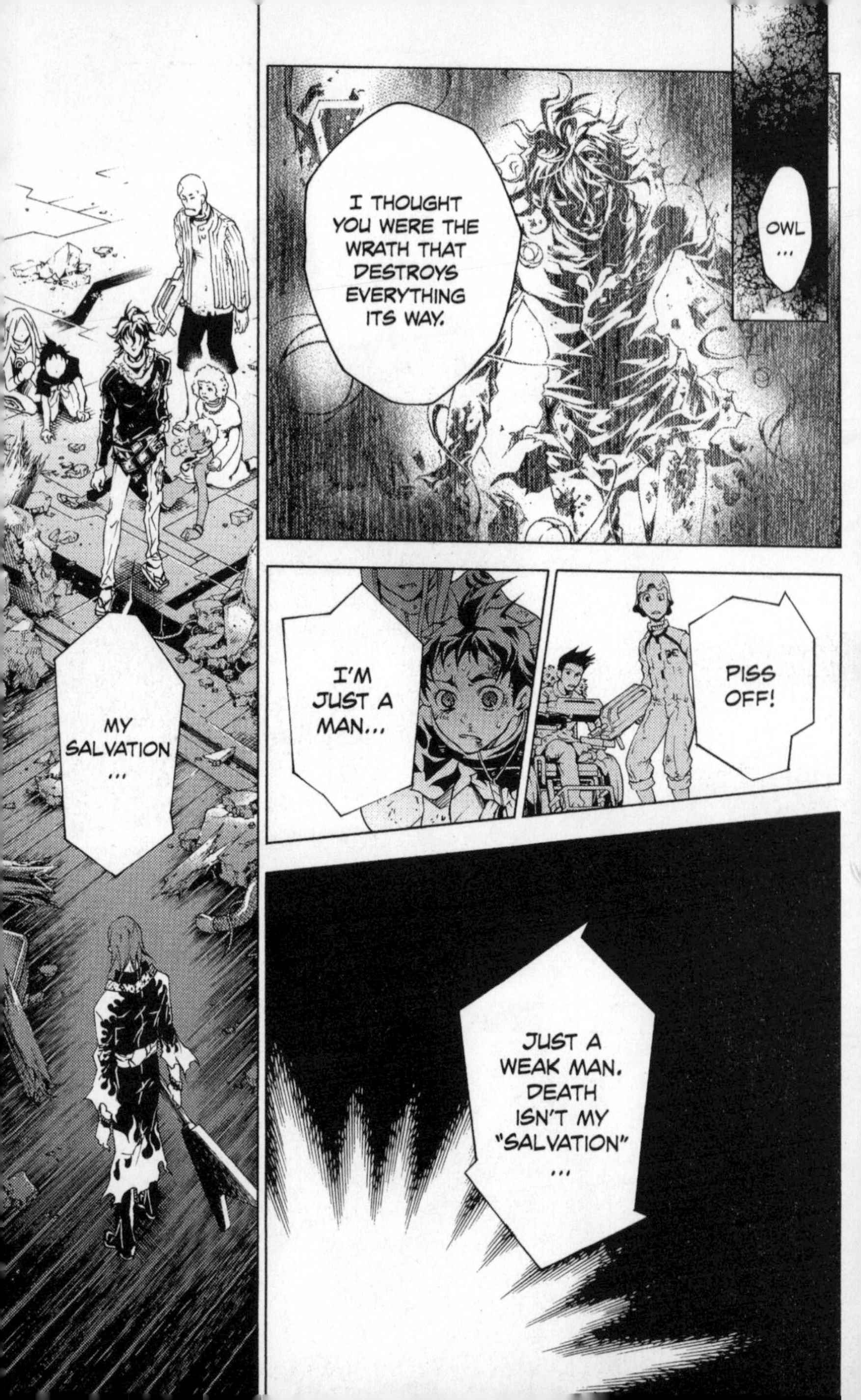
OWL
...
I THOUGHT YOU WERE THE WRATH THAT DESTROYS EVERYTHING ITS WAY.
PISS OFF!
I'M JUST A MAN...
JUST A WEAK MAN. DEATH ISN'T MY "SALVATION"
...
MY SALVATION
...

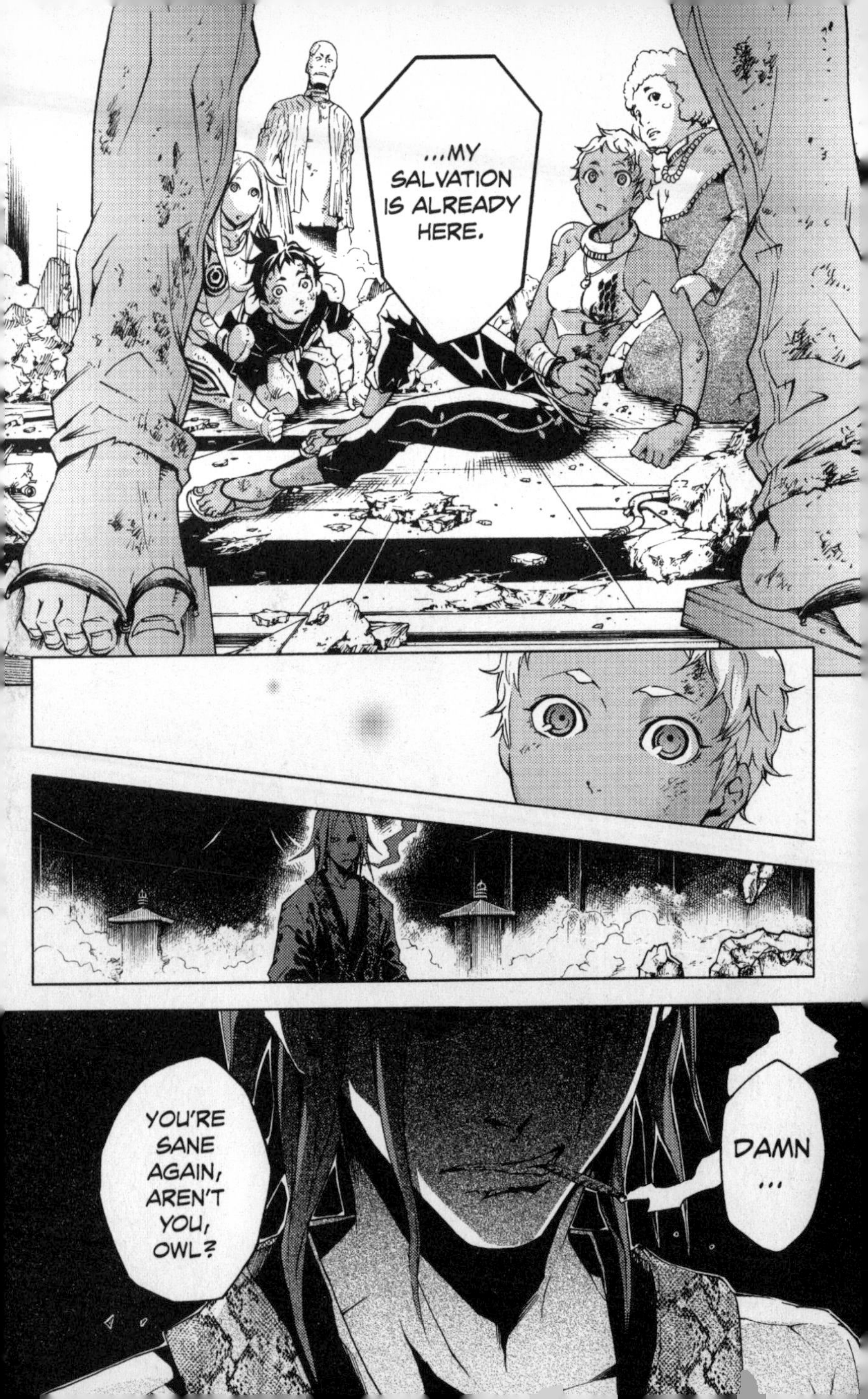
...MY SALVATION IS ALREADY HERE.
DAMN...
YOU'RE SANE AGAIN, AREN'T YOU, OWL?

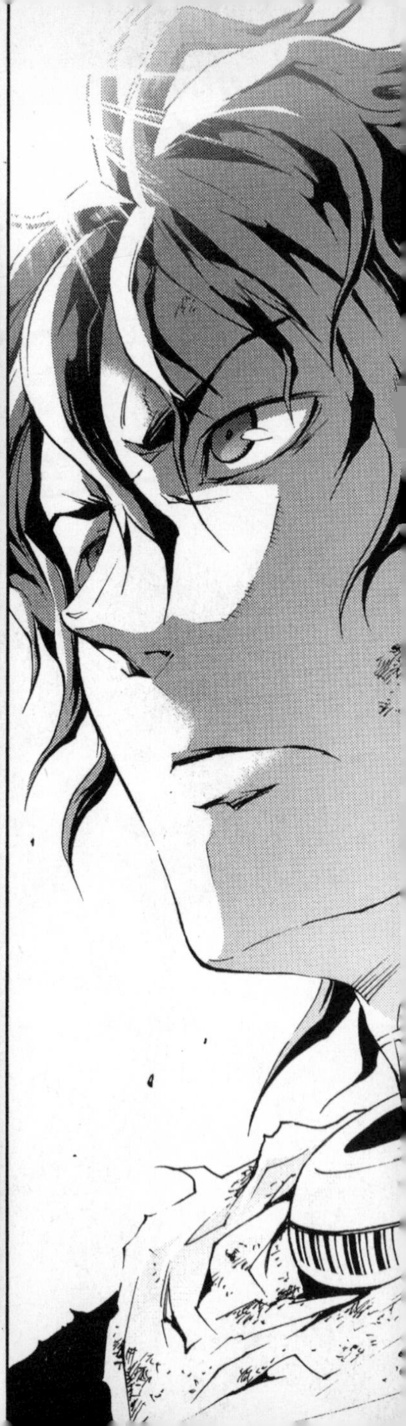
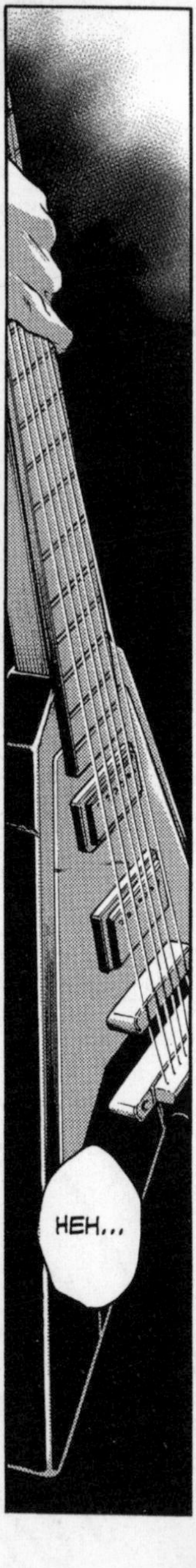
HEH...
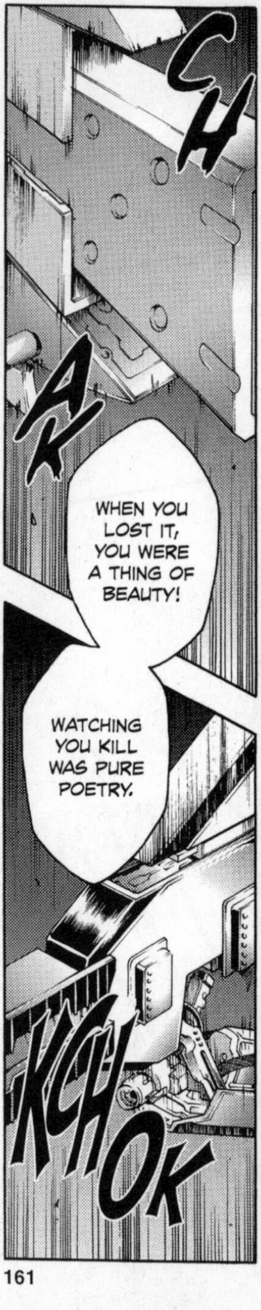
CHAK
WHEN YOU LOST IT, YOU WERE A THING OF BEAUTY!
WATCHING YOU KILL WAS PURE POETRY.
KCHOK

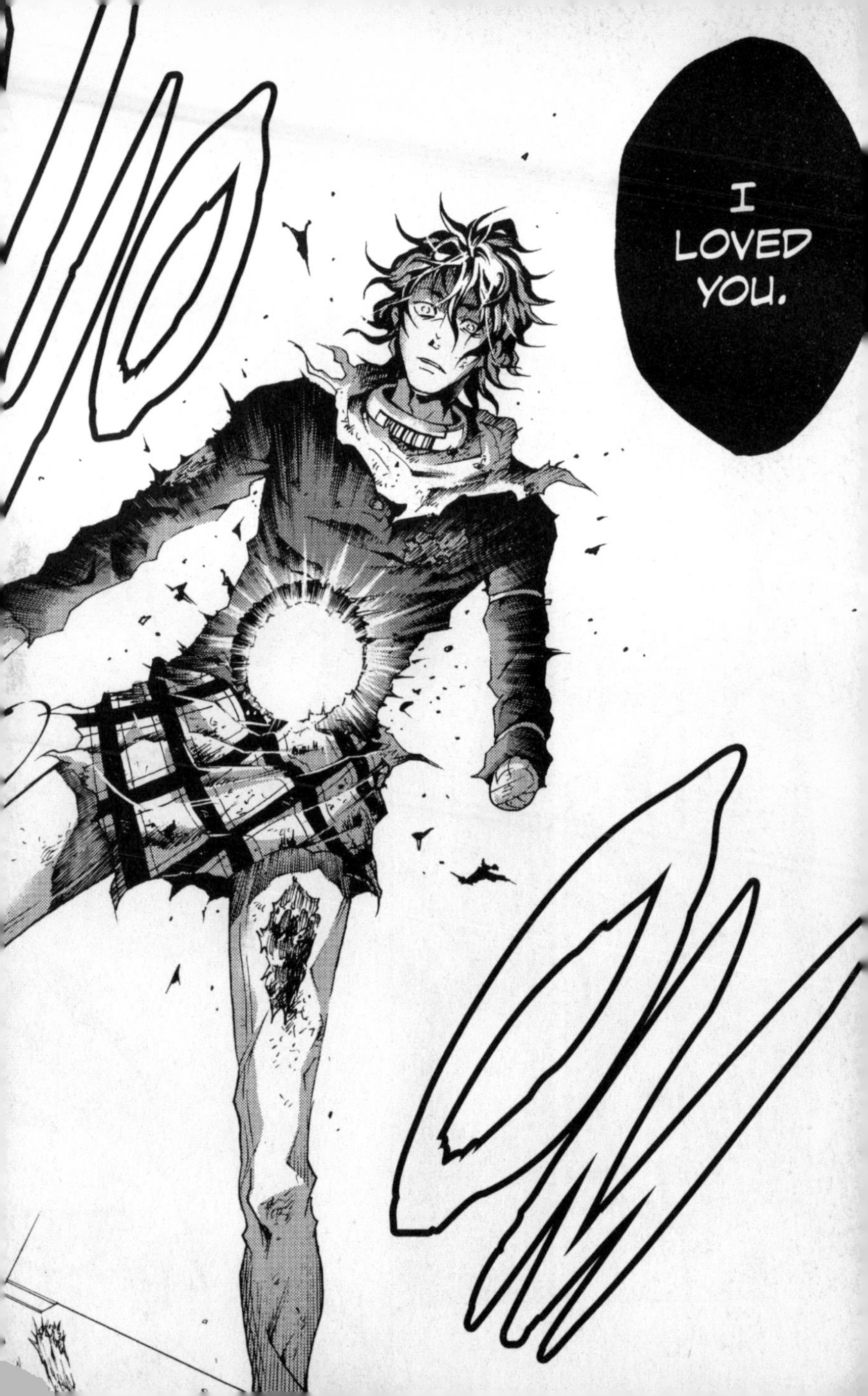
I LOVED YOU.

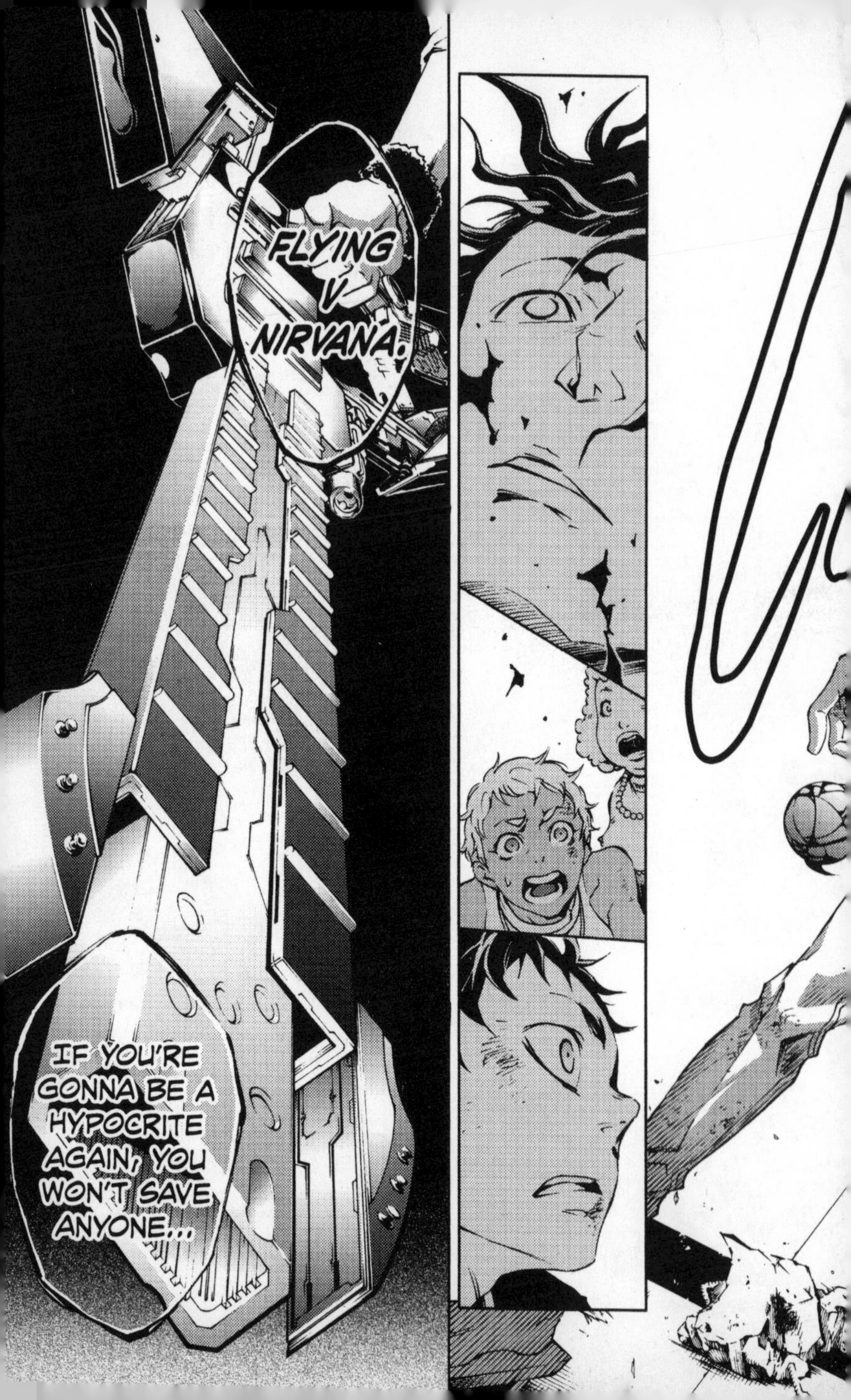
FLYING V NIRVANA.
IF YOU'RE GONNA BE A HYPOCRITE AGAIN, YOU WON'T SAVE ANYONE...

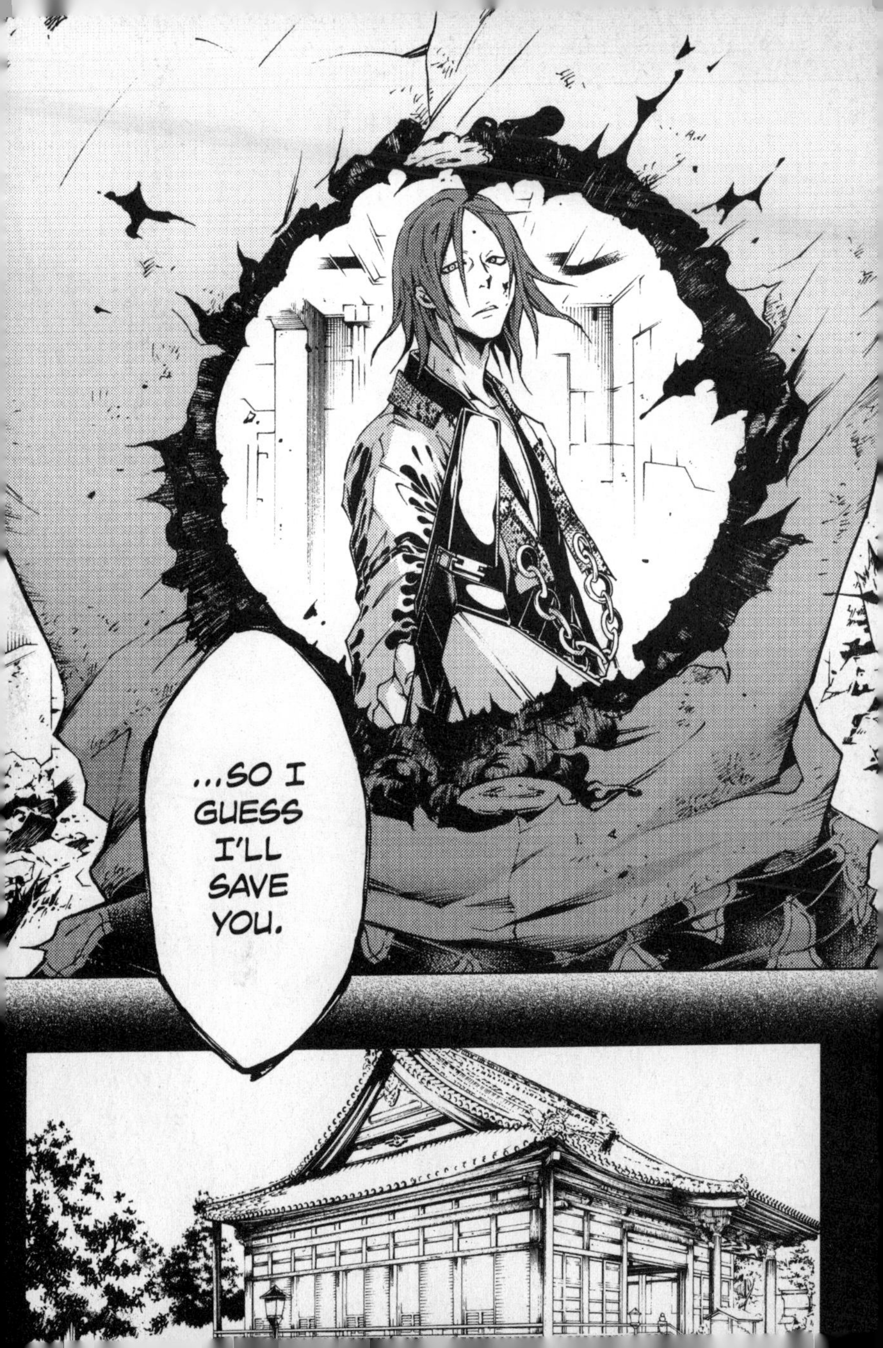
...SO I GUESS I'LL SAVE YOU.

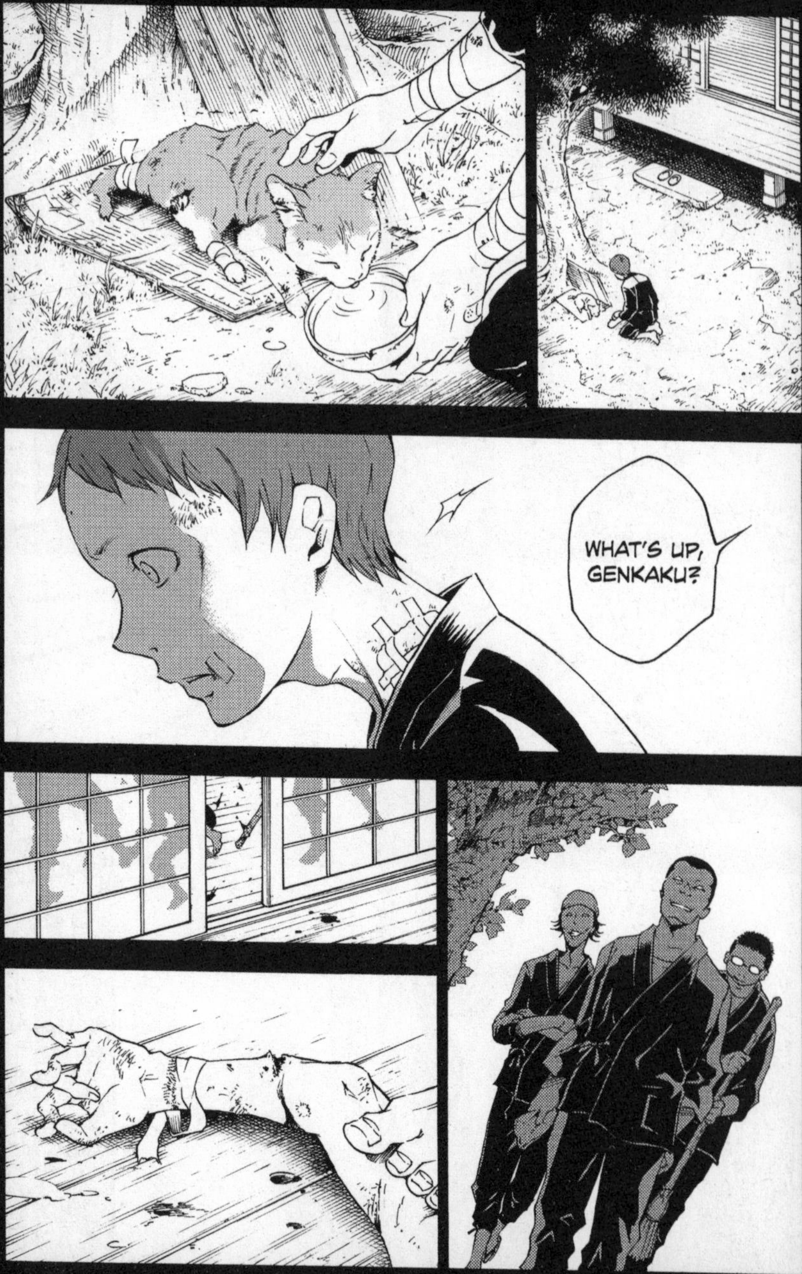
WHAT'S UP, GENKAKU?

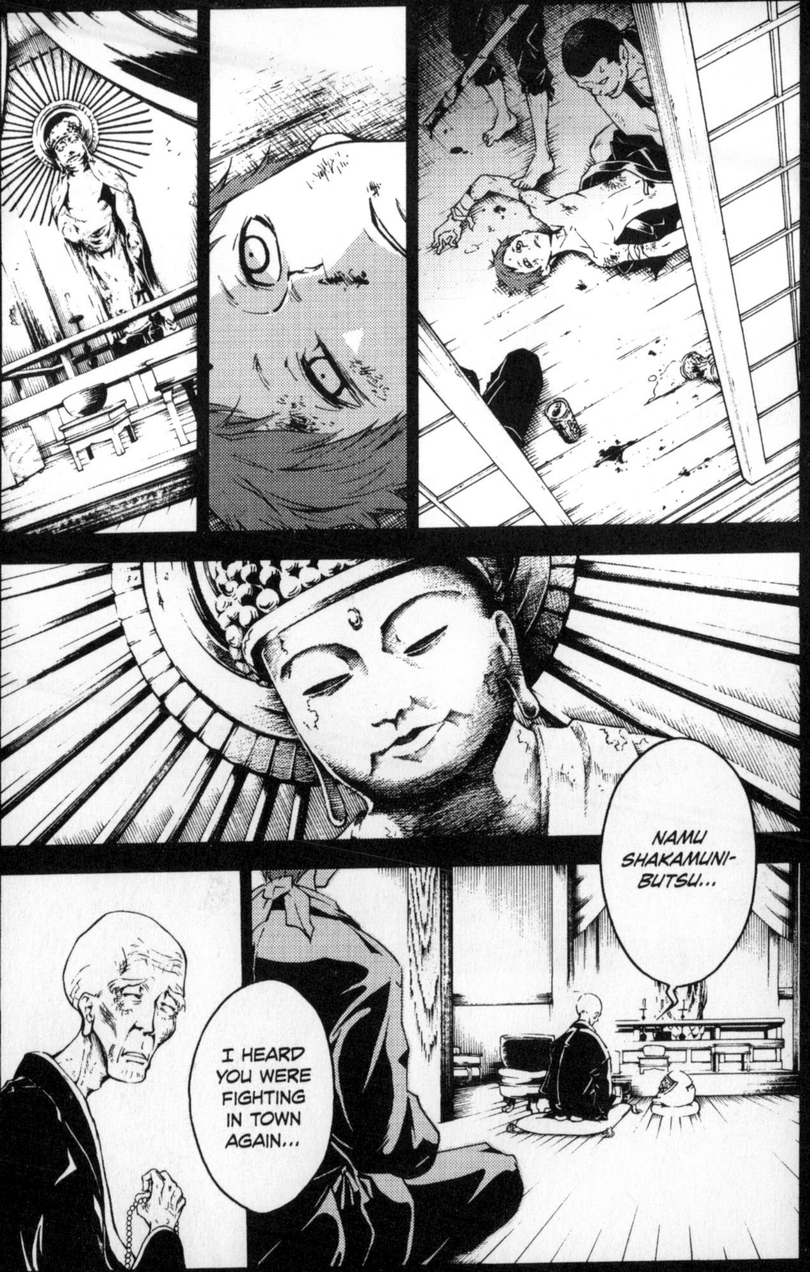
NAMU SHAKAMUNI-BUTSU...
I HEARD YOU WERE FIGHTING IN TOWN AGAIN...

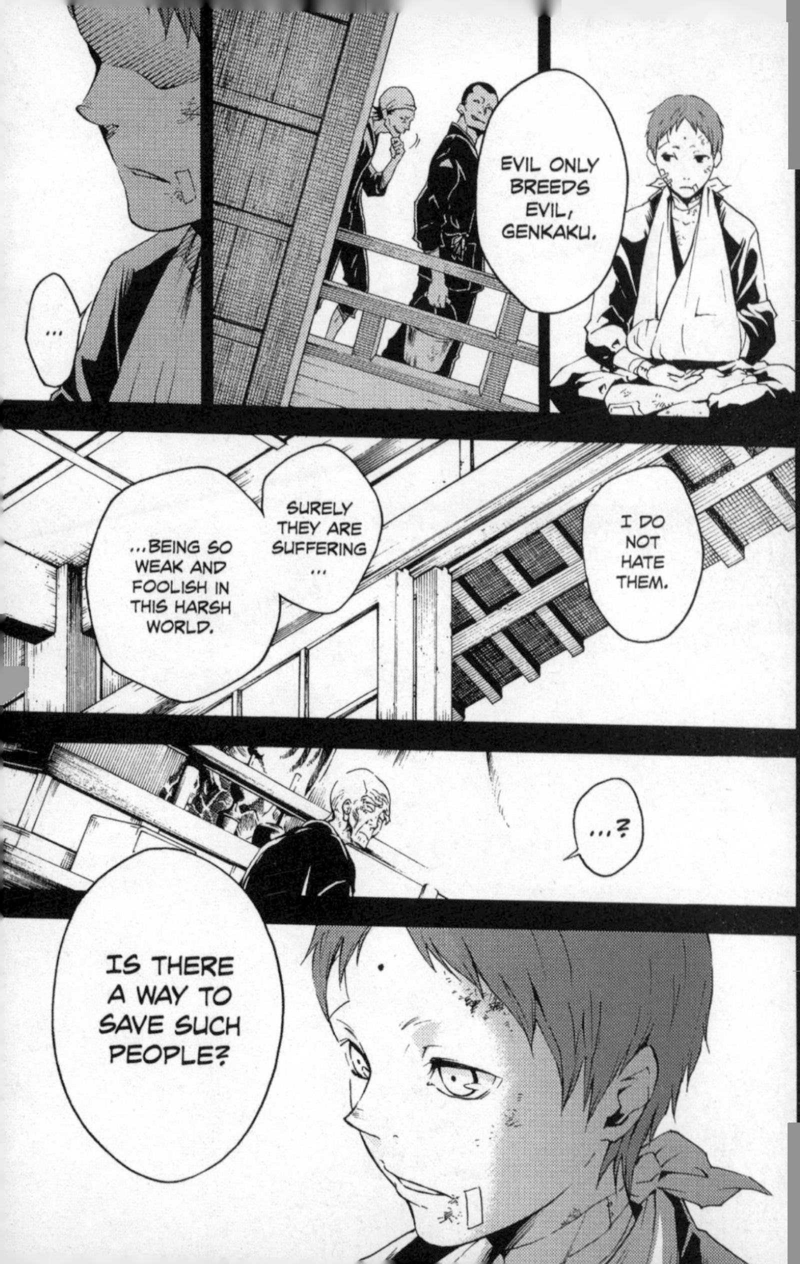
EVIL ONLY BREEDS EVIL, GENKAKU.
...
I DO NOT HATE THEM.
SURELY THEY ARE SUFFERING ...
...BEING SO WEAK AND FOOLISH IN THIS HARSH WORLD.
...?
IS THERE A WAY TO SAVE SUCH PEOPLE?

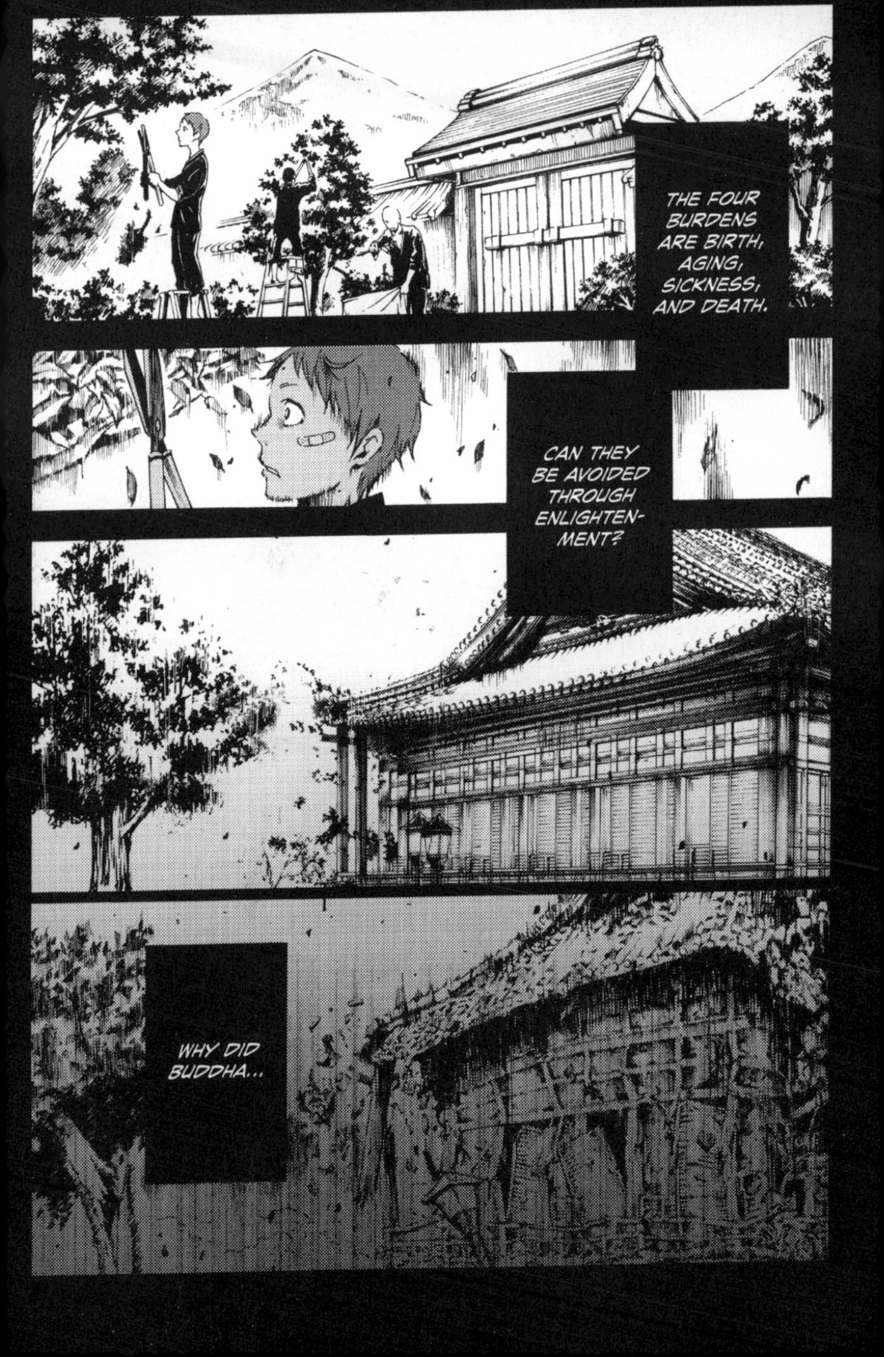
THE FOUR BURDENS ARE BIRTH, AGING, SICKNESS, AND DEATH.
CAN THEY BE AVOIDED THROUGH ENLIGHTEN-MENT?
WHY DID BUDDHA...

WAS A "BURDEN"
EVEN THOUGH HE
NEVER EXPERIENCED
IT HIMSELF?

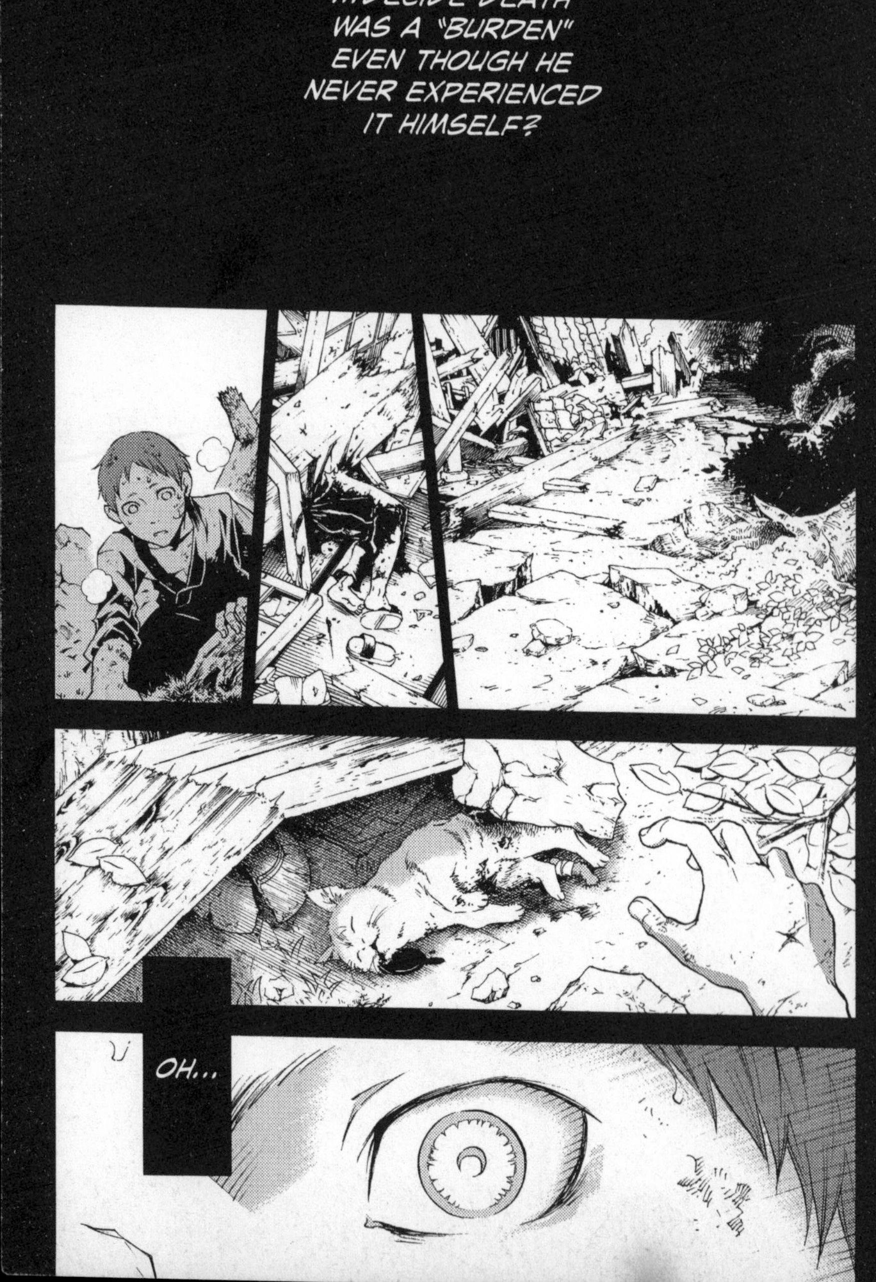
OH...

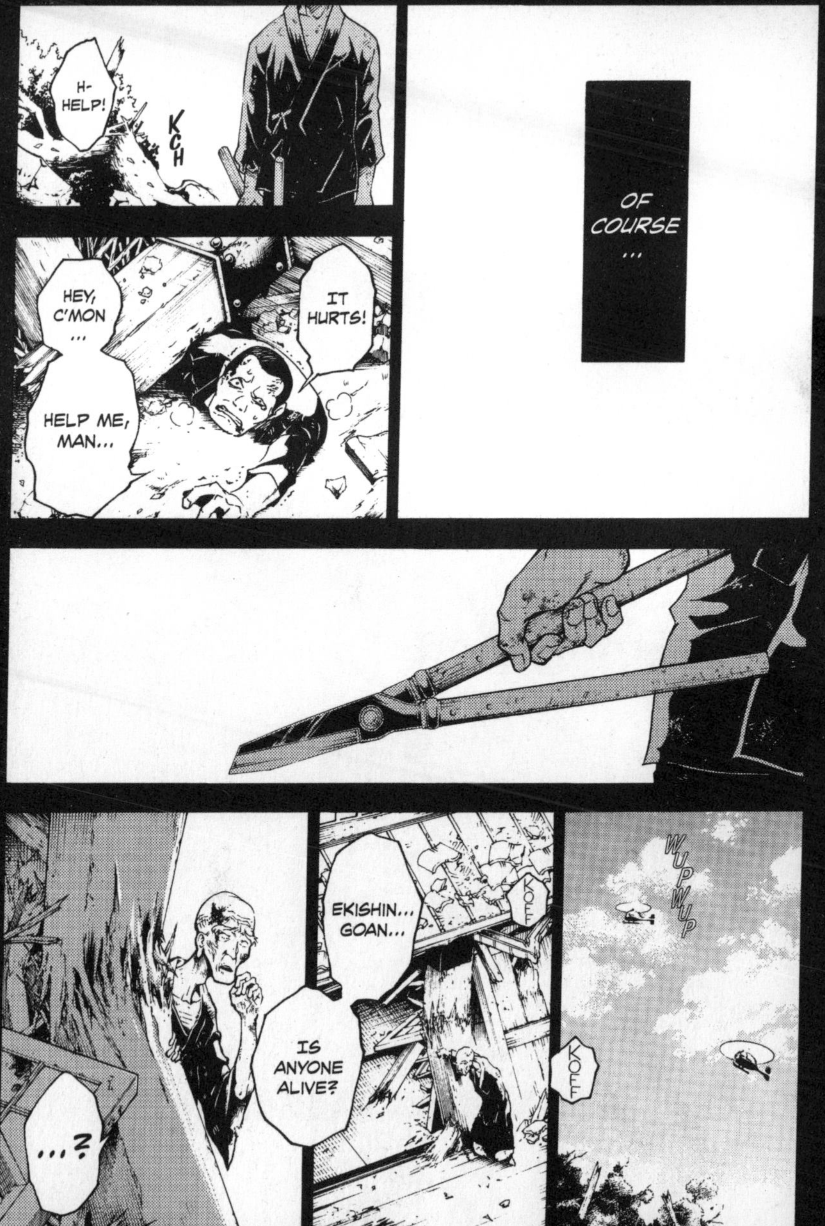
OF COURSE ...
H-HELP!
KCH
HEY, C'MON ...
HELP ME, MAN...
IT HURTS!
WUPWUP
KOFF
KOFF
EKISHIN... GOAN...
IS ANYONE ALIVE?
...?

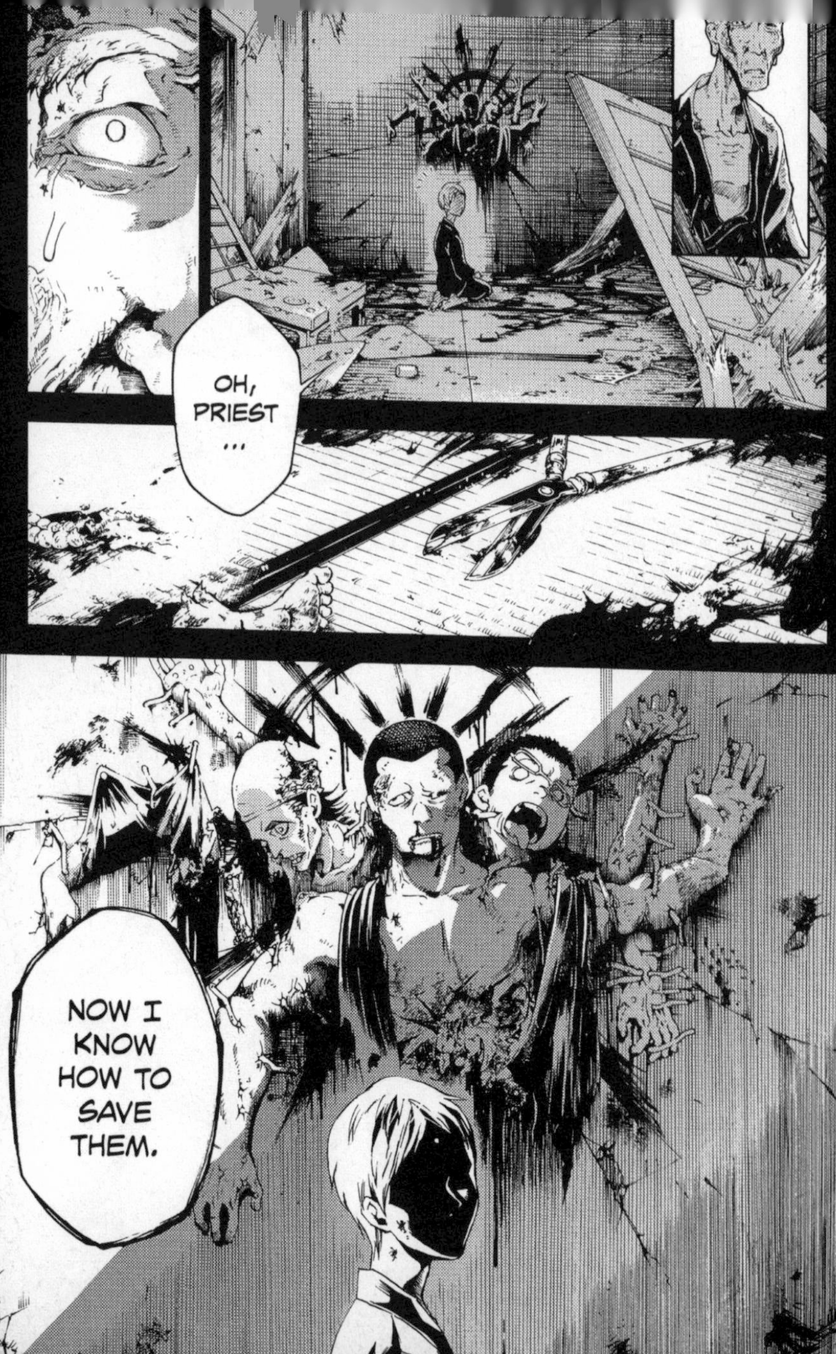
OH, PRIEST ...
NOW I KNOW HOW TO SAVE THEM.

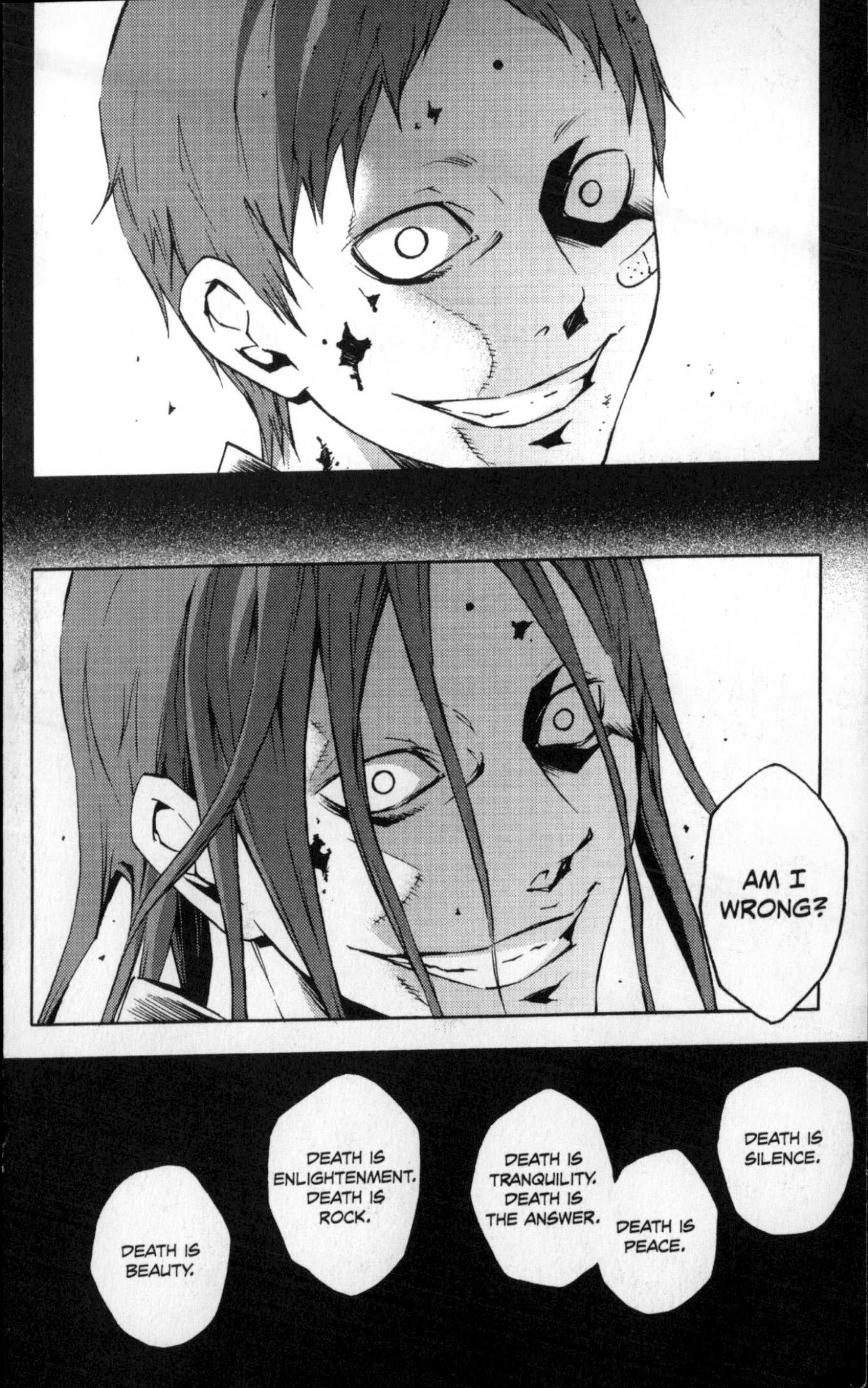
AM I WRONG?
DEATH IS SILENCE.
DEATH IS PEACE.
DEATH IS TRANQUILITY. DEATH IS THE ANSWER.
DEATH IS ENLIGHTENMENT. DEATH IS ROCK.
DEATH IS BEAUTY.

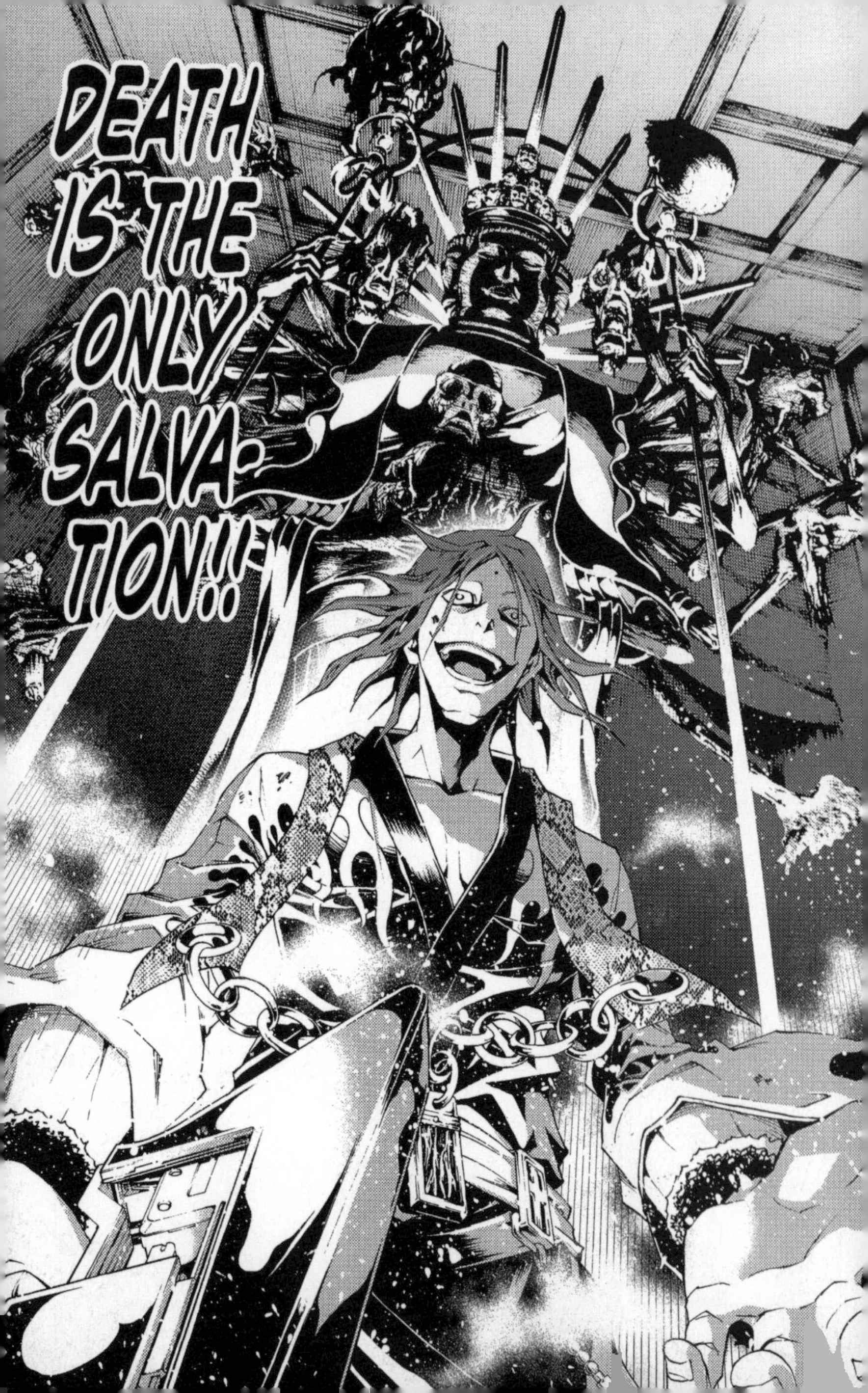
DEATH IS THE ONLY SALVA-TION!!

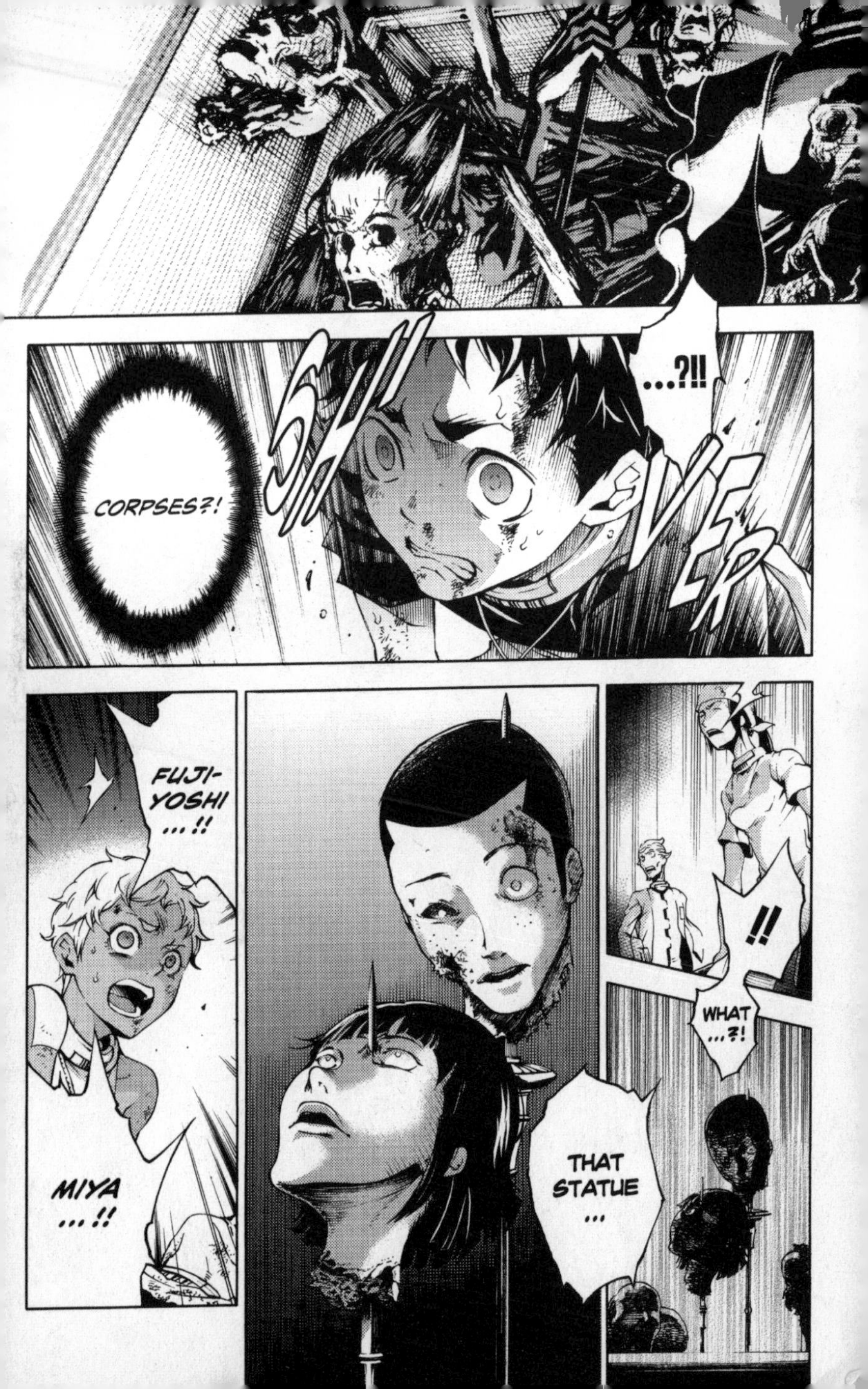
...?!!
SHIVER
CORPSES?!
!!
WHAT ...?!
THAT STATUE ...
FUJI-YOSHI ...!!
MIYA ...!!

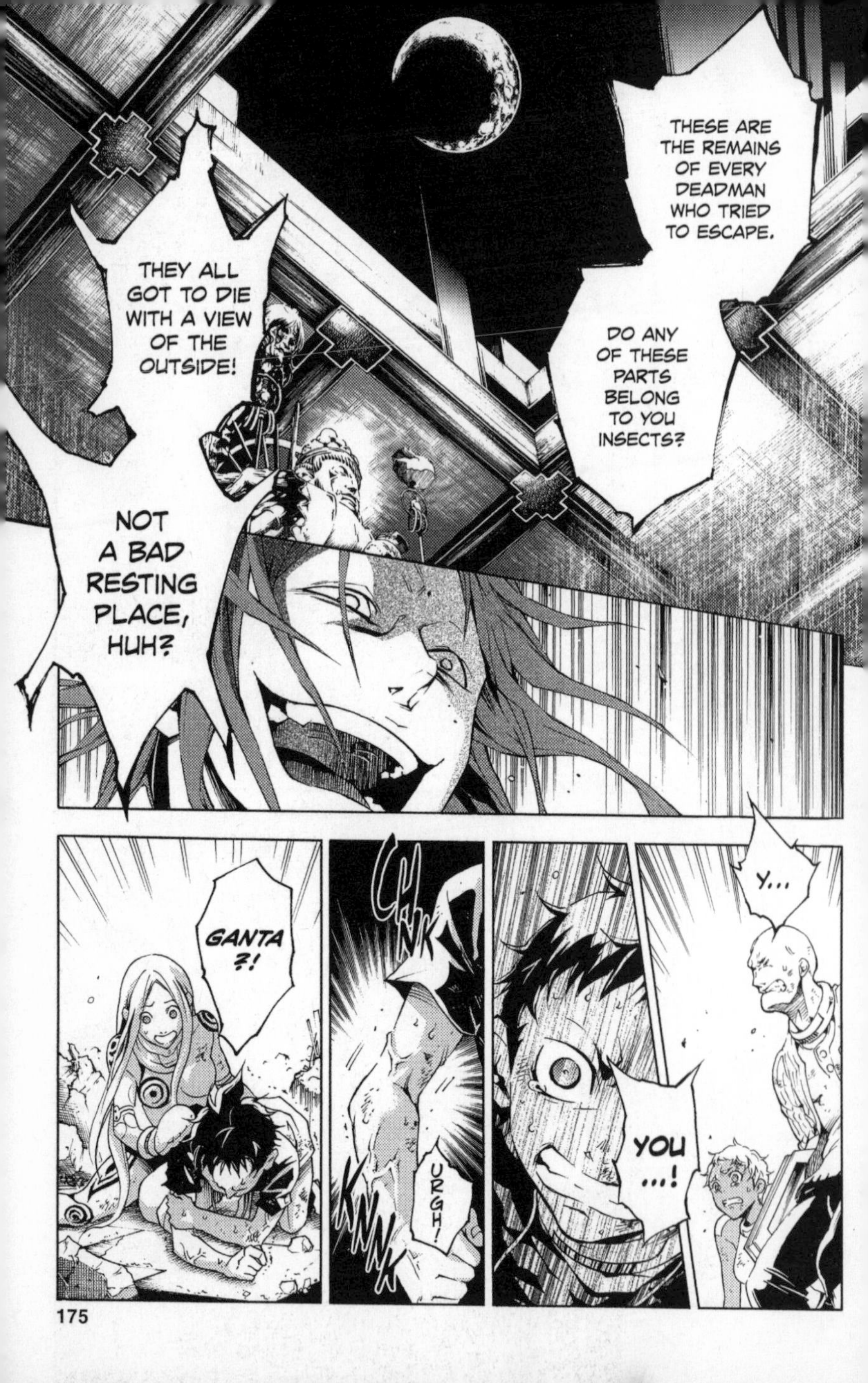
THESE ARE THE REMAINS OF EVERY DEADMAN WHO TRIED TO ESCAPE.
DO ANY OF THESE PARTS BELONG TO YOU INSECTS?
THEY ALL GOT TO DIE WITH A VIEW OF THE OUTSIDE!
NOT A BAD RESTING PLACE, HUH?
Y...
YOU ...!
CHINK
URGH!
KNNNK
GANTA ?!

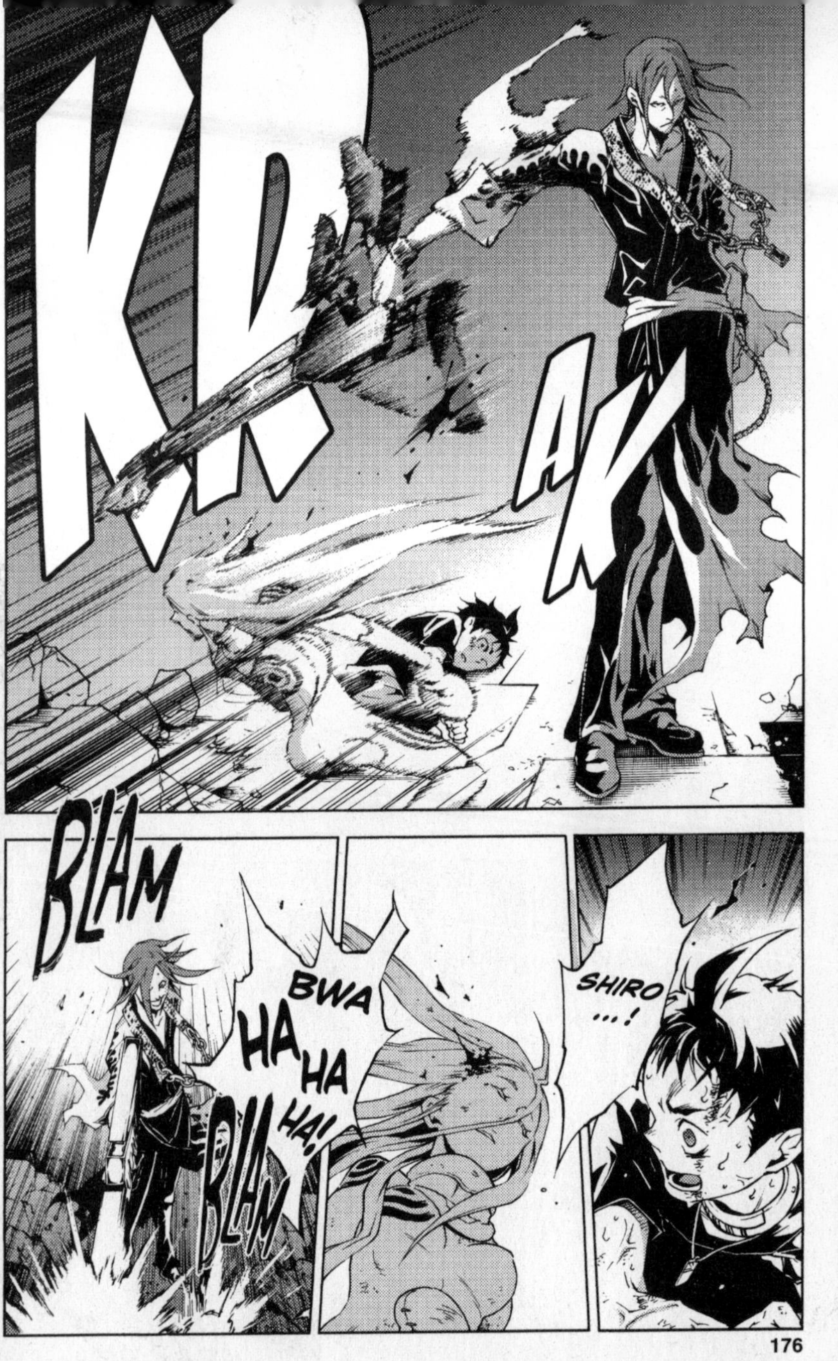
KRAK
SHIRO ...!
BWA HA HA HA!
BLAM
BLAM

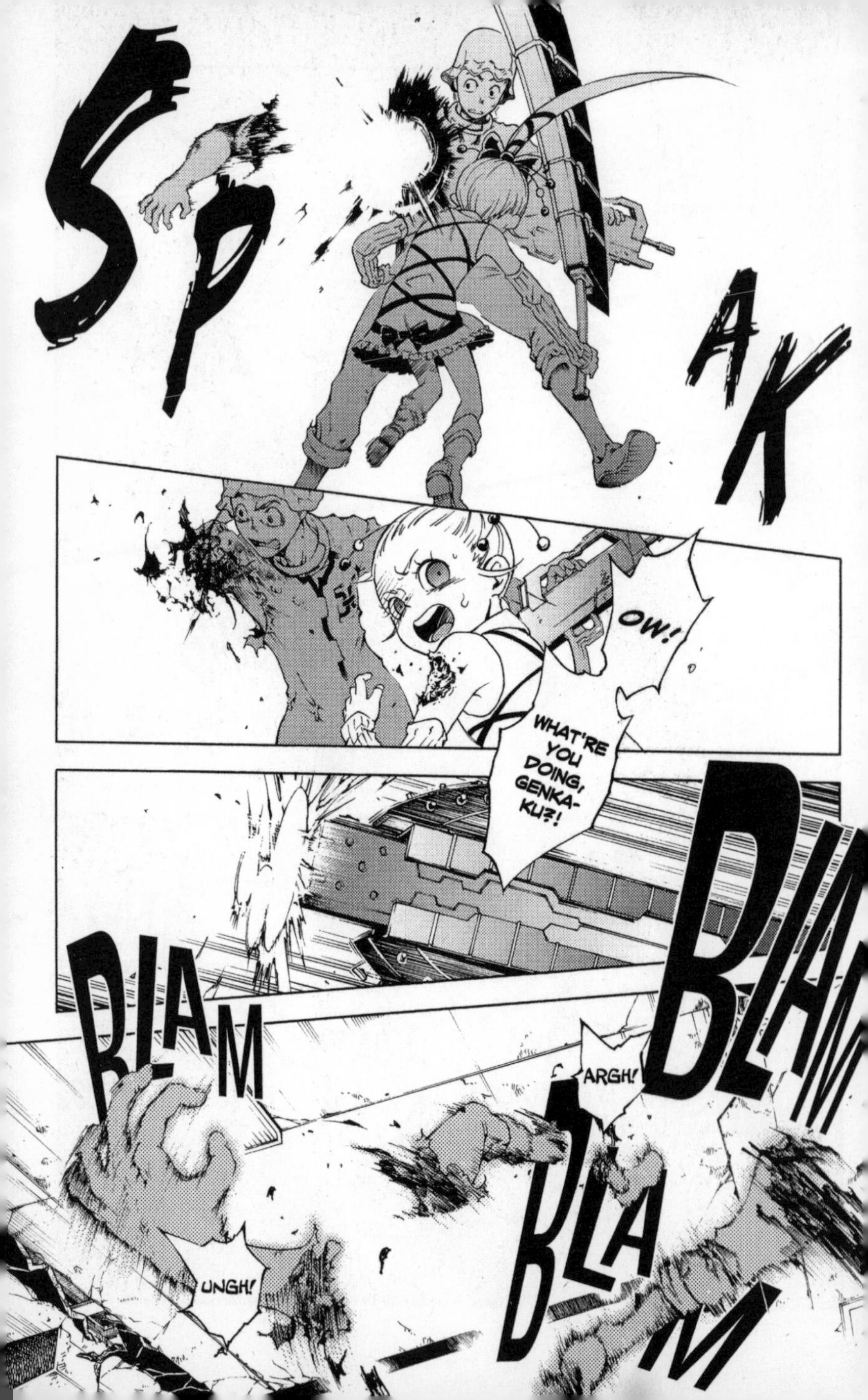
SPAK
OW!
WHAT'RE YOU DOING, GENKAKU?!
BLAM
BLAM
ARGH!
BLAM
UNGH!

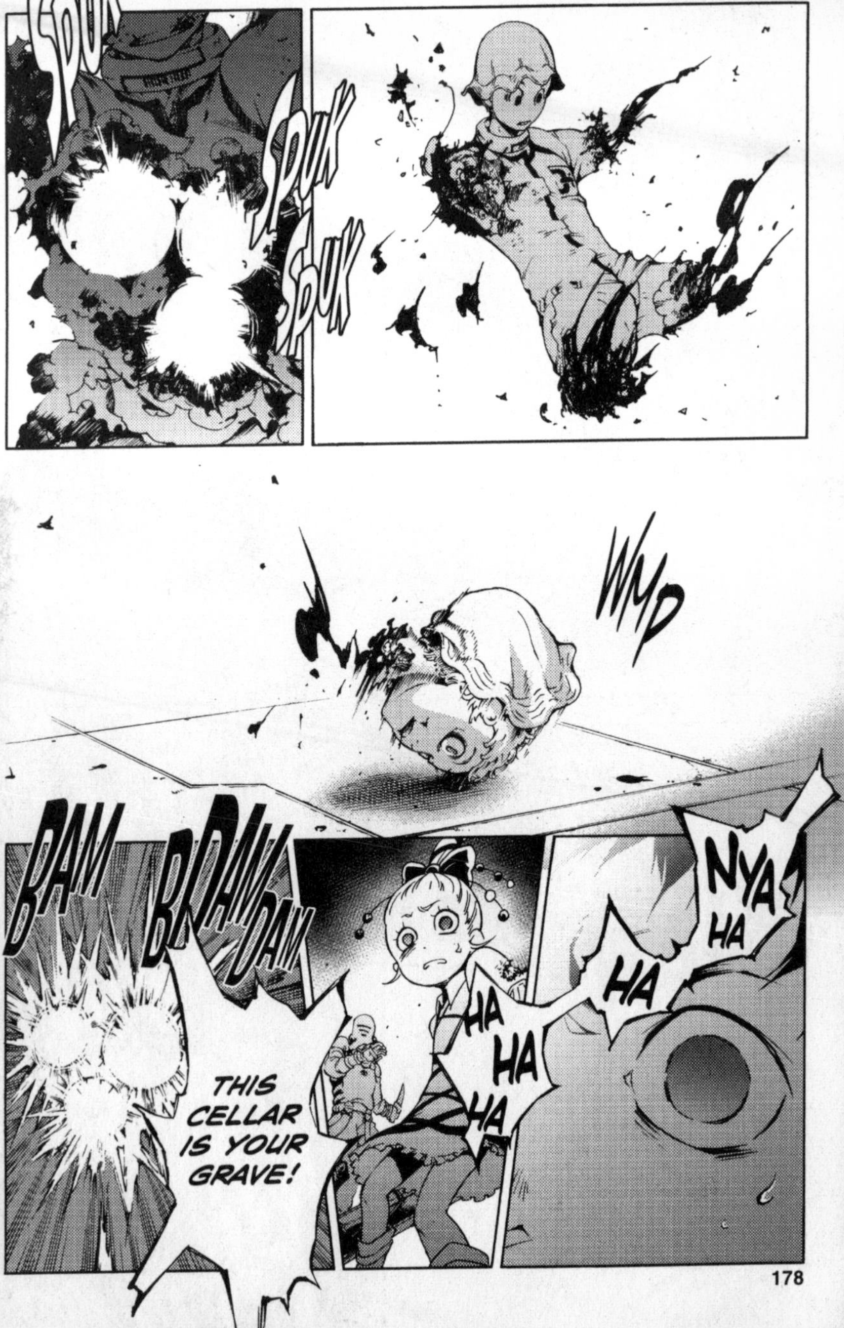
SPUK
SPUK
SPUK
WMP
NYA HA
HA
HA HA HA HA
BAM
BDAM DAM
THIS CELLAR IS YOUR GRAVE!

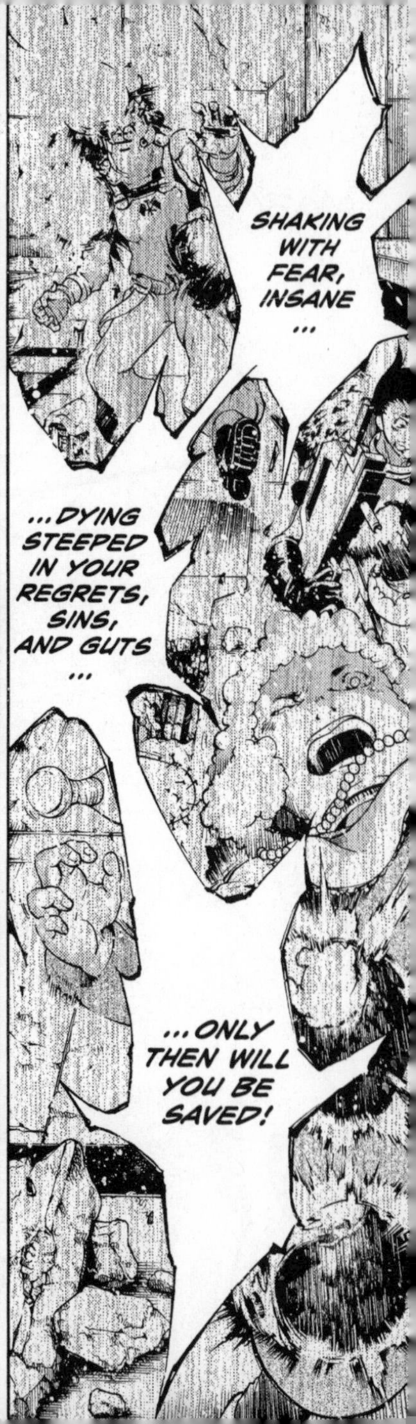
SHAKING WITH FEAR, INSANE ...
...DYING STEEPED IN YOUR REGRETS, SINS, AND GUTS ...
...ONLY THEN WILL YOU BE SAVED!
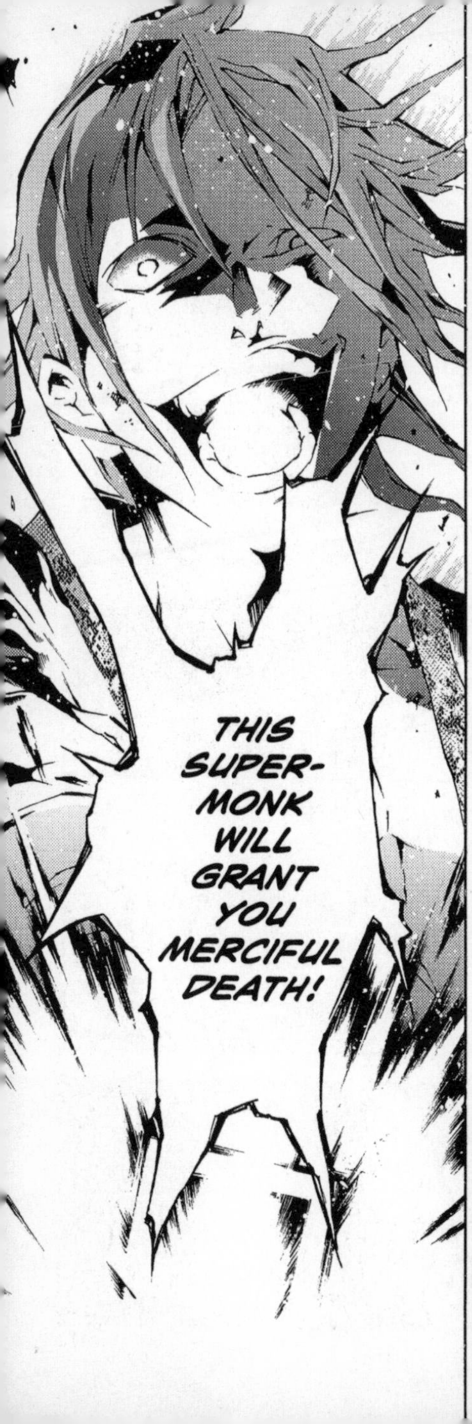
THIS SUPER-MONK WILL GRANT YOU MERCIFUL DEATH!

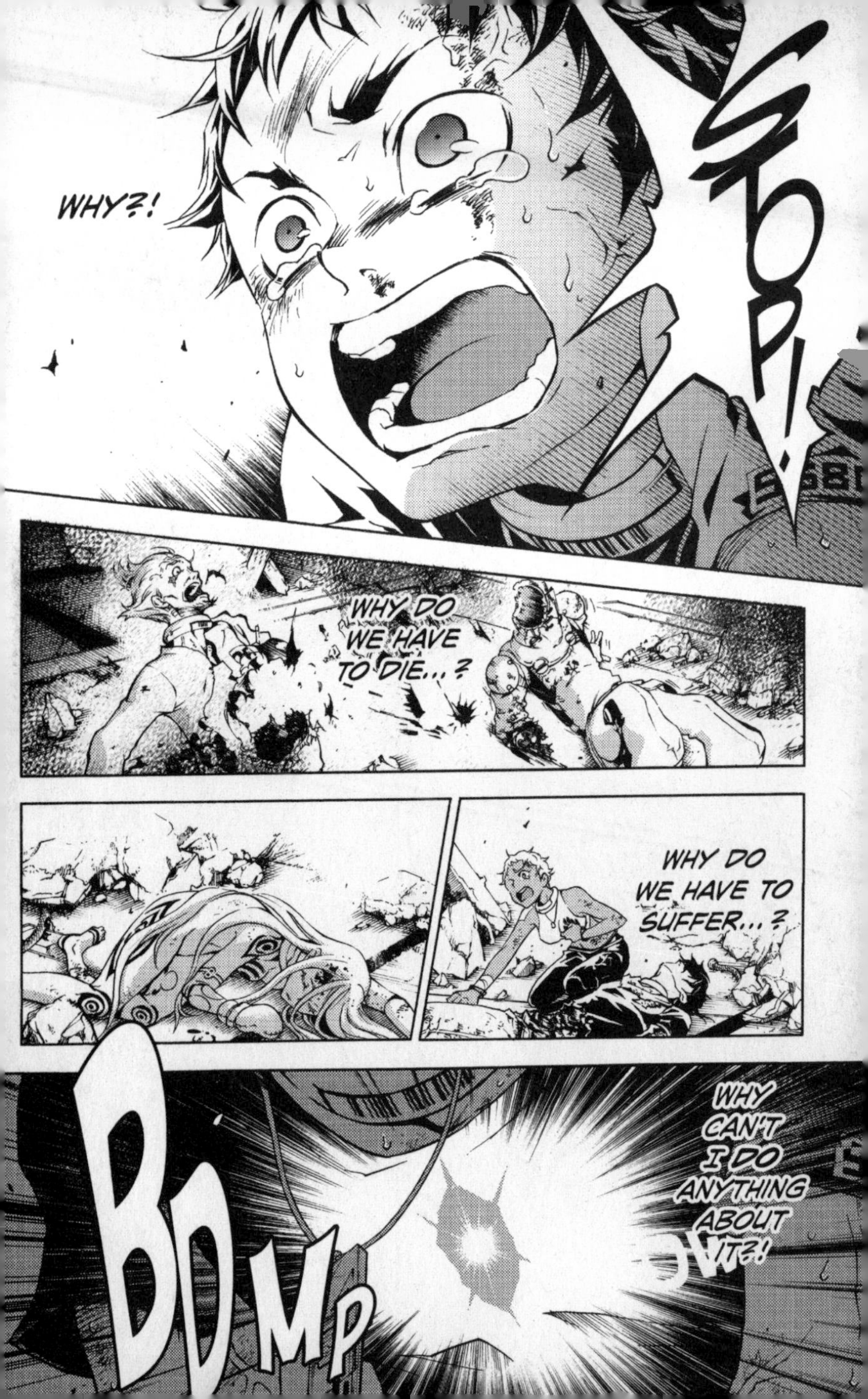
STOP!
WHY?!
WHY DO WE HAVE TO DIE...?
WHY DO WE HAVE TO SUFFER...?
WHY CAN'T I DO ANYTHING ABOUT IT?!
BADUMP

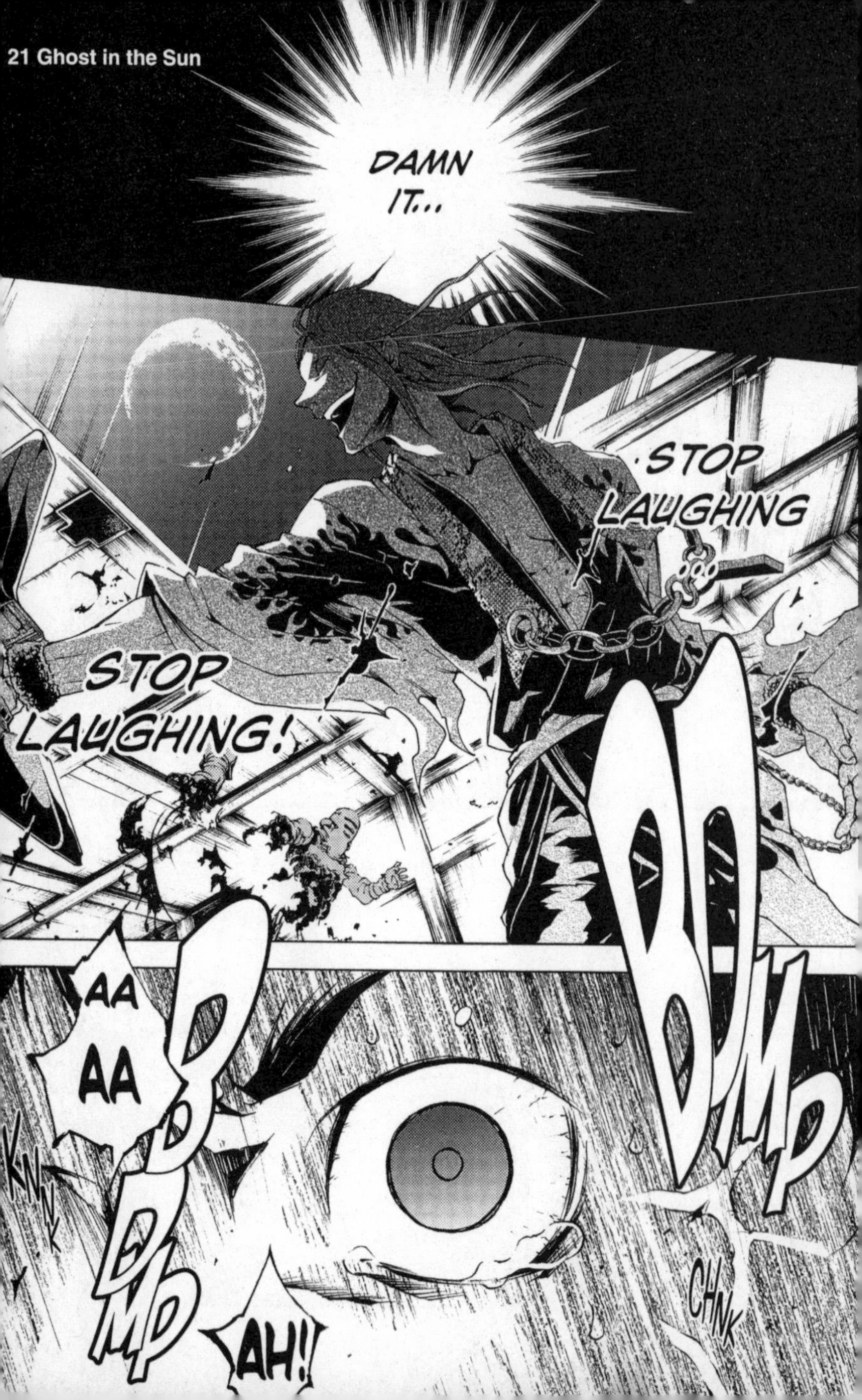
DAMN IT...
STOP LAUGHING
STOP LAUGHING!
BUMP
CHNK
AA AA
AH!

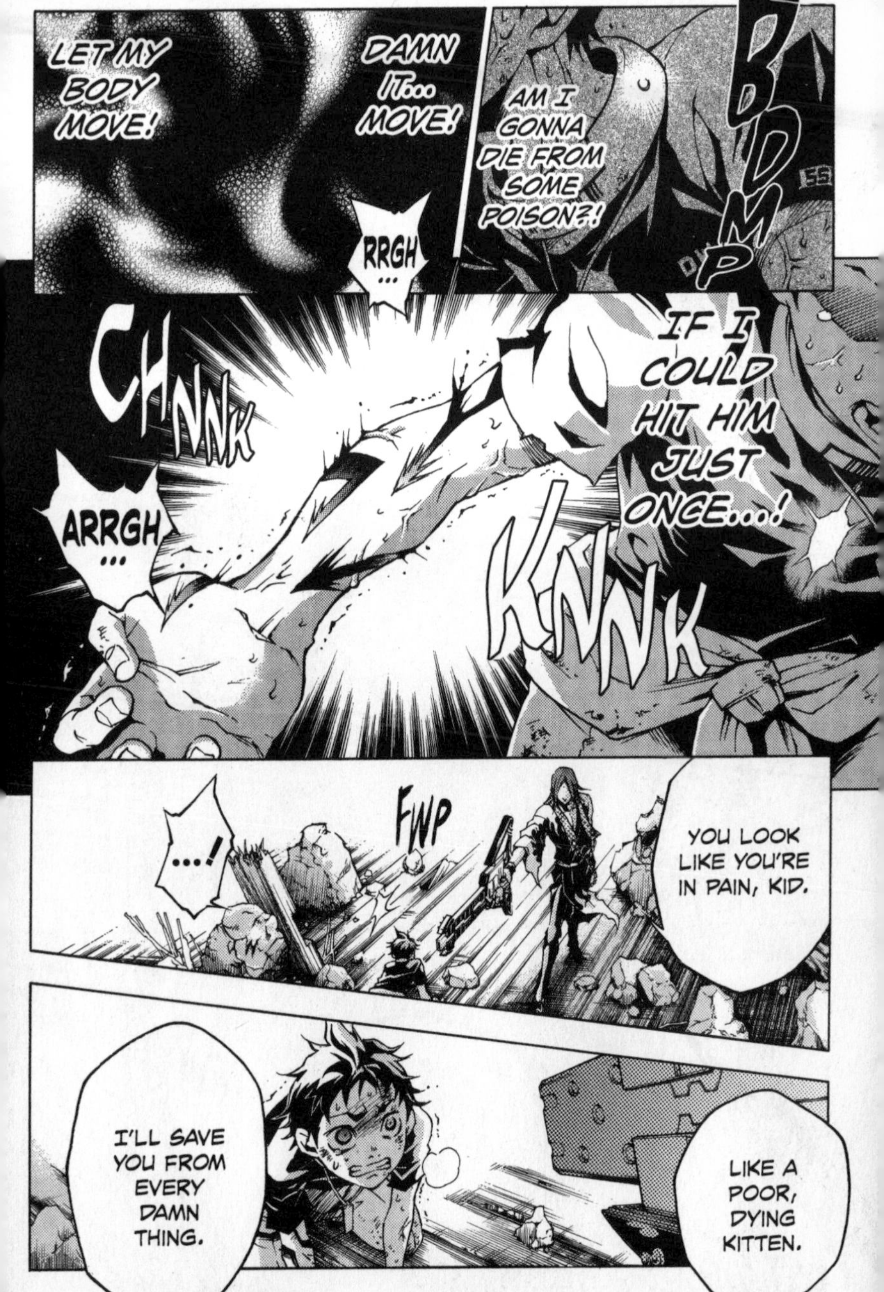
BDMP
AM I GONNA DIE FROM SOME POISON?!
DAMN IT... MOVE!
RRGH...
LET MY BODY MOVE!
IF I COULD HIT HIM JUST ONCE...!
KNNK
CHNNK
ARRGH...
YOU LOOK LIKE YOU'RE IN PAIN, KID.
FWP
...!
LIKE A POOR, DYING KITTEN.
I'LL SAVE YOU FROM EVERY DAMN THING.

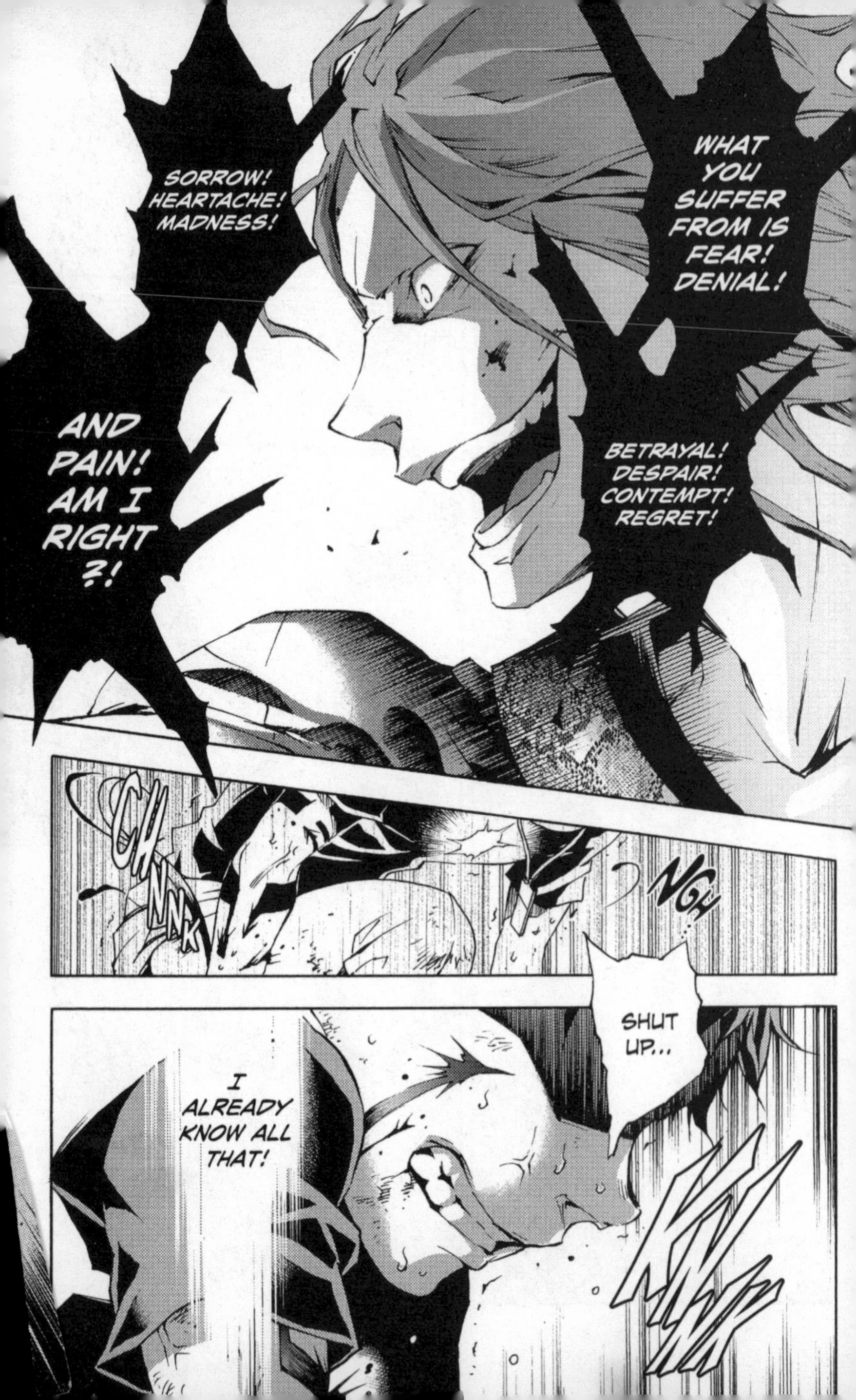
WHAT YOU SUFFER FROM IS FEAR! DENIAL!
SORROW! HEARTACHE! MADNESS!
BETRAYAL! DESPAIR! CONTEMPT! REGRET!
AND PAIN! AM I RIGHT?!
NGH
CHNNNK
SHUT UP...
I ALREADY KNOW ALL THAT!

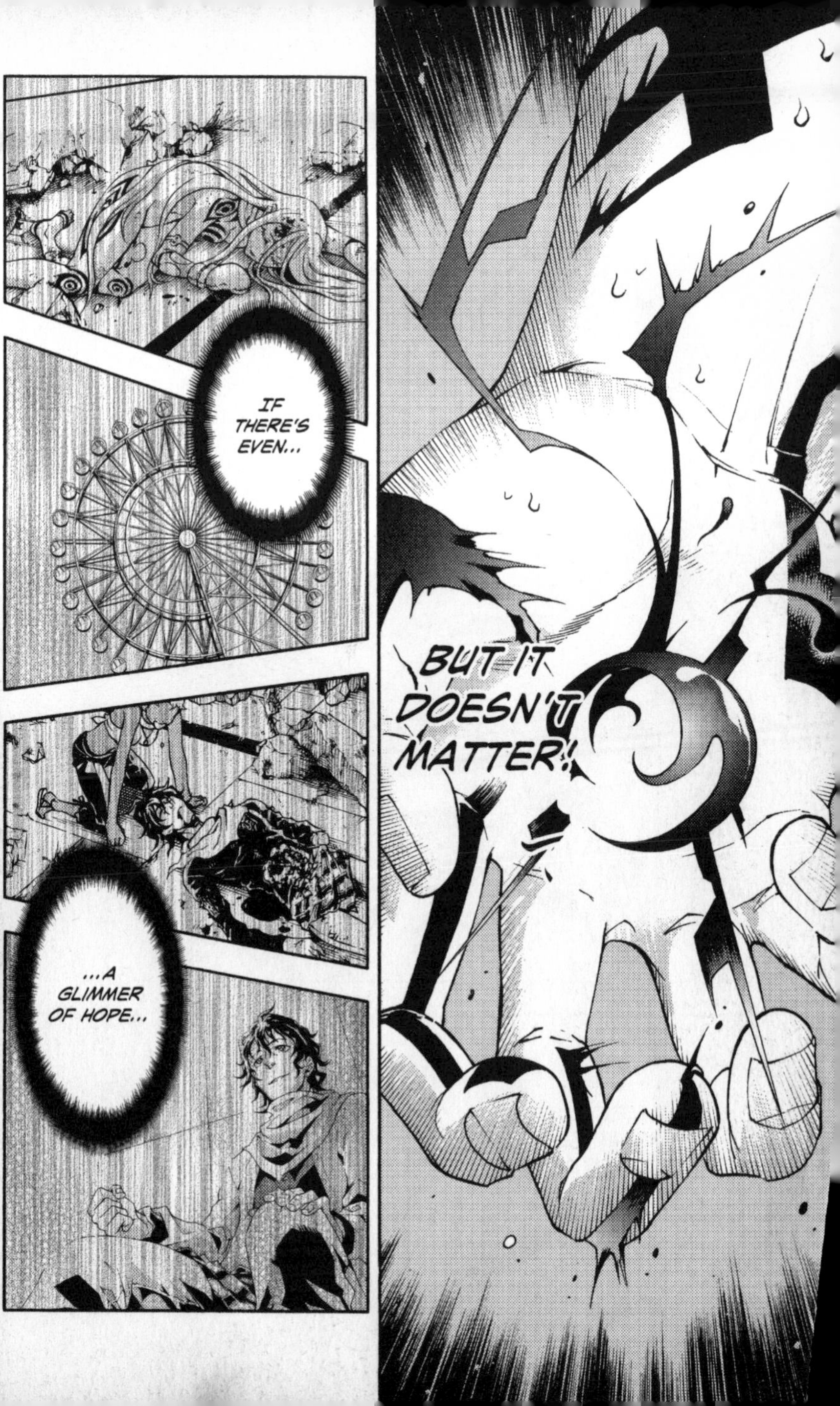
BUT IT DOESN'T MATTER!
IF THERE'S EVEN...
...A GLIMMER OF HOPE...

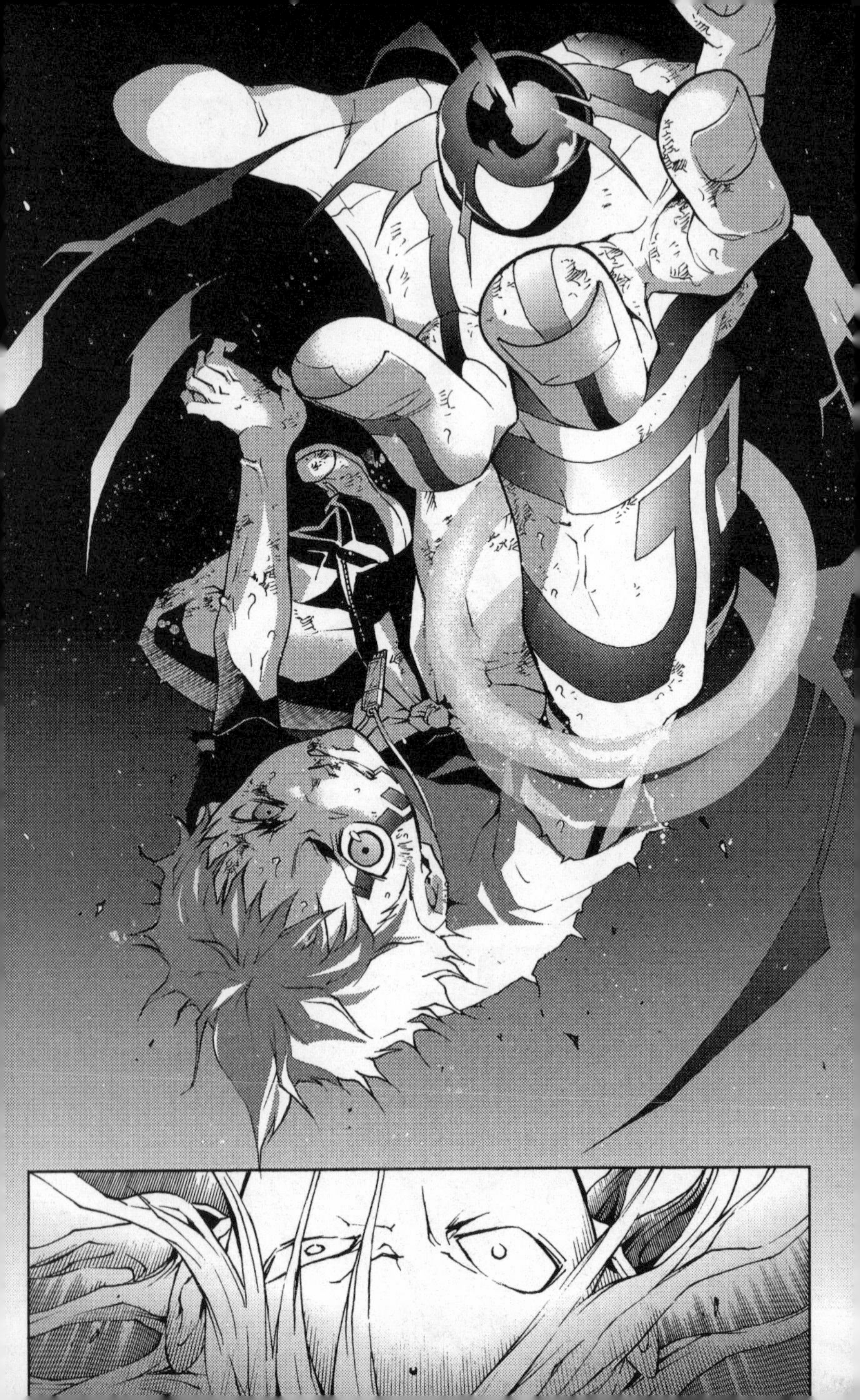

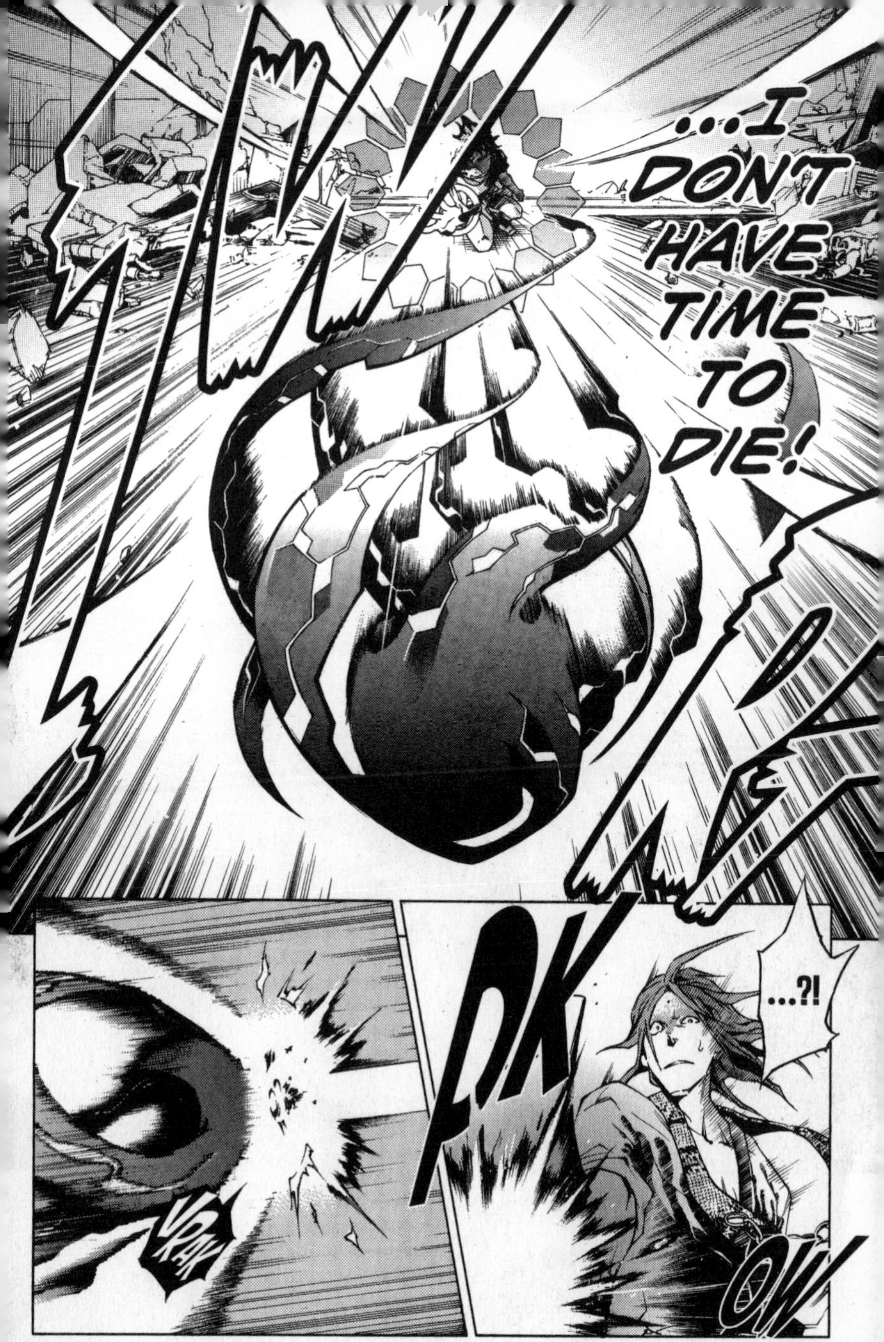
...I DON'T HAVE TIME TO DIE!
...?!
VRAK

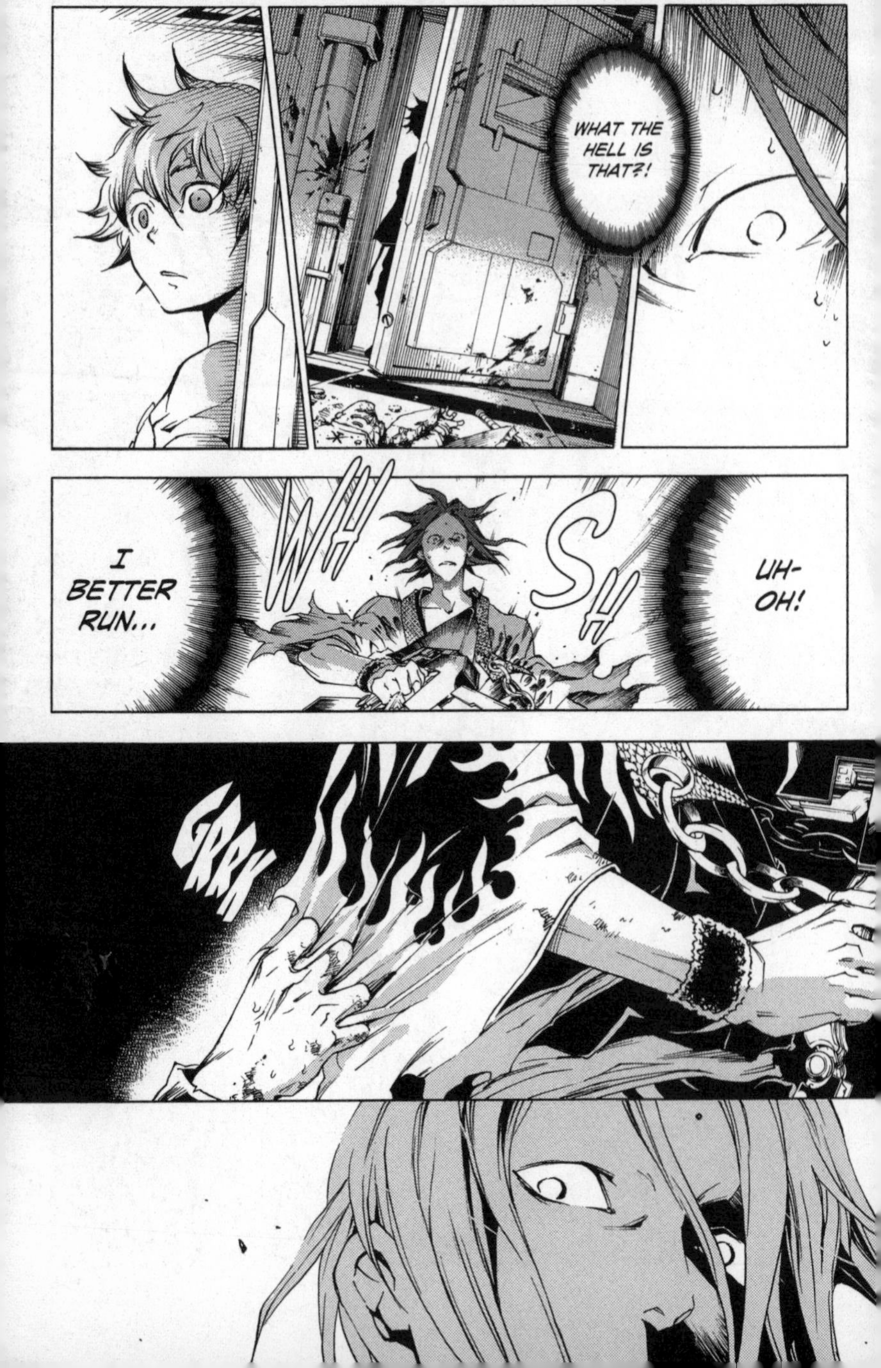
WHAT THE HELL IS THAT?!
UH-OH!
WHSH
I BETTER RUN...
GRRK

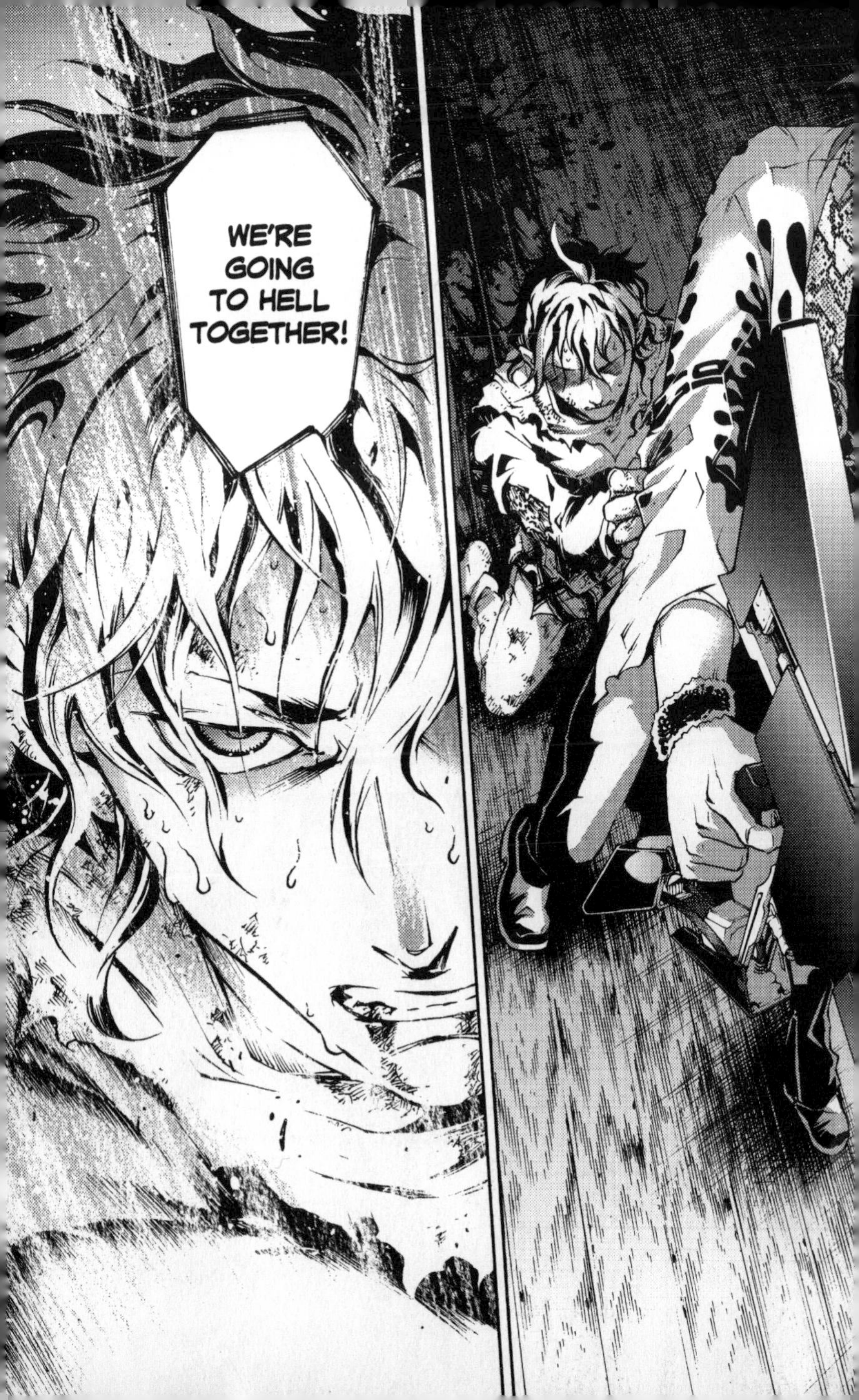
WE'RE GOING TO HELL TOGETHER!

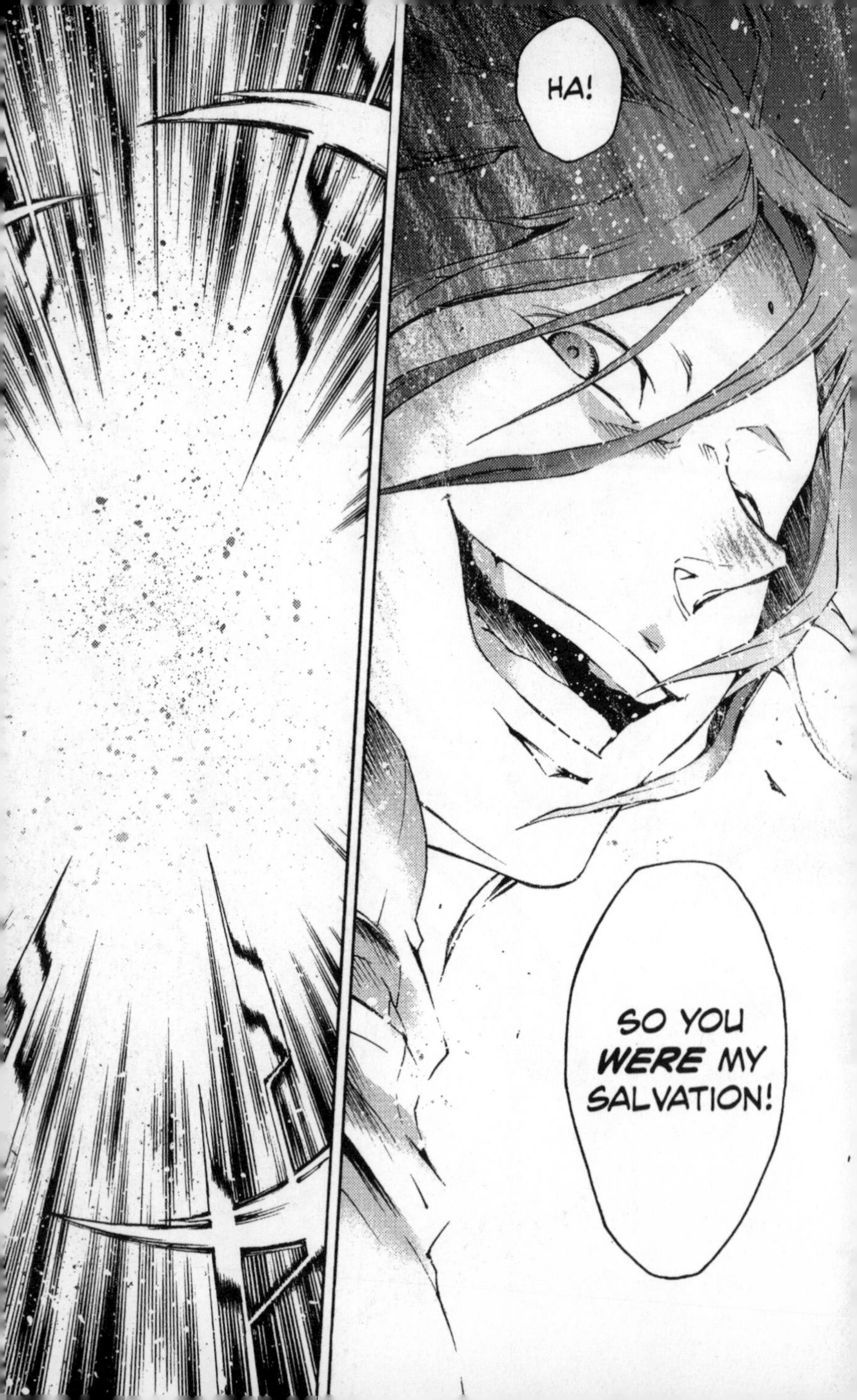
HA!
SO YOU *WERE* MY SALVATION!

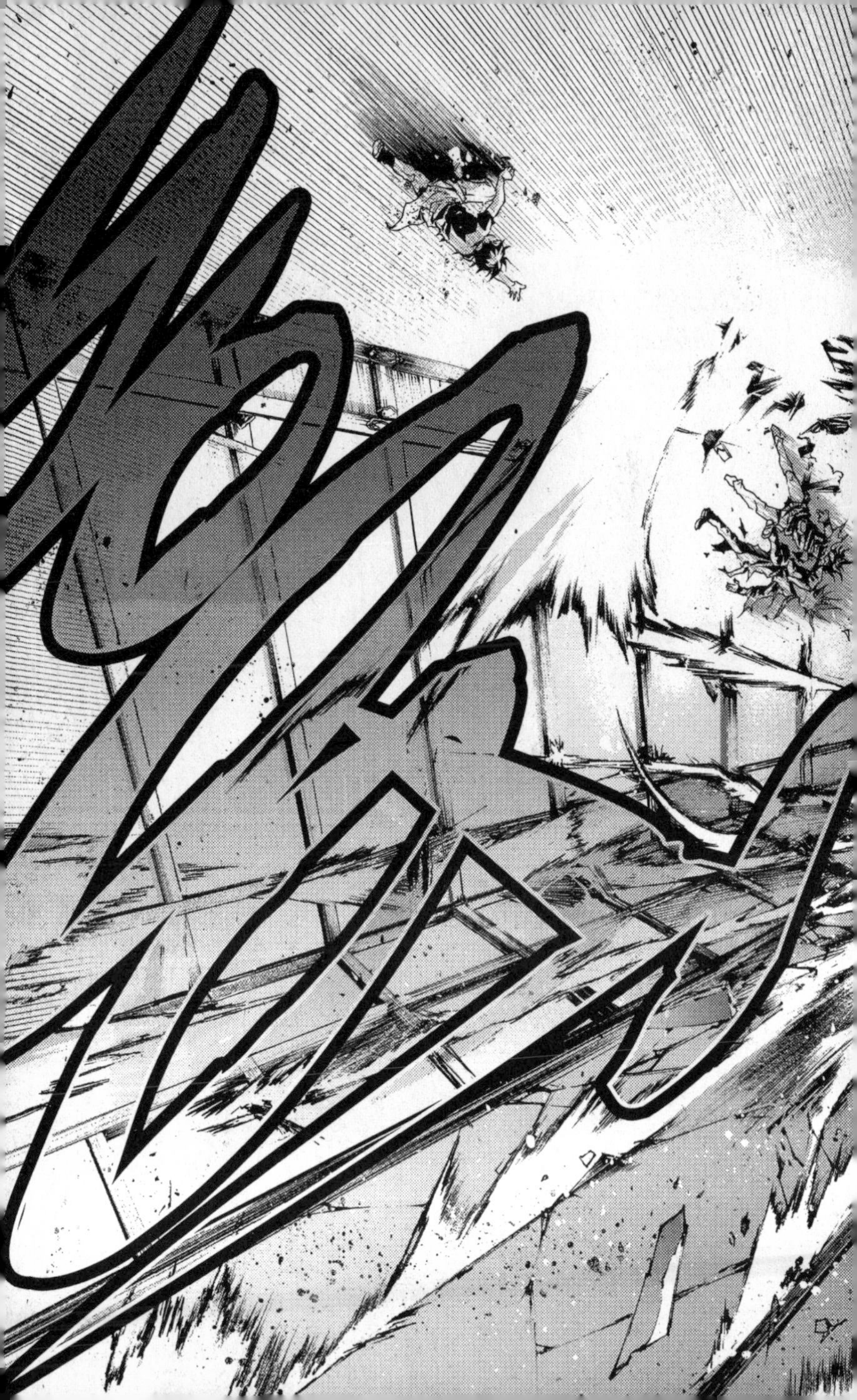

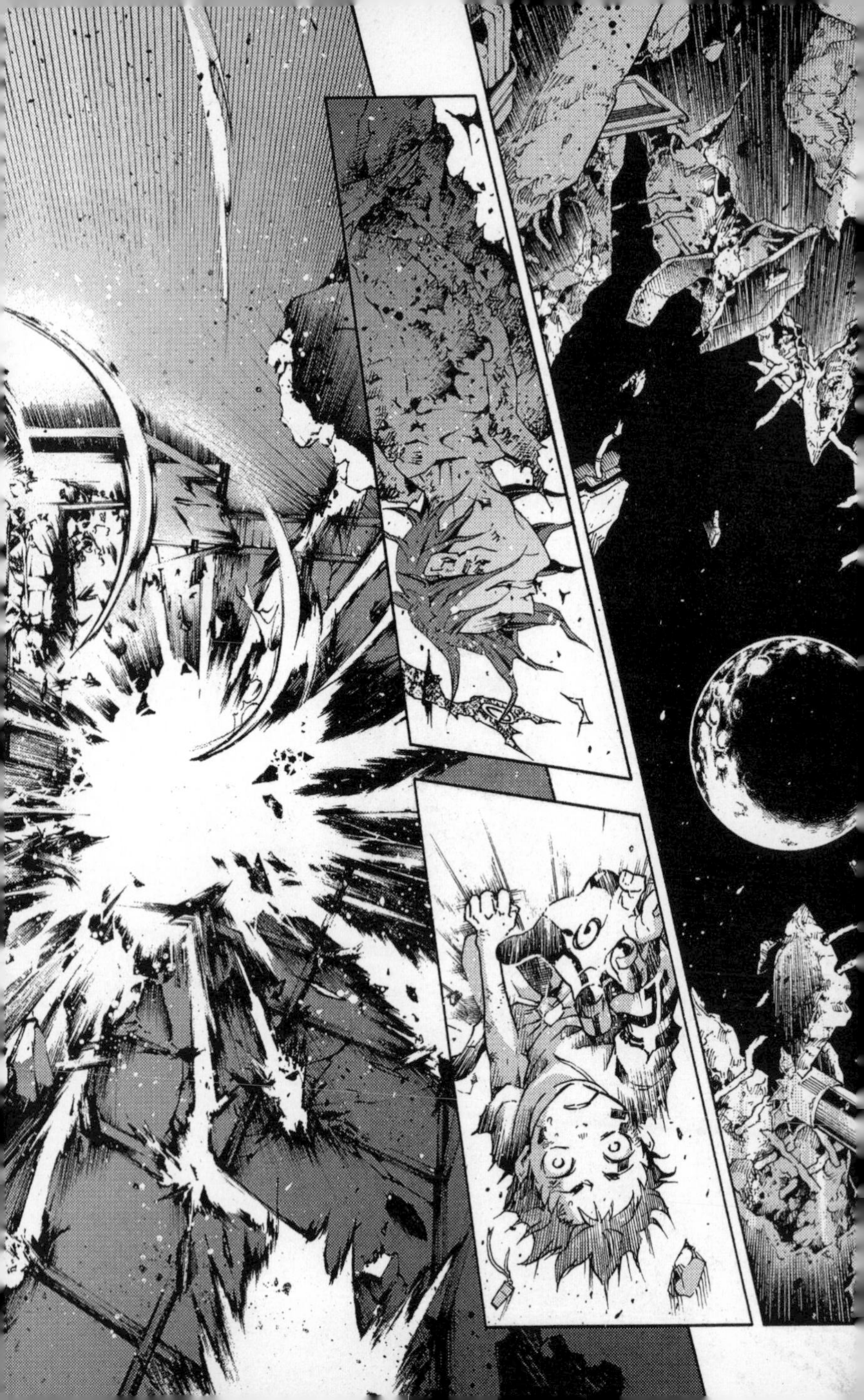

KR. KKK...
YOU'RE KIDDING ME...
GENKA-KU'S...
WHOA
WHAT BRANCH OF SIN WAS THAT?
NO ONE SAID ANYTHING ABOUT THIS!
RKK
NAGI!

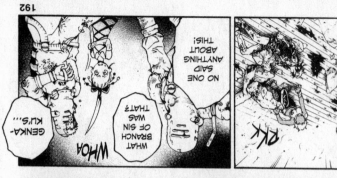

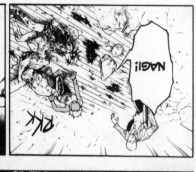

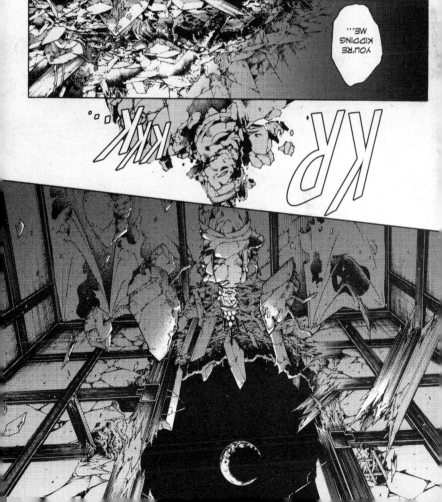

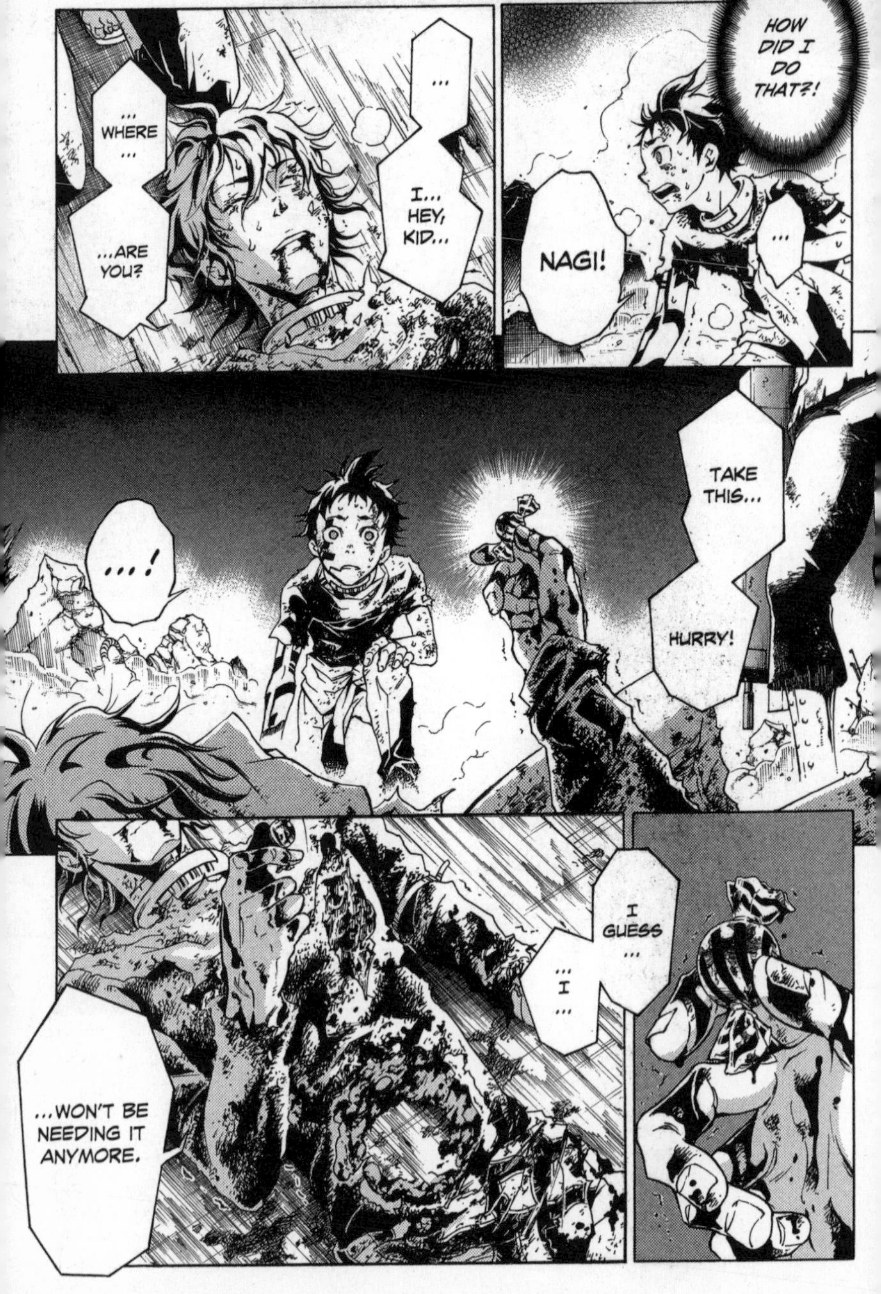
HOW DID I DO THAT?!
...
NAGI!
...
...WHERE...
I... HEY, KID...
...ARE YOU?
TAKE THIS...
HURRY!
...!
I GUESS...
...I...
...WON'T BE NEEDING IT ANYMORE.

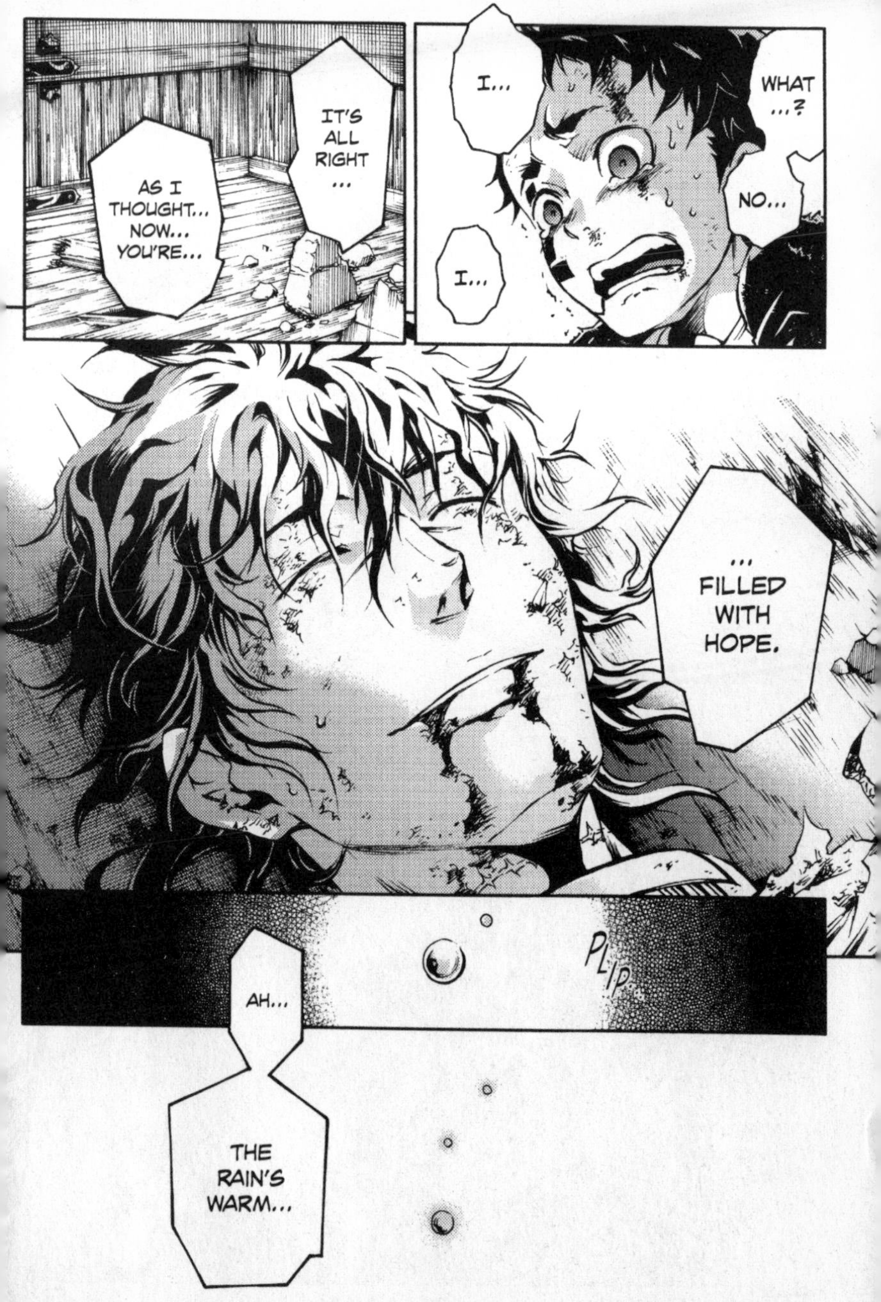
WHAT ...?
NO...
I...
I...
IT'S ALL RIGHT ...
AS I THOUGHT... NOW... YOU'RE...
... FILLED WITH HOPE.
PLIP
AH...
THE RAIN'S WARM...

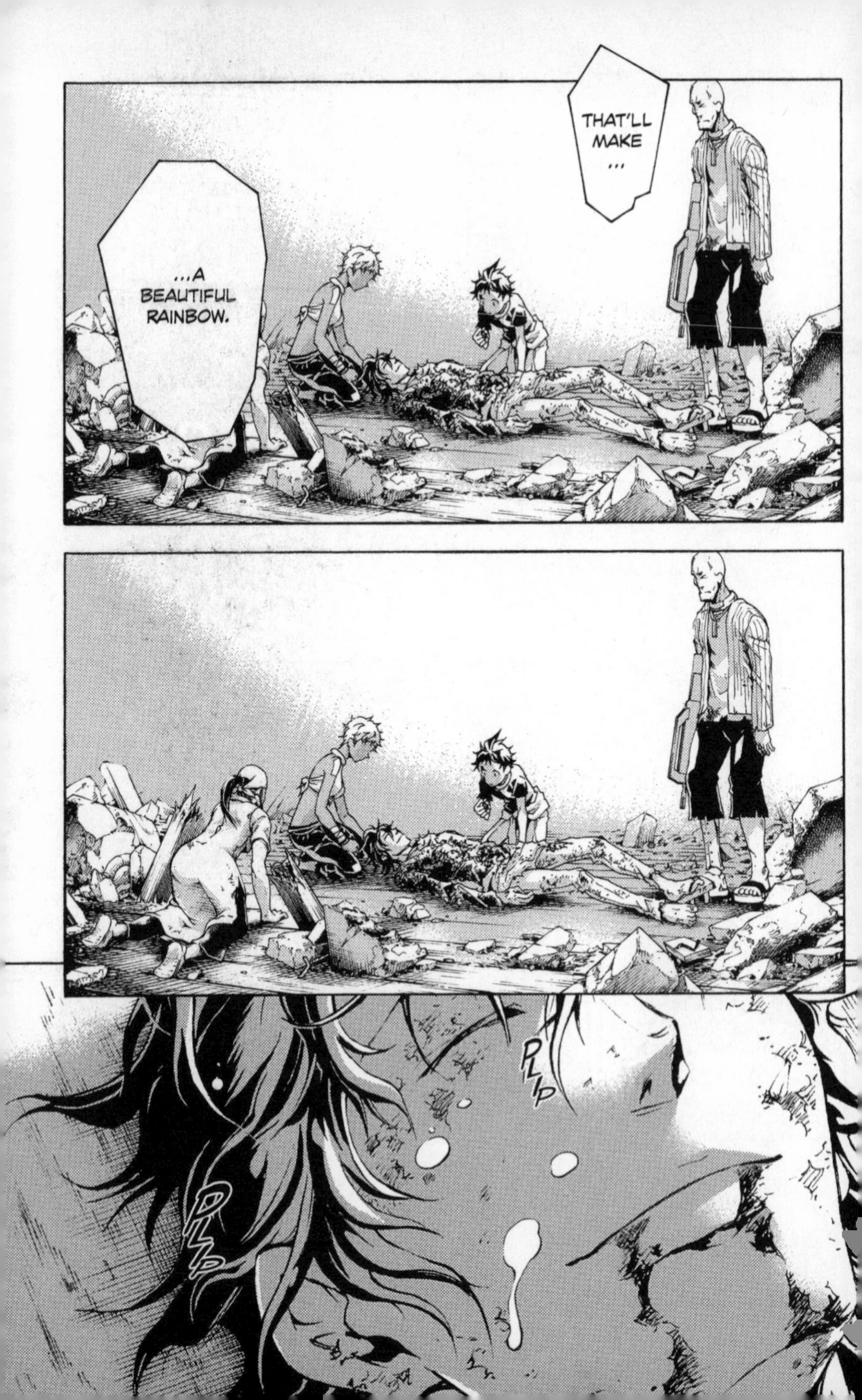
THAT'LL MAKE ...
...A BEAUTIFUL RAINBOW.
PLIP
PLIP

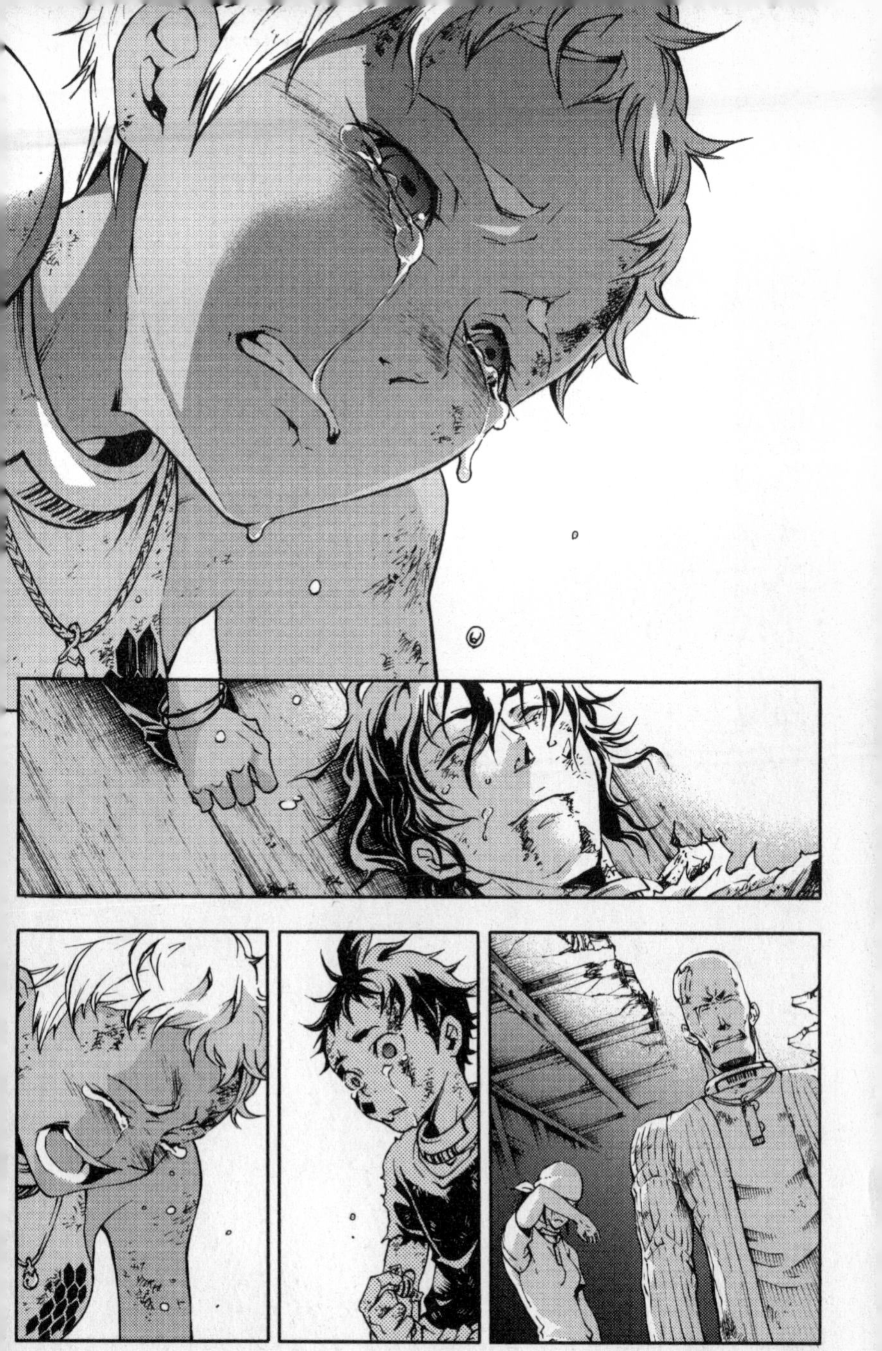

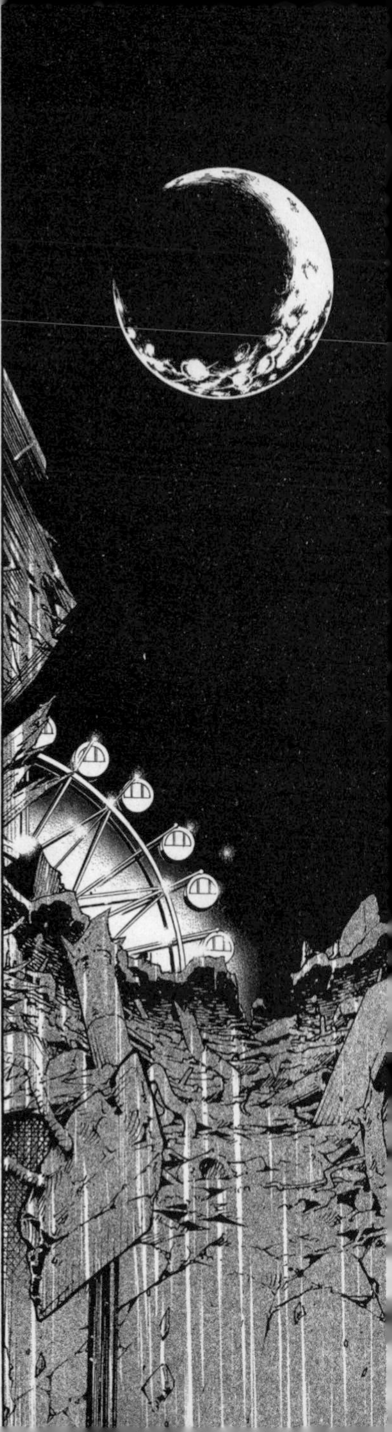
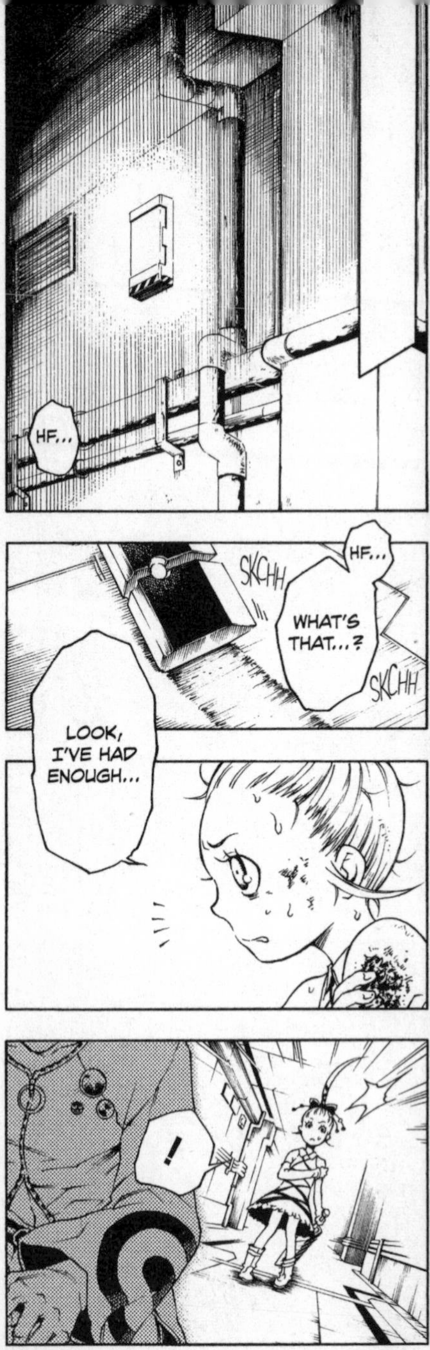
HF...
HF...
SKCHH
WHAT'S THAT...?
SKCHH
LOOK, I'VE HAD ENOUGH...
!

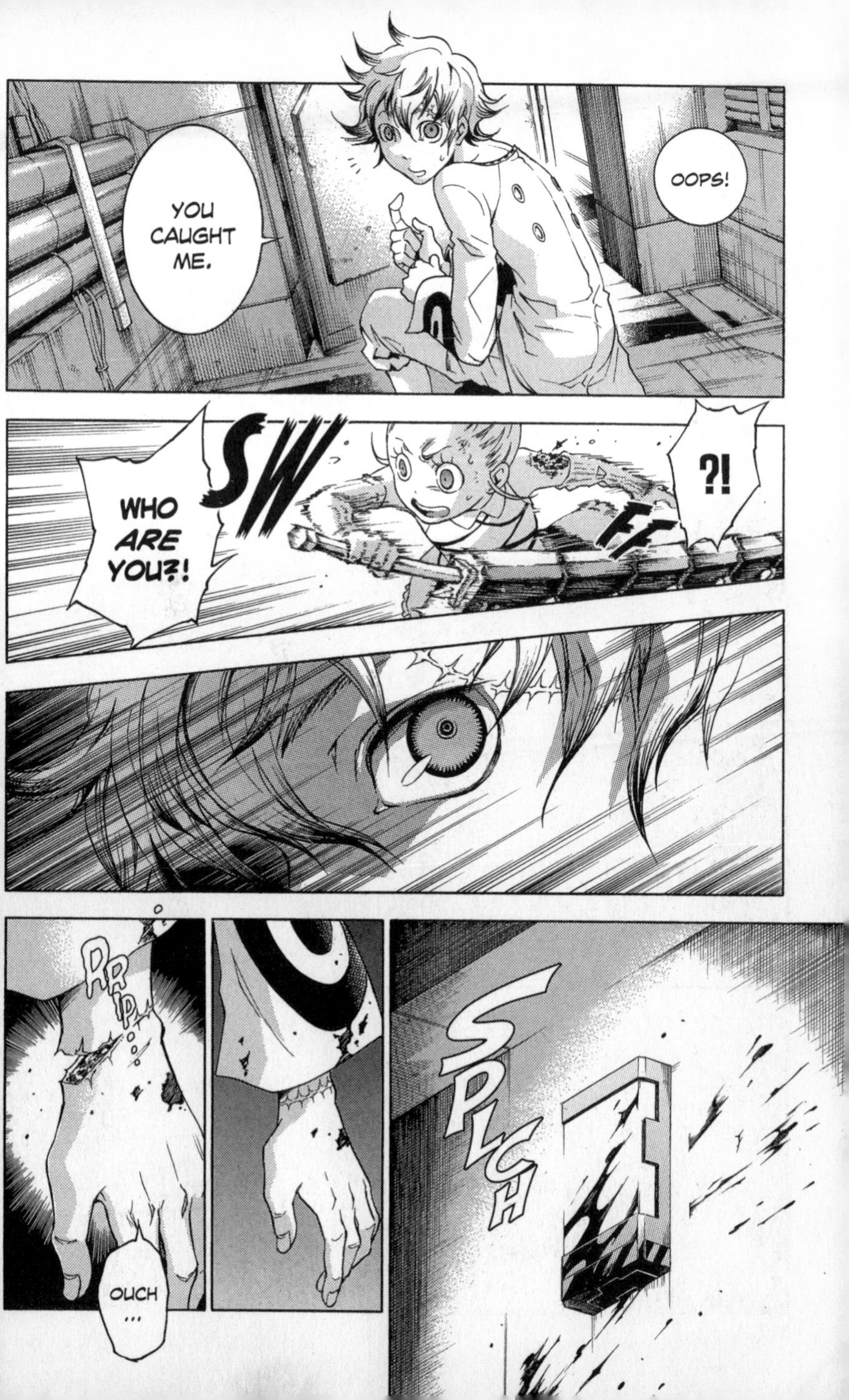
OOPS!
YOU CAUGHT ME.
?!
SWFF
WHO ARE YOU?!
SPLCH
RRIP
OUCH ...

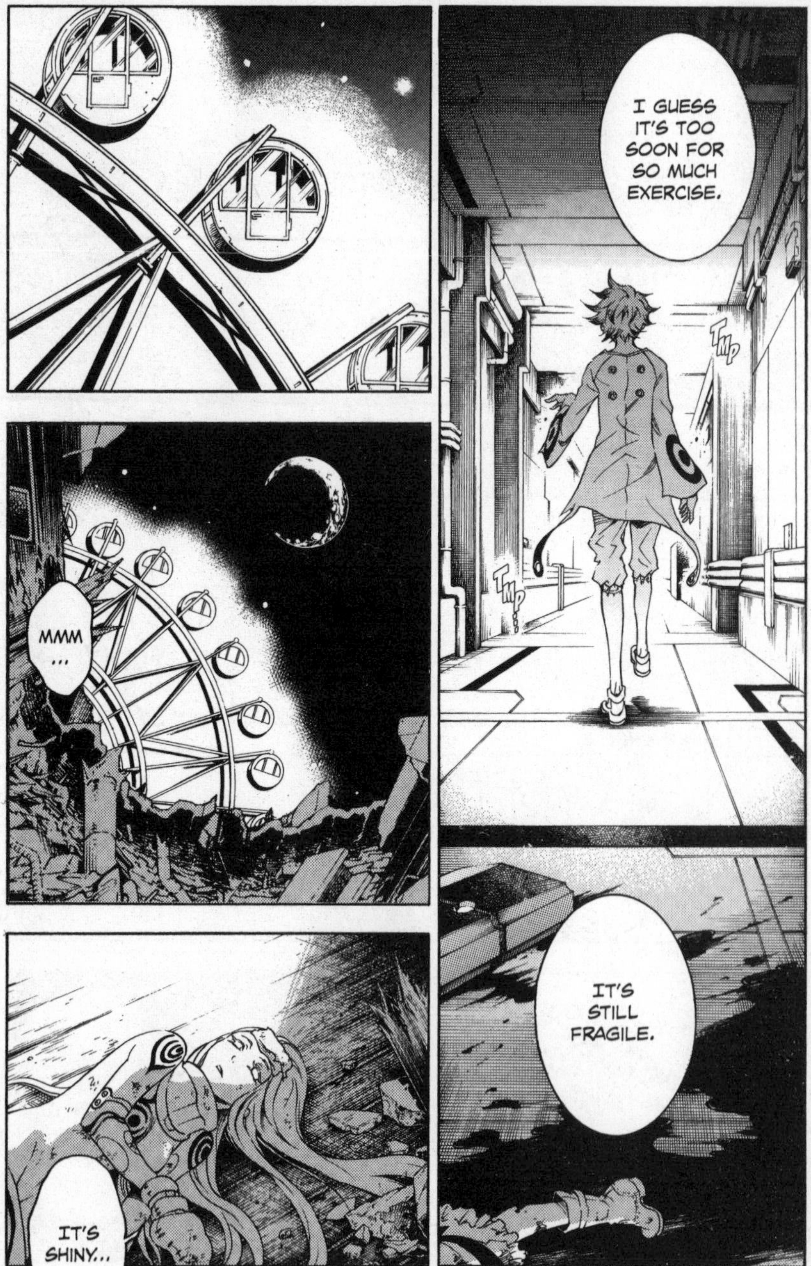
I GUESS IT'S TOO SOON FOR SO MUCH EXERCISE.
TMP
TMP
IT'S STILL FRAGILE.
MMM ...
IT'S SHINY...

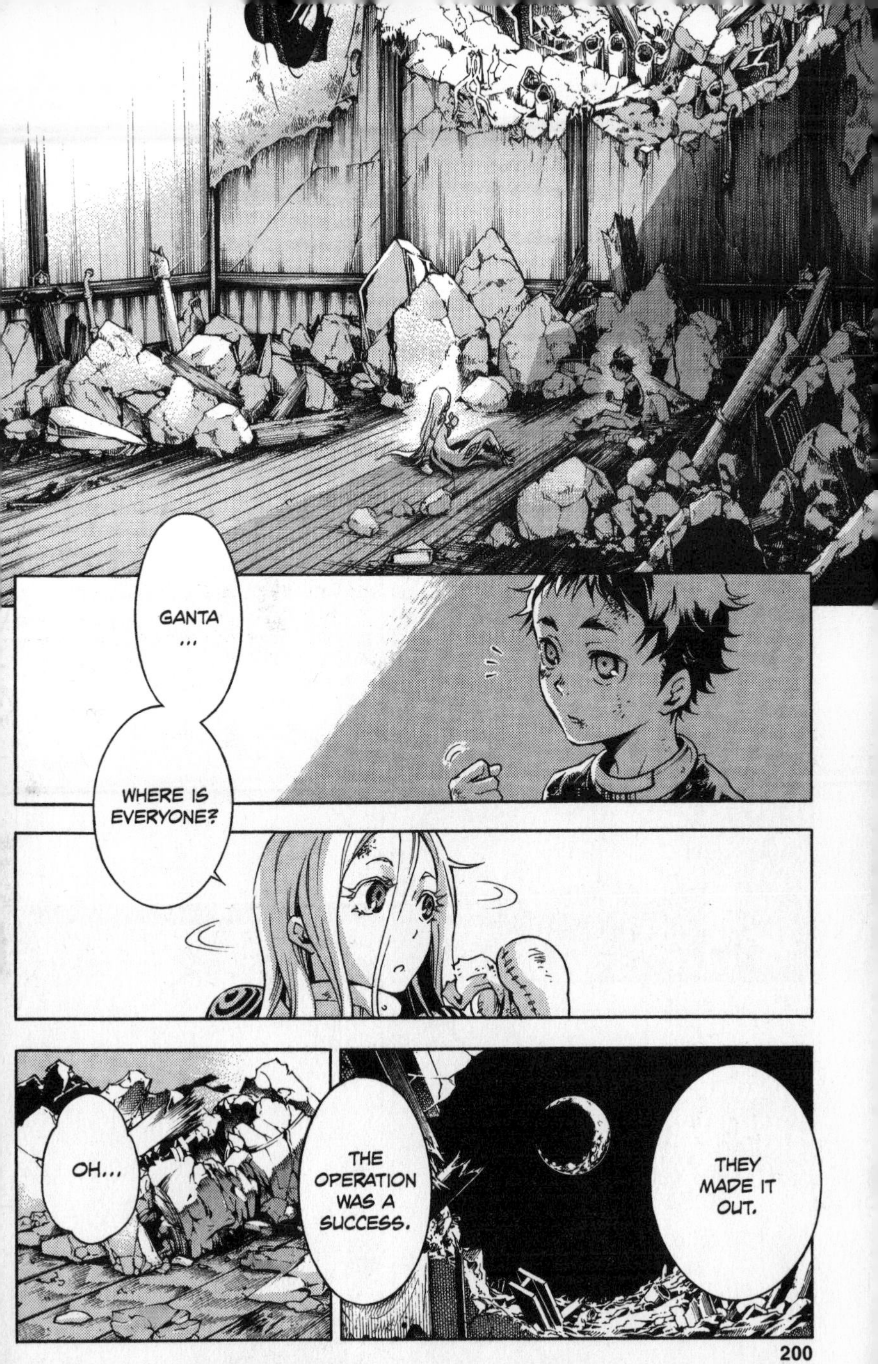
GANTA ...
WHERE IS EVERYONE?
THEY MADE IT OUT.
THE OPERATION WAS A SUCCESS.
OH...

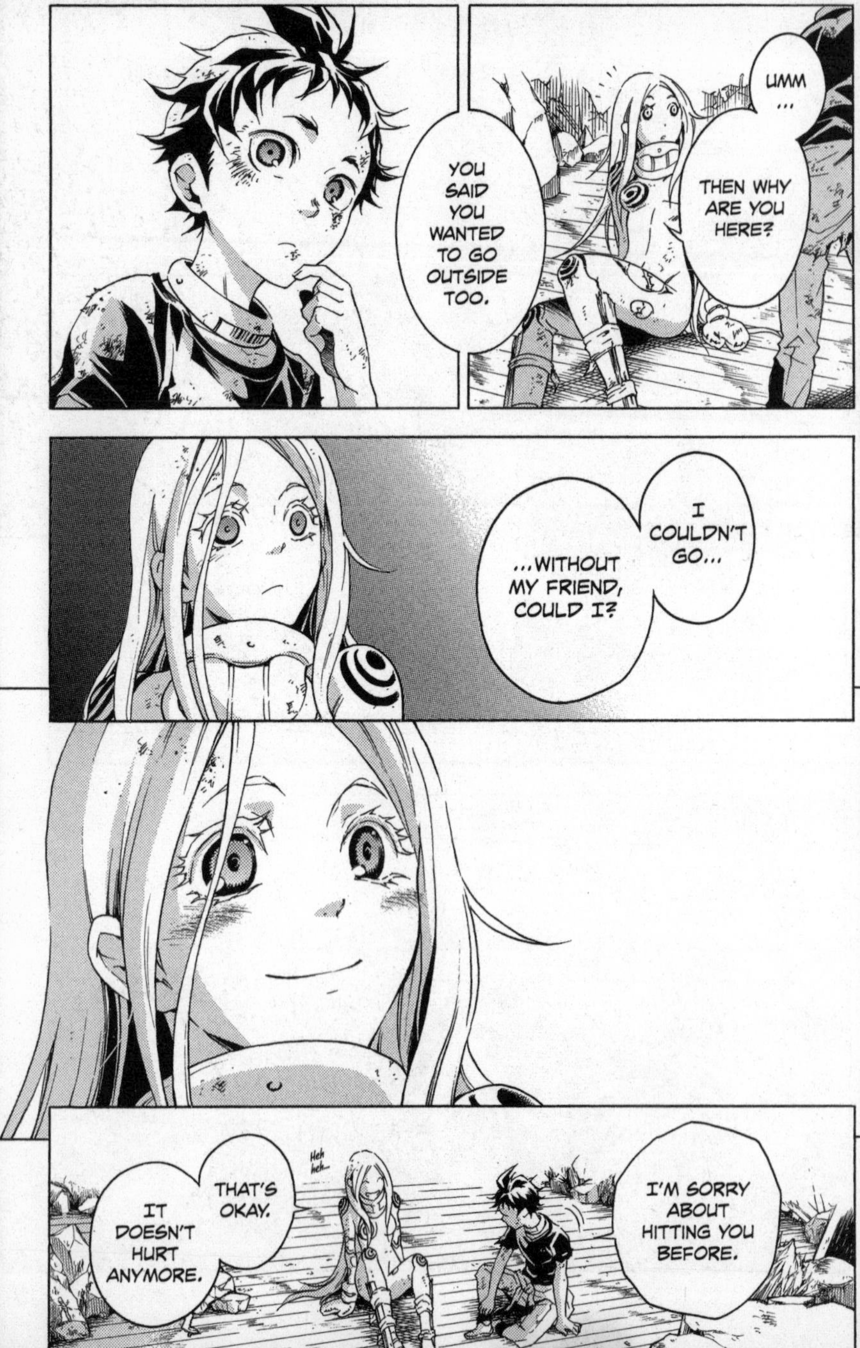
UMM ...
THEN WHY ARE YOU HERE?
YOU SAID YOU WANTED TO GO OUTSIDE TOO.
I COULDN'T GO...
...WITHOUT MY FRIEND, COULD I?
I'M SORRY ABOUT HITTING YOU BEFORE.
Heh heh...
THAT'S OKAY.
IT DOESN'T HURT ANYMORE.

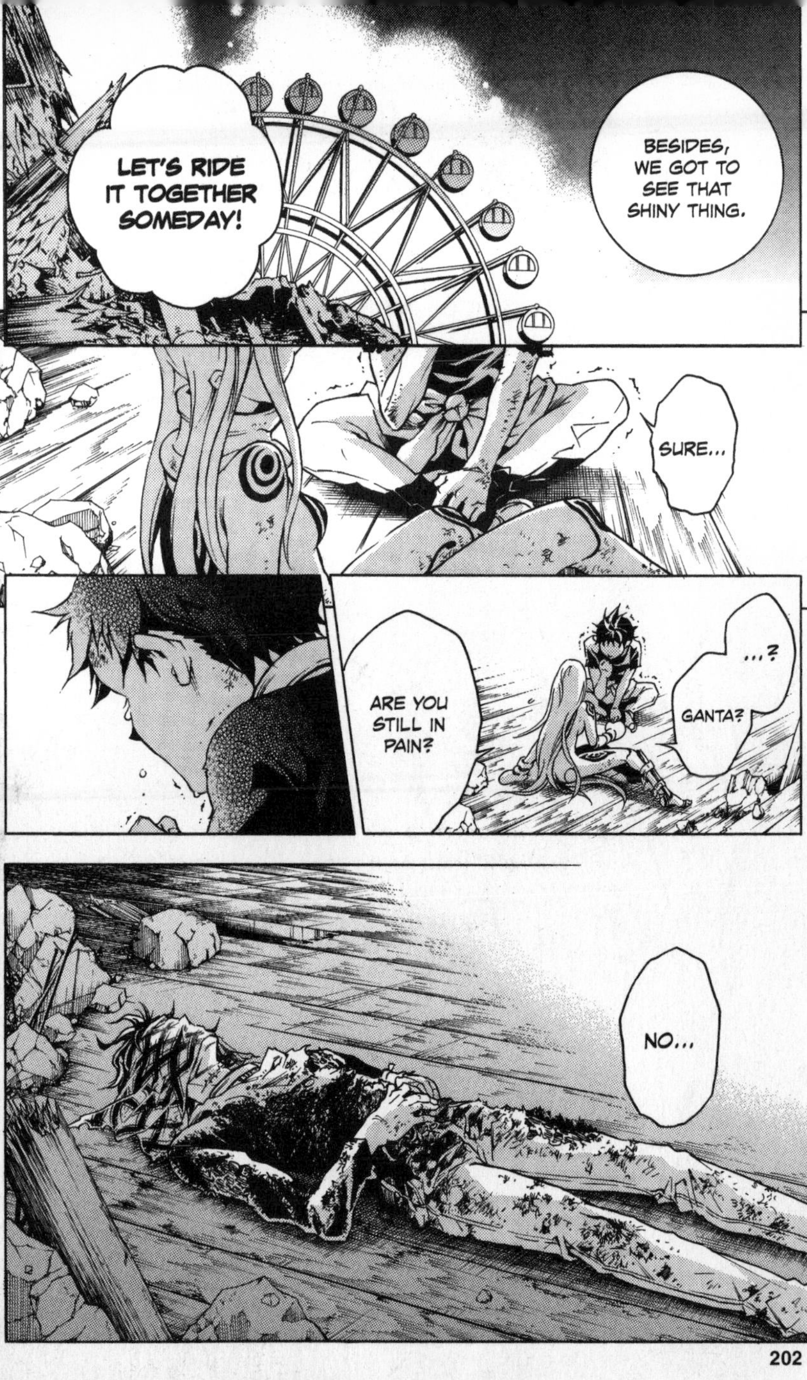
BESIDES, WE GOT TO SEE THAT SHINY THING.
LET'S RIDE IT TOGETHER SOMEDAY!
SURE...
...?
GANTA?
ARE YOU STILL IN PAIN?
NO...

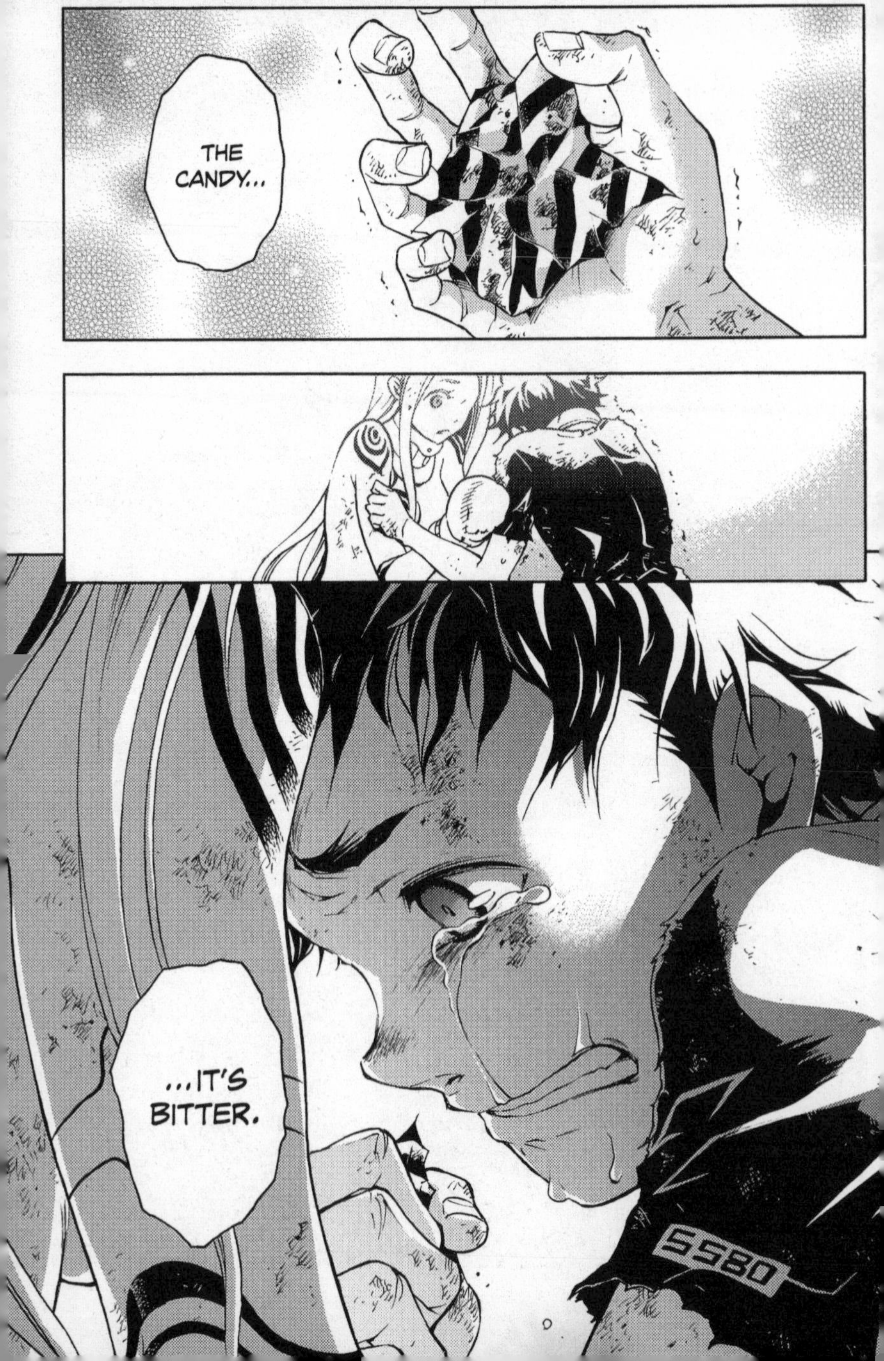
THE CANDY...
...IT'S BITTER.
5580

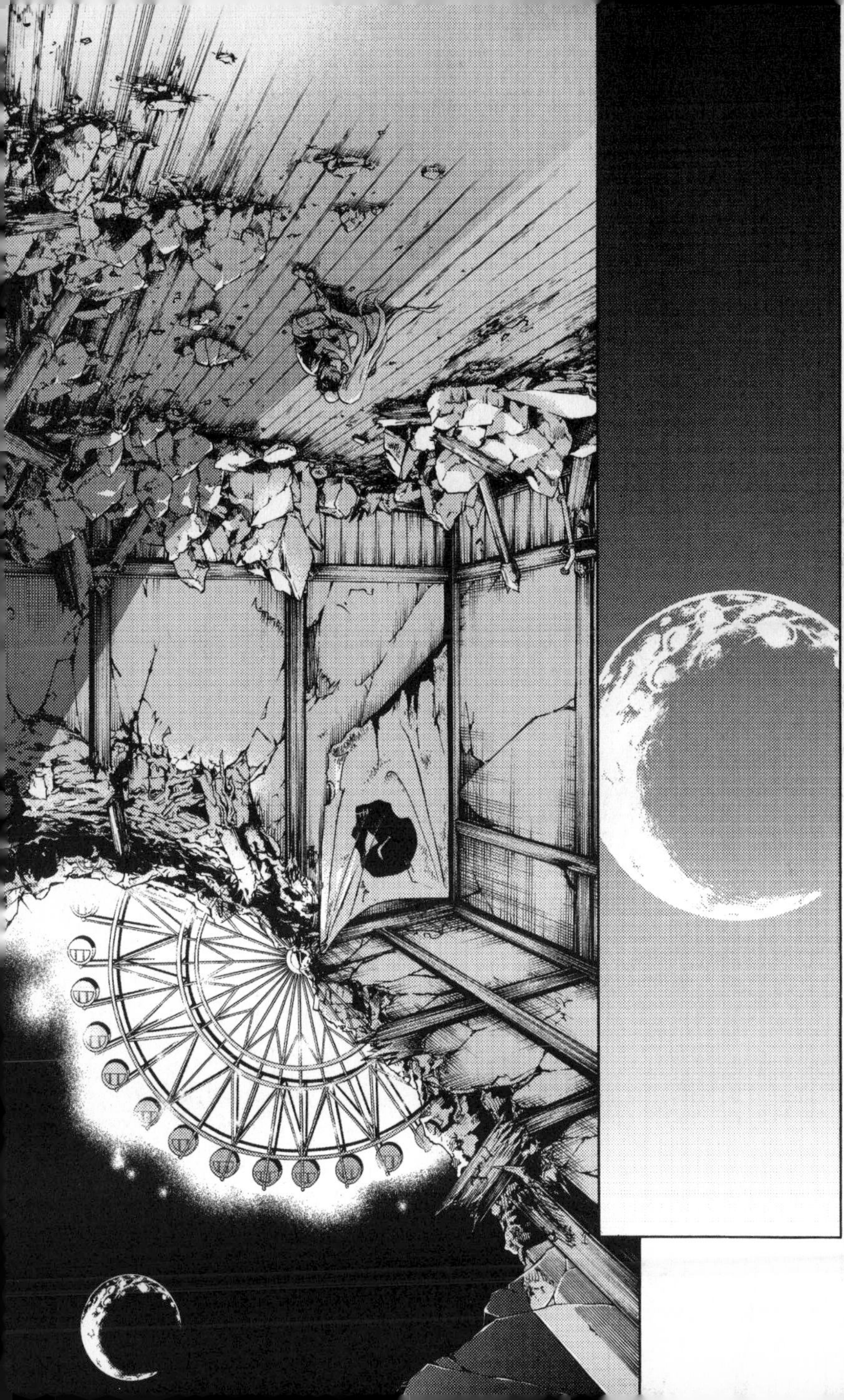

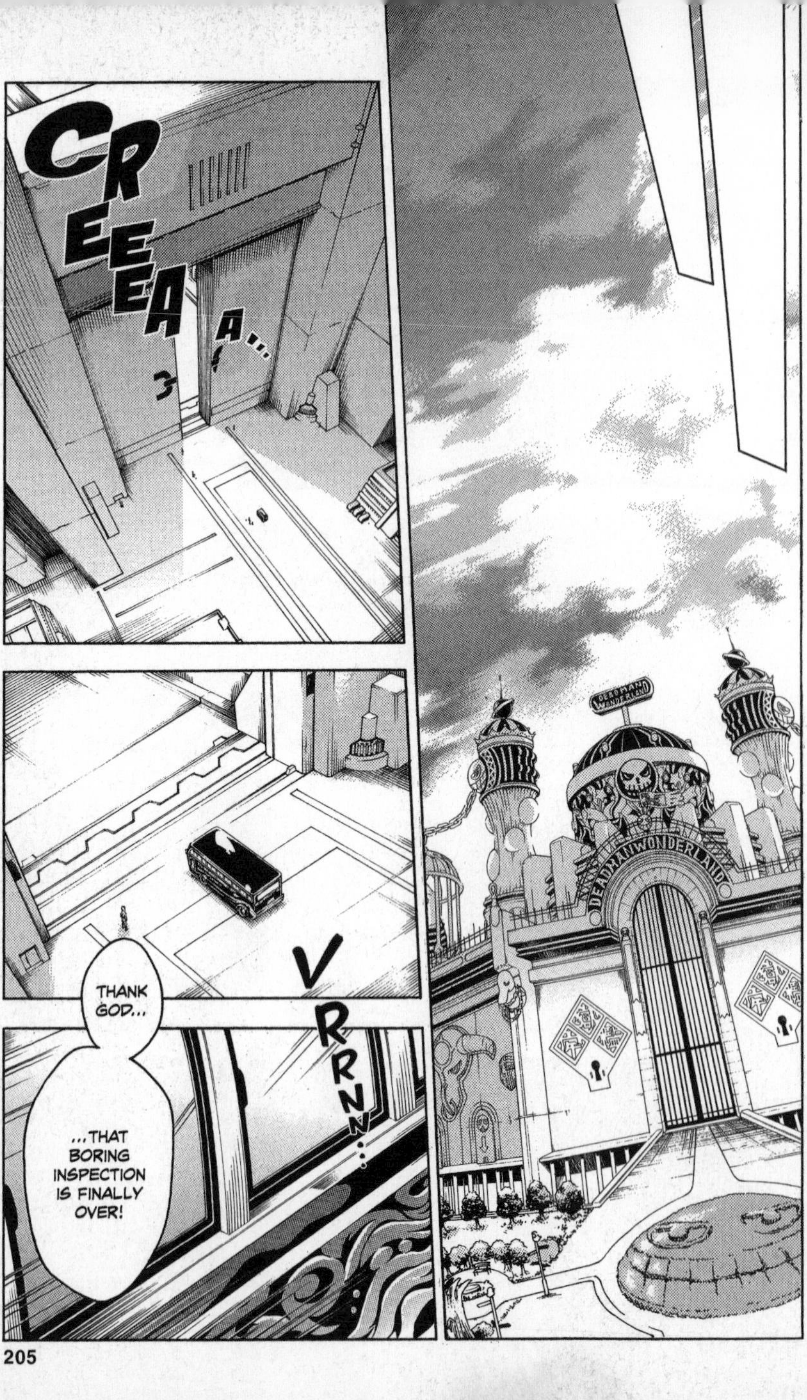
DEADMANWONDERLAND
CREEEAA...
VRRNN...
THANK GOD...
...THAT BORING INSPECTION IS FINALLY OVER!

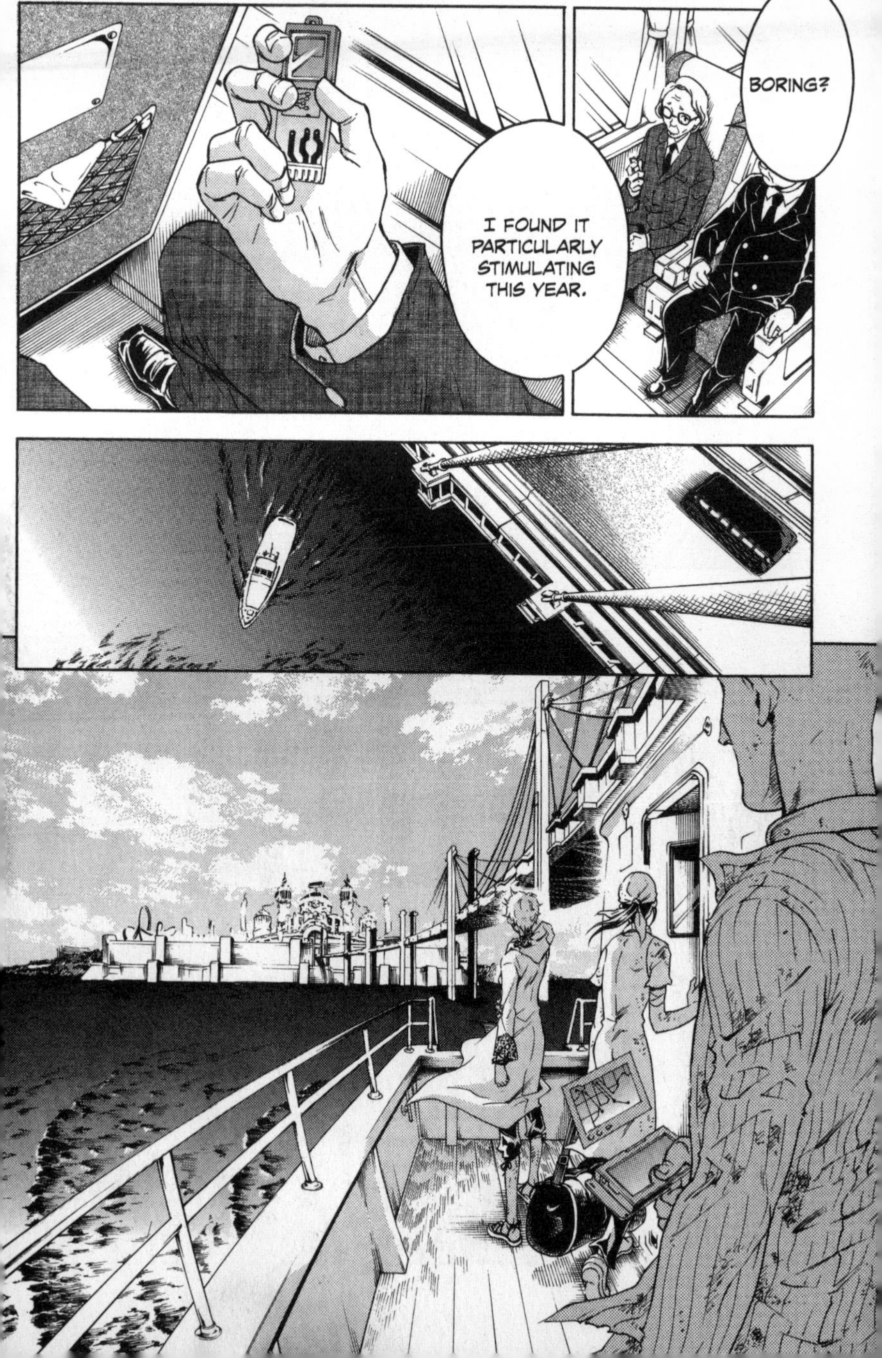
BORING?
I FOUND IT PARTICULARLY STIMULATING THIS YEAR.

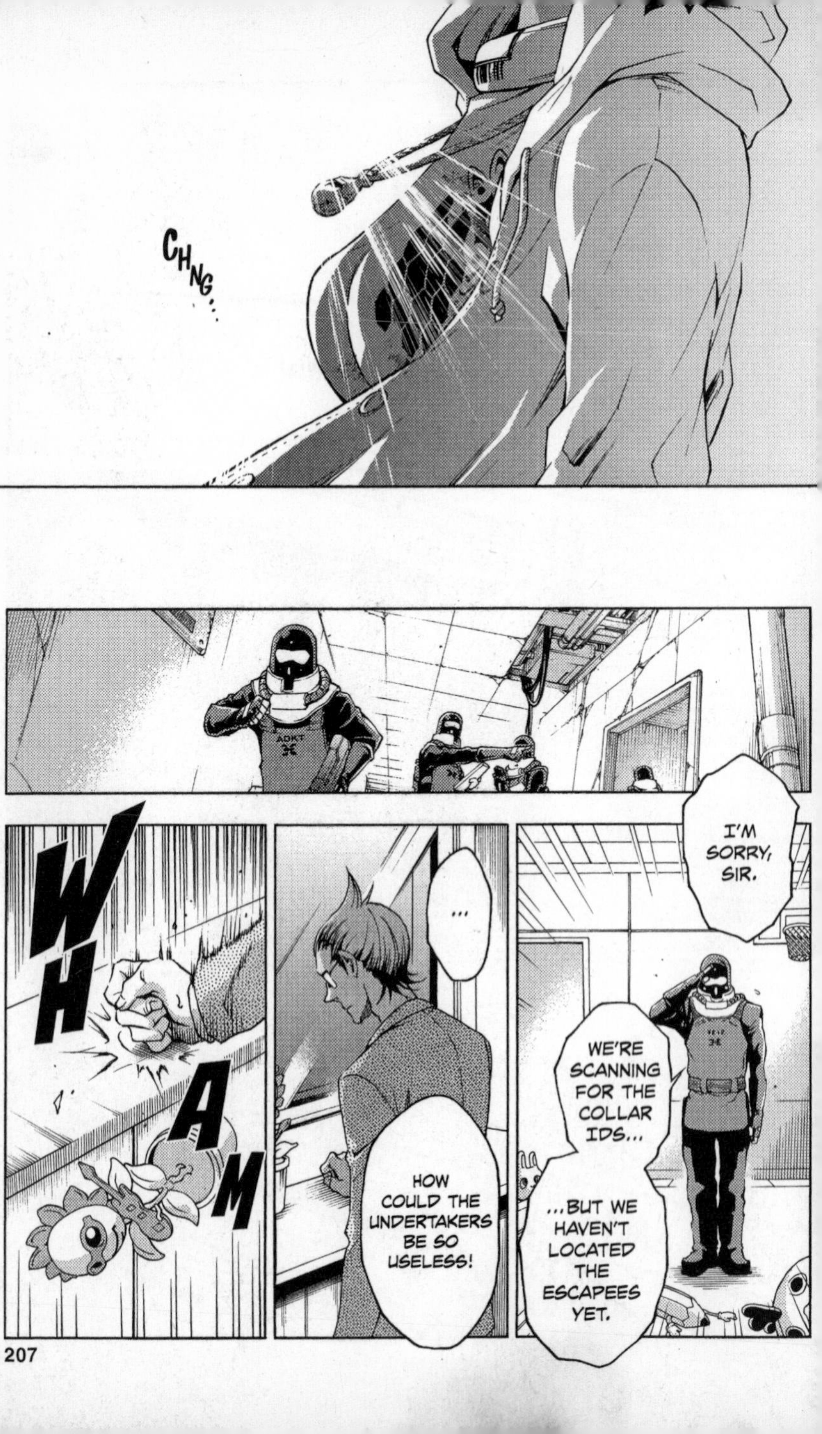
CHNG...
I'M SORRY, SIR.
WE'RE SCANNING FOR THE COLLAR IDS...
...BUT WE HAVEN'T LOCATED THE ESCAPEES YET.
...
HOW COULD THE UNDERTAKERS BE SO USELESS!
WHAM

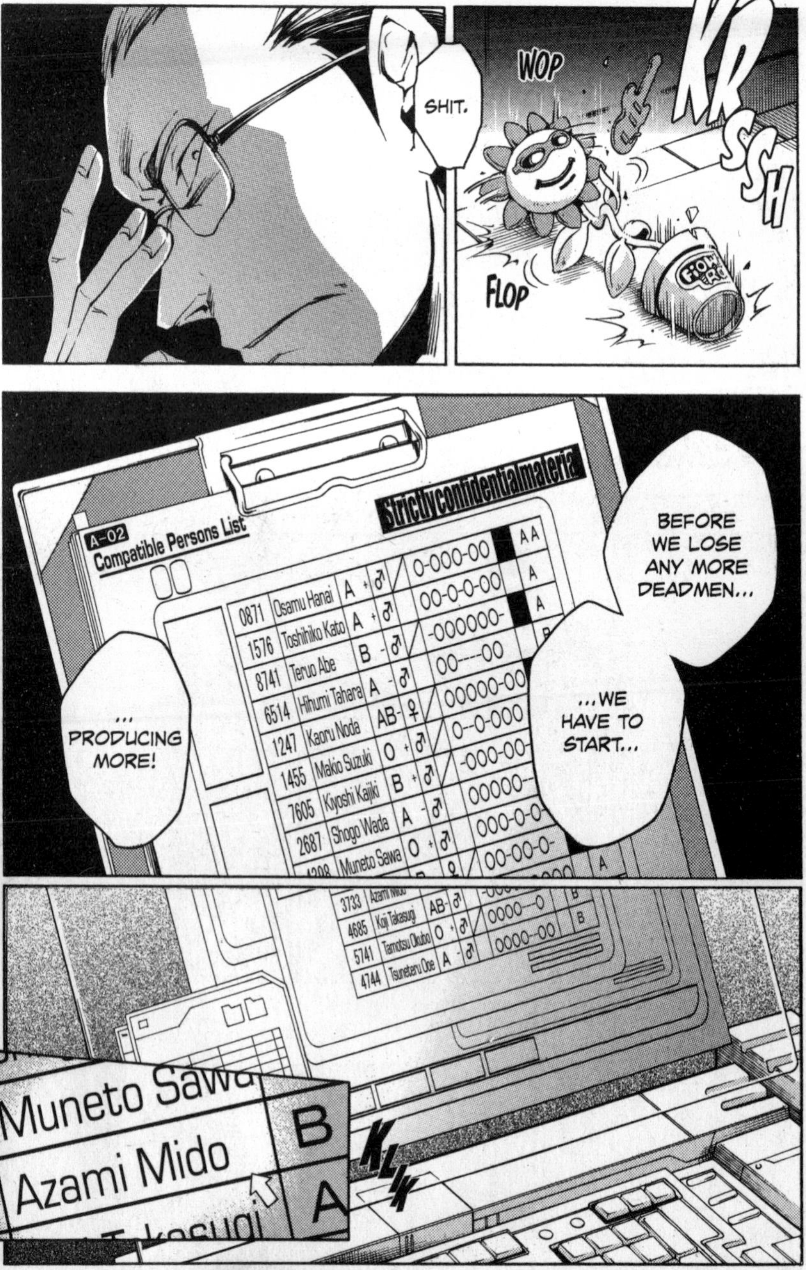
KRSSH
WOP
FLOP
SHIT.
Strictlyconfidentialmateria
A-02
Compatible Persons List
BEFORE WE LOSE ANY MORE DEADMEN...
...WE HAVE TO START...
... PRODUCING MORE!
Muneto Sawa
Azami Mido
KLIK

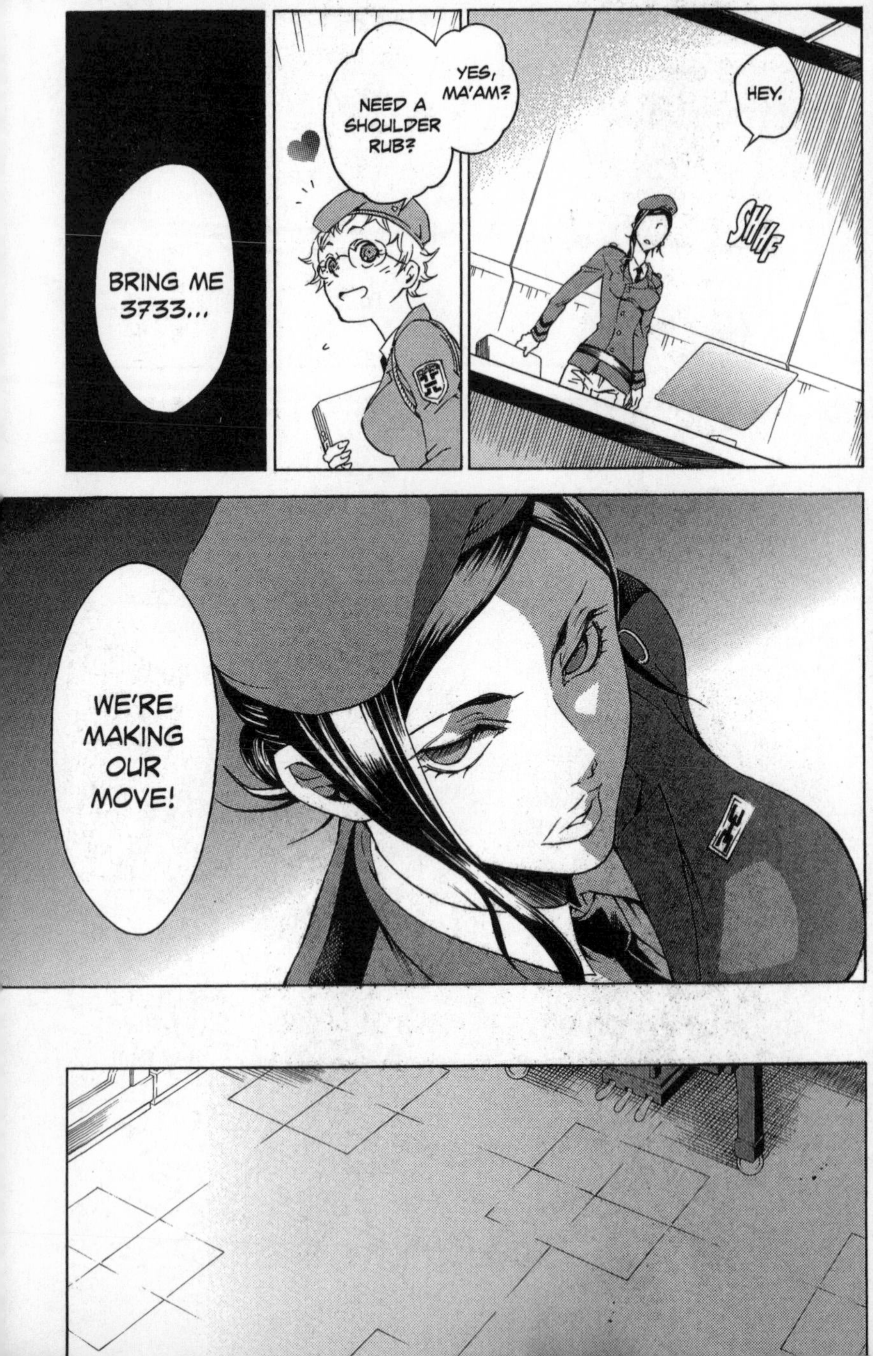
HEY.
SHHF
YES, MA'AM?
NEED A SHOULDER RUB?
BRING ME 3733...
WE'RE MAKING OUR MOVE!

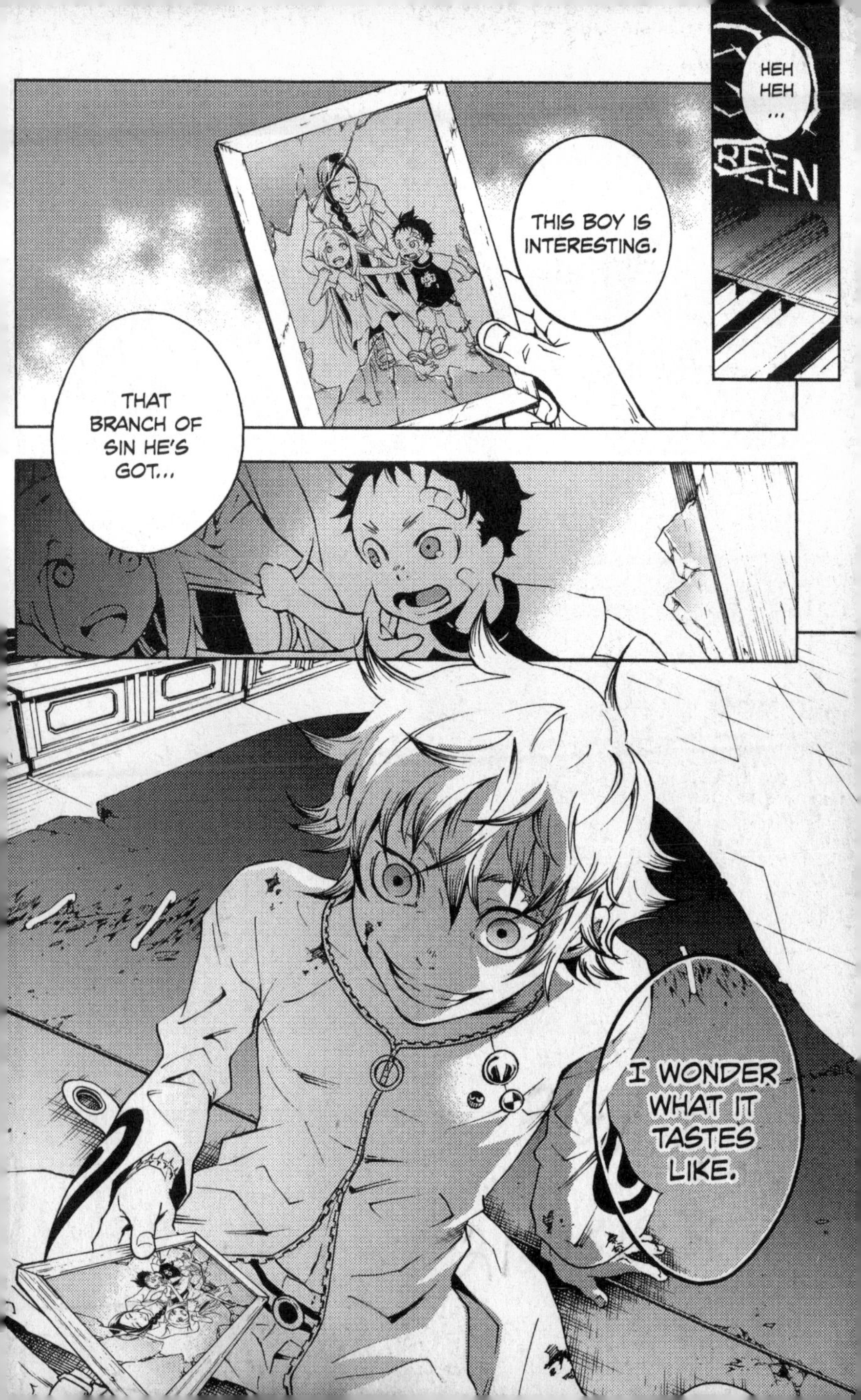
HEH HEH ...
BEEN
THIS BOY IS INTERESTING.
THAT BRANCH OF SIN HE'S GOT...
I WONDER WHAT IT TASTES LIKE.

DEADMAN WONDERLAND 5

Jinsei Kataoka
Kazuma Kondou

STAFF

Karaiko
Ryuichi Saitaniya
Shinji Sato
Ai Takahashi
Taro Tsuchiya
Toshihiro Noguchi

CONTINUED IN VOLUME 6

DE...

FORTY-SEVEN

STORY & ART BY
JINSEI KATAOKA, KAZUMA KONDOU

DEADMAN WONDERLAND
©JINSEI KATAOKA 2009 ©KAZU...
EDITED BY KADOKAWA...
FIRST PUBLISHED IN JAPAN IN 2009 BY KAD...
ENGLISH TRANSLATION RIGHTS ARRANGED WITH...

TRANSLATION/JOE Y...
ENGLISH ADAPTATION...
TOUCH-UP ART & LETTERING/JAMES GAUBATZ
DESIGN/SAM ELZWAY
EDITOR/MIKE MONTESA

PRINTED IN THE U.S.A.

PUBLISHED BY VIZ MEDIA, LLC
P.O. BOX 77010
SAN FRANCISCO, CA 94107

10 9 8 7 6 5 4 3 2 1
FIRST PRINTING, OCTOBER 2014

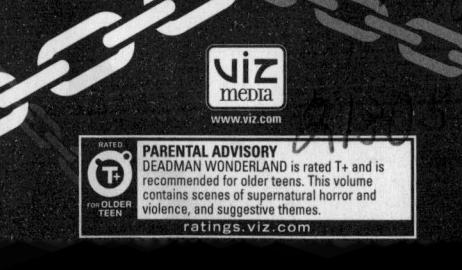

viz
media
www.viz.com